iPhone®

ALL-IN-ONE

FOR

DUMMIES®

A Wiley Brand

4th Edition

iPhone®

ALL-IN-ONE

FOR

DUMMIES®

A Wiley Brand

4th Edition

by Joe Hutsko
and Barbara Boyd

iPhone® All-in-One For Dummies®, 4th Edition

Published by: **John Wiley & Sons, Inc.,** 111 River Street, Hoboken, NJ 07030-5774, www.wiley.com

Copyright © 2015 by John Wiley & Sons, Inc., Hoboken, New Jersey

Published simultaneously in Canada

For general information on our other products and services, please contact our Customer Care Department within the U.S. at 877-762-2974, outside the U.S. at 317-572-3993, or fax 317-572-4002. For technical support, please visit www.wiley.com/techsupport.

Wiley publishes in a variety of print and electronic formats and by print-on-demand. Some material included with standard print versions of this book may not be included in e-books or in print-on-demand. If this book refers to media such as a CD or DVD that is not included in the version you purchased, you may download this material at http://booksupport.wiley.com. For more information about Wiley products, visit www.wiley.com.

Library of Congress Control Number: 2014945014

ISBN 978-1-118-93218-6 (pbk); ISBN 978-1-118-93346-6 (ebk); ISBN 978-1-118-93219-3 (ebk)

Manufactured in the United States of America

10 9 8 7 6 5 4 3 2 1

Contents at a Glance

Table of Contents

Introduction

You hear a lot about tech taking over and smartphones — with iPhone at the lead — getting in the way of personal relationships. We won't lie to you: We love tech and telling people about it, but our goal is not for tech to take charge of your life: We want you to take charge of tech.

In this book, we try to find the balance between simple, practical information for new users and new information for experienced users. Whatever your iPhone user level, we want this book to bring you to a point of using your iPhone at the maximum potential for you. For some that might mean using three or four apps such as Phone, Camera, and Messages, whereas for others, it might mean using most of the preinstalled apps.

About This Book

To write this book, we looked into every nook and cranny of iPhone, and then we asked friends and family with iPhones to tell us their weirdest, most confusing, and most confounding iPhone circumstances, which we tried to solve. Armed with that information, we revised the previous edition of this book and believe we get pretty darn close to telling you all there is to know. That said, Apple releases iOS updates frequently — this book is based on iOS 8.0 — and we encourage you to keep your iPhone and app software up to date and stay informed as to how to use features that may be added with updates.

We're not perfect, so we undoubtedly missed something. Let us know. Your comments, questions, and compliments help us to improve future editions. Drop a note to us at babsboyd@icloud.com. And to learn about changes that occur after the book is printed, join our Facebook page at www.facebook.com/iPhoneAIOFD.

Finally, throughout this book, you see sidebars (text in gray boxes). Sidebars present technical information that you don't have to know but that might interest you if you want to understand the technology behind the function. Also, you may note that some web addresses break across two lines of text. If you're reading this book in print and want to visit one of these web pages, simply key in the web address exactly as it's noted in the text, pretending as though the line break doesn't exist. If you're reading this as an e-book, you've got it easy — just click the web address to be taken directly to the web page.

Foolish Assumptions

We made a few assumptions about you when writing this book. To make sure we're on the same page, we assume that

- You know something, but not necessarily a lot, about cellphones and you want to learn the basics and more about iPhone.

- You have at least a general concept of how to use the web and email.

- You acknowledge that it's up to you to go on the web to find updated information about the products described throughout this book.

- You'll check with your cellular service provider to know how many minutes or megabytes are included in your monthly allotment and under what circumstances you might incur additional charges (although we do give you some warnings throughout the book when additional charges are more likely).

- You know that technology is changing faster than we can keep up and even geeks like us can't stay on top of everything. You will, therefore, let us know about cool stuff you find along the way of your iPhone journey so we can consider it for future editions of this book.

- You're not all work and no play. You want to have some fun with your iPhone and maybe even be entertained while you're learning how to use it.

Icons Used in This Book

To help emphasize certain information, this book displays different icons in the page margins.

The Tip icon points out bits of information that can help you do things better and more efficiently or tells you something useful that you might not know.

The Technical Stuff icon highlights interesting information that isn't necessary to know, but can help explain why certain things work the way they do on your iPhone. Like sidebars, you can skip this information if you're in a hurry. On the other hand, you might find something helpful here.

The Warning icon gives you a heads-up about something that can go wrong if you're not careful. Be sure to read the warning fully before following related instructions.

The Remember icon points out information that's been mentioned some-where else in the book but is related to the topic nearby. If you ignore it, you won't cause problems, but you could miss something useful.

Beyond the Book

You can find additional features of this book online. Visit the web to find these extras:

- ✔ **Cheat Sheet:** Go to www.dummies.com/cheatsheet/iphoneaio to find this book's Cheat Sheet. Here, you can find references on the uses of the iPhone Home button, info on the functions of the icons and buttons of your iPhone, useful websites for iPhone owners, tips on using Siri, and info on Home screen apps.

- ✔ **Dummies.com online extras:** Go to www.dummies.com/extras/iphoneaio to find the Extras for this book. Three separate articles give you specific, task-oriented information — and ideas — for using your iPhone in ways you may not know about, such as making custom ring-tones for your iPhone, using your iPhone as a remote control when making a presentation, and using your iPhone to keep tabs on your home security.

- ✔ **Bonus chapters on the web:** The bonus chapters show you how to expand your iPhone beyond the standard Apple apps. Each chapter presents a selection of apps that add a feature or function to your iPhone, or enhance something it already does. For the business user or busy household manager, there are budgeting, task management, and faxing apps. For the social butterfly, there are communications and net-working apps. Quiet types might enjoy e-reader and radio apps. There's something for everyone in the leisure, fitness, health, home, and travel apps. You'll also find a chapter dedicated to accessories such as covers, speakers, and keyboards that enhance your iPhone. Access the online content at www.dummies.com/extras/iphoneaio.

Where to Go from Here

If you're new to iPhone, closely read the first few chapters to get an under-standing of how your iPhone works, the command conventions it uses, and how to perform the basic functions. Then move on to chapters that interest you, perhaps starting with the phone and messaging functions before mov-ing up to Internet access, and lastly looking at the multimedia apps like Music, Podcasts, and Camera.

If you're familiar with your iPhone already, skim through the opening chapters to learn about the recent iOS 8 changes, and then go where you want — for example, to a chapter on a function you haven't used before, which might be the new video camera functions or Health, or to a function you use a lot but would like to know better, such as Messages.

No matter where you begin, our goal is to give you the tools to get the most out of your iPhone and encourage you to expand your knowledge and explore the many ways of iPhone.

Book I
Getting Started with iPhone

getting started with

iPhone

Contents at a Glance

Chapter 1: Exploring the Many Faces of iPhone

In This Chapter

- Taking a look at the hardware
- Considering iPhone carriers
- Making phone calls
- Sending messages
- Surfing the web
- Taking photos and videos
- Entertaining yourself with apps

The more you use your iPhone, the more you discover how powerful it is and how many handy, helpful things it can do. We know people — and you probably do, too — who resisted the iPhone craze and then, after having had an iPhone for a week (or a day), never leave it out of arm's reach.

In this chapter, we try to pique your curiosity about things you may not have thought of doing with your iPhone by introducing you to all your iPhone can do. We talk about the hardware, review your cellular carrier options, and summarize the apps that come with your iPhone. You can then pick and choose the topics and tasks where you want to dive deeper and go to those chapters for the details. We'd like you to think about how you can incorporate your iPhone into your day-to-day activities but don't worry: We don't want technology to take charge of your life. We want you to take charge of the technology.

Looking at Your iPhone from Every Angle

With the release of iPhone 6, iPhone models come in different sizes, but the overall function of each model is the same. Here we take a look at the hardware and give you a closer look at what's inside.

Front, back, top, bottom

This book explains how to use iOS 8, the latest iPhone operating system. iPhone models 4s or later work with iOS 8. The iPhone screen and body materials vary slightly from model to model, but rest assured that each is scratch- and shatter-resistant, although that doesn't mean they'll survive a beating with a hammer or being dropped from a sixth-floor window.

A metal band around the edge of the iPhone (which you may or may not see, depending on the model) not only gives stability and structure to your iPhone, but also functions as two antennae. In addition to the antennae, the buttons and holes around the edges and on the front and back, which we explain in detail in Book I, Chapter 2, have the following functions:

- ✒ Sleep/Wake button
- ✒ Microphones
- ✒ Lightning port for connecting various cables and connectors (Dock connector on 4s)
- ✒ Volume buttons
- ✒ Silent/ring switch
- ✒ Two video/still camera lenses
- ✒ LED flash/light or dual LED True Tone flash/light
- ✒ SIM tray
- ✒ Speaker
- ✒ Headset jack
- ✒ Home button (with fingerprint sensor on iPhone models with Touch ID)

What you don't see can help you

Your iPhone has antennae and sensors to support the functions of the apps you use. One antenna is the metal band around the outside that connects to the cellular network. The iPhone actually switches between two antennae to receive and transmit, which increases data transfer speeds and call quality. Here's what those visible and not-so-visible parts do:

- ✒ **GPS and GLONASS:** Finds your location, gives you directions in Maps, and geotags your photos. In Book IV, Chapter 1, we explain how geotagging identifies your location when you take a photo.
- ✒ **Wi-Fi:** Connects to available Wi-Fi networks.
- ✒ **Cellular antenna:** Connects you to a selection of the following networks: LTE, GSM/EDGE, CDMA EV-DO, UMTS/HSPA +/DC_HSDPA, 2G, 3G, or 4G networks. We explain the different types of cellular networks, and what all these nerdy terms and acronyms mean, in Book I, Chapter 2.

- **Three-axis gyroscope:** Used to find your location when GPS or GLONASS aren't accessible.

- **Magnetic-field sensor:** Positions the compass.

- **Proximity sensor:** Turns the touchscreen off when you hold the phone close to your ear, so you don't accidentally tap the mute button or call another number while you're in the middle of a conversation. As soon as you move iPhone a few 16ths of an inch from your head, the screen is activated.

- **Tilt sensor:** Senses motion, which is particularly useful when playing games that involve driving or flying.

- **Accelerometer:** Allows for landscape display.

- **Bluetooth:** Connects to other Bluetooth 4.0–enabled devices.

- **Ambient light sensor:** Adjusts the screen when you're using your iPhone in low- or bright-light situations.

- **Fingerprint identity sensor (models with Touch ID):** Recognizes authorized fingers pressed to the Home button to unlock iPhone and make purchases in the iTunes and Apps Stores, as well as iTunes U and Newsstand. Third-party apps may use this sensor to authorize actions, too.

- **NFC antenna (iPhone 6 and 6 Plus):** In conjunction with Apple Pay, this antenna allows you to use your iPhone to charge purchases to a credit card already associated with your iTunes account, or another card you add, simply by pointing your iPhone at an NFC reader, and then authorizing the purchase with Touch ID.

- **Barometer (iPhone 6 and 6 Plus):** Measures relative elevation, so, for example, the Health app can tell you not only the number of steps you took but the distance you ran and how many flights of stairs you climbed.

- **Moisture sensor:** Lets Apple know if your iPhone has gone for a swim. If you purchased AppleCare+, Apple may replace or repair your phone for up to two accidents after you pay a deductible. Learn about AppleCare in Book I, Chapter 5.

Other stuff in the box

Your iPhone comes with a few nice accessories, too. Here's what you'll find when you open the box:

- **EarPods:** Stereo headphones with a built-in microphone and volume control buttons.

- **USB cable connector:** Connects your iPhone to a USB port on your computer, in your car, and on the USB power adapter. iPhone 5 and later models have the 9-pin reversible Lightning connector, whereas iPhone 4s and earlier have a 30-pin, one-way Dock connector.

✔ **USB power adapter:** Connects to the USB cable connector and plugs into an outlet to charge your iPhone's battery.

✔ **Finger Tips guide:** Apple's quick guide to iPhone functions and features.

✔ **Product info:** Legal and technical information.

Considering iPhone Carriers and Configurations

In the United States, four national carriers support iPhone — AT&T, Sprint, T-Mobile, and Verizon — as well as smaller regional carriers. That's made a situation that is both competitive and confusing for the consumer. In Europe, Vodafone is popular, although many countries also have country-specific carriers with competitive pricing.

Unlocked iPhones (iPhones you purchase outright without a service contract) work with carriers that use the GSM standard (see the following paragraph). In the United States, AT&T, T-Mobile, and 30 or so regional carriers use GSM, as do most of the carriers outside the U.S. Although Verizon CDMA phones are unlocked for international use, a Sprint customer in good standing can request that his CDMA carrier unlock his iPhone so it can access the GSM networks overseas, but nonetheless remains tied to the national and roaming costs associated with the cellular service contract.

Your iPhone doesn't only make phone calls. In fact, many of the things you do with your iPhone use the Internet, which you connect to via either Wi-Fi or a cellular data connection. Many carriers boast an LTE (Long Term Evolution) cellular data connection, which is sometimes referred to as 4G (for fourth-generation); it's designed to use different radio frequencies at higher speeds. The iPhone 5c can access up to 13 LTE bands and iPhone 6 accesses between 16 and 20 LTE bands (depending on the carrier), giving greater possibility of finding LTE wherever you are. Without getting into a bunch of technical gobbledygook, LTE means your web page, email, video streaming, and any other stuff you do online works faster — sometimes even faster than the Wi-Fi connection depending on your location. In North America, Europe, Japan, Russia, India, Australia, and Brazil, you find pretty good coverage in metropolitan areas, whereas in China, Mexico, and some emerging African and South American countries, 4G LTE support is in the works.

With so many different plans available from multiple national and regional carriers, we can't take responsibility for advising you on which to choose. We can, however, give you some things to think about — and questions to ask prospective providers — when choosing. Here are a few things to consider so you can compare plans from different carriers and make an informed decision:

- **How much time do you spend on the phone?** Most plans offer unlimited calling, so this question is almost moot. If you're considering a plan that offers a set number of minutes, consider how you use your phone: Do you make many calls or just check in now and then? Three hundred and sixty minutes for a month is 12 minutes a day, whereas 1,000 minutes is just over a half-hour a day. If you're thinking about replacing your landline with a cellphone, an unlimited calling plan may be a better choice.

- **Who do you call?** Some plans offer a you-and-me or family discount for one number, or a group of numbers, that you call more than any other. Some offer unlimited mobile-to-mobile calls, even to other carriers.

- **Where do you use your phone?** If you travel around the country, you probably want a call plan with nationwide coverage.

- **Do you travel overseas?** If you do, shop around for the best roaming rate or, if you frequently go to the same country, consider getting a local, rechargeable SIM card and using that in your iPhone when you're out of the United States.

- **Do you send text messages?** Again, most plans offer unlimited texting (SMS), however, text messages may be billed at a per-message rate or your plan may include a limited number of messages or kilobytes and you pay a per-message or per-kilobyte rate if you exceed the limited number. iMessage lets you send text messages over the Wi-Fi or cellular data network to other iPhone, iPad, and iPod touch users (as well as users of Macs running OS X 10.8 or later) without incurring SMS charges.

- **How much cellular data usage do you need?** Wi-Fi is widespread in the United States. Even the smallest one-café town seems to offer free Wi-Fi if you buy a cup of coffee, which makes cellular data less necessary. Most plans these days offer unlimited Internet access, although 50MB is the file size limit for downloading over a 3G or LTE cellular network.

When contracting with a cellular service provider, make sure to ask what charges you'll incur if you go over the minutes or data transfer limits — even going slightly over can cost a lot. Some carriers send an alert when you reach your limit; you can also refer to the Cellular Data Usage section of the Settings app (open the Settings app and tap Cellular), but most carriers offer free apps that track your calling and data usage.

The Winning Combination: Hardware and Apps

Your iPhone is more than just a phone. It's your online communications tool, personal digital assistant, GPS navigation system, entertainment source, camera, and flashlight. With each new generation, iPhone has added more functions and features. iPhone itself is the hardware, and the iOS and apps are the software that let you do so many things. Here we take a look at all your iPhone has to offer.

Phone

Clearly, iPhone is a cellular telephone (see Figure 1-1) that makes voice calls and offers text messaging. So what? All cellphones do that. Things get interesting when you send and receive multimedia messages with active links to web pages or a video of the pop fly your granddaughter just caught at the softball championship. Visual voicemail displays a list of messages so you can listen to the most important ones first rather than go through them in chronological order. Add to that more ways to communicate cost-free with other iOS device owners: FaceTime lets you make audio and video calls, and iMessage, which is part of Messages, gives you multimedia message exchanges. We explain the ins and outs of phoning and messaging in Book III, Chapters 1 and 2. For those times you don't feel like talking to anyone, there's Do Not Disturb, which blocks incoming calls and alerts.

Figure 1-1: iPhone as phone.

Music and videos

With the great display and excellent stereophonic output, your iPhone plays music, movies, podcasts, and more with crisp, clear sound and images. From the iTunes Store, you can download music, movies, TV shows, and audiobooks.

iTunes Radio lets you create a personalized radio station. Download the Trailers app to see movies that will be out in the coming months. Podcasts and iTunes U have their very own apps to enjoy podcasts and courseware. Connect your iPhone to a monitor or television with a cable or via AirPlay or Apple TV to watch everything on a big screen. All you have to do is pop the popcorn. Check out Book IV, Chapters 2, 3, and 4 to learn all about the audio and video functions.

Camera and video camcorder

The iSight camera places the iPhone 4s and later in the same class as many digital cameras. The enhanced lens, ten frames per second burst mode for capturing action shots, and dual-color LED flash of the 5s and later models may tempt even professional photographers to leave their DSLRs home some-times. What's more, the rear-facing camera captures 240-degree panoramic photos and high-definition video in 1,080 rows of pixels (also known as 1080p). With iOS 8, video recording has evolved even further and offers improved video stabilization, slow-motion capture, and time-lapse videos. The LED flash next to the objective lens on the back of your iPhone illuminates both still photos and videos. The Photos app organizes your photos and videos after you capture them and gives you good editing options. To create professional-looking movies and trailers, you can download the iMovie app. Go to Book IV, Chapters 1 and 4 for detailed information.

Personal digital assistant

With Siri, the voice-recognition interface that's available on any iPhone that can run iOS 8, iPhone is your personal digital assistant (PDA for short). Just speak your commands to Siri and she — or he, if you choose a male voice — does what you ask, such as reading your messages and then typing and sending a dictated reply, finding a florist, or identifying a new song you hear on the radio. We explain how to use the Siri interface in Book I, Chapter 3, and throughout this book, we sprinkle tips for using Siri with specific apps.

Don't overlook iPhone's other PDA features. The resident apps complete iPhone's PDA role. Contacts eliminates the need for a paper address book. Calendar replaces your time management system, and Notes makes all those scraps of ideas and grocery lists obsolete, while Reminders makes sure no task or appointment is forgotten. We show you how to use your iPhone's PDA apps along with Voice Memos, Clock, and Calculator in Book IV.

Passbook manages apps that track store cards, coupons, and boarding passes so you can (almost) leave your wallet at home and never miss out on a discount or point-accumulation opportunity. See Book IV, Chapter 5 for how to use it.

If you recently purchased a new iPhone, you can download the iWork suite gratis, which includes the Pages word processing app and Keynote presentation creation app, which we explain in Book III, Chapter 5, and the Numbers spreadsheet app, which we talk about in Book III, Chapter 4.

Internet communicator

The real power of your iPhone shows up when you go online. Able to access the Internet via either your cellular network or Wi-Fi, you never have to miss another time-sensitive email or tweet. You can search the Internet with Safari as you would on any computer. For example, you can search for movie times, book airline tickets, settle bets with Wikipedia, and read the news from your favorite news outlets. Safari's Reading List function lets you store a link to an article to read later. With iCloud, you can share tabs and bookmarks between all your devices. Book II, Chapter 3 explains Safari.

You access your email accounts through Mail. If you have multiple accounts, you can sync them all with Mail and see them individually or all together. Learn all about Mail in Book II, Chapter 4.

Tap open the Share Sheet from apps like Photos, Maps, and Safari to send information via AirDrop (iPhone 5 or later) to other iOS devices or Macs, attached to a Mail or Messages message, or upload to Facebook or Twitter. From the Share Sheet, you can also copy or print a document or image.

Your iPhone comes with some specific apps that gather information from the Internet. Weather leans on the Weather Channel to bring you the weather forecast for cities you want to know about. Stocks lets you follow international investment markets, as well as your personal investments. We take you through these apps in Book III, Chapters 3 and 4, respectively.

Personal GPS navigator

Between the Compass and Maps apps and the GPS, Wi-Fi, and cellular sensors, 99 percent of the time, your iPhone can tell you where you are and tell you how to get where you want to go. What's more, in coordination with Yelp, Maps and Siri can give you suggestions for vendors and services, like bookstores, museums, and restaurants, based on your location. The links in Maps are active — as they are in most iPhone apps — so you just click on the suggested vendor and the website for that vendor opens in Safari. We explain how to use Maps and Compass in Book III, Chapter 3.

E-book and document reader

Your iPhone's document-reading capabilities make reading on your iPhone easier than ever — instead of leafing through outdated tabloids in a waiting room, you have the latest news and novels at your fingertips. We talk about

Newsstand, which organizes and updates your magazine and newspaper app subscriptions, in Book IV, Chapter 5. For your reading pleasure, you have iBooks, which we explain in Book IV, Chapter 2.

You can read many types of documents on your iPhone. If a colleague sends you a PowerPoint presentation or a Pages document as an email attachment, just tap the attachment and your iPhone opens it so you can review it. With the iWork productivity apps, you can edit the document (without an additional app), and even without iWork, you can print the documents if there's an AirPrint-enabled printer on your wireless network.

Health maintenance organizer

We dedicate Book III, Chapter 6 to staying healthy. We show you how to manage your health records and statistics with the new Health app (see Figure 1-2). We also talk about the Nike+ iPod app, which tracks the distances and times of your runs or walks by receiving information from a sensor in certain models of Nike running shoes. That's not the only app that helps you stay fit. The App Store boasts dozens of apps that create workout routines or track your progress toward fitness goals and work in conjunction with Health. In Bonus Chapter 5, which you find online, we tell you about a few of our favorite fitness apps. For more on this book's online content, see the Introduction.

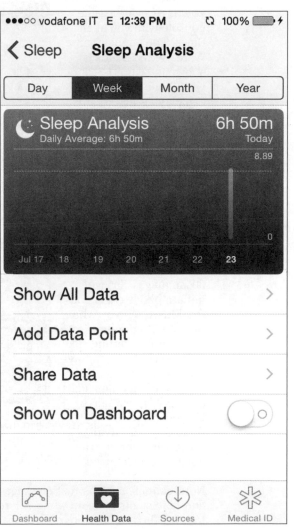

Figure 1-2: The Health app helps you stay, well, healthy.

Pocket video game console

With all the ruckus, you might think Candy Crush Saga is the only game in town. Actually, the App Store boasts more than 100,000 games, and many are free. Take that, Nintendo DS! With iPhone, you have a video game console with you at all times. The popular game Words With Friends is shown in Figure 1-3, and with Game Center, you can play against friends online and see who has the highest score. We tell you about Game Center in Book IV, Chapter 5.

Systemwide functions

The keyboard, used in any app where typing is involved, supports 50 languages. Siri can initiate phone calls, control Music, tell you what time it is, and more. Accessibility settings like enlarged font sizes, grayscale, custom vibration signals for incoming calls, and spoken text make iPhone easier to use. Guided Access helps those with learning disabilities stay focused on one task.

Figure 1-3: Your iPhone is also a tiny game console.

Notifications, such as text messages, Facebook status updates, reminders, and voicemails come in while you're doing other things; you can respond by tapping the notification, regardless of what app you're using. Just swipe down the screen and you see your upcoming appointments, stock activity, and the weather forecast along with a list of notifications. You choose to which and when you want to respond.

Swipe up from the bottom of the screen and you open the Control Center, as shown in Figure 1-4. Turn Wi-Fi and Bluetooth on or off, activate Do Not Disturb, adjust brightness and volume, and shine a light on your path with the flashlight — all just a tap away.

iCloud syncs your contacts, calendars, notes, browser tabs, photos, and documents across Apple and third-party apps on all your devices, including Mac and Windows computers, and you can store your files in iCloud Drive. With iCloud Keychain, AutoFill information such as usernames, passwords, and credit card information for secure access to your favorite websites and shopping haunts is shared across all your iCloud-enabled devices.

If you want to find something, Spotlight searches the contents of your phone from within many of the apps on your iPhone.

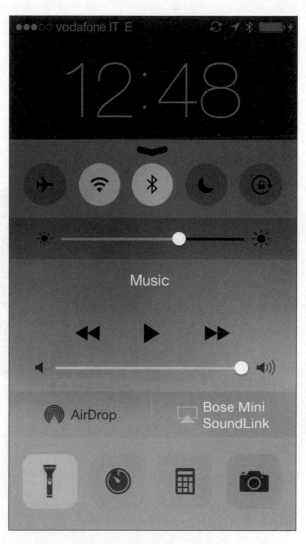

Figure 1-4: The Control Center gives you instant access to often-used system controls.

And a thousand other things!

Even if you never add another app to your iPhone, it can do a lot, but adding third-party apps moves the potential even higher. In the bonus chapters on this book's companion website, we try to knock your socks off by introducing some of the newest and most innovative problem-solving apps available. The online minibook is divided into six chapters ranging from practical business solutions and creativity tools to apps for sports, cooking, and travel. (For more on how to access the companion website, see this book's Introduction.) We certainly found apps we never imagined existed when we were researching them for this book, and we hope this nudges you to do some research on your own. Figure 1-5 shows one of Barbara's favorites, StarWalk.

We also include a chapter on hardware you can add to your iPhone, such as protective cases, supports and stands, speakers, and more.

With that, dear reader, you should have some idea of where you want to go.

Figure 1-5: StarWalk is a location-based astronomy guide.

Chapter 2: Activating and Understanding Your iPhone

In This Chapter

- Activating your iPhone
- Turning iPhone on and off
- Adjusting the volume
- Charging the battery
- Interpreting screen communications
- Making connections
- Adjusting Accessibility options for easier operation

*A*re you itching to get started with all things iPhone? In this chapter, we tell you how to use your iPhone's hardware and understand the interface. We begin with the most obvious tasks: turning your iPhone on and off, adjusting the volume level, and charging the battery. Then we review the basic layout of iPhone's screen and define the Status bar icons, notifications, and badges. We explain different types of connections you make with your iPhone — Internet and network connections, GPS connections, and printer connections. At the end of the chapter, we take a look at some of the ways you can modify your iPhone to make it easier to use if you have vision, hearing, or tactile challenges or if a young person who uses your iPhone has learning disabilities.

‿ıⱤ E 4:54 PM

ꜱage   **Battery Usage**

TIME SINCE LAST FULL CHARGE

Usage   3 Hours, 8 M

Standby   19 Hours, 21 M

ʰone has been plugged in since tʰ ʰarge.

Activating Your iPhone

To make phone calls and send SMS text messages, your iPhone must be connected to a cellular network through your cellular service provider. You can purchase an iPhone with a cellular network contract or without a contract, which is called an *unlocked iPhone* — not to be confused with the Unlocked/ Wake mode, which we explain in the next section.

Here's the difference:

✔ **Contract:** iPhone is activated when you sign up for a service plan with an iPhone service. There are several cellular network carrier choices. The most common that offer contracts are AT&T, which uses the GSM (Global System for Mobile Communications) cellular communications protocol, and Verizon and Sprint, which use the CDMA (Code Division Multiple Access) cellular communications protocol. We explain both GSM and CDMA in the "Making Connections" section of this chapter. You register your phone with the network and pick a plan for the calling, text messages, and Internet service usage you want.

If you bought your iPhone with a cellular service contract, it was already activated when you bought it; you only need to turn your iPhone on and follow the onscreen instructions. You can skip ahead to the section "Turning iPhone On and Off."

✔ **Unlocked:** You purchase a SIM card (that's the little chip inside that gives you access to the cellular network) from a service provider. The provider needs to know which iPhone model you have in order to give you the correct SIM: iPhone 5 or later requires a nano-SIM, while iPhone 4s uses a micro-SIM. You then purchase prepaid calling minutes in a pay-as-you-go option or monthly plan that automatically renews until you cancel it, which you can do at any time. Cellular broadband Internet access may be sold separately or bundled with the calling and text message allotment. You can sign up for a contract even if you have an unlocked iPhone; in that case, you bought your iPhone outright so the monthly charge should cost less than iPhone plus a cellular service fee. Unlocked iPhones work only with carriers who use the GSM cellular communications standard. AT&T and T-Mobile are the most common in the United States, but there are others, which you can find by searching "no contract cellphones" or "prepaid cellphones" on the Internet.

If you bought an unlocked iPhone and then signed up for a renewable or contractual cellular service, you need to install the SIM card and do some of the legwork your self. To insert the nano-SIM, do the following:

1. Insert the end of a paper clip into the hole on the SIM card tray on the right side of your iPhone.

   The SIM card tray pops open.

2. Place the SIM card in the tray, matching the cut corner of the SIM card to the cut corner in the tray.

3. Push the SIM card tray closed.

If you spend a lot of time overseas, you can purchase a prepaid SIM in that country, which you put in your iPhone when you're there. (Check with your U.S. service provider to see if unlocking has to be performed stateside first.) When you're in the United States, you put the U.S.-based SIM in your iPhone.

Press and hold the Sleep/Wake button (at the top right of iPhone 4s or 5 models; at the top right of iPhone 6 models) to turn it on. When you turn on your iPhone for the first time, the Setup Assistant takes you through a series of screens where you type in the requested information or choose from a list and tap Next or Done. You have to have a Wi-Fi or cellular network data connection to complete activation. The Setup Assistant asks for the following information:

- **Language:** Tap your selection in the list.

- **Country:** Tap your selection in the list.

- **Wi-Fi network:** A list of available Wi-Fi networks appears. Tap the one you use and enter the password. If Wi-Fi is unavailable, you can skip this step and do it later, or you can connect you iPhone to your computer with the USB connector cable and choose Connect to iTunes.

- **Location Services:** We recommend that you choose Enable Location Services, which lets various iPhone apps such as Maps and Reminders use your location to better perform operations.

- **Set Up iPhone:** If this is your first iPhone, you can choose Set Up as New iPhone or you can restore from a backup of your iPad or iPod touch, which puts your apps, data, and media on your iPhone. If you're moving from an older iPhone to a newer model, first back up your old phone and then choose Restore from iCloud Backup or Restore from iTunes Backup (whichever you use). Learn all the details of syncing, restoring, and using iCloud in Book I, Chapter 5.

- **Sign in or create an Apple ID:** Although you can choose to skip this step, your Apple ID lets you

  - Store your iPhone backup on iCloud, Apple's remote storage site.

  - Make purchases from the iTunes Store and the App Store.

  - Sign in to FaceTime.

  - Sync documents, calendars, notes, reminders, passwords, and more automatically across your iOS devices.

  You can have separate Apple IDs for iTunes and iCloud, but you need to follow the onscreen instructions to sign in to both. iCloud requires ID with an email format, such as `babsboyd@icloud.com`, so you may have to create a new account to activate iCloud. The Setup Assistant asks you to create an ID and password and set up three security questions — questions only you know the answer to that Apple asks if you forget your password or if you call for customer service and the technician wants to verify your identity.

  If you don't have an Apple ID and aren't sure what we're talking about, skip this step and go to Book I, Chapter 4, where we explain how to create and use an Apple ID in more detail.

✔ **Set Up Touch ID (only on models with this function):** Tap Set Up Now to go through the process that allows an iPhone 5s, 6, or 6 Plus to memorize your fingerprint. (Tap Set Up Later if you prefer to postpone this action; we show you how in Book I, Chapter 4.) After setting up Touch ID, touching the Home button unlocks your iPhone and can also be used in place of your Apple ID password to authorize purchases.

✔ **iTunes Store Sign in:** Type your Apple ID and password and agree to the Terms and Conditions when asked.

✔ **iCloud Setup:** You can choose to use iCloud or decline and then set up iCloud later, as explained in Book I, Chapter 5.

✔ **Messaging:** Choose which phone number and email address other people can use to reach you on iMessage, iPhone's text messaging service, and FaceTime, iPhone's audio and video calling service. Both can use cellular data or Wi-Fi.

✔ **Diagnostics:** We recommend you choose Automatically Send. Tap Start Using iPhone after you complete the setup procedure.

Turning iPhone On and Off

When you bought your iPhone, the salesperson probably showed you a few basic tasks, such as turning your iPhone on and off. For good measure, we review it here in our review of the iPhone's external buttons. But first, throughout the book we use a few terms regarding your iPhone's state of consciousness, or modes, that warrant an explanation because they could be a bit confusing:

✔ **Sleep:** Your iPhone is asleep when it's on but the screen is dark. It can receive incoming calls, email, messages, and notifications, which push it into Wake mode.

✔ **Wake:** Your iPhone screen displays something, which could be the Lock screen (Figure 2-1) or the Home screen (Figure 2-2) or an app screen. It can receive incoming communications.

✔ **Locked (or Lock screen):** Your iPhone is awake, but you only see an image with some basic information (explained later in this chapter). You can open the Notification Center or the Control Center (Book I, Chapter 4) or slide the Camera icon up to use the camera, but you have to slide your finger across the screen or across a notification to go into Unlocked mode.

✔ **Unlocked:** Your screen is awake and active. You see either the Home screen or an app screen and interact with them with all the touchscreen gestures we explain in Book I, Chapter 3.

Your iPhone is on in all four modes and in combination may be in Sleep/Locked mode, Wake/Locked mode, or Wake/Unlocked mode (but not Sleep/Unlocked).

The Home button is found in the same place on all iPhone models. You find the Sleep/Wake button on the top of iPhone 5 and earlier models and on the right side of iPhone 6 and 6 Plus. When you press and hold it, it turns iPhone on or off, and when you press and release it, it either wakes iPhone (and you see the Lock screen) or puts iPhone to sleep. Here are the specifics for those actions:

✔ **To turn iPhone on:** Press and hold the Sleep/Wake button. The Apple logo appears in the center of the screen. After 30 seconds or so, the Lock screen appears (refer to Figure 2-1). Depending on whether you set a passcode, you see one of the following:

• *With Passcode:* Drag your finger across the screen and then, on the keypad that appears (a keyboard if you used a complex passcode), tap the passcode you assigned during setup. After you enter the correct passcode, the last Home or app screen you were using appears.

Figure 2-1: The Lock screen appears when you first wake your phone from its Sleep state.

• Even if you have an iPhone with Touch ID, when you turn your iPhone on, you have to use your passcode.

• *Without Passcode:* Drag your finger from left to right across the screen and the Home screen (or the last app you were using) opens.

- If you have a SIM card, with a personal identification number (PIN), a message comes up with two buttons: OK and Unlock. Tap the right button to open a keypad where you enter the PIN of your SIM card to unlock it. Tap the left OK button, and you can use iPhone apps but not any of the phone, message, or Internet features.

✔ **To turn iPhone off:** Press and hold the Sleep/Wake button until the bar appears with the message *Slide to Power Off.* Drag your finger from left to right across this bar to turn iPhone off. Tap the Cancel button at the bottom of the screen if you change your mind.

✔ **To put iPhone to sleep:** Press the Sleep/Wake button once.

✔ **To wake iPhone:** Press either the Sleep/Wake button or the Home button, which is the round button below the screen that we explain in a couple of paragraphs. Then do one of the following to reach the Home screen or the app you were using before your iPhone went to sleep:

- *Without passcode:* Slide your finger across the Lock screen.

- *With passcode:* Slide your finger across the Lock screen and then tap your passcode on the keypad that appears.

- *With Touch ID:* Rest your finger on the Home key (without sliding your finger across the Lock screen).

iPhone goes to sleep and locks (not to be confused with the SIM lock) automatically when you don't touch the screen for one minute. You can change this setting to up to five minutes or never in the Settings app by tapping General and then tapping Auto-Lock. This saves battery power and keeps you from unintentionally opening an app or making a call by accidentally touching the Home screen. When iPhone is asleep or locked, you still receive phone calls, messages, and alerts — unless you have the Do Not Disturb function activated — and can listen to music. You can also adjust the volume of a call or music with the volume buttons on the side of the phone.

Incoming communications such as a phone call, text message, or notification from an app like Facebook or Mail also wake your iPhone and present an action to take on the Lock screen.

The Home button is the round, central button on the front of iPhone, below the screen. You can do the following:

✔ **When iPhone is awake:** Press this button once to return to the Home screen at any time from any app.

Quickly press the Home button twice, also known as a double-click, to open the App Switcher and switch from one app to another. More about that in Book I, Chapter 3.

✔ **When iPhone is asleep/locked:** Press this button once to wake iPhone the same way as the Sleep/Wake button does.

If you have an iPhone with Touch ID, the Home button performs the above functions and houses the Touch ID sensor, which uses your finger to authorize iPhone access and purchases in place of a passcode or Apple ID.

Turning Up the Volume

When you're in a noisy place and you don't want to miss a call, you might want to have the ringer at full volume. On the other hand, if you're in a meeting but waiting for an important call, you may want to keep your iPhone silent and choose to respond only to that one not-to-be-missed call. Likewise, you may want to increase the speaker volume to better hear the person you're speaking with on a call in a noisy place. Here we explain how the three buttons on the left of your iPhone control volume:

✔ **Volume buttons:** You find the volume buttons — two round, slightly raised buttons — on the left side of iPhone. The button on top with the plus sign increases volume; the lower button with the minus sign lowers volume. When iPhone is awake, but not otherwise engaged in a noisy activity, these buttons control the volume of both the ringer and alerts, unless you've turned that feature off within the sound settings, as we explain in Book I, Chapter 4. When you're engaged in a call or using an app that has volume — be it music, a video, or a game — these buttons control the volume of the thing you're listening to, watching, or playing.

Both volume buttons double as shutter buttons for the Camera. (Refer to Book IV, Chapters 1 and 4 to learn about using your iPhone's camera and video recorder.)

✔ **Silent/Ring switch:** The switch above the volume buttons is a mute button. Push it to the back and you see a red bar. This is the off or silent position. Pushed to the front is the on or ring position. When iPhone is in silent mode, it vibrates when calls or alerts come in. If your iPhone rings and you prefer not to answer, you can turn the Silent/Ring switch off. Your caller continues to hear the phone ring until he decides to hang up or leave a voicemail message, but your iPhone will be silent although it will continue to vibrate. See Book II, Chapter 1 for information about declining calls.

When iPhone is in silent mode, alarms you set are still audible, which means you can put your iPhone in silent mode when you go to sleep but you'll hear the alarm you set to wake you in the morning. The audio for Music and some games will be heard through the speaker or earphones, if you happen to have those plugged into your iPhone (and into your ears, of course).

Charging Your iPhone Battery

Like all battery-powered gadgets, your iPhone is useless with an uncharged battery. The good news is that iPhone recharges in less than an hour, and you can charge the battery in several ways, which we describe here. Even though it recharges quickly, sometimes you want to conserve that charge for as long as possible; check out the sidebar at the end of this section for tips on helping your iPhone hold the battery charge longer.

Plugging into the USB charger

Your iPhone comes with a USB connection cable and a USB power adapter. To charge the battery, plug the dock connector into the dock port at the base of your iPhone, plug the USB end into the USB power adapter and plug the power adapter into an electrical outlet. iPhone beeps, which lets you know it's actively charging.

The power adapter automatically adjusts to 110 or 220 voltage, based on the voltage for the location you're plugging into. If you're using your iPhone outside the United States, you have to purchase an adapter that changes the plug conformation to meet the outlet style of the country you're visiting. You can find a kit at the Apple Store (http://store.apple.com/us) or single adapters at TravelProducts.com (www.travelproducts.com). If you use a MacBook, PlugBug World from Twelve South (www.twelvesouth.com) connects to the Mac's power block and houses a USB port so you can charge your Mac and iPhone on the same outlet. Or you can charge your iPhone with your computer's USB port, as we explain next.

Charging with your Mac or PC's USB port

When you connect your iPhone to a USB port on your computer to sync or transfer photos, the battery automatically begins taking a charge. Again, iPhone beeps, which lets you know this is going on.

If your computer is turned off or is sleeping, your iPhone battery may drain instead of charge, so make sure your computer is on whenever you connect your iPhone to it.

Although plugging your iPhone into any recent or new Mac can charge your iPhone, the same isn't necessarily true for recent or new Windows desktop and laptop computers or older Macs. Apple explains that's because the USB ports on certain models don't pass through enough wattage to charge your iPhone. If connecting your iPhone to your USB port doesn't yield a charge — you know it's charging because it beeps and there's a lightning bolt next to the battery in the Status bar — try plugging into a port dock on a powered USB hub. If that doesn't work, you'll have to plug into a charger to charge your iPhone.

Don't pull the cable to detach your iPhone from your computer. Always grasp the hard, square part of either end of the USB cable to remove it.

If iPhone's battery charge drops very low or runs down completely, your iPhone automatically shuts itself off. To bring your iPhone back to life, you must attach the USB cable to a power source (your computer or an electrical outlet). When your iPhone shuts itself off because the battery charge is too low or nearly empty, you won't be able to use your iPhone until the battery reaches a minimal charge level. Usually you only have to wait a few minutes before your iPhone turns itself on again.

To preserve the overall life, you should cycle the battery on a monthly basis. *Cycling* is letting the battery completely discharge and then charging it fully.

More charging options

Apple and other third-party vendors make charging accessories. You can use an iPhone dock, which is a type of base that you set your iPhone in to charge the battery — it's convenient to have on your desk to keep your iPhone close at hand. Make sure you purchase the dock that's appropriate for the iPhone model you use. You can also purchase battery packs that attach to your iPhone to get a longer charge. And, if you spend a lot of time in your car, another option is a USB adapter that plugs into the cigarette lighter to charge your iPhone. Many newer car models come with a built-in USB port that both charges your iPhone and lets you listen to audio from your iPhone through the car's stereo speakers.

You can replace standard electrical outlets with USB-enabled outlets, so all you have to do is plug in the cable. We've seen USB outlets more frequently in hotels and airplanes, too, which makes charging while traveling super easy. If charging in a hotel room, make sure the USB outlet still works when you turn out the lights.

Keeping an eye on your charges

The battery icon in the Status bar indicates roughly how much battery power you have. If you want to see a specific percentage, open the Settings app, tap General, tap Usage, and tap the Battery Percentage switch on.

You can see detailed battery charge consumption in the Settings app by tapping General, tapping Usage, and tapping Battery Usage. The screen shown in Figure 2-2 opens. You see how much time has passed since your last charge, specified in two ways:

- **Usage:** How much you've used it
- **Standby:** How much time your iPhone spent sleeping

The list shows which apps have been the top battery consumers in the last 24 hours. As in Figure 2-2, low (cellular data) signal is the cause for a high usage of apps that use the Internet like Facebook and Mail.

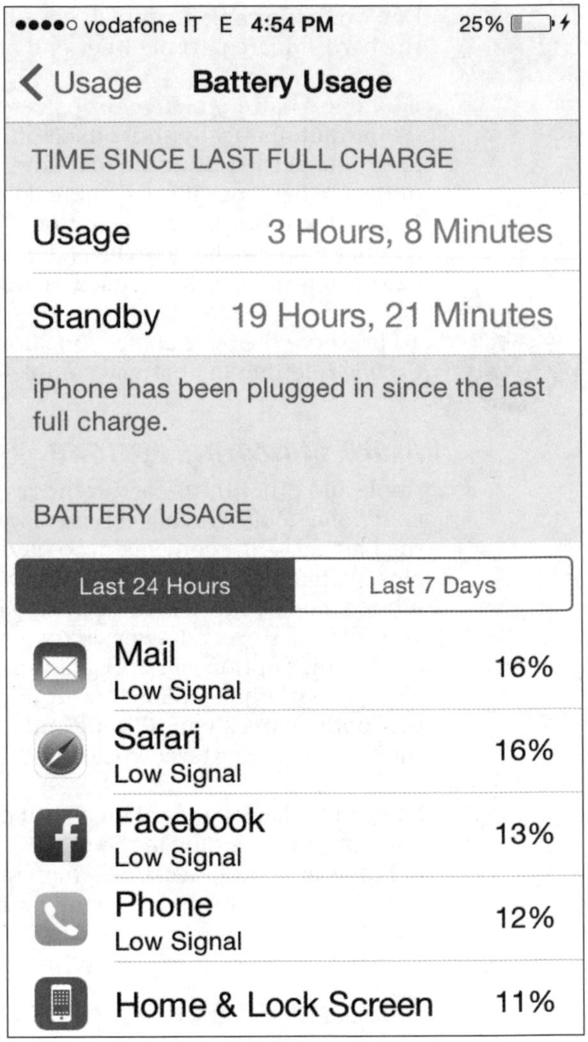

Changing the battery

If you keep your iPhone for many years, sooner or later, you'll need to replace the battery. Despite our do-it-yourself (DIY) world, you can't replace the battery yourself. You have to send it in to the Battery Replacement Program. For $85 (as of this writing), you send your iPhone to Apple or take it to an Apple Store, the battery is replaced, and Apple takes care of disposing of the old one. This service is covered if your iPhone is still under the one-year warranty or you extended the warranty to two years with the AppleCare protection plan, which we explain in Book I, Chapter 5.

●●●●○ vodafone IT E 4:54 PM	25% 🔋⚡
‹ Usage Battery Usage	

TIME SINCE LAST FULL CHARGE

Usage	3 Hours, 8 Minutes
Standby	19 Hours, 21 Minutes

iPhone has been plugged in since the last full charge.

BATTERY USAGE

Last 24 Hours	Last 7 Days

✉	**Mail** Low Signal	16%
🧭	**Safari** Low Signal	16%
f	**Facebook** Low Signal	13%
📞	**Phone** Low Signal	12%
📱	**Home & Lock Screen**	11%

Figure 2-2: Battery Usage shows which apps are power hogs.

Gaming, watching videos, and surfing the web use big chunks of battery power. Playing a game helps pass the time on a long trip, but make sure you leave enough battery power to call your ride when you arrive at your destination, or that there's a power source into which to plug your iPhone.

Charging Your iPhone Battery *Charging Your iPhone Battery* **29**

Keeping the battery charged

Technically, you should get about eight hours of talk time on an iPhone 5 on the 3G network. Realistically, if you play games and go on the Internet, you probably get less. Here are some tips for keeping the battery charged longer and for maintaining long battery life:

✔ **Turn off Location Services.** Open the Settings app, tap Privacy, and tap Location Services. (Remember though that the apps that use it do so only when you're using them, so you're not saving a ton of battery life this way.)

✔ **Turn off Wi-Fi.** If you have Wi-Fi turned on and there's no Wi-Fi network, your iPhone keeps searching and searching and consuming battery power. To turn off Wi-Fi, open the Settings app, tap Wi-Fi, and tap the Wi-Fi switch off, or just swipe up from the bottom of any screen to open the Control Center and tap the Wi-Fi button.

✔ **Turn off 4G/LTE.** If 4G or LTE isn't available where you are or you don't need to access the 4G network, turn it off. Sometimes this actually improves access to your cellular calling network. It doubles your battery charge. Open the Settings app, tap Cellular, and tap the Enable 4G/LTE switch off.

✔ **Turn off Siri.** If you don't need Siri's assistance, you may as well send her out to lunch since she's a power hog. Open the Settings app, tap General, tap Siri, and tap the Siri switch off.

✔ **Turn on Airplane Mode.** If you happen to be out of your network range, your iPhone consumes a lot of battery power as it continually searches for the cellular network. Eventually the words *No Service* appear instead of the carrier name, and your iPhone settles down and stops searching. Consider putting your iPhone in Airplane Mode: Open the Settings app and tap the Airplane Mode switch on, or just swipe up from the bottom of any screen to open the Control Center and tap the Airplane Mode button. Both cellular and Wi-Fi are turned off, but you can still use other apps that don't need those services.

✔ **Use fetch instead of push.** Instead of having your iPhone constantly check for new information with push, you can set your iPhone to sync with whichever cloud service you use — such as iCloud, Yahoo! Mail, or MS-Exchange — at set time intervals, or sync manually. Open the Settings app; tap Mail, Contacts, Calendars; tap Fetch New Data; and tap the Push switch off.

✔ **Use Auto-Brightness.** Dimming your screen also improves the length of a charge. The ambient light sensor dims or brightens your screen based on the light it senses. You can turn the automatic adjustment on in the Settings app by tapping Display & Brightness and then tapping the Auto-Brightness switch on.

✔ **Turn off Bluetooth.** If you don't have any Bluetooth devices connected and don't plan to use any for a while, open the Settings app, tap Bluetooth, and tap the Bluetooth switch off, or just swipe up from the bottom of any screen to open the Control Center and tap the Bluetooth button.

✔ **Turn off cellular data.** Open the Settings app, tap Cellular, and tap the Cellular Data switch off. You can still use the phone and Wi-Fi connection.

Interpreting the (Visual) Signs

In this section, we explain what you see on the Home screen, how to interpret the Status bar icons, and how to read and respond to notifications iPhone sends you when it has something important to communicate.

Home screen

The point of departure for everything iPhone is the Home screen, which features three basic parts (or zones), as you can see in Figure 2-3. At the very top is the *Status bar,* which we get to in just a few paragraphs. The bulk of the screen holds 16 or more app buttons and folders; the number varies with screen size. Four of the Home screen's apps stay tacked at the bottom of the screen in what's called the *Dock,* which makes it easy to get to your most-favorite apps no matter which Home screen you're viewing.

Figure 2-3: The Home screen is the point of departure for iPhone.

When a Home screen is filled with apps and/or folders, a new Home screen is added, up to 15 Home screens in all. Between the last row of apps and the Dock is a line of dots (one of which is white, the others are gray). These represent the number of Home screens you have. The white dot tells you which of the Home screens you're on. In Figure 2-3, you see the first dot is white followed by three gray dots, which means this is Home screen one of four. Flick the current Home screen to the left, and the screen moves one screen to the left; flick the Home screen to the right, and the screen moves one screen to the right. Touch the dots toward the left, and the screen moves one screen to the left; touch the dots to the right, and the screen moves one screen to the right.

Tap any of the app icons on the Home screen, and the associated app opens. If you tap a folder, it opens. Then you tap the app inside the folder that you want to launch. Double-click the Home button and the apps that are open appear in the App Switcher and contact icons for your favorite folks or those with whom you've recently exchanged a phone call or message appear at the top.

iPhone 6 Plus lets you view the Home screen in landscape (horizontal) mode.

Staying informed with Status bar icons

The Status bar runs across the very top of your iPhone in either portrait or landscape view, in apps that support landscape view. Its icons give you information about your cellular and/or wireless network connection, battery life, and auxiliary functions you may have turned on, such as Do Not Disturb and the alarm clock. Here is an explanation of each one. Remember, you won't see them all at once on your iPhone, and some you may never see:

 ✔ **Airplane Mode:** You see this icon if you've turned Airplane mode on in Settings. See Book I, Chapter 4 for more details on Airplane Mode.

 ✔ **Alarm:** Appears if you set an alarm using the Clock app; we explore the Clock app in Book III, Chapter 2.

 ✔ **Battery:** The filled amount indicates approximately how much charge remains on the battery. A more accurate percentage appears next to the icon if you turn on Battery Percentage in the Settings app by tapping General and then tapping Usage. A lightning bolt next to the battery tells you it's being charged. Refer to the earlier section, "Charging Your iPhone Battery" to read more about battery usage.

 ✔ **Bluetooth:** Shows that Bluetooth is turned on. When it's black or white, you're connected to another Bluetooth device such as a headset. When it's gray, Bluetooth is on but no device is connected. Some Bluetooth-enabled headsets add their own battery charge indicator to the Status bar, so you know when you need to charge your headset.

 ✔ **Call Forwarding:** On GSM models (an unlocked Apple iPhone or an AT&T iPhone, refer to the "Considering iPhone Carriers and Configurations" section in Book I, Chapter 1), appears when you've forwarded your calls to another phone number. The call forwarding settings are explained in Book II, Chapter 1.

 ✔ **Cell Signal:** Indicates the strength of the cellular signal your iPhone is connected to. If you have no filled-in circles or just one, the signal is weak — more solid circles, stronger signal. *No Service* appears when iPhone is unable to pick up a signal from your cellular provider. If Airplane Mode is turned on, you see the airplane icon instead of the cell signal circles. If your carrier offers Wi-Fi calling, you've activated it as an option with your carrier, and you turn it on in the Phone section of the Settings app, you see *carrier name* Wi-Fi.

✓ **Do Not Disturb:** Reminds you that you've activated the Do Not Disturb feature.

 ✓ **EDGE (E):** Appears when iPhone is connected to your cellular provider's EDGE data network for accessing the Internet. GSM models support EDGE networks. Read more about Internet access later in this chapter.

 ✓ **GPRS/1xRTT:** GSM models use the GPRS (General Packet Radio Service) network and CDMA models use the 1xRTT (1x Radio Transmission Technology) network to access the Internet when those networks are available. Read more about Internet access in the "Making Connections" section, later in this chapter.

 ✓ **Location Services:** When you see this icon, an app, such as Maps or Reminders, is tracking your current location coordinates in order to provide you with nearby information or other services.

 ✓ **LTE:** Lets you know you have an LTE cellular connection; this icon may be 4G, depending on your carrier.

 ✓ **Network Activity:** Spins when iPhone is accessing a cellular or Wi-Fi network for any app that uses the Internet, such as Safari or the App Store. It also appears when iPhone is syncing iCloud information over the air, or sometimes when an app is performing other data-related activities.

 ✓ **Personal Hotspot:** This icon is active when you've connected to another iPhone or a 3G/4G iPad that is providing a Personal Hotspot.

 ✓ **Orientation Lock:** This reminds you that you've turned off the landscape view feature. You can turn your iPhone every which way, but the screen remains in portrait position — unless you open an app that only works in landscape position, such as some games or videos.

 ✓ **Syncing:** Indicates that your iPhone is syncing with iTunes or iCloud.

 ✓ **TTY:** Indicates your iPhone is configured to work with a Teletype (TTY) machine.

 ✓ **UMTS/EV-DO (3G):** Indicates when GSM models are connected to the UMTS (Universal Mobile Telecommunications System) network, or CDMA models are connected to the EV-DO (Evolution-Data Optimized) network to access the Internet when those networks are available. Read more about Internet access in the "Making Connections" section later in this chapter.

 ✓ **VPN:** Indicates iPhone is connected to a VPN (Virtual Private Network).

✓ **Wi-Fi:** Indicates iPhone is connected to a Wi-Fi network. The more bars, the merrier — er, we mean, the more stable — the connection. Read more about wireless connections in the "Making Connections" section of this chapter.

Understanding Status bar colors

The text of the Status bar may be black or white, whichever shows up better on the background of the app or Home screen. In some situations, however, the background color changes behind the status bar when you're engaged in one activity, such as a phone call, and begin another activity, such as opening Notes to jot down something your caller is telling you. These are what the different colors mean:

- ✔ **Green:** A phone or FaceTime call is active but you're doing something else. You can continue to converse while you do the other activity; it's helpful to put the call on speakerphone before opening another app.

- ✔ **Red:** Voice Memos or another recording app is recording while you're doing other things. Tap the red bar to return to Voice Memos, or the recording app, and stop recording.

- ✔ **Blue:** Your iPhone is set up as a Personal Hotspot and its Internet connection is being accessed by another device.

Noticing notifications and badges

When iPhone wants to get your attention and tell you something, it communicates via badges and notification alerts (see Figure 2-4) and banners. These are different from alerts, alarms, and reminders that you set on your iPhone in that they contain information iPhone wants to give you.

A *badge* appears as a white number inside a red circle in the corner of certain app icons, such as Mail and Podcasts (refer to Figure 2-3). The number indicates how many unread messages or status updates await you in those apps.

Figure 2-4: Notification alerts often have buttons that give you a choice of actions to take.

Alerts require a response and appear when you want to do something but iPhone needs something else to happen before it can complete the task. Alerts appear in rectangular boxes in the middle of the screen and typically display buttons you can tap to respond to with a certain action. In the example in Figure 2-4, for instance, you have the choice o f acknowledging the alert by tapping Cancel, or by tapping Disable to turn off Airplane Mode.

Banners appear when you're doing one thing — say, reading an article on a website — and another thing happens — say, you get an incoming email. You see a banner across the top of your iPhone's screen. You can choose to respond or ignore it. You can ignore the banner, and it disappears in a few seconds, tap it to open the app that wants your attention, or in apps that offer interactive notifications, like Messages or Facebook, swipe down to respond. For example, an iMessage comes in while you're reading the news on Safari; pull the banner down and a field opens so you can type your response, tap Send, and then return to the article you were reading, without ever having left Safari or pull down on a Facebook banner, tap Like or write a comment, and then return to what you were doing. iPhone saves notifications you don't respond to in the Notification Center, which you can see by swiping down from the top of the screen. You choose which apps you want to see in the Notification Center and how you want to be notified in Settings, which we cover in Book I, Chapter 4.

When a new app has been installed or an existing app updated, a blue dot appears to the left of the app name under the app icon.

Making Connections

Your iPhone has the ability to connect to a variety of signal sources, which means you can be connected to someone somewhere all the time: to the Internet via your cellular carrier's data network or via a Wi-Fi network, or to other devices like printers, keyboards, and hands-free headsets using Bluetooth, and to other iOS devices or Macs using AirDrop, which transmits over Bluetooth or Wi-Fi. To help you understand all your iPhone's many connection options, we've organized those options into three sections: cellular and wireless connections; Personal Hotspot, tethering, and AirDrop; and lastly, Bluetooth and GPS connections. You can manage these connections in the Settings app.

Cellular

When you activate your iPhone with a carrier, you gain access to that carrier's cellular voice and data network. Without boring you with too many technical details, your iPhone typically connects using one or more of the following protocols:

✔ **LTE/4G:** Long Term Evolution is the most recent cellular communications protocol. Both GSM- and CDMA-model iPhones can access the LTE network where it's available. This may be referred to as 4G when a GSM carrier accesses the 4G UMTS network.

✔ **GSM (Global System for Mobile Communications) models**

- *3G/UMTS:* 3G is the third-generation protocol standard that uses the UMTS (Universal Mobile Telecommunications System) cellular frequency. This protocol is faster than EDGE, but consumes more battery power. If 3G is on but unavailable, iPhone defaults to EDGE.

- *EDGE:* Enhanced Data for GSM Evolution is the first-generation protocol standard for connecting to the Internet over the cellular carrier network. EDGE often offers a more stable, albeit slower, connection than 3G because it offers wider network coverage.

- *GPRS:* General Packet Radio Service supports both second- (2G) and third-generation (3G) cellular telephony. Usage is based on volume rather than time. If neither EDGE nor 3G is available, iPhone defaults to GPRS.

- *HSPA+:* High-Speed Packet Access is a faster type of 3G.

✔ **CDMA (Code Division Multiple Access) models**

- *EV-DO:* The Evolution-Data Optimized is a 3G or third-generation protocol, similar to UMTS for access speed.

- *1xRTT:* 1x Radio Transmission Technology is an alternative 3G protocol.

Unlike GSM-model iPhones, if you have a CDMA iPhone and are actively transferring data over your carrier's cellular network — to check your email or browse a web page, for instance — you cannot also engage in an active phone call while those data-related activities are underway. Any calls you may receive while using your cellular carrier's data connection are sent directly to your voicemail. You can make and receive calls while doing those data-related things on your CDMA iPhone if you're connected to a Wi-Fi network.

When your iPhone is connected to the Internet with one of these protocols, the associated icon appears in the Status bar, as mentioned earlier in this chapter.

If you happen to be outside your carrier's network, you can try to access the Internet through another carrier. This is called Data Roaming and is enabled by opening the Settings app, tapping Cellular, and tapping the Data Roaming switch on.

Data roaming, especially if you're out of the country, can rack up sizeable surcharges. Check with your carrier for data roaming fees before being surprised with a whopping bill at the end of the month.

If your cellular carrier contract has a data transfer limit, you want to keep track of how much data you're consuming. Your carrier may have a dedicated website or app that tracks the information for you or you can monitor your cellular data usage by opening the Settings app and tapping Cellular.

Scroll down the screen to see the Call Time and Cellular Data Usage, which indicate the number of days and hours you spent on your iPhone during that period and during the total span of your relationship with your carrier plan and the amount of data you've shuttled back and forth over your cellular carrier's network. At the very bottom of the screen, you find the Reset Statistics button that resets the aforementioned stats so you can start tracking those figures.

You should tap Reset Statistics at the end of the month or on the day when your period renews. Using Wi-Fi for data access is an alternative if you have free or low-cost Wi-Fi service in places where you use your iPhone.

Wi-Fi

You may want to say that cellular is wireless, and you'd be right. But Wi-Fi is wireless, only better. Connecting to the Internet using iPhone's Wi-Fi feature is one of the fastest — and cheapest — ways to connect to the Internet. Wi-Fi networks blast their typically close-range signals from a device known as a *wireless router,* which is connected to a broadband modem, which in turn is typically connected to your cable or phone company's broadband Internet service (or whatever the Wi-Fi router you tap into is connected to, be it at your favorite cafe, on a train, or a public library, for example). Other people can connect their Wi-Fi enabled devices as well, making the group of you a network, as opposed to a single connection. You may need a password to access a Wi-Fi network, and some Wi-Fi services charge an hourly or daily fee to access their networks.

To join a Wi-Fi network, follow these steps:

1. **Open the Settings app and tap Wi-Fi.**

   The Wi-Fi Networks screen opens.

2. **Tap the Wi-Fi switch on.**

   The screen expands to give you the option to Choose a Network, as seen in Figure 2-5. iPhone detects servers in the area, and the Wi-Fi symbol indicates how strong the signal is: the more waves, the stronger the signal. Servers that require a password have a closed lock icon next to them.

   Some Wi-Fi networks may require you to agree to the provider's terms before you can use the network. In those cases, a prompt appears, asking for your permission to launch Safari to view the provider's web page, where you typically tap a check box indicating you agree to the legal mumbo jumbo listed on the web page. In other cases, you have to type in a username and password in order to agree to the provider's terms.

   If you know the name of the network you want to join and it's not in the list, follow these steps:

1. **Tap Other.**

   The Other Network pane opens.

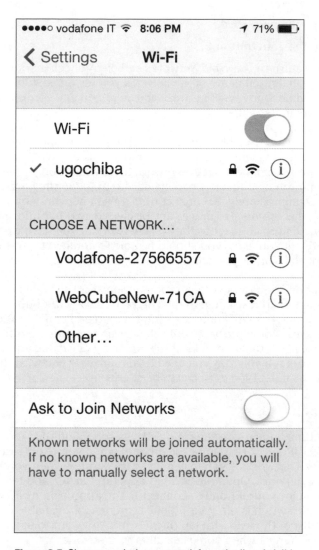

Figure 2-5: Choose a wireless network from the list of visible servers.

2. **Type the name of the network in the Name field.**

3. **If the network has a password, tap Security.**

   The Security screen opens.

4. **Choose the type of password this network uses and tap the back button that reads Other Network.**

   The Other Network screen reopens, and the cursor is blinking in the Password field.

3. **Type the password.**

4. **Tap the Join button.**

> You return to the Wi-Fi Networks screen. A check mark appears next to the highlighted name of the network you've joined. iPhone automatically remembers any Wi-Fi network you've joined and connects to it whenever you're in its range.

iPhone remembers Wi-Fi networks you previously connected to and automatically reconnects whenever you're in range of those Wi-Fi networks, unless you're already connected to a network that has a stronger signal. Tap the Info (i) button next to a network name and then tap the Forget This Network button to immediately disconnect from a Wi-Fi network you're connected to. Tapping this option also erases any password or other information you may have typed in to connect to the Wi-Fi network. If you have trouble connecting to a network you *know* you should be able to connect to, try forgetting the network and signing in again.

Information about and configuration options for the Wi-Fi network you're connected to appear beneath the Forget This Network button. Scroll down the list to see the Wi-Fi network's information and configuration options. Chances are, you'll probably only view or change these additional Wi-Fi network settings if the tech folks at the company or organization that operates the network tell you that you need to and provide you with the necessary details you must type in to make the connection.

Carrier

This setting appears on the main Settings screen on GSM models (such as the AT&T iPhone or an unlocked iPhone) when you're outside your service provider's network — you may not see this option when you're within your carrier's network. Open the Settings app, tap Carrier, and tap the Automatic switch on for your iPhone to connect to the appropriate carrier. When the Automatic switch is off, your iPhone searches for available carriers and presents a list of those found; tap the network you want to use. You may incur roaming charges when you use a different network.

Many apps download and upload data with a remote server and use either Wi-Fi or the cellular data network to make those exchanges. For example, Facebook accesses the Facebook server to show you the latest status updates and let you post your own; likewise, the App Store exists in the virtual realm of the Internet and when you access it from your iPhone, your browsing and shopping activity travels on the cellular data network or Wi-Fi. You can better control how you consume your contractual cellular data allotment by choosing which apps use cellular data. Open the Settings app, tap Cellular, scroll down to the Use Cellular Data For section, and tap the switches on or off for the apps you want to allow cellular data access. Even if you tap an app's switch to the off position, it can still perform its data functions when you're connected to Wi-Fi.

AirDrop

AirDrop creates a connection between your iPhone 5 or later and one or more iOS devices such as iPhones (5 or later), iPads (fourth generation or Mini), or iPod touches (fifth generation), or newer Macs running OS X (10.10) Yosemite or later. You can then exchange documents and data from apps, such as a contact card in Contacts, an address in Maps, or an event in Calendar. To use AirDrop, follow these steps:

1. **Drag up from the bottom of the screen to open the Control Center.**

2. **Tap AirDrop.**

   When you turn AirDrop on, both Wi-Fi and Bluetooth are activated because sharing takes place with either of these types of connections.

3. **Choose one of the choices:**
   - *Off* to turn AirDrop off
   - *Contacts Only* to give access to your iPhone only to people with iCloud accounts who are in your Contacts
   - *Everyone* to let everyone on the same Wi-Fi network with an iCloud account see your iPhone

4. **Open whatever it is you want to share — say, a photo in Photos.**

5. **Tap the Share button.**

6. **Tap the icon for the person you want to share with.**

   The person receives a notification that you want to share something with her, and she can choose to Decline or Accept your shared item.

Personal Hotspot and tethering

When another device uses your iPhone's Internet connection to connect to the Internet, that's called *tethering.* Tethering essentially turns your iPhone into a miniature Wi-Fi router that broadcasts a signal that you or a few others can tap into with your laptop computer, your iPad, or most any other Wi-Fi–enabled gadget. A Wi-Fi network you can connect to is typically referred to as a *hotspot,* and on your iPhone, this feature is called Personal Hotspot. You can also connect your computer to iPhone's Personal Hotspot feature using a USB cable, instead of connecting using Wi-Fi.

To use iPhone's Personal Hotspot feature, you must pay your cellular service provider a separate fee in addition to your existing cellular service plan. Contact your provider for details. Personal Hotspot also quickly consumes the battery charge.

To share an Internet connection using your iPhone's Personal Hotspot feature, follow these steps:

1. **Open the Settings app.**
2. **Tap Personal Hotspot.**
3. **Tap the Personal Hotspot switch on.**

   Take note of the Wi-Fi Password given on the Personal Hotspot screen.

   If Bluetooth is turned off, a notification appears asking if you want to turn on Wi-Fi and Bluetooth or use Personal Hotspot only with USB.

4. **Choose one of the following options to connect:**

   * *To connect a computer using the Personal Hotspot feature's direct cable option, connect iPhone to your computer with the USB cable.* In Network Preferences, choose iPhone. Follow the onscreen instructions to configure the connection if this is the first time.

   * *To connect a computer or other device (such as an iPad, another iPhone, or an iPod touch) using that device's built-in Wi-Fi feature, choose your iPhone from the list of Wi-Fi networks that appears on the device.* Type the Wi-Fi password shown in the Personal Hotspot settings.

   A blue band appears at the top of your iPhone screen whenever a device is connected.

Bluetooth

The iPhone uses the Bluetooth 4.0 protocol. Bluetooth is a short-range (up to 300 feet) wireless protocol used to attach, or *pair,* devices to your iPhone. Unlike Wi-Fi, which broadcasts its availability continuously, Bluetooth has to be turned on to make your iPhone or other device discoverable so that they can see each other. A passkey or PIN is used to make that connection private.

The most common devices paired with iPhone are a wireless, or hands-free, headset or wireless speakers. Other devices that you may want to pair with your iPhone are earphones for listening to music, a physical keyboard, or your car so you can answer calls by tapping a button on the steering wheel or radio. If you pair two iPhones, you can share photos, files, and even an Internet connection between them. To connect devices to your iPhone via Bluetooth,

1. **On your iPhone, open the Settings app, tap Bluetooth, and tap the Bluetooth switch on, or just drag up from the bottom of the screen to open the Control Center and tap the Bluetooth button.**

   The Bluetooth screen opens, as shown in Figure 2-6. Tapping Bluetooth on makes your iPhone discoverable, which means other devices with Bluetooth turned on can see your iPhone. The Bluetooth icon appears in the Status bar.

2. **Turn on Bluetooth on the device you want to connect so it's discoverable.**

   If the device is another iPhone or computer, you have to turn on Bluetooth on that iPhone or computer, too. Active devices show up in a list on the Bluetooth screen on your iPhone.

   A Bluetooth headset only needs to be turned on. Obviously a headset doesn't have a keypad to enter a passkey, but it may come with an assigned passkey, which you need to pair with your iPhone. Check the instructions that came with the headset for the passkey code or try 0000. (It's usually the default code.)

3. **In the list, tap the device you want to pair with your iPhone.**

4. **Enter the passkey on the keypad that appears on your iPhone, if requested.**

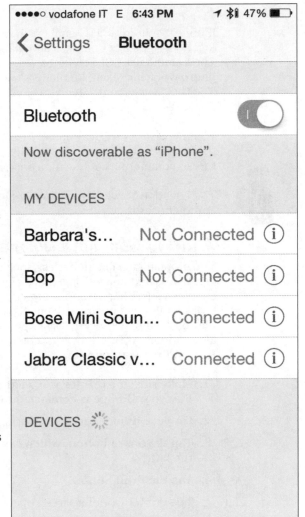

Figure 2-6: Bluetooth lets you connect devices to your iPhone.

The two devices can now communicate across the Bluetooth connection.

5. **To turn Bluetooth off and make your iPhone undiscoverable, open the Settings app, tap Bluetooth, and tap the Bluetooth switch off, or just drag up from the bottom of the screen to open the Control Center and tap the Bluetooth button.**

   The Bluetooth button on the Control Center is dimmed and the Bluetooth icon disappears from the Status bar.

GPS

iPhone's built-in GPS (Global Positioning System) sensor determines your location. Apps like Compass and Maps use GPS to pinpoint your location. The Camera uses GPS to do *geotagging,* which is adding the location to a photo when it's taken. Reminders uses GPS to provide location-based alerts. The GPS is accessed when you check in to some third-party apps or social networks.

When you turn on Location Services in the Settings app (tap Privacy and then tap Location Services), the GPS sensor is activated. We explain the features and functions of Location Services in Book I, Chapter 4.

The Location Services icon appears in the Status bar when you're using an app that uses it.

Printing from your iPhone

The utopian idea of a paperless society may be near, but it hasn't arrived yet. Words and images on a piece of paper are sometimes necessary. AirPrint enables your iPhone to print directly to an AirPrint-enabled printer. Many types of files can be printed: email messages and any readable attachments, photos, web pages, even PDFs. Apps you download from the App Store may also support AirPrint. AirPrint couldn't be easier. Here are the steps to take to print from your phone:

1. **Make sure the printer you want to use is on the same Wi-Fi network that your iPhone is connected to.**

2. **On your iPhone, open the document you want to print.**

 3. **Tap the Share button, which can be one of the two icons you see to the left.**

 4. **Tap the Print button.**

   The Printer Options screen opens.

5. **Tap the Printer button to select the printer you want to use.**

   Another screen opens, showing the printers that are available in the Wi-Fi vicinity.

6. **Tap the printer you want to use and then tap the Back button at the top left of the screen.**

7. **Select the number of copies you want to print by tapping the plus and minus buttons.**

   Depending on the app and the printer, you may also have the option to choose double-sided printing and/or a range of pages.

8. **Tap Print and walk over to the printer to pick up your page.**

Adjusting Accessibility Options for Easier Operation

With the Accessibility settings, Apple addresses the physical challenges that some users may have with iPhone's interface. They've created optional features that customize the interface to make iPhone more accessible. Open the Settings app, tap General, and tap Accessibility. Many of the options have subsequent settings when tapped in the list. We recommend that you consult Chapter 32 of iPhone's User Guide (http://manuals.info.apple.com/ en_US/iphone_user_guide.pdf or in the iBooks Store for free) for complete instructions on how to get the most out of the Accessibility features. The features are divided into five categories: Vision, Hearing, Media, Learning, and Interaction. Here we briefly explain each feature:

- **VoiceOver:** Turn this setting on to hear an audible description of the buttons on the screen. With some practice, vision-impaired iPhone users can learn the tapping, double-tapping, and flicking movements necessary to use apps. Within VoiceOver, you can adjust the speaking rate, attach a Braille device, select which parts of a web screen you want to have read to you, and which language you want VoiceOver to speak.

- **Zoom:** The Zoom feature enlarges the entire iPhone screen when you double-tap with three fingers. Use three fingers to move from left to right on the screen and one finger to move the screen up and down. Double-tap again with three fingers to return to normal size.

  You can't use VoiceOver and Zoom simultaneously.

- **Invert Colors:** Turn this feature on and all color on the display is inverted, like a photo negative.

- **Grayscale:** Change your onscreen colors to black, white, and gray.

- **Speech:** Within this option, you can choose one or more ways to have iPhone read to you: selected text, screen contents, and auto-corrections, even if VoiceOver is turned off.

- **Larger Text:** Tap this item and then tap Larger Accessibility Sizes to the On position. Move the slider as shown in Figure 2-7 to choose the type size that's comfortable for you. Your choice is reflected in Calendar, Contacts, Mail, Messages, Notes, and Reader, as well as any other app that supports dynamic type. You can also open the Settings app, tap Display & Brightness, and tap Text Size to make a similar adjustment.

- **Bold Text:** Tap this option on and your iPhone restarts, and then all text on your iPhone shows up in a heavier, more pronounced typeface. (Figure 2-7 shows Bold Text activated.)

- **Button Shapes:** Buttons have a filled shape so they're more easily seen (Figure 2-7 shows this feature.)

- **Increase Contrast:** When tapped on, the contrast on some backgrounds will be increased for better legibility.

✔ **Reduce Motion:** You may have noticed that as you tilt your iPhone it seems that the buttons or the background move a bit. This is called a *parallax effect* and can be turned off by tapping this option on.

✔ **On/Off Labels:** Tap on to show the On and Off symbols on the switches, in addition to the white (off) and green or gray (on) backgrounds and moving switch. Refer to Figure 2-7.

✔ **Hearing Aids:** For those who use a hearing aid, turning this feature on may reduce interference.

✔ **LED Flash for Alerts:** When this feature is turned on, the LED next to the camera lens on the back of your iPhone flashes when iPhone is locked or asleep. It works whether the ring volume is on or not.

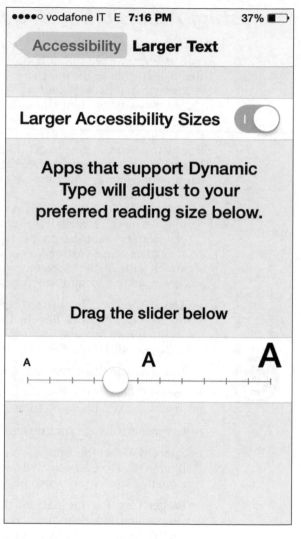

Figure 2-7: Larger Text makes reading on your iPhone easier on the eyes.

✔ **Mono Audio:** This feature changes the left and right sound channels into a mono channel that comes through both sides so those who can hear with only one ear hear both channels.

✔ **Phone Noise Cancellation (iPhone 5 or later):** When on, this function helps reduce ambient noise when you're on a phone call and the phone is near your ear.

✔ **Volume Balance Slider:** Move the slider right or left to increase the volume on one side or another.

✔ **Subtitles & Captioning:** When this option is on and subtitles or closed captioning are available, they appear onscreen.

✔ **Video Descriptions:** When this option is on and video descriptions are available, they're played.

✔ **Guided Access:** Lets you limit iPhone use to one app and even limit features within that app so someone with attention or learning disabilities can stay focused on one task.

✔ **Switch Control:** Allows you to set up new controls and gestures for the various iPhone commands and iPhone functions with an adaptive accessory.

✔ **AssistiveTouch:** Lets you use an adaptive accessory, such as a joystick, to control your iPhone. You can also adjust tracking speed or create custom gestures to make them easier.

✔ **Home-Click Speed:** Adjust the double- and triple-click speed of the Home button.

✔ **Call Audio Routing:** Lets you designate the headset or speaker as the default device for incoming calls.

✔ **Accessibility Shortcut:** You can choose to associate a triple-click of the Home button with up to five Accessibility functions: VoiceOver, Invert Colors, Zoom, Switch Control, or AssistiveTouch. If you choose more than one, when you triple-click the Home button, a menu lets you choose which option you want.

Chapter 3: Controlling the Touch and Voice Recognition Interfaces

In This Chapter

✓ Learning the moves: tapping, scrolling, and zooming

✓ Leaving Home and going Home again

✓ Organizing apps and folders

✓ Commandeering the keyboard

✓ Talking to your iPhone

✓ Searching here, there, and everywhere

If you explored some of the options we discuss in the first two chapters of this book, you've already intuitively used a couple of the touch gestures — tap and possibly scroll. You also used the onscreen keyboard to type your Apple ID and maybe you tried talking to Siri.

In this chapter, we describe the gestures you use to control your iPhone — gestures you'll come across time and again throughout the rest of the book. We explain how the Home screen is organized and what the Home button does, and show you how to organize apps and folders on the Home screen. Then we introduce you to Siri, your iPhone's voice-commanded virtual assistant, and give you examples of how Siri can work for you. For the times when you don't have Wi-Fi or a strong enough data signal, we explain the Voice Control option. Although you're probably familiar with a keyboard layout, we show you how to use the QuickType keyboard and give you some tricks that can make typing and editing easier. At the end of the chapter, we shine a light on Spotlight Search so you can find apps, phone numbers, music, and more on your iPhone and beyond.

Learning the Moves

Your iPhone's touchscreen is similar to other touchscreens you may have used, such as an ATM or the custom sandwich selector at your local mini-market. You need just a few good moves to make iPhone do all the things you're used to doing with a phone and more. These are the finger gestures that control everything on your iPhone:

- ✔ **Tapping:** A tap is lighter than pressing a button. It's a quick touch without any holding. Tap an app button on the Home screen to open the app. Tap an item in a list to select it. Variations on tapping are

  - **Double-tap:** Two quick taps zooms in and out of a web page, email message, or photo. A double-tap also changes the Shift key to a Caps Lock if you enable that function in the Settings app (tap General and then tap Keyboard).

  - **Two-finger tap:** A two-finger tap zooms out of the app you're viewing.

    In Maps, the one finger double-tap only zooms in, and the two-finger double-tap zooms out.

- ✔ **Scrolling:** Scrolling is a dragging motion done with one finger, or more if that's more comfortable for you. You can even rest one finger on the screen and scroll with another one. Touch the screen and drag up or down. In some apps and websites, you can scroll left or right, too. Scrolling is most often used when reading something online or a document, to go through a list, such as Contacts, or to rotate a rotor like the one used to set the alarm clock, which we explain in Book III, Chapter 2. Scrolling doesn't select or open anything; it only moves the list. You must tap to select.

- ✔ **Swiping:** Swiping is a scroll with a specific starting point. Place your fingertip on the Status bar and swipe, or pull, down to open the Notification Center, swipe up from the bottom of the screen to open the Control Center, or pull your list of messages down as far as they go. They refresh.

- ✔ **Flicking:** Touch your finger to the screen and quickly flick it up, or left, or right, and down. Flicking left and right on the Home screen moves to the next or previous screen, flicking down the middle of the Home screen opens Spotlight Search. Flicking in a list, instead of scrolling, moves the list up and down more quickly. You can wait for it to stop or tap when you see what you're looking for, and then tap the item you want to select.

Your iPhone has many options to make gestures easier for people with visual, auditory, or manual dexterity challenges. You adjust those settings by opening the Settings app, tapping General, and tapping Accessibility. Read about them in Book I, Chapter 2.

- ✔ **Zooming in and out:** Pinch (draw two fingers together) to zoom in and expand (spread two fingers apart) to zoom out on photos, maps, web pages, email messages, and other elements.

- ✔ **Sliding:** Slider bars show up when you want to turn your iPhone on or off. They also appear on the Lock screen when your iPhone rings. Touch and hold the slider bar on the left and slide your finger across the bar to the right. The action listed on the slider bar happens. Some sliding actions take place without a slider bar, such as when you unlock your iPhone as in Figure 3-1; just slide your finger across the screen. You can also slide switches to turn functions on and off.

Book I
Chapter 3

Controlling the
Touch and Voice
Recognition
Interfaces

✔ **Pressing:** Press the physical buttons on your iPhone: the Home, Sleep/Wake, or volume buttons. You switch the Silent/Ring switch on and off. We explain these buttons in Book I, Chapter 2.

✔ **Double-click:** Double-clicking the Home button reveals the App Switcher, which shows apps that are running, as well as favorite and recent contacts. You can then tap the app you want to switch to or the person you want to call or message.

✔ **Triple-click Home:** This option is activated in the Accessibility screen in the Settings app

Figure 3-1: Use the sliding move to unlock your iPhone.

and allows you to press the Home button three times to activate selected functions such as VoiceOver, Invert Colors, Zoom, and/or AssistiveTouch.

✔ **Double-tap Home (iPhone 6 and 6 Plus):** When you double-tap the Home button, the top of the screen drops down so you can tap the fields, text, or images that reside there. Known as Reachability, this feature helps you singlehandedly access the upper part of the larger screen on the iPhone 6 and 6 Plus.

Home, Away from Home, and Home Again

The Home screen is what you see when your iPhone is awake and you aren't using an app. The Home screen is actually more than one screen. You move between one Home screen and the next by flicking or scrolling left or right. See Book I, Chapter 2 to learn more about the Home screen.

The round, slightly depressed button centered beneath the screen is the Home button. When you press this button, different things may happen, depending on your point of departure:

- ✔ From an open app, you return to the Home screen you most recently viewed, so if you tap an app on the fifth Home screen and then press the Home button, you return to the fifth Home screen.

- ✔ From the second to the fifteenth Home screen (if you have multiple Home screens), you return to the first Home screen.

- ✔ When your iPhone is sleeping or locked, pressing the Home button wakes it (refer to Figure 3-1). Slide your finger to the right, and the last screen you were viewing appears. It could be a Home screen or a running app.

If you have an iPhone with Touch ID, you can use your fingerprint to unlock your iPhone and authorize iTunes, App, and iBooks Store transactions. Set up Touch ID by tapping Touch ID and Passcode in the Settings app.

Launching and Managing Apps

Apps are the applications on your iPhone. Book I, Chapter 4 summarizes the apps that come with your iPhone, and other chapters throughout the book cover each app in depth. The online bonus content for this book presents some third-party apps we think you'll like. (See this book's Introduction for more about the bonus content.) Here, we tell you how to launch and close apps, and how to organize the app buttons on your Home screen.

Launching apps

To launch or open an app on the Home screen, tap the app icon. You can also ask Siri to open an app for you. You may see icons that are squares with tiny app icons on them; these are folders, which can contain many apps and multiple pages — you see dots at the bottom just like those that indicate the number of Home screens and flick to move between one folder page and another. To launch an app that resides in a folder, tap the folder to open it, and then tap the app button you want to launch. To close the folder, tap it or the Home screen.

Switching between apps

Instead of opening an app, closing it, returning to the Home screen, and then opening another app, you can have multiple apps open at the same time — although you just see one app at a time on your screen. When you double-click the Home button, the App Switcher appears, as shown in Figure 3-2. These are the apps that you most recently used that haven't been shut down. This is especially helpful when you want to cut and paste from one app to another, which we explain in the section about using the keyboard.

Flick left and right to move through the apps. Tap the app you want to switch to.

To close an app alto-gether, double-click the Home button and then swipe up the app you want to close. Or — check this out — use two or three fingers to close several apps, simultaneously.

Figure 3-2: The App Switcher reveals open apps and favorite and recent contacts.

TIP

Across the top of the App Switcher screen you see icons for contacts you identify as Favorites and those whom you recently called or messaged. Tap a contact and then tap the buttons for how you want to interact with that person: tap a phone button (there's one for each number you have stored for that contact) to initiate a call; tap the message button to send an SMS or iMessage, or tap the FaceTime button to begin a FaceTime call. See Book II, Chapters 1 and 2 to learn about phoning and messaging.

Organizing Apps and Folders

Icons for the apps that come preinstalled on your iPhone occupy the first Home screen and part of the second. You may want to rearrange the apps so that the ones you use most frequently are at the top of the Home screen, you may want to group similar apps in a folder, or you may want to change the apps that are in the Dock. As you add new apps, you'll want to arrange them in a way that makes sense to you. You can move apps around on your iPhone and from iTunes.

Organizing apps on your iPhone

To organize apps from your iPhone, follow these steps:

1. **Press and hold any app button on your Home screen.**

   This part is fun, especially if you're new to iPhone. Try it — we'll wait.

2. **Any of the apps that have circled Xs on the upper-left corner can be deleted. (Preinstalled apps can't be deleted so they don't have an X.) To delete an app, just tap the circled X.**

   A message opens asking if you really want to delete that app. Tap the appropriate button: Delete, if you want to delete that app, or Cancel, if you tapped the circled X by mistake.

   If you delete an app by mistake, the App Store maintains a copy of all your apps, free or purchased, so you can reinstall it, but you could lose data or documents created with the app if they aren't backed up to your computer or iCloud.

3. **Touch and drag the app buttons around to arrange them in a way you like, even from one Home screen to another.**

   For example, the Maps app button is being moved in Figure 3-3.

4. **To change the four apps that are in the Dock, you first have to drag one out, and then you can replace it with another app.**

   You don't have to have four apps in the Dock. If you prefer three or two or none, you can move the buttons out of the Dock onto a Home screen. Or you can place up to four folders on the Dock instead of single apps.

Folders

Folders give you the option of putting like-minded apps together in one place so you can find them quickly and easily. You can even put the Apple apps you don't use in a folder so they're out of sight.

Book I
Chapter 3

Controlling the
Touch and Voice
Recognition
Interfaces

Adding folders

To add a folder, press and hold your finger on an app on the Home screen until they start a-wigglin' and a-jigglin'. Then, follow these steps:

1. **Lift your finger.**

2. **Touch and drag one app button over another app button.**

   A square is formed around both apps as shown in Figure 3-4.

3. **(Optional) iPhone assigns a name to the folder but you can change it now or later, with the following steps:**

   1. Tap the circled X on the right of the field where the name is written. The field is erased. A cursor appears at the beginning of the field and the keyboard opens.

   2. Type the name you want to give this folder.

   3. Tap the Done key on the keyboard.

4. **Tap anywhere on the screen outside of the folder.**

   The folder closes.

Figure 3-3: Delete apps with an X or drag the app icon to a new position.

5. **(Optional) Touch and drag another app into the folder.**

6. **Tap the Home button to save the folder and stop the app dance.**

If a folder has already been created but you want to add apps to it, press and hold an app to make them wiggle and then drag the app you want into the folder. To remove apps, while the apps are wiggling, tap the folder you want to change to open it. Drag apps out of the folder onto the Home screen. A folder is automatically deleted when all apps are moved out and it's empty.

If your apps folder has a badge on the upper-right corner, the number on the badge is a cumulative number of items that need attending to, such as unread messages, app updates, or information updates.

Figure 3-4: Drag one app over another to create a folder.

Managing apps with iTunes

When you have a lot of apps and folders, moving them around from screen to screen can be tedious. Luckily, you can also organize your Home screens, apps, and folders in iTunes (see Figure 3-5). Connect your iPhone to your computer with the USB connector cable, and open iTunes. Click the Devices icon in the Toolbar, select your iPhone, and then click Apps in the Sidebar. Drag an app from the list to the Home screen or folder where you want it to

Book I
Chapter 3

Controlling the
Touch and Voice
Recognition
Interfaces

reside, and it moves from its old location to the new one. You can even move an entire Home screen to a new position in the lineup or add a blank Home screen — and you can do those maneuvers only in iTunes. After you make your changes and the Home screens are organized just the way you like, click the Sync button to sync your changes with your iPhone. Learn more about managing apps in Book IV, Chapter 5.

Toolbar   Devices

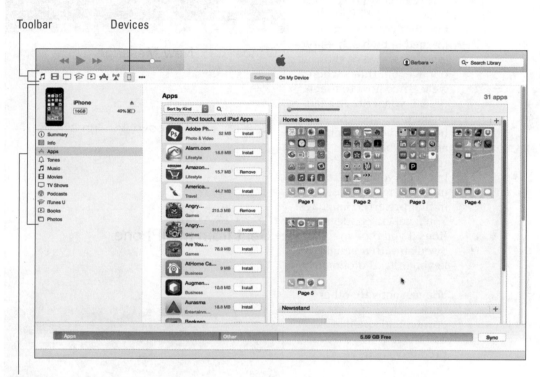

Sidebar

Figure 3-5: Organize your apps and folders via iTunes.

Commandeering the Keyboard

For many iPhone users, the keyboard is the hardest thing to get used to — all of a sudden, you have gorilla fingers. Don't despair. With a little practice, the keyboard becomes second nature in no time. Any time you tap in a blank text field, the keyboard opens and a blinking cursor appears in that empty field. Some short fields, for example the URL field in Safari or the Search field, have a small X in a circle to the right; tapping the X deletes any text so you can type new text

The keyboard functions we describe here work in any app that uses the keyboard, so, like most things iPhone, after you hone your skills in one app, they apply across the board in all your iPhone apps.

Keyboard settings

The default keyboard has the classic QWERTY format that you may have learned in high school typing class — we're showing our age, but that's where we learned how to touch type. If you write in a language other than English, however, you'll want to add a keyboard that reflects the alphabet of the language you want to type in — and recognizes words in that preferred language. You'll get crazy suggestions if you type in Swedish with an English keyboard and dictionary.

You can activate other options, too, such as autocorrect and spellcheck, and the new iOS 8 feature, predictive text.

Adding languages

Your iPhone comes with two languages activated: English (or the language of the country where you purchased your iPhone) and Emoji, which lets you add smiley faces, hearts, monkeys, and flowers to your text, as shown in Figure 3-6. To add keyboards for additional languages, do the following:

Figure 3-6: Use the Emoji language to add smiley faces and more to your missives.

1. **Open the Settings app, tap General, tap Keyboard, and tap Keyboards.**

2. **Tap Add New Keyboard to add another language-specific keyboard.**

   A list of languages opens. Many languages have multiple options, such as the Chinese handwriting option or the Swiss or Canadian French option.

3. **Tap the language you want to add.**

   It automatically appears in the list of keyboards.

4. **Repeat Steps 2 and 3 to add other languages or tap Keyboard in the upper left to return to the Keyboard settings.**

5. **To change the keyboard layout, tap English or whichever language's keyboard you want to edit.**

   The screen opens and displays options such as QWERTY or QWERTZ for the Software Keyboard Layout (that is, the keyboard on your iPhone). You can choose the Software Keyboard Layout you're used to using.

6. **Swipe right or tap Keyboards in the upper left to return to the Keyboards settings.**

To rearrange the order of the languages, touch and drag the rearrange button (it looks like three stacked horizontal lines) to move the languages to the order you want. To delete a language, tap Edit, and then tap the red and white minus sign to the left of the language. Tap the Delete button that appears.

Activating keyboard options

You also have some other optional keyboard functions that you activate, or deactivate, in the Settings app. These options apply to all the keyboards you add to your iPhone. Follow these steps to change the options:

1. **Open the Settings app.**

2. **Tap General and then tap Keyboard.**

3. **You can turn the following functions on or off.**

   - *Auto-Capitalization:* Automatically capitalizes the letter *I* when it stands alone and capitalizes the first letter after any punctuation that iPhone recognizes as a new sentence (for example, a period or a return).

   - *Auto-Correction:* Automatically corrects words as you're typing using iPhone's built-in dictionary. For example, if you type **jome**, "home" appears in a box above the word. If you tap the spacebar, the Return key, or a punctuation key, the suggestion is accepted; tap the X on the box, or just keep typing to complete your word, and your typed word remains. The dictionary automatically adds names from Contacts, so it recognizes many names you type. Your iPhone learns your idiosyncrasies, adding words you type frequently, that it doesn't know, to the dictionary.

- *Check Spelling:* iPhone underlines words it thinks are spelled wrong. Tap the underlined word, and iPhone shows you possible replacement words. Tap the one you want or tap elsewhere on the screen to decline. If iPhone thinks the word is spelled wrong but doesn't have a suggestion, a flag reads *No Replacement Found* and you have to correct the word, if necessary, on your own.

- *Enable Caps Lock:* When this is on, you can quickly tap twice on the Shift key and it changes to a Caps Lock key.

- *Predictive:* Tap on to activate the QuickType function, which is the writing equivalent of speed reading — rather than type letter for letter, you tap a whole word. As you type, three words appear above the keyboard, as shown in Figure 3-7. If you see the word you want to use, tap it instead of typing it out. The Predictive option offers words that commonly follow other words — in Figure 3-7 only the *l* is typed but the word *late* appears as a choice since that often follows the word *running.* The predictive keyboard also

Figure 3-7: Turn on predictive typing to activate QuickType and tap words instead of single letters.

Book I
Chapter 3

Controlling the
Touch and Voice
Recognition
Interfaces

learns and remembers phrases you use often. Predictive text is available in general text fields, such as the body of a message or email but not in constrained text fields, such as an email address or URL.

- *"." Shortcut:* Double-tapping the spacebar inserts a period and then one space.

4. Tap Shortcuts.

Shortcuts let you type a few letters that your iPhone interprets and expands into a longer phrase. For example, type **omw** in a message and it becomes "On my way!" Type your text in the Phrase and Shortcut text fields and then tap Save.

If you add a word or phrase to Shortcuts without typing in the shortcut, the word or phrase is added to your Personal Dictionary and iPhone won't make suggestions for correcting it.

When you turn Documents and Data on in iCloud, your shortcuts sync between iOS devices and your Mac, if you use one. PDC! (That's short for "pretty darn cool.")

5. Tap General in the upper left, and then Settings in the upper left to return to the main Settings screen, or swipe right until you reach the screen you want.

Switching between languages

To simply switch from English to Emoji, tap the Emoji key. If you have more than one language activated, you see a Globe key instead of the Emoji key. Tap the Globe key to switch between languages; each tap takes you to the next language. The languages are in the same order as your keyboards are listed in Settings.

Tap and hold the Emoji/Globe key to open a pop-up list of English, Emoji, and any languages you added, as well as the option to turn Predictive text on or off, as shown in Figure 3-8. Tap to select the language you want to use or tap the Predictive switch to the on or off position. Even if you enabled predictive typing in the Settings app, you can tap it on or off while typing.

Typing tips

Apple suggests, and we concur, that you begin typing with one index finger — probably that of your dominant hand — and gradually move up to two-finger or two-thumb typing. When you tap a key, the letter appears enlarged on the screen so you know which key you actually hit. If it's the letter you want, just lift your finger and that letter appears on the message, note, or field you're typing in. If it's not the letter you want, without lifting your finger, slide your finger to the key of the letter you want. As you slide, the enlarged letter changes to show which key your finger is on.

As you become familiar with the tap typing technique with your index finger, you may want to try putting iPhone on a flat surface and typing with two index fingers. In the landscape position — where the keys are slightly bigger but the typing field is smaller — you can hold your iPhone with both hands, placing your thumbs at the bottom and your middle fingers at the top. Use both index fingers to type.

Sooner or later, most iPhone users learn to thumb-type in either portrait or landscape position, cradling the iPhone in both hands, keeping them slightly relaxed, and using their thumbs to type. Of course there's also the I-was-born-texting position: cradling your iPhone in one hand and typing with the cradling hand's thumb. This tactic is particularly useful while standing on a moving bus or stirring a pot on the stove.

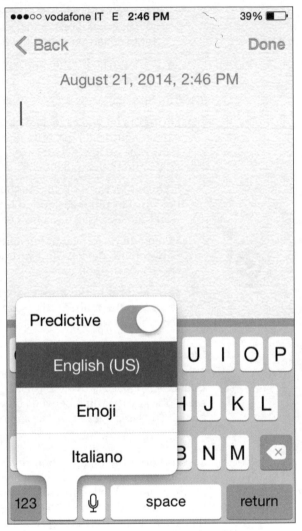

Figure 3-8: Tap and hold the Globe/Emoji key to switch languages.

After you get going, iPhone uses an algorithm to predict the word you're typing so zones of letters imperceptibly increase in size to increase the probability that you hit the letter you want. With predictive typing turned on (refer to Figure 3-8), whole words appear above the keyboard, which you tap to insert in your note or missive.

Keyboard layouts

Looking at the keyboard in Figure 3-9, moving top to bottom, left to right, you see the letters of the alphabet, the Shift key, the Delete key, the ABC/123 key, the Globe key (if you've added a language) or Emoji key (if you have not), the

Book I
Chapter 3

Controlling the
Touch and Voice
Recognition
Interfaces

Microphone key, the spacebar, and a Return key. The keyboard changes slightly depending on what function you want to perform. When you're in a To field in Mail or in the URL field in Safari, the spacebar shrinks to allow one or two more buttons next to it: an at (@) button (in Mail) and a dot (.) button (in both). This makes typing an email or website address easier. The Return key becomes the Search button in Spotlight and a Go button in Safari, and sometimes it becomes a Next, Search, or Done button when you're filling out forms, using a search engine, or signing in to a service. In addition to these visible changes that make typing easier, there are some invisible shortcuts:

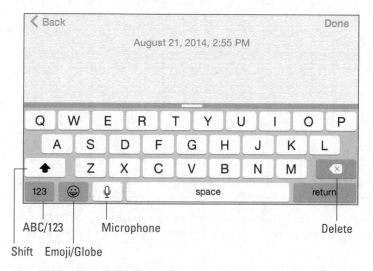

Figure 3-9: Familiarizing yourself with the keyboard layouts makes typing faster and more efficient.

- Double-tap the Shift key to turn it into a Caps Lock key so you can type in ALL CAPS. You have to turn this option on in the Keyboard settings.

- Tap the Delete key once to delete one character to the left. Tap and hold the Delete key and it begins deleting one letter after another. If you continue holding, it deletes whole words at once.

- Hold the ABC key and slide your finger to the symbol or number you want to type. The character is typed, but the keyboard reverts to letters.

- When the cursor is in the To field and you have the space, at, and dot buttons, touch and hold the dot key and a small window opens offering an assortment of the most common web suffixes: .com, .net, .edu, .org, and so on. If you've added an international keyboard, the local suffixes are included (for example, .it for Italy and .eu for European Union).

✔ Tap the 123 key to change the keyboard to show numbers, as shown in Figure 3-10. The Shift key changes to a symbols key; the 123 key changes to an ABC key. Tap the symbols key and the top row of the keyboard where the numbers were changes to show more symbols, as shown in Figure 3-10. Tap the ABC/123 key to return to the alphabet keyboard; tap the symbols key to switch between numbers and symbols.

✔ Tap the Emoji key to switch to the Emoji keyboard (refer to Figure 3-6) or the Globe key to switch to another language you added.

Tap the spacebar after typing a number or symbol, and the letter keyboard returns.

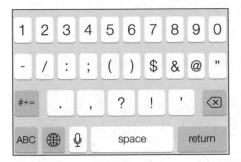 

Figure 3-10: The letters change to numbers when you tap the ABC/123 key and the numbers change to symbols when you tap the symbols key.

Some of the letters, when held, give non-English options, and some of the numbers and symbols give multiple options as well, as shown in Table 3-1. These options are from the U.S. English keyboard and may change when you change the keyboard language.

Table 3-1	Special Characters and Symbols
Key Pressed	*Special Character*
A or a	à á â ä æ ã å ā
C or c	ç ć č
E or e	è é ê ë ē e˙ e̦
I or i	ì i̧ ī í ï î
L or l	ł
N or n	n´ ñ
O or o	ō ō ø œ ó ò ö ô

Book I
Chapter 3

Controlling the
Touch and Voice
Recognition
Interfaces

Key Pressed	Special Character
S or s	ß ś š
U or u	ū ú ù ü û
Y or y	ÿ
Z or z	ž ź ż
Zero (0)	0
Period	Ellipsis (. . .)
Question mark (?)	¿
Exclamation point (!)	¡
Apostrophe (')	` ' '
Hyphen/minus sign (–)	– —
Forward slash (/)	\
Dollar sign ($)	¥, €, ¢, £, ₩
Ampersand (&)	§
Quote (")	« » „ " "
Percentage (found when you tap the symbols button after tapping the numbers button) %	‰

Editing Your Text

The longer you have your iPhone, chances are, the more you'll find yourself using it for written communications that you used to create with pencil and paper or on a computer: email, notes, to-do lists, appointments, status updates and posts to your social network of choice, and maybe even longer documents. All this writing means a greater possibility for making mistakes, changing your mind, and wanting to move sentences around — in other words, you want to edit your text. iPhone has the basic editing capabilities of copy, cut, and paste, select or select all, even undoing and redoing. In Mail, you can stylize your text by making it bold, italic, or underlined and indented. We show you how to do each of these tasks in the following sections.

Selecting

You can tap once to insert the cursor somewhere in the middle of your text, and then make changes letter by letter or you can select a word, phrase, paragraph, or the entire text and make changes with this procedure:

1. **Tap the text you want to edit.**

   The keyboard appears and the cursor blinks more or less where you tapped.

2. **Press and hold your finger in the general area where you want to insert the cursor.**

   A magnifying loupe appears over the text with the cursor in the center.

3. **Drag your finger over the text until the cursor is at the point where you want it.**

4. **Lift your finger.**

   Two or three buttons appear, including Select or Select All, along with options such as Paste, Copy, Define, or Insert Photo, which we explain in the upcoming sections.

5. **Tap Select to select the word or portion of the text; tap Select All to select the entire text.**

   The word is highlighted in blue and there are blue grab points on the upper-left and lower-right corners. (Refer to Figure 3-11.)

   If you select just one word, you can *cut* or *copy* that word, or if you tap the arrow on the far right, iPhone offers to *replace* the word with its idea of auto-correct (for example, for *creams,* the suggested replacements were *dreamy, creaky,* or *cream's*) or *define* the selected word — just tap the appropriate button.

   If you don't want to use Select or Select All, tap once on the screen and proceed to edit with the Delete key and keyboard.

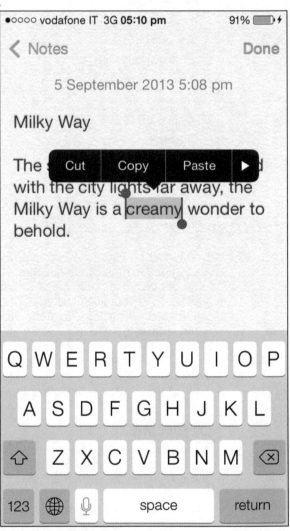

Figure 3-11: Use blue grab points to select the text you want to copy, cut, or replace with a suggested synonym.

Book I
Chapter 3

Controlling the
Touch and Voice
Recognition
Interfaces

6. **To select a portion of the text, touch and drag the blue grab points to select the text you want to cut or copy.**

7. **If you want to delete, tap the Cut button. If you want to copy or cut, and paste in another location, read on.**

Cutting, copying, and pasting

What if you want to copy something from an email message you received and paste it onto an existing list in Notes for future reference? Here's how to copy and paste into an existing document:

1. **Follow the previous steps to select the text you want to copy.**

   After you've tapped Select or Select All, a Copy button appears above the highlighted text.

2. **Tap Copy.**

3. **Open the document in the app where you want to place the copied text.**

   If, from our example, Notes is already open, double-click the Home button, and then tap the Notes screen in the App Switcher. Otherwise, press the Home button to open the Home screen and tap Notes from there.

4. **Tap and hold on the screen where you want to insert the copied text.**

   The magnifying loupe appears, allowing you to move the cursor precisely where you want it.

5. **Lift your finger.**

   A Paste button appears.

6. **Tap the Paste button.**

   Your copied text is now in a new spot.

Turn iPhone 6 Plus to landscape view, select your text as above, and then tap the special Copy and Paste keys to perform those actions.

Copying and pasting isn't only for text within apps like Notes and Mail. You can copy a portion of a web page and paste it into an email. Press and hold the part of the page you want to copy and the blue grabbers come up, along with a Copy button. Drag the grab points to select everything you want to copy, and then tap the Copy button. Open the app where you want to paste the selection. Press and hold until you see the Paste button. Tap Paste.

Undoing and redoing

To undo your edit, shake your iPhone. A message opens with the option to undo the last action or cancel. Tap the Undo button and you're home free. And if you want to redo what you thought you wanted to undo? Just shake your iPhone again and the buttons ask if you want to redo or undo or cancel.

Telling Siri What to Do

Having a personal assistant is no longer just an indispensable luxury for a few busy executives or celebrities. Siri on your iPhone is a close second to a human counterpart. After you establish a rapport with Siri, you may wonder what you ever did without her, er, or him, should you decide to give Siri a male voice. Following is a partial list of things Siri can help you with:

- Making phone calls
- Scheduling meetings
- Opening apps on your iPhone
- Writing and reading messages
- Retrieving voicemail messages
- Adjusting iPhone settings such as screen brightness or Do Not Disturb
- Relaying the weather forecast
- Identifying songs you hear
- Finding a restaurant and requesting reservations
- Using Find My Friends to see where the people you know are hanging out
- Telling you the score for last night's game and statistics for your favorite player
- Finding the nearest movie theater, telling you what's playing, and buying tickets
- Playing requested music
- Writing your grocery list
- Setting up reminders
- Making coffee and taking out the trash — just checking if you were paying attention!

Siri requires an Internet connection. When you ask Siri to do something for you, the request is sent to the remote Siri server, which interprets your request and sends the answer back. Siri's response speed depends on the speed of your Internet connection. If you have a 3G or EDGE connection, the action will take longer (sometimes 30 seconds or more) than when you have a Wi-Fi or 4G/LTE connection.

To use Siri, first you have to turn it on by following these steps. While you're in the Settings app, you can adjust some of the Siri settings:

1. **Tap General and then tap Siri.**
2. **Tap the Siri switch on.**

3. **Adjust the following optional settings:**

   - *Voice Activation:* Tap the Voice Activation switch on and when your iPhone is connected to a power source, you can say "Hey, Siri" to get Siri's attention.

   - *Language:* Tap Language and then tap the language you want to use to speak to Siri.

   - *Voice Gender:* Tap Voice Gender and decide if you want a male or female assistant.

   - *Voice Feedback:* Tap Voice Feedback to choose if you want Siri to always repeat what you say. The default is only when you're in hands-free mode, which is when you speak to Siri while using the headset, a Bluetooth device, or holding your iPhone to your ear. Otherwise, you see what you said on the screen.

   - *My Info:* Tap My Info and Contacts opens; select your Info card. Siri also uses people you indicate as related to better understand your commands. See Book III, Chapter 1 to learn how to use Contacts.

**Book I
Chapter 3**

Controlling the
Touch and Voice
Recognition
Interfaces

To talk to Siri, do the following:

1. **Press and hold the Home button, the center button on the earphones, or the button on your Bluetooth headset, until you hear the beep and the Siri screen opens.**

   You can do this from the Home screen or from within an app. Siri knows what you're doing and responds appropriately.

   Or, if you turned Voice Activation on and your iPhone is plugged in to a power source, simply say "Hey, Siri."

2. **Two rapid beeps let you know Siri is ready to listen. Following are examples of how Siri uses the apps on your iPhone. You don't have to open the app — just speak when Siri's ready:**

   - *All apps:* Say "Open StarWalk" or "Launch Mail."

   - *Calendar:* View and create events. Ask "Where is my 9 o'clock meeting?" or "Make appointment with Bill Jones for 10 a.m."

   - *Clock:* Set alarms, start the timer, find out the time in another city. Say "Set timer for 25 minutes." You can also simply ask what time it is.

   - *Contacts:* Ask for information about your contacts. Ask "What's Jim Rose's address?" If you refer to someone by first name only, Siri looks for matches in Favorites in Contacts and in Conversations in Messages, and then repeats the first and last name asking if it's the correct contact. It's quicker and easier to use both first and last names. Enter names of related people on your info card so Siri knows who "Mom" or "sister" are. Book III, Chapter 1 is about Contacts.

- *Find My Friends:* Ask Siri where your friends are or who's near your current location.

- *Facebook/Twitter:* Ask Siri to post your status update to Facebook or Twitter, just make sure both are activated in Settings. Ask to search Twitter for a topic or person.

- *Mail:* Search and send email. Say "Email Joe Hutsko about deadline."

- *Maps:* Get directions, find addresses. Ask "Where is the nearest Apple Store?" or "Give me directions from here to Paula's house."

- *Messages:* Read and send SMS and iMessage text messages. Say "Tell Darrin Smith I'm on my way."

- *Movies:* Ask "What movies are playing in Philadelphia?" or "What action films were released this week?"

- *Music:* Play artists, albums, playlists, songs, or the new iTunes Radio. Say "Play Blue" or "Play a reggae station." Siri can also identify songs for you. Activate Siri and she automatically begins listening to ambient noise, expecting a command. If you do nothing, she'll identify the song or you can speed things up a little bit and say "What song is this?" Siri connects to Shazam, the song identification service and not only tells you what's playing but provides a link to the iTunes Store so you can add the song to your music collection.

- *Notes:* Create, search, and edit notes. Say "Note tablecloth is 104 by 84."

- *Phone:* Make a phone or FaceTime call or listen to your voicemail. Say "Call Joe Hutsko" or "Get voicemail."

- *Reminders:* Create, search, and change reminders. Say "Remind me to take book to Jen when I get home."

- *Restaurants:* Say "Make a reservation at Zuni Café for 8 p.m. Saturday."

- *Safari:* Search the web. Say "Search the web for cold remedies."

- *Settings:* Change your iPhone settings. Say "Turn off Wi-Fi" or "Turn on Airplay Mode."

- *Sports Information:* Ask "Tell me Pete Rose's best batting average" or "Who won the Pac-12 game last night?"

- *Stocks:* Obtain stock info. Ask "What is the stock price for Apple?"

- *Weather:* Ask for forecasts. Ask "What is today's weather?" or "What's the forecast for Boston next week?"

- *WolframAlpha:* Answer factual, statistical, and mathematical questions. Ask your question in simple terms, such as, "How fast is the speed of light?" and Siri accesses the WolframAlpha research database to give you an answer.

These are just a few suggestions to demonstrate Siri's vast capabilities, but we encourage you to experiment — ask Siri "What can I ask you?" to get some ideas. Speak as you would to a person and see how resourceful Siri is when it comes to finding answers and assisting you in your day-to-day tasks.

Siri displays what it hears you say as you say it, as opposed to waiting until you finish speaking to show what you said. This helps it give you a faster response.

3. **Siri makes an audible response and asks for confirmation.**

Figure 3-12 shows the conversation with Siri; if the appointment were confirmed, an email would be sent to Ray for the appointment at 11 a.m. on the following Wednesday and the event would be added to Calendar. Siri shows her sense of humor when the request is cancelled.

Siri understands different ways of saying the same thing; however, if it's unsure of a command, Siri asks for clarification.

Siri often provides interactive responses, as in Figure 3-13. Tapping one of the movie selections opens theater and playing times, reviews and a link to a trailer.

When Siri asks for clarification, she waits a few seconds but then stops listening and the microphone button appears at the bottom of the screen. Tap it to speak to Siri again.

Figure 3-12: Siri reads and displays the response to your request.

Book I
Chapter 3

Controlling the
Touch and Voice
Recognition
Interfaces

4. **If Siri's interpretation of your request, which you see written on the screen, isn't exactly what you want, you can make corrections by doing the following:**

   - Tap Tap to Edit under what Siri understood and then type your request or tap the microphone and dictate the correction.

   - If a word is underlined in blue, tap the word and then choose an alternative from the choices, or tap the microphone to dictate the correction.

   - Tap the microphone to speak to Siri and clarify your request.

   - To correct a message or email before sending, dictate the changes or say "Send it" when it's correct.

Figure 3-13: Siri finds movies and restaurants.

5. **If when reading your messages or relaying voicemail, Siri mispronounces a name, say "That's not how you pronounce** *name***."**

   Siri asks how to pronounce the name, and then repeats three options so you can choose the correct one.

6. **To cancel a request, say "Cancel," tap the microphone button, or press the Home button.**

Book I
Chapter 3

Controlling the
Touch and Voice
Recognition
Interfaces

In the Settings app, tap Touch ID & Passcode, and you can allow access to Siri even when your iPhone is locked. Doing this, however, compromises some of the Passcode Lock's security features.

Siri, take a memo

Any time you want to dictate instead of type, tap the microphone key on the keyboard, dictate, and then tap Done when you finish. Siri understands your dictation best when you dictate punctuation. Pretend you're speaking to a recorder that someone will transcribe. For example, to have Siri type:

Dear John, thank you for the new iPhone 5.

Say: "dear john comma thank you for the new iPhone 5 period"

Likewise to insert paragraphs, quotation marks, and any other punctuation that might be applicable to your dictated missive.

Using Voice Control

If you find yourself in an area without adequate Internet service, you can still instruct your iPhone to do simple tasks with Voice Control. Voice Control doesn't work if Siri is turned on; to turn Siri off, open the Settings app, tap General, tap Siri, and tap the Siri switch off. Here's how to use Voice Control:

1. **Press and hold the Home button, the center button on the earphones, or the button on your Bluetooth headset, until the Voice Control screen opens, as shown in Figure 3-14.**

   The words that appear on the Voice Control screen are suggestions for commands you can give.

   Two quick beeps let you know that Voice Control is ready to listen to your command.

2. **Speak the name of the person you want to call (or the artist you want to hear).**

   Voice Control replies with the name it understood. If it found more than one match, it reads off a list of the options. Repeat the option you want.

   If you asked for music, iPhone responds with "Playing songs by *artist's or album name*," and begins playing.

3. **Repeat the option that you want.**

4. **iPhone dials that person.**

   If Voice Control offers an option you don't want, say "No" or "Cancel." Voice Control closes and you have to start over.

TIP

Voice Control also tells time. Press and hold the Home button. When Voice Control opens, ask "What time is it?" Voice Control tells you.

Shining a Light on Spotlight Searches

Spotlight is iPhone's search feature for finding things stored on your iPhone or on the web. To access Spotlight from any Home screen, flick down from the middle of the screen. Spotlight Search opens on top of the Home screen, as shown in Figure 3-15. Your search criteria can contain numbers, so you can search for a phone number, date, or address. Spotlight searches the apps, which you specify in Settings, on your iPhone for the word, phrase, or number you type. For example, if we type in the name **Bonnie**, a list appears showing all the places where that name was found: contacts named Bonnie, songs by Bonnie Raitt, the Burl Ives song "Wee Bonnie Lass,"
emails exchanged with anyone named Bonnie, appointments with Bonnie or birthdays of people named Bonnie, and any notes we may have jotted down about Bonnie.

Figure 3-14: You can command your iPhone to call someone, play a song, or tell the time with Voice Control.

TIP

If Spotlight finds an app with the word you're searching and it's in a folder, the name of the folder is displayed to the right of the result.

Book I
Chapter 3

Controlling the
Touch and Voice
Recognition
Interfaces

You also have access to Spotlight within many apps using the Spotlight Search field at the top of an app's screen. In Contacts, the Search field is always visible. In other apps, the Search field is sometimes hidden. Tap the Status bar or scroll to the very top of the app screen, to see it. To search for something within an app, do the following:

1. **Tap in the Spotlight field.**

   The blinking cursor appears and the keyboard opens.

2. **Type your word or phrase and then tap Search.**

   Spotlight searches within the app you're using and displays any items that match your search criteria.

3. **Tap an item in the list to view that item's contents.**

When you search from within an app, iPhone searches only in that app.

Figure 3-15: Spotlight Search searches all the apps on iPhone for occurrences of a word or phrase.

You can alter the Spotlight settings to limit your searches to certain apps or prioritize the order in which the apps are searched. To change Spotlight settings, follow these steps:

1. **Open the Settings app, tap General, and tap Spotlight Search.**

   The Spotlight Search list opens.

2. **Tap the name of the app in the list to make the check mark on the left appear or disappear.**

    A check mark means Spotlight will search that app when looking for something from the Spotlight search screen or within that app.

3. **To change the order of the apps, press and hold the rearrange button to the right of the app, and then drag up and down to move it.**

    Spotlight searches and shows results from the apps at the top of the list first when doing a search.

Chapter 4: Keeping Things Set and Secure

In This Chapter

✔ Getting to know preloaded apps

✔ Adjusting basic settings to suit your style

✔ Setting up passcodes and Touch ID

✔ Invoking iPhone's security and privacy features

✔ Averting panic in case your iPhone is lost or stolen

You're probably starting to realize — if you didn't already know — that your iPhone is so much more than a phone. The apps that come with it help you manage time and tasks, take photos, and entertain you. This chapter introduces you to those apps, as well as every other preinstalled app.

We close this chapter by showing you how to adjust your iPhone's basic settings to suit your personal style, explaining how to activate security features, including the Touch ID fingerprint sensor, to protect your iPhone from prying eyes, and introducing you to steps you can take to track down your iPhone (and even remotely erase your personal information) if your beloved gadget is ever lost or stolen.

Tapping into iPhone's Preinstalled Apps

Right out of the box, your iPhone is loaded with a gaggle of great apps that can do just about everything except fold your laundry or take your dog for a walk. Getting to know iPhone's apps can help you choose which ones you want to use right away.

When you turn on your iPhone for the first time, you see iPhone's apps arranged on the first Home screen page in a way Apple's iPhone designers figured probably makes sense for most people, as shown in Figure 4-1. We write about how to organize the Home screen in a way that makes sense to you, in Book I, Chapter 3.

Here's a roll-call rundown of the apps included with your iPhone, with bite-size descriptions of what each can do, and pointers to the chapters you can read to learn more about each app:

✓ **App Store:** Search, browse, and read reviews of thousands of apps that you can download for free or a fee. Review and download updates to installed apps you already own. (See Book IV, Chapter 5.)

✓ **Calculator:** Add, subtract, multiply, and divide with the basic keypad, or turn iPhone sideways to reveal a wider-ranging scientific calculator keyboard; copy and paste numbers to and from the calculator display. (See Book III, Chapter 4.)

✓ **Calendar:** Create, manage, and share calendars that you can keep in sync with calendars you maintain on your Mac or Windows PC, your other iOS devices, and with any online calendars you access using iCloud, Microsoft Exchange, and Google Calendar accounts. (See Book III, Chapter 2.)

✓ **Camera:** Take normal, square, and panoramic photos and instantly add special effects filters and record slow-motion and time-lapse videos (if your iPhone model supports those functions). Share the results with others via Messages, Mail, Facebook, Twitter, Flickr, or Vimeo. (See Book IV, Chapter 1.)

Figure 4-1: iPhone's main Home screens display built-in apps and app folders.

✔ **Clock:** View the current time in your present location and other locations with World Clock; use Alarm to wake you up; tap Stopwatch to track a timed event; and use Timer to count down the hours, minutes, and seconds remaining 'til the cows come home. (See Book III, Chapter 2.)

✔ **Contacts:** Contacts helps you create, view, and manage contact information to keep track of people and company names, addresses, phone numbers, email addresses, instant messaging account names, birthday and anniversary dates, and other contact-related bits of information. And, you can sync them with your other devices. (See Book III, Chapter 1.)

✔ **FaceTime:** Use this app to make audio and video calls to your friends with iPhones or iPads or Macs using the cellular data or Wi-Fi service. (See Book II, Chapter 1.)

✔ **Game Center:** View and compare your game score rankings and achievements with friends and leaderboard top scores; invite friends and new opponents from around the world to compete in multiplayer games; and find Game Center games to play. (See Book IV, Chapter 5.)

✔ **iBooks:** iBooks acts as your virtual doorway to Apple's iBooks Store, where you can download free classics in e-book form, like *Great Expectations* and *War and Peace,* as well as purchase the latest bestsellers and other e-books. You can also read PDF and ePub documents downloaded from other sources such as Project Gutenberg (www.gutenberg.org). (See Book IV, Chapter 2.)

✔ **iTunes Store:** Browse, search, preview, and purchase music, movies, TV shows, ringtones, and audio books. Also, rent movies. Genius makes recommendations for music, movies, and TV shows. iTunes Match upgrades existing music to better-quality audio files, and iTunes Radio offers customized listening. (See Book IV, Chapter 2.)

✔ **iTunes U:** iTunes U manages all your coursework materials, such as videos, podcasts, e-books, and presentations. iTunes U links to the iTunes Store so you can find, subscribe to, and download iTunes U lectures you want to learn from. (See Book IV, Chapter 2.)

✔ **Mail:** Send, receive, and manage email messages for multiple email account types, including Microsoft Exchange, Gmail, Yahoo!, AOL, and Outlook.com. Send, receive, and download media attachments. (See Book II, Chapter 2.)

✔ **Maps:** Locate and view your current location on a map, and get turn-by-turn directions from one place to another with traffic conditions and information about a location. Bookmark, or save as a contact, or share locations. (See Book III, Chapter 3.)

✔ **Messages:** Use this app to send, receive, and manage SMS (Short Message Service) text messages, MMS (Multimedia Message Service) messages, and iMessages that can include photos, videos, contact information, web links, and map locations. (See Book II, Chapter 2.)

- **Music:** Listen to your music and audio books through your iPhone speaker, earphones, Bluetooth speakers, or external speakers connected to your iPhone. (See Book IV, Chapters 2 and 3.)

- **Newsstand:** Keep your magazine, newspaper, and journal subscriptions in one place. Connect to the Newsstand Store to download the periodical's app and then subscribe in-app. (See Book IV, Chapter 5.)

- **Nike + iPod:** This app icon won't appear until you turn on the Nike + iPod feature in the Settings app (tap Nike + iPod, and then tap the Nike + iPod switch on). Use this app to record and monitor your walking and running workouts when linked to the Nike + iPod sensor tucked into the foot bed of your Nike+ running shoes (sensor and shoes sold separately). You can upload your workout data to the Nike+ website to view past workouts and track progress toward your running goals.

- **Notes:** Create, view, and manage text notes you can sync over the air using your iCloud, Gmail, Yahoo!, or Microsoft Exchange account. Copy and paste text to and from notes with other apps, and share and print Notes. (See Book III, Chapter 5.)

- **Passbook:** Manage your store cards, coupons, and boarding passes. Present the bar code in Passbook at the cashier or check-in counter to earn points, pay for purchases, and take advantage of discounts. (See Book IV, Chapter 5.)

- **Phone:** Use this app to place and answer calls, and even block callers you don't want to contact you. Create, search, and edit Contacts, record your voicemail personal greeting and listen to, reply to, and manage voicemail messages. (See Book II, Chapter 1.)

- **Photos:** View, share, manage, add filters, and edit photos and videos captured with your iPhone, copied from your computer, saved from other apps, or shared from other devices. Printing photos, viewing photos as a slide show, assigning a photo to a contact card, or choosing a photo as your iPhone's wallpaper are just a few things you can do with Photos. (See Book IV, Chapter 1.)

- **Podcasts:** Browse the podcast catalog to find audio and video podcasts that interest you and stream, download, and subscribe. (See Book IV, Chapter 3.)

- **Reminders:** Create and manage an interactive to-do list. Add deadlines and locations, and set up alerts so you know when you have to be somewhere. (See Book III, Chapter 2.)

- **Safari:** Access and view websites; share links you like; create a reading list that you can return to when you have more time; read without distraction in Reader; switch between web page windows; create and manage bookmarks, and sync your bookmarks and tabs between iPhone and Safari or Internet Explorer on your computer or other iPhones or iPads;

view, save, and print web pages, photo files, PDFs, and other files. (See Book II, Chapter 3.)

✔ **Settings:** The place to go to customize features for all the apps on your iPhone, not to mention the functions and features of the iPhone itself.

✔ **Tips:** To help you get up to speed with iOS 8, Tips gives you weekly tidbits and tricks that you may not find on your own — although you'll find most of them in this book!

✔ **Extras (folder):** Not an app, the Extras icon is actually a folder containing other apps. The following apps may be in the Extras folder or on the Home screen:

- **Compass:** Find out which direction you're facing, view your longitude and latitude coordinates, and switch between true north and magnetic north bearings. Swipe across the Compass to open a level. (See Book III, Chapter 3.)

- **Stocks:** Stay on top of stock prices, track trading summaries, and view detailed market data and news. (See Book III, Chapter 4.)

- **Voice Memos:** Record and replay spoken or other in-the-moment sounds you want to capture and listen to again; share your recorded ramblings or even convert them to ringtones. (See Book III, Chapter 5.)

✔ **Videos:** Watch and listen to music videos, movies, and TV shows; stream video content to your Apple TV or connect your iPhone to a monitor or HDTV with the Lightning Digital AV adapter. (See Book IV, Chapter 4.)

✔ **Weather:** View current weather conditions (including humidity level, real and perceived temperature, and wind direction), a 24-hour hourly forecast, plus a nine-day forecast for one or more locations around the world. (See Book III, Chapter 3.)

Downloading Extra Apple iPhone Apps

While we're talking about apps, we want to introduce you to a few free Apple apps that aren't preinstalled on your iPhone. The first time you use the App Store app, a notification asks "Would you like to download free Apple apps?" so you may already have some of these apps. If not, you can download them from the App Store, which we cover in Book IV, Chapter 5.

✔ **Apple Store:** Browse and order Apple products online and have them shipped to your doorstep — or reserve them at your nearest Apple Store and then drop in to fetch your new goods in person, with directions to the store brought to you by your iPhone's own Map app. The Apple Store app also lets you make a date for one-on-one training, or reserve a seat at the Genius Bar or at upcoming events and training workshops.

✔ **Find My Friends:** Download and sign in to this app with your Apple ID and you can see friends with Apple devices in the vicinity.

✔ **Find My iPhone:** In the unhappy event your iPhone is lost or stolen, all may not truly be lost if you have the Find My iPhone feature turned on. The Find My iPhone app is not required to use the Find My iPhone feature, but it lets you manage and track other iPhones or iPads. It's just so handy to have on hand to see those other gadgets, or to help a friend who may have misplaced or lost his iPhone. We tell you how to use the Find My iPhone feature and app at the end of this chapter.

✔ **Remote:** This app taps into your home Wi-Fi network to turn your iPhone into a remote control for browsing and playing content stored in your computer's iTunes library or controlling Apple TV with a better user interface than the physical remote that ships with Apple TV.

If you bought a new iPhone after September 2013, you can download complimentary copies of Apple's iWork apps (Pages, Keynote, and Numbers) along with iMovie and GarageBand. If you updated an existing iPhone to iOS 8, you can still purchase those apps separately from the App Store. We talk about iWork apps in Book III, Chapters 4 and 5; iMovie in Book IV, Chapter 4; and GarageBand in the bonus online extras.

Adjusting iPhone's Settings

In the Settings app, you adjust iPhone's numerous settings to suit your style, including date and time, screen brightness, default ringtone, and background wallpaper image options (to name a few). Turn various networking features on and off; tweak individual app settings and choose which ones can access your location or send you notification messages; create and manage email, contacts, calendar, and notes accounts; manage iCloud syncing and backup; and view information about your iPhone's system software, usage, and capacity. Settings is command central for everything your iPhone does.

You'll get the most out of this section by following along with your iPhone in hand as we describe the various settings that let you customize how you use your iPhone.

The Status bar icons (Book I, Chapter 2) can help you determine which settings you turn on, such as Wi-Fi or Bluetooth connections or an alarm.

Throughout this book's many chapters, we show you how to access and adjust iPhone's individual app settings on a need-to-know basis. For instance, in Book II, Chapter 1, we show how to adjust iPhone's Phone settings to turn on (or off) features like call forwarding and whether your caller ID is displayed when you place calls to others.

Some settings, such as the image that appears behind the buttons on the Home screen — referred to as *wallpaper* — can be changed in more than one way. For instance, when you capture a photo with Camera, you can then choose that snapshot as your Home screen or Lock screen (or both) wallpaper image. Using the Photos app to browse images you copied from your computer is another way to change iPhone's wallpaper setting.

In the rest of this chapter, we show you how to change the basic settings you may want to change now or later, straight up, no stumbling-upon necessary.

Open the Settings app to display iPhone's list of settings, as shown in Figure 4-2, and then scroll up and down the list and tap on one you want to change. We go through each setting here in order of appearance, and where we don't go into detail, we direct you to the chapter in which it's discussed.

From the first Settings screen, you tap into a specific options screen and from there you often tap again. You see the disclosure triangle (>) symbol that, when tapped, displays the selected setting's individual options (and, in some cases, additional sub-settings options for that selected top-level set-ting). There are two ways to back out of those screens:

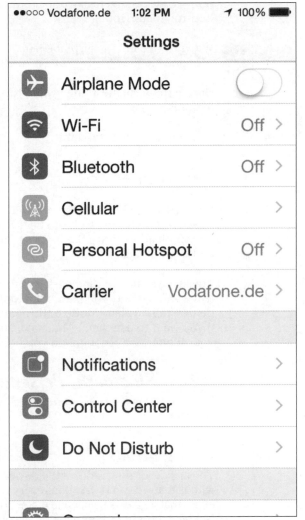

Figure 4-2: Tapping into iPhone's list of settings.

  ✓ **Tap** the button in the upper-left corner — it displays the name of the previous screen and you can tap, tap, tap until you reach the very first Settings screen.

  ✓ **Flick** right, as if turning back pages in a book with an index finger.

Airplane Mode

Airplane Mode is a top-level setting that features a single On/Off button.

Think of the Airplane Mode setting as your one-stop, instant cut-off switch for immediately disconnecting every one of your iPhone's wireless connection "cords" in one fell swoop. You find an Airplane Mode button in the Control Center, too.

 When turned on, the airplane icon appears in the Status bar, indicating Airplane Mode's "no fly" zone is in effect.

Hitting the Airplane Mode switch turns off the following wireless connection features:

- Cellular voice and data
- Wi-Fi
- Bluetooth

When Airplane Mode is on, you can't make or receive phone calls or messages, or browse the web or check your email. Nor can you use wireless Bluetooth accessories like Apple's Bluetooth Wireless Keyboard, headsets, and headphones.

These days, most airlines ask you to turn cellular connections off but let you leave your device, Wi-Fi, and Bluetooth active. So swipe up to open Control Center, tap Airplane Mode to turn it on, but then tap Wi-Fi and Bluetooth on, if you want to use them. That said, should the airline request you turn off your iPhone, we recommend you honor their request.

Wi-Fi, Bluetooth, Personal Hotspot, Carrier

These settings are presented in the "Making Connections" section of Book I, Chapter 2.

Notifications

The upside, or downside, of the devices and gadgets we surround ourselves with is that we can learn about every movement and quirk of every person or event that interests us seconds after something happens. On your iPhone, Notifications offer a combination of sounds, alert messages, and badges that can appear on the Lock screen, the Home screen, over the Status bar while you're using an app, and in the Notification Center. For each app that is somehow connected with the world, you can select how, when, and where you want to be alerted when something happens, or you can choose not to be alerted at all. The great thing about notifications is that they grab your attention even if the app that's doing the attention grabbing isn't running. iOS 8 offers interactive notifications so you can quickly respond to a message or even comment on a Facebook post without leaving the app you're using, as illustrated by Figure 4-3.

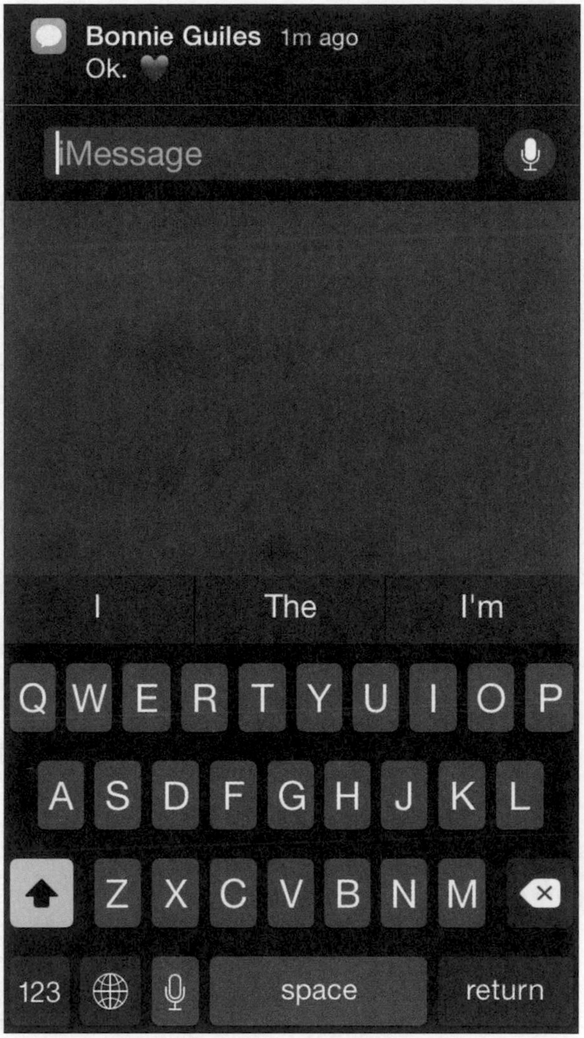

The Notification Center is a central location where all notifications are saved until you remove them. Hidden from view but always available, it appears when you swipe or pull down from the very top of the screen from the Lock screen, any Home screen, or app. If the app is in landscape view, swipe down from the top of that view.

Notice the two tabs across the top of the Notification Center as shown in Figure 4-4. Tapping each one displays information based on the settings you choose:

Figure 4-3: Interactive notifications let you respond even when you're using other apps.

- ✔ **Today:** Tap to show the items you have selected for the Today view, such as the weather forecast, any appointments you have scheduled for the day, and the current stock activity.

- ✔ **Notifications:** Tap to display all notifications, read or unread, from the apps you have associated with the Notification Center.

Today view

The Today view in the Notification Center gives you an at-a-glance overview of the weather and your appointments for the day, along with a few other handy bits of information. By default, the Today view includes the following:

- ✔ **Today Summary:** The day, date, and weather forecast.

✔ **Traffic Conditions:**
Traffic conditions for
routes you take fre-
quently, such as going
to work. You have to
turn on Frequent
Locations in the
Settings app by tap-
ping Privacy, tapping
Location Services,
and tapping System
Services. It can take
up to one month for
your iPhone to learn
your frequent loca-
tions and begin giving
you traffic reports on
the Today view.

✔ **Calendar:** Events
you have scheduled
on the Calendar app.

✔ **Reminders:** Tasks
you put in Reminders
for today as well as
any from the past
that haven't been
checked as com-
pleted. You only see
Reminders with
Remind Me On A Day
activated (see
Book III, Chapter 2).

✔ **Stocks:** Current
quotes for stocks,
funds, indexes, or
markets that you fol-
low as defined in the Stocks app. (Refer to Book III, Chapter 4.)

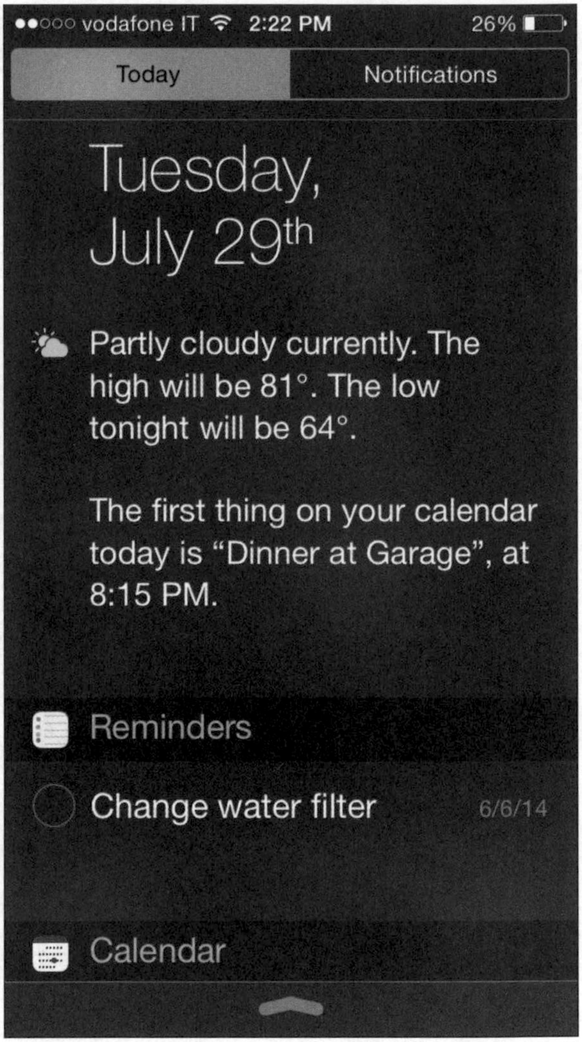

Figure 4-4: The Today view in the Notification Center.

✔ **Tomorrow Summary:** A brief narrative of anything you have scheduled
for the next day.

Tap any of the items in the Today view to open the app it came from.

You can change which of these items you see in the Today view by doing the
following:

1. **Pull down from the top of the iPhone screen to open the Notification
Center.**

Do this from the Home screen or an active app; you can't edit the Today view from the Lock screen, although you can see it.

2. **Tap the Today tab at the top of the screen, if it isn't active.**

3. **Scroll to the bottom of the screen and tap Edit.**

   A list of the default Today view items appears.

4. **Tap the Remove button (the minus sign in the red circle) to remove the app from the Today view — don't worry, you can always put it back.**

5. **Tap the Remove button.**

   The app is moved to the Do Not Include part of the list, as shown in Figure 4-5.

6. **(Optional) Touch and drag the rearrange button to the right of Calendar, Reminders, or Stocks to change the order of appearance on the Today view.**

7. **(Optional) Tap the Add button (the plus sign on the green circle) to move an app you removed back to Today view.**

8. **Tap Done.**

   The Today view appears again (refer to Figure 4-4).

9. **Press the Home button or swipe up to close the Notification Center.**

Notifications

We explain responding to notification messages in Book I, Chapter 2; here, we explain how to designate the type of notifications you want to receive for each app that offers

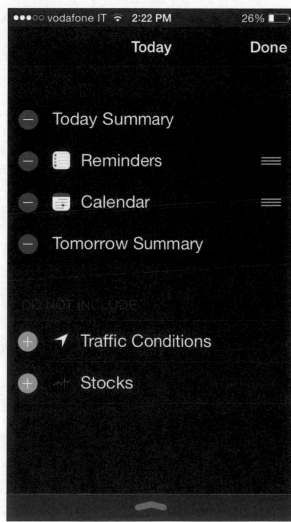

Figure 4-5: Edit the Today view from within the Notification Center.

notification options. With so many options, it can seem somewhat complicated at first, but after you set your preferred notification settings for the first few apps, you get the hang of it.

1. **Open the Settings app and tap Notifications.**

2. **In the Notifications View section, tap either Manually or By Time to choose how notifications are sorted in the Notification Center.**

3. **Refer to Figure 4-6, and notice how apps on your iPhone are divided into two sections: Include and Do Not Include.**

Apps in the Include section appear in the Notification Center when something happens, but you can still receive alerts (badges, banners, or alerts) from apps in the Do Not Include section. For example, if you turn Notification Center

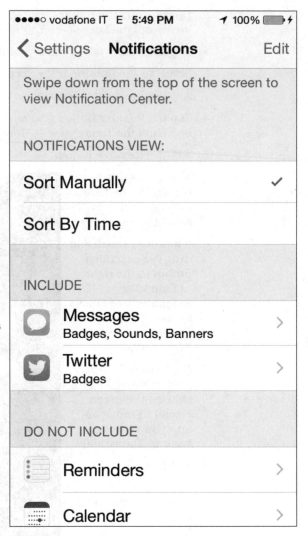

Figure 4-6: Notification settings on a per-app basis.

Off for Messages but leave badges and banners on, when a new message arrives, you see the numbered badge on the Message button on the Home screen and a banner appears on the screen for a few seconds. No record of the message appears in the Notification Center. Or you can choose to have app alerts appear only in the Notification Center and not receive any other alerts (the None option in Step 10).

4. **Tap the name of each app in the list to choose if and how you want that app to send you notifications.**

A screen similar to the one in Figure 4-7 opens.

5. **Tap the Allow Notifications switch on or off.**

   When on, you see a screen similar to Figure 4-7; when off, the options disappear.

6. **Tap Show in Notification Center, and then choose how many items from this app you want listed in the Notification Center.**

   For example, if you choose 5 for Mail, you see the five most recent messages you received in Mail listed in the Notification Center. The app then appears in the Include list on the previous screen.

   Choose No Recent Items if you don't want to see this app in the Notification Center, and it will then appear in the Do Not Include list on the previous screen. You can still see alerts, banners, or badges or hear audible alerts when the app wants your attention.

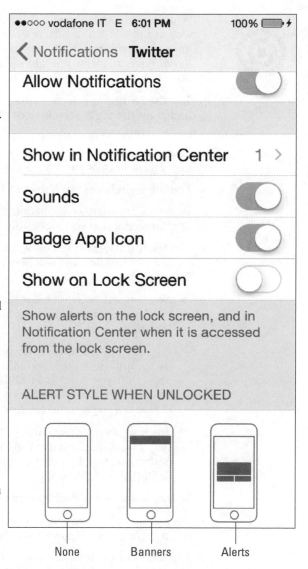

Figure 4-7: Set notifications for each app that has a notifications option.

7. **Tap the Sounds switch on to hear an audible alert when the app wants to tell you something.**

   For Reminders, Messages, Mail, Phone, and Calendar you can choose a specific sound for the app. You can also manage sounds for these apps in the Sounds part of the Settings app.

TIP

What's more, Mail allows a different sound for each email account as well as for VIP or threads. In Contacts, you can assign a special sound to individual contacts. Calendar lets you further specify a sound for the different types of alerts it might send. (See Book II, Chapter 4 and Book III, Chapters 1 and 2, respectively.)

8. **Tap the Badge App Icon switch on if you want to see the numbered badge on the right shoulder of the app's icon on the Home screen.**

   You won't see this option for all apps because those numbers tell you, for example, how many unread email messages you have in Mail or how many missed calls and unheard voicemails you have in Phone.

9. **Tap the switch next to Show on Lock Screen to the on, or off, position.**

   When on, the alert style (banner or alert) you chose will appear on the Lock screen when you wake your iPhone.

10. **Choose the Alert Style you want the app to use when your iPhone is unlocked (and on the Lock Screen if you turned that option on in Step 9):**

    • *None* means you don't want any alerts from this app — but you can have up to ten recent items appear in the Notification Center (see Step 6).

    • *Banners* appear across the top of the Home screen or app you're using, and then automatically disappear after a few seconds. For apps that you can respond to, such as a message, you can pull down the banner — before it disappears — and respond (refer to Figure 4-3) or tap the banner to open the app that notified you.

    • *Alerts* appear in the center of the screen and require an action before they disappear. You can tap Close to acknowledge the alert but do nothing or tap the other choice, which, depending on the app, may be Reply, View, or Options.

11. **You may see other Notifications options, which vary from app to app.**

    For example, Messages and Mail have a Show Preview option, which, when turned On, displays a few lines of the message in the notification.

12. **Tap the Notifications button in the upper-left corner to return to the previous screen, and then scroll through and tap the apps in both the Include and Do Not Include lists, repeating steps 5 through 11.**

13. **Tap the Edit button.**

14. **Tap and hold the rearrange button to the right of the app name, and then drag the app up or down to reorder the list as it will appear in the Notification Center.**

15. **Tap Done.**

16. **Tap Settings in the upper left or flick right to return to the Settings screen.**

Control Center

The Control Center gives you quick access to the most commonly used Settings such as Airplane Mode, Do Not Disturb, screen brightness, playback volume, and several apps, including a nifty flashlight and the Camera app. The Control Center, as shown in Figure 4-8, appears when you swipe up from the bottom of the screen. Tapping the buttons that appear activates that setting or opens the app. Pull down from the arrow at the top to close the Control Center. In these settings, you can choose to access the Control Center from the Lock screen and from within apps; just tap the switch on next to both options.

Figure 4-8: Just drag and tap to turn on settings from the Control Center.

Do Not Disturb

Barbara uses Do Not Disturb on a daily, er, nightly, basis. Living in one time zone and working in another means messages and calls sometimes come in at 3 a.m.; she sets Do Not Disturb to enjoy an interruption-free night's sleep. Incoming calls are forwarded to voicemail and alerts for incoming Messages or other apps that audibly vie for your attention are silenced. You can adjust Do Not Disturb settings to allow calls to come through while blocking other alerts.

You can also manually turn on Do Not Disturb when you need some time without any intrusions or disruptions from your iPhone. Simply open the Settings app, tap Do Not Disturb, tap the Manual switch on, or just swipe up from the bottom of the screen to open the Control Center and tap the Do Not Disturb button. To automatically activate Do Not Disturb at a scheduled time every day, follow these steps:

Switching between portrait and landscape views

You may have noticed that if you rotate your iPhone 90 degrees to the left or right, the screen rotates, too. This is considered switching between a portrait, or vertical, view and a landscape, or horizontal, view. Many games, as well as movies viewed in Videos, work only in landscape view. Some apps and the Home screen work only in portrait view. The pre-installed apps that can be viewed in both portrait and landscape are Safari, Mail, Messages, Maps, Notes, Contacts, Stocks, Photos, Camera, Calculator (changes to a scientific calculator in landscape view), Calendar (changes to a multiday calendar in landscape view), and Music in playback mode.

You can lock your iPhone so it stays in portrait view by tapping the Portrait Orientation Lock button in the Control Center. A lock appears to show that Portrait Orientation Lock is on and the same icon appears in the Status bar to remind you it's on (refer to Figure 4-8).

Repeat the steps to turn Portrait Orientation Lock off.

On iPhone 6 Plus, switching to landscape view in Messages and Mail gives you a split-screen view, listing messages on the left and showing the contents of one message on the right. In the Weather and Calendar apps, you see more days.

1. **Open the Settings app, and tap Do Not Disturb.**

2. **Tap the Scheduled switch to the on position and then tap the From/To field to open a Quiet Hours (love that!) rotor where you choose the starting and ending time for Do Not Disturb to automatically activate.**

3. **Tap Back in the upper left to return to the previous screen.**

4. **Tap Allow Calls From.**

   The following options appear:

   - *Everyone:* This lets calls come through but blocks other alerts, such as incoming messages and Facebook updates.

   - *No One:* Silences all incoming calls and messages.

   - *Favorites:* Allows calls to come through only from people you've identified as Favorites in Contacts (see Book IV, Chapter 1).

   - *Groups:* If you have groups set up in Contacts, you can choose to receive calls from people in one or more group.

5. **Tap Back in the upper left to return to the previous screen.**

6. **Tap Repeated Calls On if you want to let a second call from the same number within three minutes come through.**

7. **Select one of the choices in the Silence section (scroll down to see it):**

   - *Always* to activate Do Not Disturb whether you're using your iPhone or not.

- *Only while iPhone is locked* to silence incoming calls and notifications only when your iPhone is locked. For example, if someone calls while you're looking something up on Safari, your phone will ring.

8. **Tap Settings in the upper left, or swipe right, to return to the Settings screen.**

A quarter moon icon rises in the Status bar to indicate Do Not Disturb is on.

General

The General setting screen is actually a catch-all for more than a dozen individual settings — many of which we write about in greater detail in the chapters where those settings are called into play. The following list provides details for settings you won't find explained elsewhere in this book and points you in the right direction for the settings that are fully explained in other chapters.

Many settings in Settings have multiple levels. Tap the arrow, also known as the disclosure triangle, to the right of the item to go to a deeper level and see more options; tap the button in the upper left of the screen, or flick right, to return to the previous screen.

- **About:** Tap Name to change your iPhone's name. Beneath that, view detailed information about your iPhone, including the serial number; the phone carrier; the hardware model and software versions; the number of songs, photos, videos, and applications; the total amount of memory space storing all of those things is gobbling up (and how much memory space remains); a bunch of interesting-looking regulatory logos and glyph-like symbols that are sort of like virtual passport stamps; and page after page of tiny legal gobbledygook describing a panic-inducing laundry list of permissions, rules, regulations, warnings, disclaimers, and outright threats that, were you to actually read all of it, would probably scare you so badly you'd wind up ditching your phone contract, selling or giving away your iPhone, and switching to tribal bongos or tin cans connected by a single length of string as your preferred mode of communicating with the rest of the world.

- **Software Update:** If a new version of the operating system, also known as iOS, is available, tapping this button downloads and installs it to your iPhone. Make sure your iPhone is connected to a power source and Wi-Fi while installing.

- **Siri:** Turn Siri on or off and choose how you interact with Siri. See Book I, Chapter 3.

  Siri can adjust many of your iPhone settings but needs to be on to enable dictation and receive requests.

- **Spotlight Search:** For choosing which apps (and app contents) Spotlight searches, and the order in which they will be searched. See Book I, Chapter 3.

- **Text Size:** Certain apps support something called Dynamic Type, which means the text size changes based on your preferences. Tap this option and then slide the slider to the text size that's comfortable for your eyes. When available (for example in Mail, Messages, Contacts, and Reader), the text will appear in the size you set.

- **Handoff & Suggested Apps:** If you own or use several Apple devices with the same iCloud account, you can begin working in one app on your iPhone and then pick up where you left off on another iOS device or Mac. Tap the switch to turn Handoff on. From this screen you can also turn on Suggested Apps, which lets your iPhone use your current location to recommend apps installed on your iPhone (My Apps) or from the App Store that would help you. For example, when the App Store function is on and you visit a new city, public transportation apps for that city will be suggested to you when you open the App Store app.

- **Accessibility:** See Book I, Chapter 2.

- **Usage:** Lists how much storage each app on your iPhone uses and how much overall storage remains. Tap Manage Storage and then tap an app to delete the app (if it isn't a preloaded app) or delete the contents of an app, such as courses in iTunes U or media in the Music app. If you activated iCloud, you see the total and available iCloud storage amounts as well (refer to Book I, Chapter 5 to learn about iCloud).

  The most useful buttons are, perhaps, the Battery Usage and Percentage settings, which we discuss in detail in Book I, Chapter 2.

- **Background App Refresh:** When on, apps that pull information from the Internet (such as Weather or Stocks) or use Location Services (for example Reminders) will refresh even when they aren't open so you have up-to-date information when you do open them or so they can send you location-based updates. Tap to turn the setting on and then tap specific apps to turn the function on, or off, which helps conserve both battery and cellular data usage.

- **Auto Lock:** Tap Auto Lock and then choose the amount of time you want your iPhone to wait before it automatically locks the screen. Your choices range from one to five minutes, or you can choose Never, which means it's up to you to remember to press the Sleep/Wake button to lock your iPhone.

  Even when locked, your iPhone can still receive calls, text messages, and inbound communications — unless you activated Do Not Disturb — and you can still listen to music or other audio.

- **Restrictions:** This powerful tool is hidden in iPhone's General settings. Tap the Enable Restrictions button and then type in a secret four-digit code, and then type in the code a second time to verify your code. Tap the apps and features you want to turn off or on. App icons for any apps you restrict disappear from iPhone's Home screen.

If you share your iPhone with another person (or you're a parent or guardian who holds the keys to iPhone's kingdom), you can allow or restrict access to apps and features, or block access to content, such as songs containing explicit lyrics, or movies or TV shows based on their MPA rating. You can also allow or restrict changes to specific apps such as Contacts and Facebook. Scroll down the list to find a Volume Limit setting and Game Center limits.

Although you'd think turning off access to a certain app, such as Safari, would totally block your iPhone from accessing web pages, that isn't 100 percent true. Although the app icon disappears from the Home screen and browsing the web with Safari is therefore disabled, certain apps you may have installed on your iPhone can *still* access the web using their own web browser features. For instance, tapping a web page link that appears in the Facebook, Twitter, or Google apps opens those apps' built-in web browsers to display the content of a web page link. There are also other browser apps, such as Google Chrome, which can't be restricted with this setting.

If you want to "hide" some of the preinstalled apps that can't be deleted from your iPhone, you may be able to restrict them, which removes the app button from the Home screen. The app is still on your iPhone, but you don't see it.

- ✔ **Date & Time:** See Book III, Chapter 2.

- ✔ **Keyboard:** See Book I, Chapter 3.

- ✔ **Language & Region:** Choose the written and spoken language you want to use with your iPhone. Tap Region Format to set how dates, times, and phone numbers are displayed in apps that use that information.

- ✔ **iTunes Wi-Fi Sync:** To sync your iPhone with iTunes without using the USB connector cable, tap Wi-Fi Sync and then tap Sync Now. See Book I, Chapter 5.

- ✔ **Reset:** See Book 1, Chapter 5.

Display & Brightness

You can control the screen brightness in the Control Center, or here, in Settings. Drag the slider left or right to decrease or increase your iPhone's screen brightness. Auto-Brightness adjusts the iPhone's brightness level based on your environment.

You also access two features that enhance the text on the screen:

- ✔ **Text Size:** Tap to open and then drag the slider to adjust the size of the typeface to one that's comfortable for your eyes. Apps that support Dynamic Type (that is, adjustable typeface sizes) will use your preferred type size, such as Contacts, Mail, and Safari.

✔ **Bold Text:** When On, your on screen text will be bold. Your iPhone has to restart for this function to take effect.

Wallpaper

Wallpaper is the term used to describe the screen you see when your iPhone is locked, and the background image displayed behind app icons on the Home screen. You can choose the same image for both wallpaper choices, or you can choose a unique image for each choice. Some images display as dynamic wallpaper, which means the image moves, both on its own and in response to movements you make with your iPhone.

With the advent of iOS 7, some users reported feeling seasick while using their iPhone and the dynamic wallpaper seems to be to blame. If you're having this problem, open the Settings app, tap General, tap Accessibility, and tap the Reduce Motion switch on, which disables the so-called parallax effect (a fancy way of saying movement) of icons and alerts.

To change the wallpaper on your iPhone, open the Settings app and tap Wallpaper. The two thumbnails show your current wallpaper choice: the left is the Lock screen and the right is the Home screen. Tap Choose a New Wallpaper to display the locations you can choose to pick your new wallpaper. Tap one of the categories to see the images stored in that category. Apple Wallpaper contains pretty pictures that came preloaded on your iPhone. Photos is where you find any snapshots you captured using Camera, or any images you may have saved from web pages, email, or text messages. (See Book IV, Chapter 1.)

Tap an image to preview what your choice will look like as a wallpaper image. If you choose an image from Photos, you can move or zoom the image in or out to adjust the image to your liking. Tap Cancel if you don't want to use the image and return to your choices. Or tap Set to choose the image, and then tap Set Lock Screen, Set Home Screen, or Set Both to set the image as your wallpaper of choice for either or both screens. Swipe back to the initial Wallpaper screen to see a preview of how your wallpaper will appear in the thumbnails, as shown in Figure 4-9.

Sounds

With the number of notifications and alerts you can receive, assigning different sounds to each one can help you distinguish which ones need immediate attention and which can be attended to later. The most obvious sound your iPhone makes is that of an incoming call. By default, your iPhone is set to vibrate whenever a call comes in. You can choose whether you want that good vibration when your phone rings or when it's in silent mode or both or none.

In the Ringer and Alerts section, dragging the volume slider left or right to decrease or increase ringtone and alert message sounds has the same effect as pressing your iPhone's actual volume buttons up or down. Turn off

Change with Buttons if you don't want your iPhone's physical buttons (or, if plugged in, headset volume buttons) to change ringtone and alert volume levels. The volume buttons still let you increase or decrease the volume level of other sound-related output, such as music you're listening to, videos you're watching, and games you're playing, as well as the voice of anyone you're speaking with on the phone.

In Sounds and Vibration Patterns as shown in Figure 4-10, tap the alert in the list, such as Ringtone or Calendar Alerts, and then choose the vibration and sound you want to associate with that type of alert. You can also choose None for either or both vibration and sound. Scroll to the bottom of the Sounds screen to turn Lock Sounds (what you hear when you lock or unlock your iPhone) and Keyboard Clicks (what you hear when you type) off or on.

Figure 4-9: Wallpaper choices you can live with.

You turn Sounds on for incoming Twitter and Facebook posts in Notifications settings but choose the sound you hear when you post in the Sounds settings. Sounds settings also let you choose a Sent Mail sound, whereas Notifications manages New Mail and account specific sounds for incoming messages. You have more options for Calendar alerts in Notifications, too.

Passcode

Requiring a passcode to unlock your iPhone can help prevent others from viewing your personal data or making calls on your dime. To set it up, do the following:

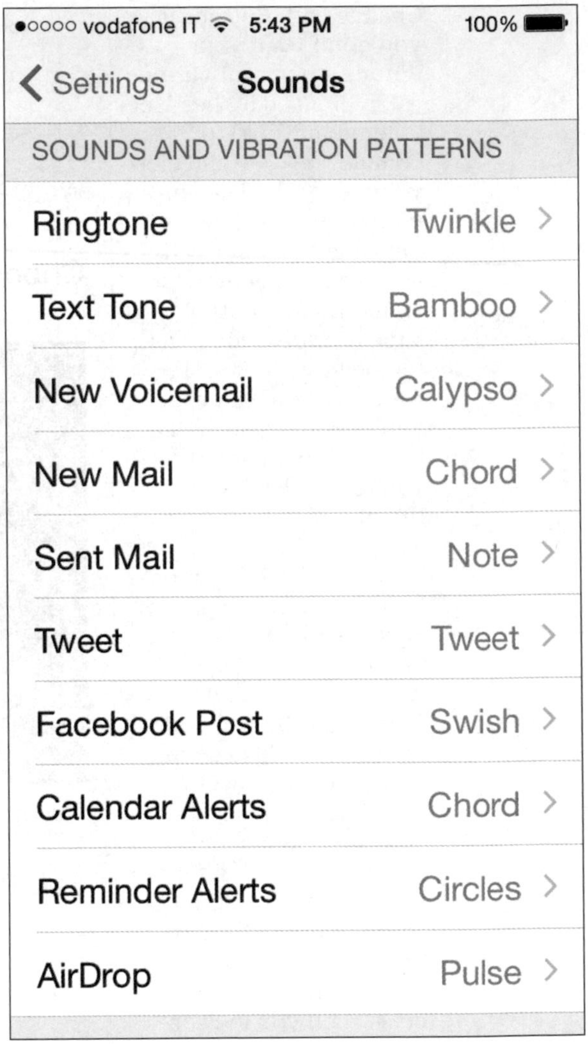

1. **Open the Settings app, tap Passcode, and tap Turn Passcode On.**

2. **Type in a four-digit passcode, and then type in the code a second time to verify your code.**

   Simple Passcodes are four digits, whereas complex passcodes can be a word or phrase, an alphanumeric combination, or only numbers (such as the phone number of a childhood friend). Complex passcodes are more secure because they are harder to guess. To use a complex passcode:

   1. Tap the Simple Passcode switch off. The Set Passcode screen opens.

   2. Type the passcode you want to use.

   3. Tap Next.

   4. Re-enter your passcode.

   5. Tap Done.

●○○○○ vodafone IT 🛜 5:43 PM   100% 🔋

❮ Settings   **Sounds**

SOUNDS AND VIBRATION PATTERNS

Ringtone	Twinkle ❯
Text Tone	Bamboo ❯
New Voicemail	Calypso ❯
New Mail	Chord ❯
Sent Mail	Note ❯
Tweet	Tweet ❯
Facebook Post	Swish ❯
Calendar Alerts	Chord ❯
Reminder Alerts	Circles ❯
AirDrop	Pulse ❯

Figure 4-10: Choose vibration patterns and sounds for different apps.

You can change your secret code anytime by tapping Change Passcode, entering your old passcode, and then entering a new passcode.

3. **Tap Require Passcode and then tap Immediately if you want your iPhone to require your passcode whenever you unlock it. Or choose one of the time-out options if you want your iPhone to require your code after the chosen amount of time has passed.**

4. **Tap the Voice Dial switch on if you want to require the passcode to make voice-controlled calls.**

5. **Tap the functions you want to work from the Lock screen to the On position: Today, Notifications View, Siri, Passbook, and/or Reply with Message.**

When Siri is accessible from the Lock Screen, security features such as the Passcode Lock are overridden and, therefore, compromised — even though your iPhone is locked, you (or someone else) can make a phone call or take another action via Siri.

And, if you use iCloud Keychain (Book I, Chapter 5) or AutoFill in Safari (see Book II, Chapter 3) to store passwords and credit card information for certain websites, without a passcode that information is readily available to anyone who might casually use your iPhone to visit, say, the Amazon shopping site. Interestingly, Apple doesn't allow you to store your Apple ID password with AutoFill.

6. **Tap the Erase Data switch on to protect your personal information in the event your iPhone falls into the wrong hands.**

Erase Data erases everything stored on your iPhone if the correct passcode isn't entered after ten tries.

If your iPhone has a SIM card, you can activate and change a personal identification number (PIN) to lock the SIM card (some SIM cards come with a preset PIN). When activated, you must type in the PIN code whenever you turn iPhone off and then on again. But unlike the Passcode Lock feature, which generously offers up to ten tries in the game of Guess Your Secret Code, the SIM PIN Lock feature is less forgiving — after three failed attempts to crack the SIM code, unlocking the SIM PIN may then require a unique Personal Unlocking Key (PUK) code to unlock your iPhone (which rightful owners may obtain by contacting their cellular carrier's customer service department). You can change the SIM PIN or turn it off completely by opening the Settings app, tapping Phone, tapping SIM PIN, and tapping the SIM PIN switch off or tapping Change PIN.

Touch ID & Passcode

The Home button, on the iPhone models with Touch ID, houses the Touch ID sensor, which gives you the option to use your fingerprint to verify authorized access to your iPhone from the Lock and to authorize purchases from the iTunes, App, and iBook Stores. With iOS 8, Apple opened this option to developers so you'll be seeing it as an option with other apps soon, too.

You may have set up Touch ID when you set up your iPhone (refer to Book I, Chapter 2). If not, follow these steps to add your fingerprint or that of someone else, like a child or significant other. We also tell you how to name or delete fingerprints.

You still have to set up a passcode to use Touch ID, for two reasons: When you turn your iPhone on, you have to enter the passcode, and if for some reason your fingerprint doesn't work, you can still unlock your iPhone.

1. **Open the Settings app and tap Touch ID &Passcode.**

   If you previously assigned a Passcode to your iPhone, you have to enter it before you can access the Fingerprint setup. If you haven't set up a passcode, you can do it at the same time you add a fingerprint.

2. **Tap Add a Fingerprint.**

3. **Place your finger, or thumb, on the Home button.**

   The fingerprint on screen begins to redden as the whorls and swirls of your finger are memorized.

4. **Lift and replace your finger on the Home button and roll it around so the Touch ID sensor can memorize the edges of your finger.**

   After registering the flat part of your finger, iPhone prompts you to adjust your grip. Tap Continue and place the tip and edges of your finger on the Touch ID sensor.

5. **When your fingerprint is successfully read, tap Continue.**

6. **If you haven't set up a passcode, tap a four-digit passcode on the keypad that appears (or type a complex passcode on the keyboard if you turned Simple Passcode off), otherwise go to Step 8.**

7. **Re-enter the passcode on the subsequent screen.**

8. **Choose when you want to use your fingerprint to authorize actions by tapping on iPhone Unlock (to use Touch ID to unlock your iPhone) and/or iTunes & App Store (to authorize purchases with Touch ID).**

9. **(Optional) To change the name or delete a fingerprint, do one of the following:**

   • *Name the fingerprint:* Tap the fingerprint and then type a name, such as "Barbara's Index" or "Lucy's Paw."

   • *Delete the fingerprint:* Tap the fingerprint in the list, and then tap Delete Fingerprint.

10. **Activate the other passcode options as explained in Steps 3 to 6 in the previous section "Passcode."**

Even when a passcode or fingerprint is required to open the Lock screen, you, or more likely someone who wants to use your iPhone because you're incapacitated, can make an emergency call by tapping the Emergency button in the bottom-left corner of the passcode screen. After tapping the Emergency button, a Medical ID button appears that lets the Good Samaritan who's helping you contact your next of kin.

Privacy

Privacy has become a hot button for many. Some say it's useless to try to maintain privacy because Big Brother knows all. We say, do what you can and don't do anything you wouldn't want your grandma to see. In this Settings section, you find Location Services, which gives your location information to apps that use it to perform their functions. Obviously, apps like Maps and Weather use your Location, but so do Reminders (to give you location-based alerts) and Camera (to geotag your photos).

Here, you also find a list of apps that have accessed information from other apps that are share-able such as Contacts, Calendar, and Photos, as well as Twitter and Facebook.

To adjust your privacy settings, tap Privacy and then tap Location Services to display the main Location Services setting switch and a list of all the apps that tap into your iPhone's Location Services features, as shown in Figure 4-11. Do the following:

✔ **Tap Share My Location.** If you want people to know where you are, tap Share My Location and then tap the switch to the on position. Tap From to choose which device you want to use to identify where you are (we can think of all sorts of espionage escape uses for this feature). You probably want to choose This Device (your iPhone) on the From list; if you have another iPhone or an iPad or iPod touch signed into the same iCloud account, you'll see them on the list. This function allows Messages to share your location with groups you create in iMessage. Tap the Back button in the upper left to return to the Location Services screen.

✔ **Scroll down the list of apps and tap each app to choose when to allow it to use Location Services.** Your options are:

  • Never, which doesn't ever allow the app to access your location.

  • While Using the App, which lets the app know where you are when it's open.

  • Always, which means the app will know where you are at all times.

If you spot the Location Services icon beside an app in the list, that means the app tapped into your iPhone's Location Services sometime over the last 24 hours.

Scroll to the bottom of the Location Services screen and tap the System Services button. These system-wide services use your location to perform functions such as calibrating the compass or providing traffic conditions in Maps. Tap the toggle switch to the off position next to the services you don't want to have access to your location.

Scroll to the very bottom of the System Services screen to turn the Location Services Status Bar Icon switch on or off. When on, the arrow appears in the Status bar whenever System Services accesses your location. Tap the back button in the upper-left corner twice to return to the Privacy settings screen.

Tap any of the apps in the Privacy list to see a list of other applications that have accessed information from that app. You can turn access to those apps on and off from this second-level screen.

Figure 4-11: Location Services helps your iPhone find its way — and yours.

At the very bottom of the Privacy settings screen, you find two settings:

- **Diagnostics and Usage:** If you want to "help" Apple improve products by letting it know how you use your iPhone, tap Automatically Send. If you'd rather keep your business to yourself, tap Don't Send. If you want to see the information that's been sent, tap Diagnostic & Usage Data.

✔ **Advertising:** Tap to open the options, and then tap the Limit Ad Tracking switch to the on position. This blocks apps from seeing what you do with your iPhone, which is information they use to send you targeted ads.

Other Apple and third-party app settings

After the Privacy button, you see five sections that list other apps. We explain the settings for each app in the first three sections in other chapters of this book. The fourth section contains social networking apps, and the fifth section contains Apple and third-party apps that you installed. Tapping the app in the list opens a settings or information screen. There's no set rule for the type of settings options an app offers, so you have to poke around when you download a new app — or read the app's instructions either on your iPhone or on the app's website.

Taking Steps if Your iPhone Is Lost or Stolen

Your worst iPhone nightmare: Your beloved iPhone is lost or stolen. Don't panic — even though your iPhone may be gone for good (er, bad), all may not be totally lost. If you back up regularly or better yet, use iCloud, a good portion of the apps and data on your iPhone is in safekeeping in a remote location.

As for the risk of untoward characters accessing your data on your iPhone, we have potentially good news, possibly great news, and maybe even fabulous news. First, the potentially good news: If you turned on the Passcode Lock or Fingerprint feature described in the previous section, whoever found or "borrowed" your iPhone must type in your secret passcode or have your live and attached-to-your-body finger before they can even unlock your iPhone and start snooping around. Second, the possibly great news: If, in addition to turning on the Passcode Lock feature, you also turned on the Erase Data option, your iPhone develops a sudden case of permanent amnesia and erases everything stored on it if, after the tenth try, the interloper fails to guess your secret code. And because you regularly back up with iCloud or iTunes, erasing what's on your iPhone isn't such a big deal.

And finally, what may be the best-case-scenario news of all: Before unexpectedly parting ways, hopefully you configured the Find My iPhone feature we explain here.

Of course, the first thing to do when you realize your iPhone is missing is borrow a phone and call yourself; you may hear your iPhone ringing nearby or someone may answer it and you can recover it quickly and simply.

To use Find My iPhone, you must have an iCloud account, and then turn on the Find My iPhone option in the Settings app by tapping iCloud and then tapping Find My iPhone. Tap the Find My iPhone switch to the on position and tap the Send Last Location switch on, too. When the battery runs dangerously low, your iPhone's position is sent to Apple so you can track it down through them.

With Find My iPhone activated, you may be able to track down your iPhone's general location on a map using a web browser on your computer or other web-savvy gadget, or by using the Find My iPhone app installed on another person's iPhone, iPad, or iPod touch, which in turn may jog your memory as to where you may have lost or misplaced your iPhone (like between the sofa cushions in the den, or in your gym locker).

When you begin searching for your iPhone from another device, Find My iPhone, even without a Passcode Lock, automatically activates the Activation Lock, which requires whomever has your iPhone to enter your Apple ID and password in order to use it, information he's unlikely to have or easily guess.

Because of Activation Lock, when you sell or give away your iPhone at some future date, you must disable Find My iPhone to deactivate the Activation Lock, otherwise no one else can use your iPhone. You should also back up your iPhone and then sign out of your iCloud account, which automatically deactivates Find My iPhone and all the other iCloud services on your iPhone.

What's more, you can command your iPhone to play a loud bleating sound to help guide you (or anyone nearby) to wherever it's hiding. You can lock your iPhone with a secret passcode you create on the fly in the event your iPhone wasn't already protected using the Passcode Lock feature before it vanished.

And finally, if you still can't find your iPhone, you can issue a "self-destruct" command that instructs your iPhone to erase everything stored on it. That way, you lose only your iPhone — which you can replace — but not your personal data and identity information.

To track down a missing iPhone, tap the Find My iPhone app on a friend's iPhone (or iPad or iPod touch), or visit www.icloud.com with your computer's web browser, and then log in using your iCloud username and password. A map appears and shows your iPhone's current location, give or take a few — or a few hundred — feet, depending on the service's ability to accurately home in on your missing iPhone. Click the Information button or Devices list button to display more information and options, shown in Figure 4-12.

Figure 4-12: Locating your iPhone.

Choose one or more of the following actions, which take place immediately if your device is online. Otherwise, the action(s) occurs as soon as the device comes online:

- **Play Sound:** Click the button to play a sound on your device. The sound plays at full volume even if your device is muted.

- **Lost Mode:** When you click this button, you're asked to create a four-digit passcode. Type the digits two times, as asked, and then enter a phone number where you can be reached, which will be displayed on the screen. Click Next and then type in a message that will appear on the screen of your lost iPhone. Click Done. The phone number and message appear on your iPhone's screen and the passcode must be entered to unlock the device. You receive an email confirming that your lost device has been locked and another email with the device's location.

- **Erase:** If repeated attempts to reach out and touch someone who may be in possession of your iPhone go unanswered, this may be your last-gasp option, especially if you have sensitive personal information on your iPhone and you have no luck retrieving it. Click Erase, and then enter your Apple ID password. Confirm by clicking Erase.

Chapter 5: Syncing, Backing Up, and Troubleshooting Your iPhone

In This Chapter

✔ **Creating an Apple ID**

✔ **Understanding the syncing relationship**

✔ **Setting up iCloud options**

✔ **Syncing and backing up with iTunes**

✔ **Buying more iCloud storage**

✔ **Creating a Family Sharing account**

✔ **Avoiding common iPhone problems**

✔ **Troubleshooting Q&A**

The information in this chapter is essential to using your iPhone. We take you through the creation of an Apple ID, your passport to everything Apple — the iTunes, iBooks, and App Stores and iCloud. We explore the options for syncing and backing up your iPhone with your Windows or Mac computer and other iOS devices such as an iPod touch or iPad using iCloud or iTunes. We show you how to use the backup should you lose everything on your iPhone. Lastly, we take you through some troubleshooting tips in case your iPhone starts misbehaving or is unresponsive.

Creating an Apple ID

Your Apple ID is your entry ticket to just about everything iPhone. You need it to sign in and make purchases at the iTunes Store, the App Store, the iBook Store, and the online Apple Store, as well as to sign in and set up iCloud, Apple's remote syncing and storage service. Chances are, you created an Apple ID when your phone was activated at the Apple Store or the retailer where you bought your iPhone or if you activated your iPhone yourself, you may have created one as part of the

Setup Assistant procedure. If you skipped that step, make sure your iPhone is connected to the Internet and create an Apple ID by doing the following:

1. **Open the Settings app and tap iCloud.**

2. **Tap Create a New Apple ID.**

   The Create an Apple ID screen opens.

3. **Scroll through the rotor to choose your birth date.**

   You have to be at least 13 years of age to create an Apple ID. If you're younger than 13, a parent must set up Family Sharing and create a new account for you.

4. **Tap Next, and then enter your first and last names in the fields.**

5. **Tap Next. This screen establishes the email address that will be used with your Apple ID. You can do one of the following:**

   - *Use your current email address:* Type in the email address you want to use as your Apple ID.

   - *Get a free iCloud email address:* Choose this, and tap Next. On the next screen you create an email address that will have an @icloud.com suffix. You can't change your iCloud email address after you create it, so choose carefully.

   If you previously set up an Apple ID with an email address but have since changed that email address, tap Change Email Address. Type your old email address and password, and then tap Next. Type in the new email address you want to use as your Apple ID and then tap Next. When you sign in, use the new email address and the old password.

6. **Tap Create to confirm your choice.**

   If someone else already uses that ID, you'll be asked if it's yours or to cancel to create another choice.

7. **Create a password that has at least eight characters and contains at least one each of uppercase and lowercase letters. Tap Next.**

8. **Add three security questions.**

   Select a question from the options and then type in the answer. Tap Next to go to the next question.

9. **Add an optional Rescue Email (different from the iCloud address you created) that will be used if you forget your password.**

10. **Turn on or off email updates, which are communications from Apple about software updates and new products and services.**

11. **Tap Agree to agree to the Terms and Conditions of your iCloud email and Apple ID.**

    Your account is created and you're automatically signed in.

12. **Tap Next.**

13. **You're asked if iCloud can use your location; we suggest you tap OK, as it will be needed to activate Find My iPhone.**

14. **Tap the switch to the on position for the features you want to use with iCloud.**

    We explain more about that later in this chapter.

15. **Make note of your @icloud.com email address and keep your password in a safe place.**

16. **Press the Home button to return to the Home screen.**

If you're more comfortable working from a computer, you can create your Apple ID from System Preferences on a Mac (open System Preferences and click iCloud) or the Control Panel for Windows on a computer with Windows 7 or 8 (in Windows 7, choose Start⇨All Programs⇨iCloud⇨iCloud; in Windows 8, go to the Start screen, and then click the iCloud file; in Windows 8.1, go to the Start screen, click the down arrow in the lower-left corner, and then click the iCloud app).

Understanding Syncing, Backing Up, and Using Cloud Storage

Syncing — short for synchronizing — is keeping your data on two or more devices, like your iPhone and your computer and other iOS devices such as an iPad or iPod touch, up-to-date and mirrored on all devices. When you sync your devices, data is evaluated and compared, and when two pieces of data are different, the newer data replaces the older data.

Backing up is creating a copy of the data that's on your device and storing it somewhere else, be it your computer or a remote server so that you can restore that data to your iPhone, should you lose the data, perform an operating system update, or upgrade to a new iPhone.

Cloud storage keeps your documents on a remote server — we talk specifically about iCloud Drive and iCloud Photo Library. Rather than store the documents, and photos, on your device or computer, you access and edit them on the cloud from your device or computer.

You have to choose either iCloud or iTunes to perform the backup but you can sync through both, however, cloud storage is only available on iCloud. We give you step-by-step instructions here so you can manage your data and meet all your backing up, syncing, and storing needs.

Working with iCloud

iCloud is Apple's over-the-air syncing, sharing, and storage service. Your data is stored in a remote Apple location, somewhere in North Carolina (at the time of writing), which is a good thing because if disaster or thieves strike your home and your computer breaks or disappears, your data is safe and sound.

iCloud comprises three elements that you can activate:

- **iCloud Photo Library:** Stores all the photos from all your devices in iCloud and then you access them from your iOS devices or the web. See Book IV, Chapter 1 to learn more about iCloud Photo Library.

- **iCloud Drive:** Stores any and all of your documents on iCloud so you can access them from your iPhone, another iOS device, or your computer. Because you're working on the same document, changes you make on one device immediately show up when you access the document from another device.

  The first 5GB of storage used by iCloud Photo Library and iCloud Drive are free. You can then purchase 20GB for $0.99 a month, 200GB for $3.99 500GB for $9.99, or a whopping 1TB for $19.99.

- **Family Sharing:** Lets you share and access iTunes media purchases with other members of your family — with different Apple IDs — but even better, it asks you to assign one credit card to the family account. The Ask to Buy feature, which requires your authorization for purchases or free downloads made by children, is automatically activated for children under 13 and can be turned on for those under 18. For example, your child taps the Buy button for a new game on his iPad but a message appears on your iPhone asking you to authorize the purchase. We show you how to set up Family Sharing in this chapter but mention using it in Book IV, Chapters 2 and 3.

 iCloud comes with Mac OS X, and the iCloud Control Panel 4.0 for Windows (Windows 7 or Windows 8) is available for download at `http://support.apple.com/kb/DL1455`.

Follow these steps to use iCloud:

1. **Open the Settings app and tap iCloud.**

   If you see the email you used to set up your Apple ID, go to Step 5.

2. **Type in your Apple ID and password, and then tap Sign In. Your account is verified.**

   iCloud only works with email-style Apple IDs. If your Apple ID is something like johnsmith, you must create a new one as explained at the beginning of this chapter.

TIP

You can still use your existing Apple ID and password for purchases in the iTunes, App, iBooks, and online Apple Stores but the Apple ID that uses *yourusername@icloud.com* will control the iCloud functions.

3. **iCloud asks if you want to merge Safari data on your iPhone with iCloud. Tap Merge.**

4. **iCloud asks to use the location of your iPhone, which enables the Find My iPhone feature. Click OK.**

5. **The iCloud screen appears, as shown in Figure 5-1.**

The switches you tap on indicate which data you want to sync with iCloud. Any changes you make on your iPhone are pulled into iCloud and pushed to the other devices, and vice versa, when your devices are signed in to iCloud and connected to the Internet. iCloud keeps all your devices in sync. When you tap out of iCloud Settings and open an app that you use and has content on another device or computer, such as Contacts or Safari, you find the information on your iPhone.

Figure 5-1: Choose the type of data you want to share with other devices using iCloud.

Activating iCloud options

Here we explain each iCloud option, what happens when you turn it on, and any further actions to take:

- **Photos:** Tap to see options to activate iCloud Photo Library, which uploads and stores all your photos and videos in iCloud, and/or My Photo Stream, which uploads new photos and automatically sends them to your other devices signed in to the same iCloud account. See Book IV, Chapter 1 for more information.

- **iCloud Drive:** Tap to open the iCloud Drive options, as shown in Figure 5-2. Tap the iCloud Drive switch on to activate iCloud Drive. When you tap the switch of an app in the list on, documents created in that app on your iPhone are stored in iCloud Drive. You can access those documents from other devices and documents created on other devices from your iPhone. See the section, "Working with documents in iCloud Drive."

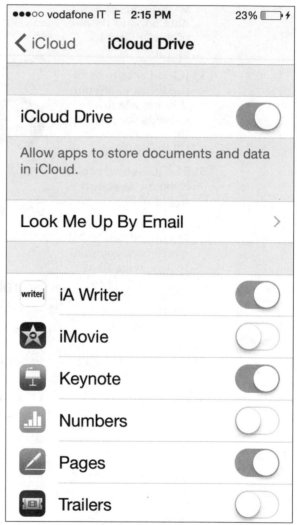

Figure 5-2: iCloud Drive lets you access your documents from any device.

Understanding Syncing, Backing Up, and Using Cloud Storage **_111_**

Book I
Chapter 5

Syncing, Backing Up,
and Troubleshooting
Your iPhone

Tap Look Me Up By Email to see a list of apps that allow other people to search for you by your Apple ID; you can tap the on/off switch next to the app to allow this feature, or not.

Tap the Use Cellular Data switch on to transfer documents and data over the cellular data network when you don't have Wi-Fi access. Be advised that this will consume your data plan's allotment faster than other types of data activity.

✔ **Mail:** Syncs and stores settings and messages.

✔ **Contacts:** Syncs and stores settings and content, including Phone Favorites and Recents.

✔ **Calendar:** Syncs and stores settings and content.

✔ **Reminders:** Syncs and stores settings and content.

✔ **Safari:** Syncs and stores bookmarks, tabs, Reading List, and history.

✔ **Notes:** Syncs and stores settings and content.

✔ **Passbook:** Syncs and stores settings and content.

✔ **Backup:** In addition to syncing and storing data from the apps you enabled for iCloud, such as Mail or Calendar, tapping this switch on will use iCloud to back up your photo library, documents, and data including accounts, ringtones, app and device settings such as wallpaper and Home screen organization, messages, iMessage, SMS, and MMS.

See the next section, "Managing iCloud Storage" to learn more about backup options.

If you're connected to a Wi-Fi network, you can tap Back Up Now to create a current backup. The first backup may take a few minutes or even close to an hour, depending on how much data you have on your iPhone. Your iPhone is backed up to iCloud. Subsequent backups take place once a day when your iPhone is attached to a power source, connected to Wi-Fi, and locked.

If you tap this option off, an alert box lets you know that your iPhone will automatically back up when you sync with iTunes.

iCloud does *not* back up the following:

* *Media that wasn't purchased in iTunes*

* *Audiobooks* (even if you purchased them in the iTunes Store, although the store remembers your purchases and you can download them again)

* *Podcasts* (again, these are available to re-download from the iTunes Store)

- *Photos and video that you transferred from your computer to your iPhone* (not such a big deal because you have the original on your computer)

- *Photos and video that are not in Photos* (unless they're stored in an app that you designate for iCloud backup as explained in the next section)

✔ **Keychain:** Tap to open the options screen. Tap the iCloud Keychain switch on to sync and store account names, passwords, and credit card information, which are encrypted and can't be read by Apple.

If you use this option, it's important to tap Advanced to activate and create an iCloud Security Code, which allows you to set up iCloud Keychain on new devices, such as one that replaces a lost iPhone or an additional device like an iPad. Tap Change Security Code, enter your Apple ID password when prompted, and then create a four-digit security code. Tap Advanced Options to create a more complex security code or have your iPhone generate a random code — we recommend complex codes as they're harder to guess in the unfortunate event that your iPhone falls into nefarious hands. Whichever you choose, write down the code and store it in a safe place because Apple cannot access it should you need to use it. A message asks if you want to use the same code as your device passcode (the code you tap in when your iPhone is locked, if you set that up). Tap Use Same Code or Don't Change Passcode.

✔ **Find My iPhone:** Tap to open the options screen and activate this function, as explained in Book I, Chapter 4.

Scroll down to see two advanced options:

✔ **Mail:** Opens the iCloud email account information, as explained in Book II, Chapter 4.

✔ **Share My Location:** Tap to access the options screen. Tap the Share My Location switch on to share your location based on where your iPhone is, in Messages (see Book II, Chapter 2) and Find My Friends.

Managing iCloud storage

The first 5GB of iCloud storage are free, but if you use iCloud Photo Library and iCloud Drive, that 5GB can fill up pretty quickly. Follow these steps to see which data occupy your storage and how to increase your space, if need be.

1. **Open the Settings app, tap iCloud, and then tap Storage toward the top of the screen.**

   The Storage screen opens and you see the Total Storage you have (5GB if you haven't purchased additional storage) and the Available Storage.

2. **Tap Manage Storage.**

The Manage Storage screen opens, which shows you what is stored on iCloud, as in Figure 5-3. You see four sections that indicate how your storage is occupied: Photos, Backups, Documents and Data, and Mail (not shown in the figure but it's at the bottom of the screen).

3. **Tap iCloud Photo Library.**

You see how many photos and videos occupy the storage, but you have to go to the Photos app to delete any of the images to free up space. If you wish to stop using iCloud Photo Library, tap Disable and Delete, which disables iCloud Photo Library on all your devices. Your photos and videos remain for 30 days, during which time you should download your photos and videos to your iPhone or another device.

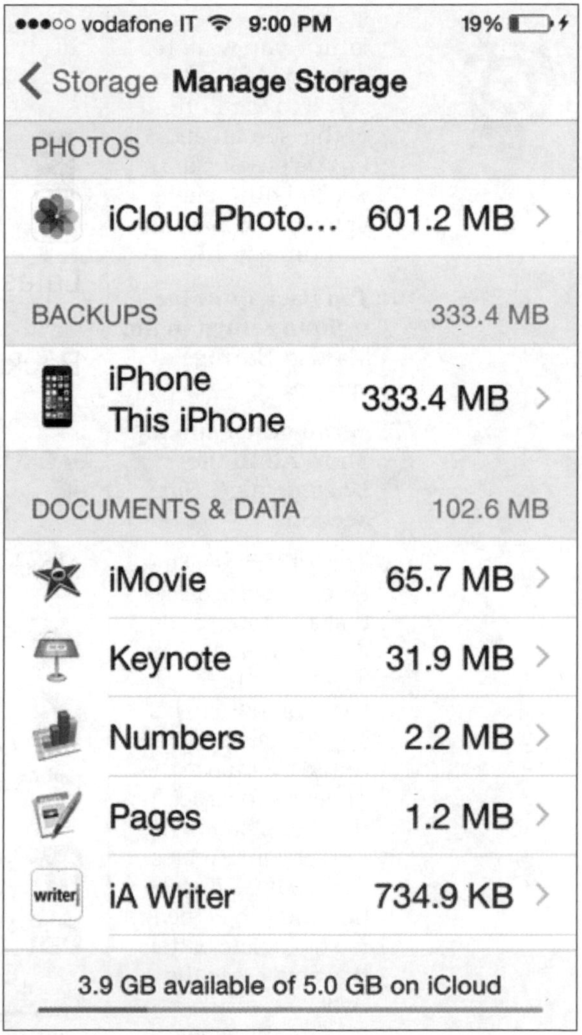

Figure 5-3: See what you have stored in iCloud from your iPhone.

4. **Tap Back or swipe right to return to the Manage Storage screen.**

5. **Tap iPhone in the Backups section.**

The Info screen shown in Figure 5-4 opens. The date and size of the last backup appear at the top. Scroll down and tap Show All Apps to see the apps for which iCloud backs up data — not the apps themselves, only the data. By default, backup is on for all apps. To shrink the size of your backup file, you can turn one or more off by tapping the switch next to it. You see how much storage the app data occupies under the name of the app.

If, at some time in the future, you want to delete your backup, scroll to the bottom of this screen and tap Delete Backup, which both deletes your iCloud backup and turns it off.

6. **Tap Back or swipe right to return to the Manage Storage screen.**

7. **Scroll down and tap Show All in the Documents & Data section.**

The list shows all the types and size of files that are stored on iCloud Drive. Tap an app to see the list of files stored from that app. To delete files, tap the Edit button in the upper-right corner. Tap the Delete button (the red and white minus sign) to the left of the document, and then tap the Delete button that appears to the right. You're asked to confirm the action as it deletes the file both from iCloud Drive and from your iPhone. Tap Delete All at the bottom to take that action.

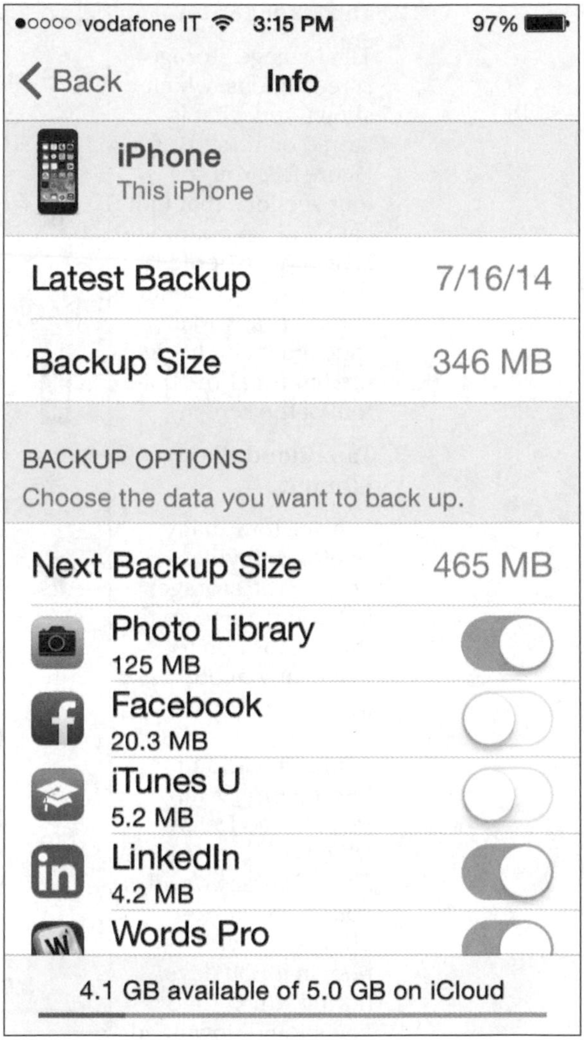

●○○○○ vodafone IT 📶 3:15 PM	97% 🔋
‹ Back **Info**	
📱 **iPhone** This iPhone	
Latest Backup	7/16/14
Backup Size	346 MB
BACKUP OPTIONS Choose the data you want to back up.	
Next Backup Size	465 MB
📷 **Photo Library** 125 MB	⬤
f **Facebook** 20.3 MB	◯
🎓 **iTunes U** 5.2 MB	◯
in **LinkedIn** 4.2 MB	⬤
W **Words Pro**	⬤
4.1 GB available of 5.0 GB on iCloud	

Figure 5-4: Choose the data you back up to iCloud.

8. **Tap Back or swipe right to return to the Manage Storage screen, and again to the Storage screen.**

9. **(Optional) If you see you're running low on available storage, you can purchase additional iCloud storage.**

iCloud Drive and iCloud Photo Library give you 5GB total storage for mail, contacts, calendars, documents, photos, and backup. Media purchased from iTunes doesn't count toward that limit. If you use Photo

Stream but not iCloud Photo Library, the images in Photo Stream don't count toward the 5GB.

Do the following to buy more storage:

1. Tap Buy More Storage.

   The Upgrade iCloud Storage screen opens. You see your current plan and upgrade options; downgrade options are available if you have a purchased plan.

2. Tap the plan you want to purchase, and then tap the Buy button.

3. Enter the password for your Apple ID, if requested, and then enter your payment information.

4. Tap Done.

   Your credit card is charged for the amount indicated immediately and on an annual basis until you downgrade, as we explain next.

If you purchase more storage and then find you don't need it, you can downgrade at any time so your credit card will be charged less or not at all when the renewal date arrives. Do the following:

1. Tap Downgrade Options.

   You may be asked to enter your Apple ID password.

2. Tap the storage plan you want when your current plan expires.

3. Tap Done.

 You can also purchase iCloud storage through the System Preferences application on your Mac (tap iCloud) or from the iCloud pane of the Control Panel in Windows.

 The alternative to buying more storage is deleting documents and files as explained in Step 7 previously. However, if the documents you delete are only stored in iCloud, you lose them completely. Open and save the documents on your computer, upload (using the Share Sheet) them to another remote storage server, or email them to yourself before deleting them from iCloud if you want to keep a copy.

Working with documents in iCloud Drive

iCloud Drive lets you save documents and files directly in iCloud and then access them from all your devices with apps that can open the file type and from your computer either in an appropriate app or from the www.icloud.com website.

To use iCloud Drive with your Mac (OS X [10.10] Yosemite) or PC (Windows 7 or later), drag the file you want into the iCloud Drive folder in the Finder (Mac) or File Explorer (Windows). To create a document on your iPhone, you must use an iCloud-enabled app. Follow these steps to create or open documents on your iPhone:

1. **Open the iCloud-enabled app on your iPhone.**

   The first time you open the app, a message asks if you want to use iCloud Drive to store documents from this app instead of storing them on your iPhone. Tap Use iCloud Drive.

2. **Create a new document or tap an existing one to open it.**

3. **Type, draw, edit, whatever you want with the document.**

4. **Press the Home button to leave the app.**

On other iOS devices such as an iPad or iPod touch, follow the same steps as for your iPhone. On your computer, do the following:

1. **On a Mac, from the Finder click the Go menu and then choose iCloud Drive or click iCloud Drive in the Finder window's Sidebar; in Windows, open the File Explorer (such as by opening a drive or folder on the Desktop) and click iCloud Drive in the Navigation pane on the left, as shown in Figure 5-5.**

   Each app from which you saved a file to iCloud Drive has a folder; your documents are inside the folder.

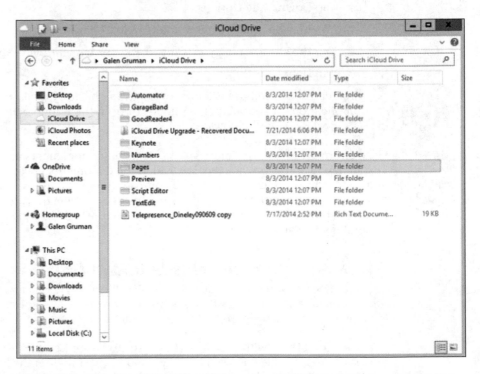

Figure 5-5: Open documents from iCloud Drive as you would those stored on your computer.

2. **Double-click the document you want to open.**

    You can also open the app, click the File menu and choose Open, and then click iCloud Drive in the Finder/File Explorer rather than your computer's hard drive.

3. **Edit the document.**

4. **Save the document as you normally would, but save it to iCloud Drive.**

    You have the option to replace the existing document with the same name or save the edited document as a new document.

To access iCloud Drive from a web browser, go to www.icloud.com, sign in with your Apple ID and password, and then click the folder where your file resides.

Backing Up and Syncing with iTunes

The current version of iTunes can back up the data on your iPhone to your computer and sync media along with the data you store in Contacts and Calendar. You can choose to sync a selection of your media, instead of syncing everything. In this section, we go through the steps for setting up both backing up and syncing with iTunes, also known as a local sync.

You can back up to iCloud but sync with iTunes or back up to iTunes and sync with iCloud.

We assume you use the latest computer operating systems — Mac OS X (10.10) Yosemite or Windows 7 or later and the latest version of iTunes (12.0). If you use a computer with an older operating system or an older version of iTunes, you have two choices: Update your software or go to Apple's Support page to read about backing up and syncing with older versions — we recommend the first choice. You can download iTunes 12 for free from the Apple website, www.apple.com/itunes.

Connecting your iPhone to iTunes

Even if you choose to back up and sync with iTunes on your computer, you can set up a daily wireless sync, which is called iTunes Wi-Fi Sync. This option makes syncing, and backing up if you want, an automatic task and you don't find yourself saying "Oh, that number I need is on my computer, I guess I should sync with my iPhone" or "I should have backed up." However, even if you plan to use iTunes Wi-Fi Sync, you must connect your iPhone to your computer one time to set up that syncing.

iTunes syncs the following:

- ✔ Music (unless you use iTunes Match, in which case music syncs with iTunes in the Cloud)
- ✔ Movies
- ✔ TV Shows
- ✔ Audiobooks
- ✔ Podcasts
- ✔ Books
- ✔ Photos from your computer to your iPhone (to copy photos from your iPhone to your computer you use a photo management app such as iPhoto or Aperture)
- ✔ Apps
- ✔ Calendar (only works if you don't use a server-based service such as iCloud or Google)
- ✔ Contacts (only works if you don't use a server-based service such as iCloud or Google)

Data from Notes, Reminders, Passbook, Safari bookmarks, Mail, and phone settings are synced only by iCloud, although you can back them up to iTunes.

The first time you connect your iPhone to your computer, iTunes opens and you can set up and perform your first sync. You also establish the criteria on which future syncing operations will be based. To begin syncing your iPhone with your computer, follow these steps:

1. **Connect your iPhone to your computer with the USB connector cable, using a port that is on your computer rather than one on the keyboard or hub (unless you have a powered hub).**

   iTunes opens. If iTunes doesn't open, open it manually.

2. **If this is the first time you connect an iPhone to iTunes, you probably want to choose Set Up As New iPhone. However, if you backup an iPod touch or iPad to iTunes, you can put that data on your iPhone.**

3. **Click Get Started on the next screen. The iPhone Summary window appears, as shown in Figure 5-6.**

   In subsequent connections, click the iPhone icon in the Navigation bar across the top of the screen.

   If iTunes doesn't recognize your iPhone, make sure the USB connector cable is firmly seated in both your iPhone and computer ports and that your iPhone is turned on.

If iTunes still doesn't see your iPhone, choose iTunes➪Preferences on a Mac or Edit➪Preferences in Windows. Click the Devices icon at the top of the window that opens. Deselect the box next to Prevent iPods, iPhones, and iPads from Syncing Automatically. Click OK to activate the new setting.

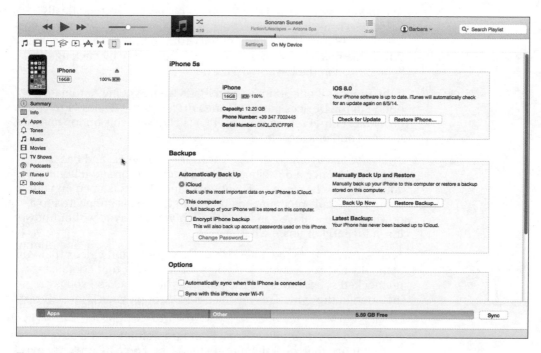

Figure 5-6: Select syncing and backup options on the Summary window.

4. **Choose one of the following in the Backups section:**

   - *iCloud:* Select this choice to use iCloud as your backup destination.

     If you're the extra-cautious type, you can select iCloud as your backup destination and then connect to iTunes and click the Back Up Now button under Manually Back Up and Restore. This gives you a backup copy on your computer as well as iCloud.

   - *This Computer:* Select this choice if you want to keep your iPhone backup on your computer. You have a subchoice of Encrypt iPhone Backup. Type a password in the dialog that appears. When you restore a backup to your iPhone, you'll be asked to enter the password. Click Back Up Now if you make this choice, and iTunes will create the first iPhone backup and save it to your computer. Each time you sync with iTunes a backup file is created.

An encrypted backup keeps your passwords so if you restore your iPhone from an encrypted backup, the passwords are restored too. If you restore from an unencrypted backup, you'll have to re-enter your passwords for apps that use them.

5. **Select from the following in the Options section:**

   • *Automatically sync when this iPhone is connected:* Automatically launches iTunes and begins syncing, and backing up, when you connect your iPhone to your computer with the USB connector cable. When this box is not checked, you sync manually by clicking the Sync button in the lower-right corner.

   If the Prevent iPods, iPhones, and iPads from Syncing Automatically option in the Devices pane of iTunes Preferences (iTunes⇨Preferences on a Mac; Edit⇨Preferences on a PC) is checked, this option appears dimmed and unavailable.

   • *Sync with this iPhone over Wi-Fi:* Your iPhone syncs, and backs up, with iTunes once a day when both your computer and iPhone are connected to the same Wi-Fi network, and iTunes is open on your computer. Apple recommends that your iPhone is connected to a power source and we concur. Although you can sync without power, it significantly drains the battery.

   • *Sync only checked songs and videos:* Only songs and videos that you manually check are synced. If you sync a playlist that contains unchecked songs and sync the playlist, the unchecked songs are not included in the sync. This means going through your iTunes library and manually selecting or deselecting all the media.

   • *Prefer standard definition videos:* Standard definition videos occupy less memory than high definition videos, so you may prefer to sync SD videos to your iPhone.

   • *Convert higher bit rate songs to 128/192/256 kbps:* iTunes automatically creates smaller audio files so you can squeeze more music onto your iPhone.

   • *Manually manage music and videos:* Select this if you want to click and drag music and videos from iTunes to your iPhone. If you want to limit the music or videos stored on your iPhone, this may be a good option to choose.

   • *Reset Warnings:* Click this button if, in the past, you've asked iTunes to stop showing you purchase and download warnings but you would like to see those warnings again.

   • *Configure Accessibility:* Click this button to turn on the various Universal Access functions, such as VoiceOver and Speak Auto-Text. We explain Universal Access in Book I, Chapter 2.

6. **Click Apply and proceed with the next sections to make choices for which data will sync.**

You can override the automatic syncing on an as-needed basis by launching iTunes before you connect your iPhone to your computer. Press and hold ⌘+Option (Mac) or Shift+Ctrl (PC) and connect your iPhone. Hold the keys until your iPhone appears on the right end of the Navigation bar below the toolbar. Your iPhone won't sync automatically, but the settings you previously established remain unchanged.

Choosing your sync options

Down the left side of the iTunes window you see a list of items: Summary, Info, Apps, Tones, Music, Movies, TV Shows, Podcasts, iTunes U, Books, and Photos. As you click each item, you make your syncing selections on the pane to the right. When you've set up the options the way you want, click the Sync button and your media from your computer will sync to your iPhone.

Summary

In addition to the backup and syncing options, the Summary pane tells you about your iPhone, the name and total storage capacity, the version of the operating system you're using, iPhone's serial number, and your iPhone's phone number.

You can see if your iPhone is up-to-date, and the next date iTunes will automatically check for an update. The Check for Update button gives you the option of checking for software updates before the date shown.

The Restore iPhone button is used when you have problems with your iPhone or if you want to reset it to its original factory settings. All the contents are erased, and your iPhone wakes up restored as if it were fresh from the factory with the latest iOS.

Info

If you prefer to sync Contacts and Calendars via iTunes instead of iCloud, make your selections here. If you sync Contacts and Calendar via iCloud or another server such as Exchange, Google, or Outlook.com, you have no options to choose in this window.

  ✔ **Contacts:** Choose which app you want to sync with, and if your contacts are divided into groups, choose to sync all your contacts or only subsets or groups of contacts. There is also an option to instruct iTunes what to do if, when syncing, it finds a new contact that's been created on your iPhone but hasn't been assigned to a group. Next to Add Contacts Created Outside of Groups on This iPhone To, choose a location from the pop-up menu.

✔ **Calendar:** You can sync calendars from more than one application, including Microsoft Outlook 2003, 2007, or 2010 and Google Calendar. Windows users must have Outlook installed in order to sync Calendars. If you have more than one calendar created, you can pick and choose which to sync with your iPhone. You can also establish a cut-off date for old syncs, such as not syncing events older than 15 days.

If you use Microsoft Outlook on a Mac, you must first turn on Sync Services in Outlook by choosing Tools⇨Sync Services and then selecting the items you want to sync, such as Calendar, Contacts, Tasks, and Notes. This syncs anything in Outlook with Calendar and Contacts on your Mac, which you then sync with your iPhone with iTunes.

Apps

You use the Apps pane, shown in Figure 5-7, to sync apps you buy in the Apps Store. If you set up automatic downloads for apps, you'll use this section only for rearranging apps and folders. In this pane, you can also copy documents between your iPhone and your computer with the Share Files feature.

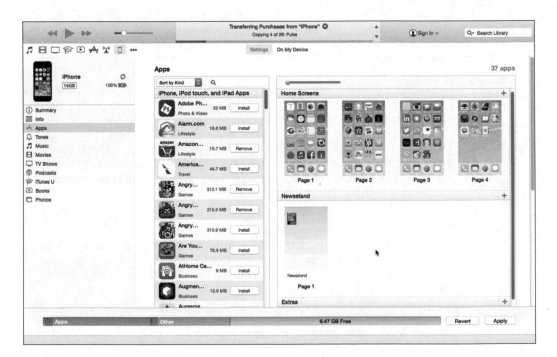

Figure 5-7: Manage your apps and share files in the Apps pane.

Select the Automatically Install New Apps check box (you may have to scroll the window a bit to see it) to sync new apps to your iPhone that you downloaded to your computer. You don't need to select this if you set up automatic downloads on your iPhone in the Settings app by tapping iTunes & App Store, tapping Automatic Downloads, and tapping the Apps switch on.

Use the pop-up menu to change how the list of apps is sorted. Click Install next to the apps you want on your iPhone or click and drag the icon from the list to the Home screen (on the right) where you want the app to reside. To delete an app, click Remove in the apps list so it will be deleted from your iPhone during the next sync.

The scrollable pane on the right reflects the setup of your Home screens. Scroll down to see folders on your iPhone, including Newsstand, and their contents. Use the slider at the top of the section to zoom in or out of the screens and folders window.

Click and drag the Home screens to rearrange their order, and click the plus sign to add a new Home screen. Like on your iPhone, click and drag apps and folders to new positions on the Home screens, and drag one app over another to create a new folder that contains the two apps.

In the lower half of the Apps pane, as shown in Figure 5-8, you see File Sharing, which lets you share documents, created with apps that support file sharing, to and from your computer and iPhone. On the left are the apps you have that support file sharing; on the right are the files on your iPhone. To transfer files from your iPhone to your computer, follow these steps:

1. **Connect your iPhone to your computer and open iTunes, click the phone icon in the Navigation bar, and then click the Apps tab.**

2. **From the list on the left, select the app that supports the document you want to share. We selected iA Writer in Figure 5-8.**

   A list of available documents appears on the right. If you use iCloud Drive to share documents, they won't appear in the documents list of iTunes.

3. **Click the document(s) you want to transfer from your iPhone to your computer.**

4. **Click the Save To button at the bottom of the list.**

   Select the destination where you want to save the document(s).

5. **Click Open (Mac) or OK (Windows).**

   The file is transferred to your computer.

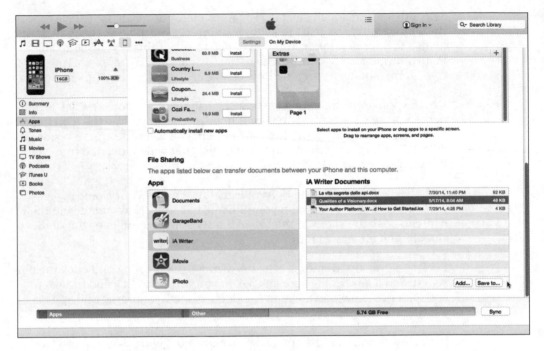

Figure 5-8: Manage file transfers from the Apps pane.

To transfer files from your computer to your iPhone:

1. **Repeat Steps 1 and 2 of the previous list.**

2. **Click the Add button at the bottom of the list.**

   Select the file from your computer that you want to transfer from your computer to your iPhone.

3. **Click Open (Mac) or OK (Windows).**

   The file is transferred to your iPhone and can be opened with an app that supports that type of document. Select additional files to transfer more than one.

To delete a file from your iPhone, select the file in the list and then tap the Delete key (Mac) or Backspace key (Windows) on the keyboard.

You can also share documents between your iPhone and computer with iCloud Drive and, if you use a Mac, with AirDrop.

Selecting media

Each of these sections gives you options to sync all of that type of media — for example, all ringtones or all TV shows — stored on your computer to your iPhone or choose a selection of the media. Click each item in the list and then click to make your selection. Here are the types of options each offers:

✔ **Music:** Sync the entire music library, or selected playlists, artists, albums, and genres. Choose to include music videos and/or voice memos.

Two other specific ways to sync music are specified in the Summary window:

- *Sync Only Checked Songs and Videos:* Choose iTunes➪Preferences➪ General (Mac) or Edit➪Preferences➪General (Windows), select Show List Checkboxes under Views, and click OK. Click Summary in the source list and choose this option. Click Music in the source list and then select Song List in the upper-right corner. Check all the songs and videos you want to sync to your iPhone. Uncheck any you don't want to sync, if they're checked. When you finish your selection, click your iPhone in the Navigation bar. Click the Sync button in the bot-tom-right corner.

- *Manually Manage Music and Videos:* Choose this option on the Summary pane, and then click the On My Device tab at the top of the iTunes window. Click the media type you want to add to your iPhone from the source list on the left. Click the Add To button in the upper-right corner; the window splits into two panes. The pane on the left is iTunes on your computer, and the pane on the right is your iPhone. Click and drag the items you want to move to your iPhone. You can navigate through different media types, as well as change the views with the tabs at the top of the page. Click Done when you finish your selection.

✔ **Movies:** Syncing gives you the option of downloading and beginning to watch a movie on one device and then syncing and watching through to the end on the other device. Click Movies in the source list and then choose to sync all movies, a selection of watched or unwatched movies, or specific movies you select one by one.

✔ **TV Shows:** As with movies, you can select to sync all TV shows or a selection of watched, unwatched, newest, or oldest episodes. You can also apply those choices to all the shows in your iTunes library or only selected shows. You can also choose single shows or single episodes.

✔ **Podcasts and iTunes U:** Choose to sync all or use the pop-up menus to set criteria to sync all or a set number of played or unplayed episodes or lec-tures. Alternatively, select series one by one or episodes within a series.

Printed material associated with iTunes U courses is found in the iBooks app.

TIP

In Movies, TV Shows, Podcasts, and iTunes U, when you set your sync options using one of the numbered selections (five most recent unplayed, or ten least recent unwatched), the selection changes as you download new media to iTunes. If you choose a specific episode or movie, it remains selected for subsequent syncs until you deselect it (or it expires, in the case of a rented movie).

- **Audiobooks:** Audiobooks manages, you guessed it, audiobooks. Again, select to sync all or select the single audiobooks, in whichever form, you want to sync.

- **Photos:** The Photos pane lets you move photos from your computer to your iPhone (from one computer only — if you try to move photos from a second computer, the originals are erased from your iPhone). First, choose the photo management app you want to sync photos from (this is where your photos reside), and then click choice to sync all photos or scroll through the panes to sync specific albums or photos by date (or face, if you use a Mac). The number of photos included in the selection appears in gray next to the selection.

Responding to a dialog to copy your photos or videos

If you've taken any photos with your iPhone since the last sync, your photo management software may automatically open and ask if you want to import the photos from your iPhone. To turn this function on, or off, do the following:

On a Mac:

1. Choose Go⇨Applications from the Finder or click Launchpad on the Dock.

2. Open Image Capture.

3. Click your iPhone in the Devices list.

4. In the Connecting This iPhone Opens pop-up menu, choose No Application if you want no application to open when you connect your iPhone to your computer. Alternatively, you can choose from one of the applications shown to open that application when you connect your iPhone.

5. Choose Image Capture⇨Quit Image Capture to exit Image Capture. The new setting is saved and occurs the next time you connect your iPhone.

On Windows:

1. Open the Control Panel.

2. Choose Hardware and Sound.

3. Choose AutoPlay.

4. Open the Apple iPhone list in the Devices section.

5. Choose Take No Action if you want no application to open when you connect your iPhone to your computer. Alternatively, you can choose from one of the applications shown to open that application when you connect your iPhone.

To do the reverse (that is, move photos from your iPhone to your computer), you use your photo management program such as iPhoto or Photoshop Elements, which considers your iPhone a digital camera or external drive with images. Another option is the Photo Stream, where your photos are stored in Photo Stream on iCloud and then pushed to your devices, such as your iPhone or your computer, or iCloud Photo Library, which stores all photos from all devices in the cloud, making them accessible from all devices.

iPhone supports many common image file types including GIF, PNG, and JPG, although iTunes doesn't sync exact copies of your photos but files that have been converted to fit iPhone's screen size. This conversion gives you better viewing quality and uses less storage space on your iPhone.

Checking your iPhone's storage capacity

With all this syncing, your iPhone can fill up pretty darn quick. There are two considerations to think about with regard to storage. One is how much space is available on your iPhone for syncing your apps, media, documents, and data. The second is whether your backup location offers enough storage. If you use iTunes and back up to your computer, this probably isn't a concern; if you use iCloud Drive, you may need to purchase storage beyond the complimentary 5GB, which we explained earlier when we talked about iCloud.

When you're ready to sync, make sure you have enough room on your iPhone before actually hitting the Sync button. Your iPhone's storage capacity depends on which version of iPhone you have.

Considering that the operating system itself takes up about 1GB of memory and another half a gigabyte is kept as a reserve for apps running in the background, that leaves you with 14.5GB on a 16GB phone, 30.5GB on a 32GB phone, or 62.5GB on a 64GB phone. That sounds like a warehouse of storage, until you start loading apps, movies, TV shows, podcasts, games, photos, and videos, when you find out it fills up fast.

There are two ways to know how much space you have on your iPhone:

- **On iPhone:** Open the Settings app, tap General, and tap Usage; here, you see how much storage is Available and Used. Tap Manage Storage to open the list as shown in Figure 5-9, which shows you how much memory is occupied by specific types of files and apps such as Videos, Photos & Camera, and Music with the biggest space hogs at the top of the list. Click one of the items in the list and you see how much the app itself occupies and how much the data occupies. A few apps give you the option for deleting parts of the data, such as your viewing history in Safari or specific songs in Music, but most of the apps only give you the option to delete the app, which means deleting its data, too.

✔ **On iTunes:** When your iPhone is connected to iTunes and selected in the Navigation bar, you see a colored bar near the bottom of the iTunes window that illustrates how much space each type of data will occupy on your iPhone when you perform the sync you've set up. If you're in the Music pane and you deselect the Sync Music box, the blue section of the bar that represents audio files shrinks. If your iPhone is nearly full, you can play with your syncing options for different media and see how they affect the storage capacity. Click once on one of the titles under the bar and the number of items in each category is displayed. Click a second time and it displays how long it will take to listen to all the audio and video in your library. Click a third time to return to the gigabyte numbers.

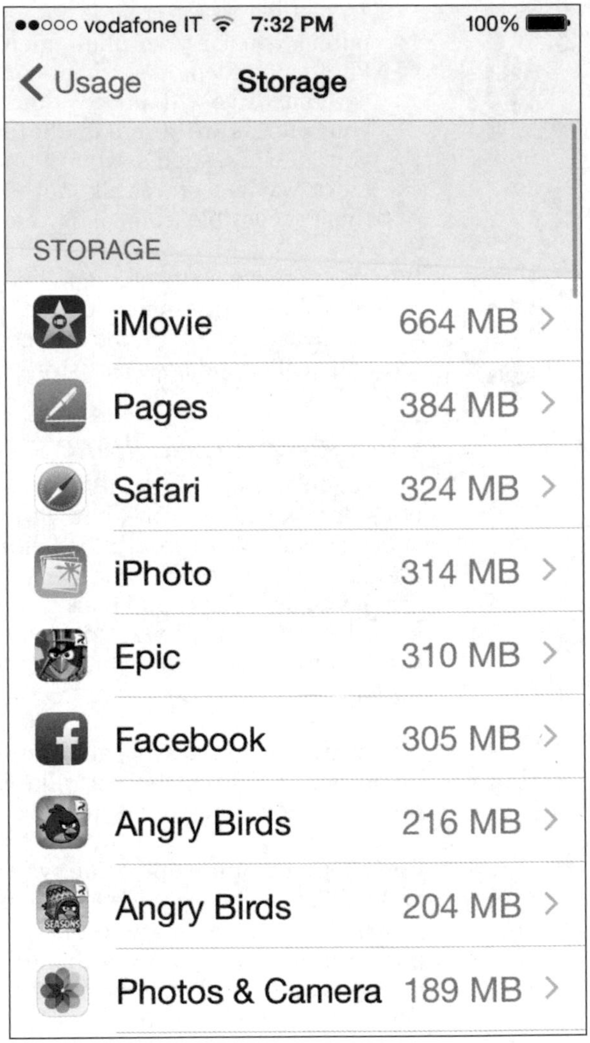

●●○○○ vodafone IT 7:32 PM   100% ▇

〈 Usage   **Storage**

STORAGE

⭐ iMovie   664 MB 〉

✏️ Pages   384 MB 〉

🧭 Safari   324 MB 〉

🖼️ iPhoto   314 MB 〉

Epic   310 MB 〉

f Facebook   305 MB 〉

Angry Birds   216 MB 〉

Angry Birds   204 MB 〉

Photos & Camera 189 MB 〉

Figure 5-9: See what bits are occupying the gigabytes on your iPhone.

If you have more media than memory, you have a couple choices for managing and choosing which data to sync:

✔ Manually select which music, videos, and podcasts you want on your iPhone and sync only those.

✔ Listen to music and watch videos in streaming from iTunes in the Cloud, as explained in Book IV, Chapters 3 and 4. Subscribe to iTunes Match if much of your music comes from sources other than the iTunes Store.

✔ Move your documents to iCloud Drive.

✔ Move your photos to your computer or iCloud Photo Library.

The iTunes sync

Now that you've set the criteria for your sync, all that remains is to click the Sync or Apply button in the bottom-right corner. Sync changes to Apply when you make changes to your Sync options.

When you connect your iPhone to your computer in the future, click your iPhone in the Navigation bar at the top of the iTunes window, and then click Sync to perform a sync that uses the criteria you established. If you select Automatically Sync When This iPhone Is Connected on the Summary pane, the sync happens without clicking the Sync button. If you also select Sync with This iPhone Over Wi-Fi, your iPhone syncs with iTunes once a day when both your computer and your iPhone are connected to the same Wi-Fi network and to a power source. The spinning sync icon in the Status bar of your iPhone lets you know syncing is happening.

When you click Sync (or Apply), iTunes syncs the categories where you've selected the Sync check box at the top of the pane. If you deselect the Sync check box at the top of the Music pane, for example, when you sync, all the music on your iPhone will be deleted, although it remains on iTunes.

Disconnecting iPhone

To disconnect your iPhone from your computer, disconnect the cable. You can disconnect your phone mid-sync and later reconnect; iTunes and iPhone take up syncing where they left off like old friends. If you get a call while you're syncing, your iPhone is so smart that it pauses the syncing session when the phone rings and picks up when the call is finished.

When the Automatic Downloads function is on, music, apps, and books that you download or purchase from the iTunes, iBooks, or App Stores from any device are transferred to the other devices. On your iPhone or other iOS device, open the Settings app, tap iTunes & App Store, and tap the Music, Apps, and/or Books switches on. On your computer, choose iTunes⇨Preferences⇨Store (Mac) or Edit⇨Preferences⇨Store (Windows) and select Music, Books, and/or Apps in the Automatic Downloads section.

Syncing with More Than One iPhone or Computer

Used to be that you had one computer every two and a half households and the only music you heard through the phone was your father singing "Happy Birthday" to you. Today, you probably have a computer at home and one at work, and maybe a laptop computer, too. Perhaps you share your home computer with your significant other or children and each of them has an iPhone. Here we give you a way to use multiple computers with one iPhone as well as multiple iPhones with one computer.

One iPhone, multiple computers

The fact is, different pieces of our lives often overlap. You want the contacts on your notebook and desktop computers and your iPhone and iPad to be the same, and you want the option of making changes in either of those places and syncing with the other two. The simplest solution is an over-the-air (OTA) syncing and storage service, like iCloud as explained at the beginning of this chapter. Just sign in to the same iCloud account on all your devices and everything is kept in sync.

If you absolutely want to use iTunes to connect your iPhone to two computers to sync apps, contacts, and calendars, make sure both computers and your iPhone use the same Apple ID, and do the following:

1. **Follow the instructions outlined previously in this chapter, sync your iPhone and one of your computers — for example, a laptop.**

2. **Connect and sync your iPhone with the other computer — say, a desktop. Set the same preferences in the Info pane as you did on your laptop. iTunes give you two options:**

   • *Merge Info:* iPhone keeps the information from your notebook and merges it with the information on your desktop.

   • *Replace Info:* The information that was synced from the first computer is replaced by the information on the second computer.

You can't sync music or other media with more than one computer. If you try to sync media from a second computer to your iPhone, you will be asked if you want to erase existing media and replace it with the new or cancel the operation.

One computer, multiple iPhones

Your family members share one computer and each of you has an iPhone. You can sync more than one iPhone with the same computer. Each device is recognized by its unique name.

On a Mac, each iPhone can use different sync settings; on Windows, each phone has to use the same settings. Each person has a separate Apple account because each iPhone has an Apple account associated with it. You probably each have different media that you'd like to sync with your respective iPhones.

The ideal solution — the one we highly recommend — is to set up separate user accounts on the Mac or Windows computer for each user, who in turn would have his own iTunes library for media and iCloud account for data to sync to his iPhone.

If for some reason the idea of separate user accounts doesn't work for you, you can sync different sets of media by setting up a different iTunes library for each family member:

1. **Hold down the Option key (Mac) or the Shift key (Windows) and open iTunes.**

   A dialog gives you the options of creating a new library or choosing which you want to open.

2. **Select Create Library.**

   Type in a name and location for the library.

3. **Whenever you start up iTunes, hold down the Option key (Mac) or Shift (Windows) key to open your personal library.**

4. **Sync your iPhone with your library.**

Make sure you uncheck Copy Files to iTunes Media Folder When Adding to Library. On Mac, this is found under iTunes⇨Preferences⇨Advanced; on Windows, Edit⇨Preferences⇨Advanced.

Perhaps you have an iPhone for business and another one for your personal use. You can sync more than one iPhone with the same account and even sync different things to each. Give each iPhone a different name and when you open iTunes, iTunes remembers which sync goes with which phone.

Sharing Across Many Devices

With iOS 8, Apple offers a function within iCloud called Family Sharing, which lets you:

- Designate one credit card for all family purchases
- Require purchase authorization for children (or big spenders)
- Share music, movies, books, and eligible apps purchased in the iTunes, App, and iBook Stores
- Share photos and videos in the family photo stream
- Share locations between members — which means you can know where your child is
- Locate family members' missing devices
- Share a family calendar that each member can edit and see

If you don't have a payment method associated with the Apple ID you use to make purchases, follow these steps to add one before setting up Family Sharing:

1. **Open the Settings app, tap iTunes & App Store, and tap Apple ID.**
2. **Tap View Apple ID in the dialog that appears.**
3. **Sign in to your iTunes Store account.**
4. **Tap Payment Information.**
5. **Tap the Payment Type you want to use.**
6. **Fill in the card number, expiration date, and billing address in the fields provided.**

   Although you can use a debit card as your payment method for yourself, you must use a credit card as your payment method in order to add children to your family.

7. **Tap Done, and swipe back to the Settings screen.**

You can now follow these steps to activate Family Sharing:

1. **Open the Settings app, tap iCloud, and tap Set Up Family Sharing.**
2. **Tap Get Started.**

   The Family Setup screen opens and shows you as the Family Organizer. The family organizer invites other members into the family and agrees to pay for purchases they initiate. Don't worry — you can set it up so that you have to approve the purchases first.

   If you want someone else to be the family organizer, set up Family Sharing on his or her device.

3. **Tap Continue.**
4. **Sign in with the Apple ID you want to use to share your iTunes, iBooks, and App Store purchases, and then tap Next.**

   Use the ID that you use to make purchases, which could be different from the Apple ID you use to sign in to iCloud.

   The payment method you use for your iTunes account appears.

5. **Tap Continue.**
6. **Tap Add Family Member, as shown in Figure 5-10.**
7. **Type the member's email address and then choose one of the following:**

   - *Enter a password:* The member you added can sign in to iTunes with the email address you used and then enter the password you assign.
   - *Send an invitation:* An invitation will be sent to the person with instructions to access the account.

8. **To add a child who doesn't have an account, tap Create an Apple ID for a Child at the bottom of the screen (see Figure 5-10).**

When you add a child, the account is part of your family until the child is at least 13 years old. Tap Next and then agree to parental consent on the following screen. Enter the name and age of the child; Ask to Buy is on by default for children under 13. When the child wants to purchase something in the iTunes, iBooks, or App Store, a message is sent to you and you have to approve the purchase before it's fulfilled. The charge will be made to the credit card associated with your iTunes account.

You can set additional parental controls in the Settings app by tapping General and then tapping Restrictions, as explained in Book I, Chapter 4.

Book I
Chapter 5

Syncing, Backing Up, and Troubleshooting Your iPhone

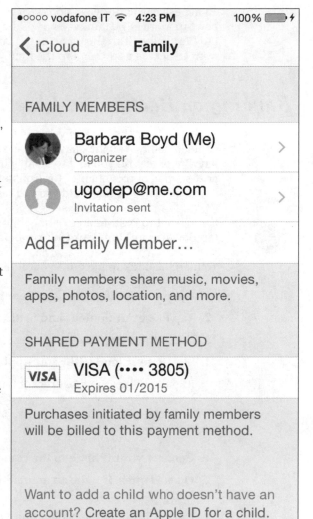

Figure 5-10: Adding a child who doesn't have an account.

9. **To delete a family member at any time, tap the name in the Family Members list and then tap Remove at the bottom of the screen.**

10. **To cancel Family Sharing, tap your name in the Family Members list and tap Stop Family Sharing at the bottom of the screen.**

To access music, movies, books, or apps purchased by another family member, tap More in the Browse bar of the iTunes, iBooks, or App Store, and then tap Purchased. Tap the name of the family member whose purchases you want to access and then tap the item you want to use.

Banking on Backups in Case Things Go Kerflooey

Sooner or later the backup you created using either iCloud or iTunes may come in handy. You may have to erase and reset your iPhone because it's gone haywire or maybe you had to send your iPhone in for repairs. (Refer to the next section of this chapter for troubleshooting tips.) The best-case scenario is you got a new iPhone and want to restore your old data to your new phone.

If you want to restore an existing iPhone, open the Settings app, tap iCloud, tap Backup, and tap Back Up Now before doing the following.

To load the backup file onto your iPhone, old or new, from iCloud:

1. **Open the Settings app, tap General, and tap Reset.**

2. **Tap Erase All Content and Settings.**

3. **When the Setup Assistant opens, tap Restore from iCloud Backup.**

4. **Sign in to iCloud with your Apple ID and password.**

   iCloud pushes the most recent backup to your iPhone.

If your backup is on your computer, and you use iTunes to restore the backup to your iPhone:

1. **Connect your iPhone to the computer you usually use to sync.**

2. **Open iTunes, if it didn't automatically open (depends on how you set it up).**

3. **Click iPhone in the Navigation bar.**

4. **Click Summary in the list on the left.**

5. **Click Restore Backup.**

   iTunes gives you a chance to back out of your choice or go ahead. Clicking Restore iPhone will erase your iPhone and re-install the most up-to-date operating system. You then must restore from a backup or start over with your iPhone. Choosing to set up as a new iPhone is a good option if you plan to give your iPhone to someone else and want it to have a clean slate.

6. **If you see multiple backup files, choose the most recent one associated with your iPhone.**

7. **Sync your media with iTunes as we explain earlier in this chapter.**

8. **On your iPhone, open the Settings app, tap iCloud, and sign in to your iCloud account to sync your Contacts, Calendar, Notes, bookmarks, and all the other data that iCloud manages.**

If you like to keep things minimalistic, you can delete older backups. Choose iTunes⇨Preferences (Mac) or Edit⇨Preferences (Windows), and click Devices. You see a list of your backups. Just click the one or ones you want to delete then click Delete Backup. Poof! Gone.

Tackling iPhone Troubles

You may think that near the beginning of a book is a strange place for the troubleshooting information. We decided to do things a little differently.

Often, when something goes awry, you panic — it's human nature. No one likes a glitch, or feeling unprepared or stupid. That's why we put this information upfront. You can skim through the topics so if one of the problems we mention occurs, you won't be surprised or panicked. You'll know where to look to resolve the problem calmly and quickly.

We include some information here to help you avoid problems, along with the traditional troubleshooting question-and-answer format. In each chapter, we include some warnings of things that could happen and tips for how to resolve problems specific to the chapter at hand.

Avoiding common iPhone problems

With iCloud syncing, your version of iOS and your apps should always be current. If you're having problems, however, open the Settings app, tap General, and tap Software Update just to be sure your iOS is current. If a badge appears on the App Store icon, chances are, the Automatic Downloads option isn't on for Apps. Open the Settings app, tap iTunes & App Store, and tap both the Apps and Updates switches on under Automatic Downloads. Refer to Book IV, Chapter 5 to learn about the App Store.

Make sure the SIM card is properly installed (if your iPhone uses one). If you dropped your iPhone, the SIM card may be slightly dislodged. Carefully insert the end of a paper clip in the hole of the SIM tray to open the tray. Take out the SIM card and re-insert it and then gently push the tray closed.

Here are a few other things to consider if you have a problem:

✔ **The headset is plugged in but you can't hear anything. First, make sure the Mute switch isn't on.** Then, make sure the headset is plugged in all the way — you hear a little "click" when it is. It may not be compatible with the cover or bumper (those colored frames that go around iPhone's outer edge) you use; that is, the cover keeps the plug from going all the way into the hole. Although ⅛-inch plugs work most of the time, the specifications call for a 3.5mm plug.

Make sure the jack is clean. If you use your iPhone in a dusty workshop or in the yard, or eat toast while texting, crumbs and particles can build up and block the audio jack. Ever-so-gently tap your iPhone on a not-too-hard surface (a placemat on a table, for example, or a mousepad) or use a hand pump with the nozzle for inflating a basketball to blow into the jack.

✔ **The words *No Service* appear where your carrier's name usually appears.** First, make sure you aren't in Airplane Mode (you see the airplane icon in the Status bar if you are). Try moving closer to a window or going outside. Then, open the Settings app, tap Cellular, and try turning 4G on or off. Try turning Airplane Mode on and then off. Try turning your iPhone off and on again. Finally, open the Settings app, tap General, tap Reset, and tap Reset Network Settings. If you have a weak signal, turning 4G on can bring a stronger signal. If you're in a crowded area with lots of other cellphone users, turning 4G off gives you access to a larger network.

✔ **You don't have Internet access.** Assuming you have data service as part of your cellular contract, make sure you have a cellular data signal or are in a Wi-Fi zone. You see the icons in the Status bar (see Book I, Chapter 2). Without one of these options, you can't get online. Try these tactics to solve the problem:

- *Disconnect and reconnect to the network.* Drag up from the bottom of the screen to open the Control Center. Tap Wi-Fi off, wait a minute, and then tap Wi-Fi on.

- *Try forgetting the network and joining again.* Open the Settings app, tap Wi-Fi, and then tap the name of the network. Tap Forget This Network and then sign in again.

- *Try renewing the Dynamic Host Control Protocol (DHCP) lease, which is the access point that allows your iPhone to access a Wi-Fi network.* Open the Settings app, tap Wi-Fi, tap the Info (i) button to the right of the connected Wi-Fi network, and then tap the DHCP tab. Scroll down the screen and tap the Renew Lease button, as shown in Figure 5-11.

- *Reset network settings.* Open the Settings app, tap General, and then scroll down to Reset, which is the last button on the screen. Tap Reset Network Settings.

- *Look for interference from devices like walkie-talkies or baby monitors.*

- *Check your home network.* If you know Wi-Fi should be available because, say, you're home, and none of these procedures work, the problem could be with the Wi-Fi router, modem, or incoming DSL line. Try turning your router off and on again or call your service provider.

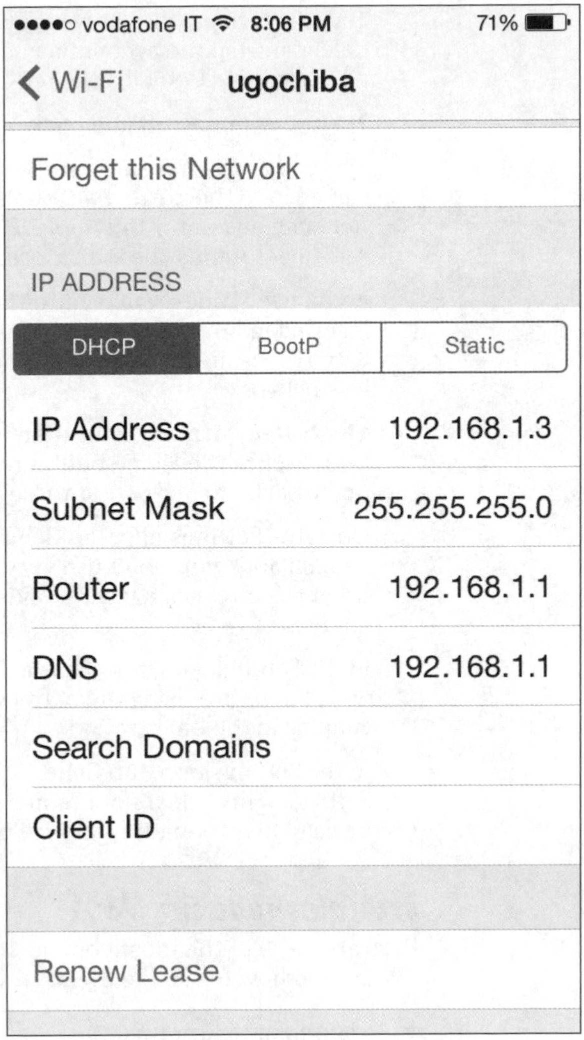

✔ **You can't send text messages.** For SMS and MMS messages, make sure you have cellular service. iMessage requires a Wi-Fi or cellular data connection, and iMessage has to be turned on in the Settings app by tapping Messages and then tapping the iMessage switch on. Check that the recipient's phone number has an area code and that you typed your message in the message field and not the subject line. When using an email address to send an iMessage, make sure it's blue, which means iMessage-enabled. Refer to Book II, Chapter 2 to find out more about text messaging.

●●●●○ vodafone IT 🛜 8:06 PM	71% ■▮
‹ Wi-Fi	**ugochiba**

Forget this Network

IP ADDRESS

DHCP	BootP	Static

IP Address	192.168.1.3
Subnet Mask	255.255.255.0
Router	192.168.1.1
DNS	192.168.1.1
Search Domains	
Client ID	

Renew Lease

Figure 5-11: Sometimes your lease is up and you have to renew to get Wi-Fi.

✔ **You can send SMS but iMessage doesn't work.** Open the Settings app, tap General, tap Reset, and tap Reset Network Settings.

✔ **You can't receive or send email or you see messages but you can't open them.** Make sure you have an Internet connection, either through your cellular data network or Wi-Fi.

Try re-entering your password. Open the Settings app, tap Mail, Contacts, Calendars, tap the account name, and tap Account. Delete and retype the password. See Book II, Chapter 4 for information about the Mail app.

Turn your phone off and back on.

✔ **Syncing doesn't seem to work.** If you use iCloud, make sure you're signed in to the correct account: Open the Settings app, tap iCloud, tap Account, and enter the Apple ID and password you use with iCloud — remember it must be in the form of an email address.

If you use iTunes, make sure the USB connector cable is properly inserted in both your computer and your iPhone. If you sync wirelessly with iTunes, make sure your iPhone and computer are on the same wireless network.

✔ **The battery drains faster than usual, especially after an iOS update.** Double-click the Home button to see the apps in the App Switcher. Swipe up on each one, or two or three at a time, until you've closed all of them.

Open the Settings app, tap General, tap Background App Refresh, and turn off apps you don't use very often; they'll refresh when you open them, which takes a few seconds more but helps conserve the battery charge.

In the Settings app, tap General, tap Usage, and tap Battery Usage to see which apps are using the battery the most and make sure they're not running in the background.

In the Settings app, tap General, tap Reset, and then tap Reset All Settings. This "clears out" some of the cobwebs in your iPhone's memory and may fix battery charge problems.

Troubleshooting Q&A

Here are some of the most common difficulties you may encounter with your iPhone and how to handle them:

Q: My iPhone won't turn on.

A: Probably the battery needs to be charged. Connect your iPhone to the USB connector cable and power adapter and begin charging. It takes about ten minutes for a completely dead battery to have enough charge to show signs of life. A lightning bolt appears on the screen, followed by the Apple logo, and you can turn your iPhone on at that point.

If you take your iPhone to the beach and leave it in your bag hanging on the back of your lounge chair (as Barbara's friend's teenage daughter did and then called in tears because her beloved iPhone wouldn't work), you risk overheating your iPhone. Likewise, leaving it out in the cold can send your iPhone into hypothermia. Signs of iPhone heat stroke or frostbite are a dimmed screen, weak cellular signal, and in the case of heat stroke, a temperature warning screen as your iPhone tries to cool itself. You cannot use your iPhone — except for an emergency call — when the temperature warning screen is visible. If your iPhone can't cool or warm itself, it goes into a deep sleep — a sort of iPhone coma — until it cools off or warms up. Put your iPhone in a cooler or warmer location. It will wake up once its internal temperature returns to normal.

Q: An app is frozen on my screen. Nothing closes it, the Home button doesn't work — it just sits there.

A: Force-quit the app. Hold down the Sleep/Wake button until the Slide to Power Off message appears, and then hold the Home button until the frozen program quits and you return to the Home screen. The app should be fine the next time you open it.

Q: Um, force-quitting the app didn't work.

A: Force-restart your iPhone. Hold down the Home button and the Sleep/ Wake button simultaneously for about ten seconds. Release when you see the Apple logo, which means your iPhone is restarting.

Q: The same app or apps keep giving me trouble.

A: Check to see if there's an update for the app or apps. If you aren't using Automatic Downloads for the App Store, a badge on the App Store button indicates you have apps to update; tap App Store and then tap the Updates button. Scroll through the list to see if the offending app is there, and if so, tap Update and then Open.

If that doesn't work, try removing and reinstalling the troublesome app or apps. Press and hold any app on the Home screen until they begin to wiggle, and then tap the X on the app you want to remove. Even after you remove an app, you can install it again because the App Store keeps a record of all the apps you installed.

Q: An app or apps stopped in the middle of an installation or update, and it neither opens nor allows me to remove it.

A: This may happen when you try to use the Update All function of the App Store, and you have more than a few apps to update. Connect your iPhone to your computer with the USB connector cable and open iTunes. Select your iPhone from the pop-up menu in the upper right of the window, and then click the Apps tab. Click the Remove button next to the offending app or apps and then click Sync. Install the app while connected to iTunes by clicking the Install button next to the apps you want to install and then clicking Sync. Alternatively, click the eject button next to your iPhone on iTunes, and disconnect your iPhone from your computer. Open the App Store from the Home screen, and tap Updates at the bottom of the screen, tap Purchased, and then tap Not on This iPhone. Tap the download icon (it looks like a cloud with a downward-pointing arrow) to download the app to your iPhone. See Book IV, Chapter 5 to learn more about the App Store and installing and updating apps.

Q: **I'm still having problems.**

A: Try resetting your iPhone settings. Open the Settings app, tap General, tap Reset, and tap Reset All Settings, as shown in Figure 5-12. This takes your settings back to how they were when you took your iPhone out of the box, or if upgrades have been released since you bought your iPhone, to the default settings for the most recent upgrade you performed. It doesn't remove any data, but you do have to redo any settings you had altered.

Q: **Nope, that didn't help.**

A: Tap Erase All Content and Settings. This does just what it says. This resets all settings and erases all your information and media by removing the encryption key to the data (which is encrypted using 256-bit AES encryption).

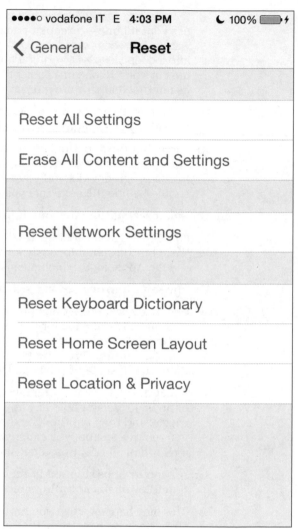

Figure 5-12: Sometimes resetting is your best option for solving a problem.

Make sure you back up your iPhone with iCloud or iTunes before tapping Erase All Content and Settings so you can sync after.

Q: **Nothing seems to work.**

A: Restore your phone. Restore erases your iPhone and returns it to the state it was in out of the box, but better than new because the most recent operating system (the software that makes your iPhone work) will be installed. All contacts, photos, music, TV shows, calendars, emails, notes, bookmarks, and third-party apps are deleted. This sounds like a drastic measure, and in a way it is, but it's not as bad as it seems. If you use iCloud to back up, you can restore from your iCloud account. If you use iTunes, try to sync with iTunes before restoring your iPhone. Even if you can't sync, your most recent backup is stored on iTunes on your computer, as explained earlier in this chapter.

When you Reset All Settings or Erase All Content and Settings or Restore, you repeat the activation process as explained in Book I, Chapter 2.

Q: iTunes doesn't recognize my iPhone.

A: Do a Device Firmware Upgrade (DFU). DFU wipes out the old OS (but not your content) and installs a new one. You can then sync and restore as explained previously. Here's the DFU procedure:

1. Turn off your iPhone.

2. Connect your iPhone to your computer.

3. Open iTunes.

4. Press and hold the Sleep/Wake and Home buttons for exactly ten seconds.

5. After ten seconds, release the Sleep/Wake button, but continue to hold the Home button for another ten seconds.

6. After ten seconds, release the Home button. iTunes now recognizes your iPhone.

7. Click OK. iTunes asks you to confirm.

8. Click Restore and Update.

Getting more help

The previous tactics usually fix typical iPhone problems. If you have a problem we didn't talk about or none of the previously discussed tactics work, you can still find more help on the Internet. Chances are, someone else has encountered the same problem. Your first stop should be Apple's iPhone Support page at www.apple.com/support/iphone. You can contact Apple's technical support group for personalized attention. If your iPhone is your sole connection to the Internet, ask to use a friend or relative's computer or return to the store where you purchased your iPhone.

You can also search the discussion forums where questions and answers are submitted by other iPhone users. Type in a few words that describe your problem and peruse the discussions. If you don't find a discussion pertinent to your problem, you can submit your question and usually an answer from another user is available within a day.

If you still don't find a satisfying answer, type a few keywords about your problem in to one of the Internet search engines like Google (www.google.com) or Bing (www.bing.com).

Wherever you search, you may be surprised to find that you aren't the first person to have the problem you're having.

Getting repairs if you need them

We're always impressed with the seriousness and efficiency of Apple's warranty and repair service. Your iPhone includes a one-year limited warranty and 90 days of complimentary support. You can get two years of coverage and support if you buy AppleCare+ ($99), which now includes no-fault insurance that covers up to two accidental damage incidents, so if you accidently drop your iPhone in the fish pond at the park, as long as you can scoop it out and take it to your local Apple Store, it will be repaired, or replaced, for a $79 deductible. You have to purchase AppleCare+ within 60 days of your iPhone purchase date. If anything goes wrong with your iPhone, call Apple or take it to an Apple Store.

If you can, back everything up before you leave your iPhone with Apple so you can re-sync on the repaired, or new, iPhone.

If you can't be without a cellular phone for two or three days, the Apple Store offers what's called the Express Replacement Service (ERS). Within two or three business days of your call, a replacement iPhone (the same model as your broken one) is sent to you, and you must return your damaged iPhone within ten days. If your iPhone is covered under AppleCare or AppleCare+, ERS is included. If your iPhone is not covered, you have to pay a $29 fee and a reserve for the value of a replacement phone is placed on your credit card. If you return your damaged iPhone after 10 days but within 20 days, you're charged a late fee, and if you don't send your damaged iPhone at all, the whole cost of a new iPhone is charged to your credit card. You're also charged the cost of a new iPhone if the damage to your phone isn't eligible for Apple-Care or warranty service. When the replacement phone arrives, you just have to insert your SIM card and sync what was on your broken iPhone to the replacement iPhone.

Book II
Communication Central: Calls, Messages, and the Web

Contents at a Glance

Chapter 1: Managing Phone and FaceTime Calls

In This Chapter

✔ Making and receiving calls

✔ Blocking unwanted callers

✔ Juggling call options and conference calls

✔ Listening to and managing voicemail messages

✔ Perusing and adjusting phone-related settings

✔ Audio and video chatting with FaceTime

W e're guessing you've already made and received phone calls with your iPhone before you arrived at this chapter, but this chapter is all about maximizing your up-close-and-personal relationship with iPhone's phone-related features.

In this chapter, we introduce you to — and explain the difference between — the Phone and FaceTime apps you use to place a call or answer one. We tell you how to use call-waiting to switch between an active call and an incoming call, politely decline a call that you can't respond to at that moment, or block callers who have become a nuisance. We show you how to listen to and manage your voicemails, and explain the different ways iPhone notifies you when you miss a call. At the end of the chapter, we review the phone-related settings you may want to familiarize yourself with before you start making calls — especially if you're traveling overseas.

Homing in on Phone

 Tapping the Phone icon on the Home screen is indisputably the most obvious way to use your iPhone as, well, a phone. When the app opens, you see the screen associated with the phone-calling method you most recently used. Figure 1-1 shows the Favorites screen, but if you make a call with the keypad and then switch to another app, when you return to the Phone app, the keypad appears.

Some not-so-obvious ways that can also land you on the Phone screen include answering an incoming call, tapping a phone number in an email or web page to call that number, tapping a number in the Contacts app, or speaking the name or number you want Siri to dial on your behalf (or Voice Control, if you disabled Siri because of a weak data signal).

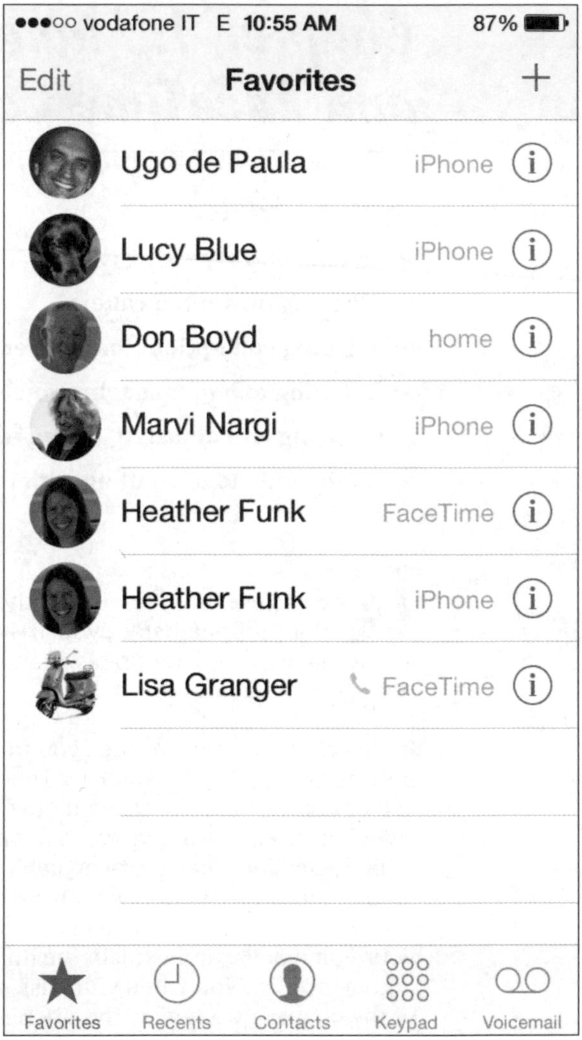

●●●○○ We assume that your iPhone currently enjoys an active connection with your provider's cellular network, as indicated by the cell signal strength icon in the top-left corner of iPhone's Status bar. The more filled-in circles you see, the better the signal. If instead of circles you see No Signal or No Service or the Airplane Mode icon, you won't be able to make or receive calls until you're once again in range of your provider's cellular network signal or Airplane Mode is disabled. To familiarize yourself with other icons you see in the status bar, check out Book I, Chapter 2.

●●●○○ vodafone IT E 10:55 AM		87% 🔋
Edit	**Favorites**	+
🧑 Ugo de Paula	iPhone	ⓘ
🧑 Lucy Blue	iPhone	ⓘ
🧑 Don Boyd	home	ⓘ
🧑 Marvi Nargi	iPhone	ⓘ
🧑 Heather Funk	FaceTime	ⓘ
🧑 Heather Funk	iPhone	ⓘ
🛵 Lisa Granger	📞 FaceTime	ⓘ
★ Favorites	🕐 Recents ⓘ Contacts	⣿ Keypad ◯◯ Voicemail

Figure 1-1: The Phone app: More ways to make calls than meets the eye.

However you reach the Phone screen, you always see the following icons at the bottom of the screen that activate the Phone app's main features:

 ✓ **Favorites:** iPhone's version of speed dial, offering quick, one-tap dialing or FaceTime access to the 50 people you call the most.

 ✓ **Recents:** A roll-call list displays up to 75 of the most recent calls you placed, answered, missed, or hung up on.

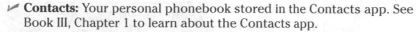

Contacts

- **Contacts:** Your personal phonebook stored in the Contacts app. See Book III, Chapter 1 to learn about the Contacts app.

Keypad

- **Keypad:** An onscreen keypad that works like the physical keypads introduced in the 1960s for dialing phone numbers.

Voicemail

- **Voicemail:** Your inbox for listening to, replying to, managing, deleting, and getting more information about voicemail messages you receive.

We write about the first four of these Phone features (as well as using Siri) in the next section and cover Voicemail in the section "Visiting Voicemail."

Making Calls

To simply make a phone call in the traditional way, tap the Phone app on the Home screen, tap the Keypad button at the bottom of the Phone screen (refer to Figure 1-1), tap out the number you want to call, and then tap Call. If you don't want to use the keypad, there are several other ways iPhone lets you make calls. Here's a quick rundown of the ways to make calls (all of which we cover in depth in the following sections):

- Tap Favorites, and then tap the contact you want to call.

- Tap Recents, and then tap the name or number you want to call.

- Tap Contacts, find and tap the contact you want to call to display his contact card, and then tap the phone number you want to dial.

- Tap Voicemail, tap the name or number you want to call, and then tap Call Back.

- Double-click the Home button to see buttons for your Favorites and Recents contacts across the top of the screen, as shown in Figure 1-2. Tap the person you want to call, and then tap the icon for the number and type of call you want to make.

- Press and hold the Home button to activate Siri (or Voice Control), and then say the name or number you want to call.

Using Favorites

Tapping Favorites displays the names of up to 50 people and organizations you deem important enough to score a spot on what is essentially iPhone's version of your speed-dial list, as shown in Figure 1-1. Each number counts as one, so if you have a work number and a home number for the same person, that equals two Favorites. The same goes for FaceTime and phone numbers. You can add, edit, rearrange, remove, and — most important — make phone calls with Favorites.

Add a Favorite

To add a Favorite, follow these steps:

1. **Tap the + (plus sign) button to display your contacts, and then search or scroll through your contacts to find the one you want to add.**

2. **Tap the contact you want to add to your Favorites list. (See Book III, Chapter 1 to learn about Contacts.)**

   If you have only one number for that contact, go to Step 3.

   If you have more than one number, the contact card opens so you can tap the phone number you want to add to Favorites.

3. **A dialog asks if you want to add the number as a Favorite for Voice Call, FaceTime Audio, or FaceTime (video). Tap the one you want.**

   The person's name is added to your Favorites list. A label

Figure 1-2: Double-click the Home button to quickly call the people you talk to the most.

indicates the type of number it is, referring to the label used in Contacts, such as *mobile, home,* or *iPhone.* FaceTime means a FaceTime video chat will be initiated, whereas a phone icon next to FaceTime (refer to Figure 1-1) means tapping that Favorite will initiate a FaceTime audio call. We explain FaceTime just a bit later in this chapter.

 Add Favorites directly from Contacts by scrolling down a contact's info card and tapping Add to Favorites. If there are multiple numbers for the contact, a menu prompts you to choose the number you want to add; then you select Voice, FaceTime Audio, or FaceTime.

Call a Favorite

To call a Favorite, tap a name in the list and the outgoing call is placed. If you tap a Favorite's FaceTime number, an audio or video FaceTime call is placed.

Delete or rearrange Favorites

To delete or rearrange Favorites, follow these steps:

1. **Tap the Edit button in the upper left.**

2. **Tap the red button to the left of a name you want to delete, and then tap the Delete button that appears to the right, as shown in Figure 1-3.**

   Your out-of-favor contact's name only vanishes from your Favorites list, but her card is not deleted from your saved Contacts.

3. **Next to a name you want to move to a new position in the list, tap and drag the rearrange button up or down your list and then let go to save your Favorite in its new location.**

4. **Tap the Done button when you finish.**

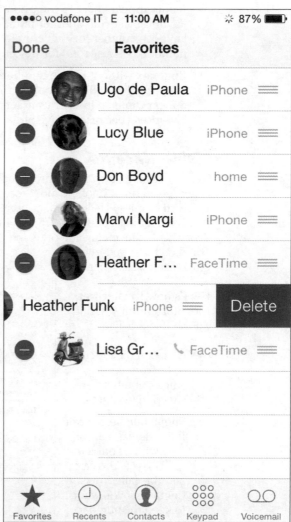

You're limited to 50 Favorites, so the + (plus sign) button doesn't appear after you've reached the limit. You'll need to delete an existing Favorite from your list to make the + appear again.

Figure 1-3: The Favorites edit screen.

Get More Info

Tap the Info button on the far right of the Favorite's name to display an Info screen. The person's contact card displays any information you filled in for that contact, including phone numbers and email addresses. We explain Contacts more in Book III, Chapter 1, but you'll notice two things in Contacts after you add a person to your Favorites list:

✔ A star appears next to the phone number that's been saved in your Favorites list. Tap another number for that contact to add a second Favorite number for that contact (for instance, one for Mom's mobile number, and a second for her home number).

✔ Contacts without phone numbers or those already added to your Favorites list with no second or remaining phone numbers to add appear dimmed in your Contacts list when adding new contacts to Favorites (because you've already added them).

Using Recents

Tapping Recents displays a chronological list — also referred to as your phone's call log — of up to 75 of the most recent numbers your iPhone has called, received or missed calls from, or hung up on (more than one call from the same number counts as one of the 75), as shown in Figure 1-4. Tap the All tab to view every kind of incoming and outgoing call or tap Missed to see only those calls you didn't respond to for one reason or another.

Here's how to interpret the information you find on the Recents list:

✔ Names indicate calls to or from people whose numbers are saved in Contacts.

✔ Phone numbers mean the caller isn't associated with a contact card — yet. You can add the caller to Contacts if you want to keep the number.

Because the Recents lists doesn't retain caller ID (for numbers that aren't in Contacts), you can download the

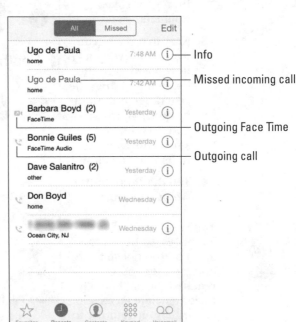

Figure 1-4: Recents displays a list of all incoming and outgoing phone activity.

Reverse Phone Lookup app to look for the identities of incoming calls, particularly missed calls when you didn't have a chance to see the caller ID.

- ✔ The label under the recent caller/callee's number — such as home, mobile, or other — is displayed if you assigned that label to the number in Contacts or the contact management app from which you imported the contact.

- ✔ Calls you place with the Phone app and FaceTime audio calls are marked with the outgoing phone call icon.

- ✔ Missed calls are hard to miss on your list because they're the items displayed in red type.

- ✔ Incoming and outgoing calls from or to the same phone number are displayed together as one item in the list, missed calls from the same number are their own item. The number in parentheses next to the name or number (refer to Figure 1-4) tells you how many calls were placed.

- ✔ The time of calls from today and the day of other calls are shown to the right of the name.

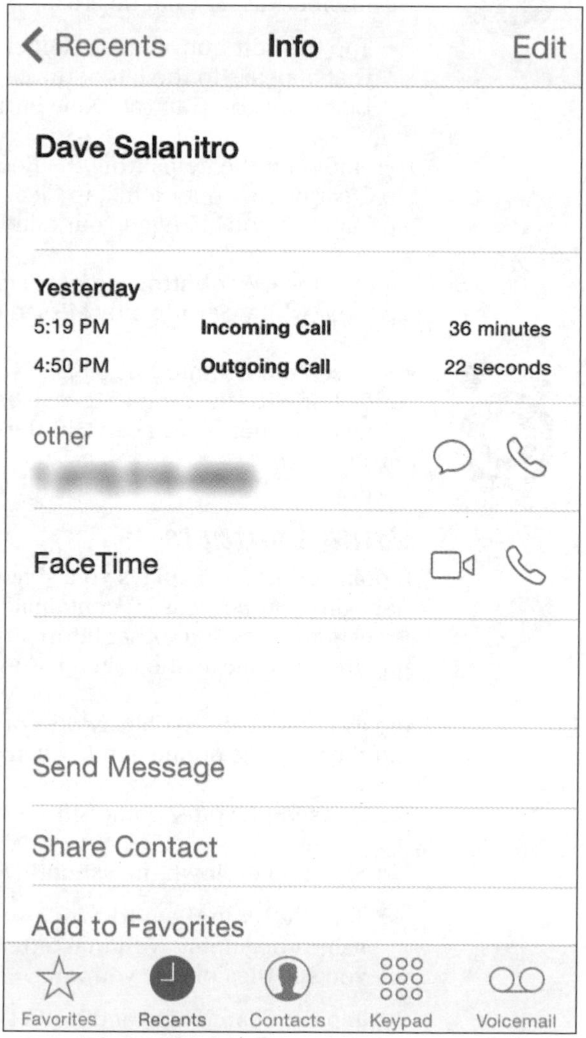

Tap the Info button (the i icon) to see detailed information about the call activity: the day and time (or consecutive times) a contact or phone number reached out to you (or you reached out to them), as shown in Figure 1-5. You also see any additional phone numbers, email or street addresses, and other details from the contacts card in Contacts.

Figure 1-5: Tap the Info button to see the time and duration of calls from the same number.

To remove items from the list, one at a time, do one of the following:

✔ Swipe right to left across the middle of an individual call and then tap the Delete button to delete only that recent call from the list.

Your iPhone's touchscreen is very sensitive, if you swipe left to right or from too close to the edge, either nothing will happen or you'll call the number rather than delete it.

✔ Tap the Edit button in the upper right. Tap the red and white minus sign that appears to the left of the call you want to delete, and then tap the Delete button. Tap the Done button in the upper right.

To remove all the items from the Recents list, tap the Edit button and then tap Clear in the upper left. Tap Clear All Recents in the dialog that appears or tap Cancel if you changed your mind.

Tapping the Clear button clears *all* items from the Recents list even if you tap Clear while viewing only Missed calls.

When you tap the Info button next to a phone number, you can create a new contact or add the number to an existing contact. When you tap the Info button next to a name, you can edit the contact information by tapping the Edit button.

Using Contacts

Tapping Contacts displays your iPhone's central directory for storing and managing contact "cards" containing the names, phone numbers, email and street addresses, and other information. The contacts you see in the Phone app are the same as those in the Contacts app.

Tap a contact card to display the contact's Info screen, as shown in Figure 1-6, and then tap the phone number you want to call to dial that number.

You can search your contacts from the Contacts list in three ways:

✔ Scroll up or down the list until you see the contact you want.

✔ Tap a letter in the A-to-Z index on the right edge to jump to contact names beginning with that letter, and then scroll through the list until you see the contact you want.

✔ Tap the Search field and begin typing the name of the person or company you're searching for to display any contacts that match what you type, and then tap the contact that matches the one you're looking for, as shown in Figure 1-7.

The Search function searches all fields so matches for street names, relations, or notes appear in the results list. This helps you find a business when you remember the location but not the name.

From the Home screen, you can use Spotlight search to find a contact; pull down the middle of the screen and type the name you want to find. We tell you everything about using Spotlight in Book I, Chapter 3.

Blocking callers

If you receive unwanted calls from a specific person or entity, you can block incoming calls from that contact. The information remains in Contacts and you can make outgoing phone or FaceTime calls, but you won't receive any incoming communications via phone, FaceTime, or Messages from that contact. Open the contact in one of the following ways:

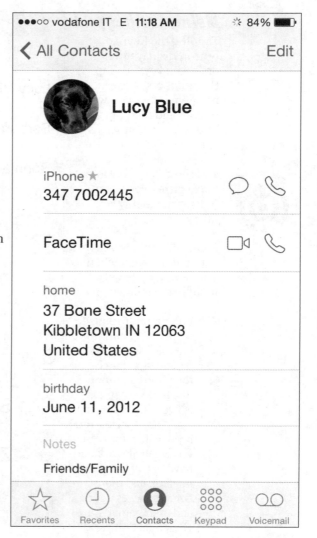

Figure 1-6: Tap a contact's phone number to call that number.

- ✔ Tap Contacts on the Home screen, and then tap the undesired contact in the list.

- ✔ Tap the Info button next to the person in the Favorites list.

- ✔ Tap the Info button next to the person or number in the Recents list.

Scroll to the bottom of the Info screen and tap Block This Caller, and then tap Block Contact in the menu that appears as in Figure 1-8. Incoming phone calls and messages from any number associated with that contact will be blocked.

If you ever want to unblock someone, follow the same steps and tap Unblock This Caller — presto change-o, they're back on your good list.

**Book II
Chapter 1**

**Managing Phone
and FaceTime Calls**

Using the keypad

Tapping the Keypad button displays the onscreen keypad. Tap the numbers of the phone number you want to call, and then tap Call to dial your number, as shown in Figure 1-9.

Tap the delete button to backspace over a number (or numbers) you mistyped.

Some nifty things you can do (and see!) when you're using keypad include the following:

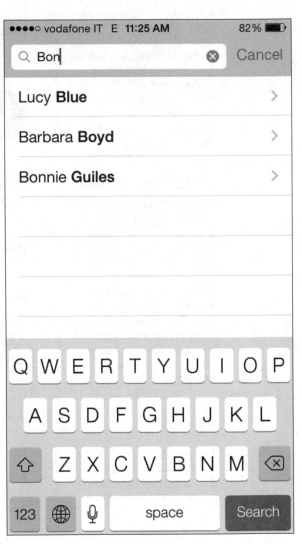

Figure 1-7: Homing in on contacts with the Search feature.

- ✓ **Enter a "soft" pause by pressing and holding the * key until a comma appears in the phone number display.** A soft pause is two seconds. You could use this feature if you call in for your voicemail at work and have to call the phone number, and then enter an access code, and then perhaps a passcode. Putting a soft pause between the phone number and each code gives the system time to receive the information and go to the next step.

- ✓ **Enter a "hard" pause by pressing and holding the # key until a semicolon appears in the phone number display.** A hard pause waits for your confirmation (tap the Call button) before transmitting the next series of numbers. For example, when calling a company, you have to wait for the line to be answered before entering an extension.

- ✓ **Paste a phone number you copied from another app into the keypad by holding your finger on the display zone above the numeric keys, and then tapping Paste when it appears.**

✔ **Press the Call button (the green button at the bottom) to bring up the last number you dialed, and then press Call again to dial it.**

✔ **See the contact name magically appear beneath a number you tap if that number is on any contact's card.**

✔ **Tap the Add button to the left of the number you enter to either create a new contact card with the phone number you're typing or add the phone number to an existing contact.**

Using Voicemail

One of our favorite things about the Phone app's Voicemail feature is how *seeing* those messages in the voicemail inbox helps to remind us to call back any of those people we want to chat with.

Tap a name or number in the Voicemail list screen and then tap Call Back to call that person or phone number.

Figure 1-8: Block unwanted incoming communications from specific contacts.

To learn about the other things you can do on the Voicemail screen besides returning phone calls, check out the section "Visiting Voicemail," later in this chapter.

Using Siri or Voice Control

Siri is all ears when it comes to using your voice to make your iPhone do things for you — including making phone calls, and if your data connection is weak, Voice Control can take over for simple commands. In Book I, Chapter 3, we explain all the other things Siri, and Voice Control, can do for you. Here, we explain phone calls.

Siri is enabled by default in iOS 8, but you need either a cellular data or Wi-Fi Internet connection to use Siri. If you lack a strong connection, open the Settings app, tap General and then tap Siri and tap the switch to the off position; Voice Control will fill in for Siri, doing tasks that don't require a data connection — such as making phone calls.

Siri

Siri is a bit more intelligent than Voice Control, or perhaps Siri is just a better listener. Siri is on by default but should you need to turn Siri off and back on again, open the Settings app, tap General, tap Siri, and then tap the switch On, or Off. Do one of the following to solicit Siri:

Figure 1-9: Dialing phone numbers the "old-fashioned" way.

✔ Press and hold the Home button until the Siri screen opens.

✔ Press and hold the center button on the EarPods controls until you hear a double-beep.

✔ Press the Attention button on your Bluetooth headset.

✔ Say "Hey Siri." This works when the Voice Activation function is enabled in the Siri settings and your iPhone is connected to a power source.

Speak your command, more or less as if you were talking with a person. You can give simple instructions, like "Call Lucy," or more complex commands such as "Call my sister at work." Siri looks for matches in Favorites and Contacts. When a match is found, Siri responds along the lines of "Calling Lucy Blue's iPhone." If there is no match or if there's more than one phone number for the contact you want to call, Siri asks for more information, as shown in Figure 1-10.

When there are multiple choices for the phone number, Siri reads the label and the number for the contact, and you can then repeat the label or say "the second one" and the call will be put through. Speak the requested information and Siri makes the phone call when she finds the number. If the person you want to call isn't in your Contacts or somewhere else on your iPhone, Siri can search the Internet for the number and then connect you. You get the picture. If the person isn't available, you can ask Siri to send the person an email or text message.

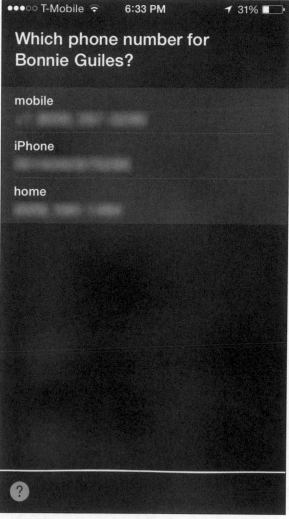

Figure 1-10: The Siri calling screen.

Book II
Chapter 1

Managing Phone
and FaceTime Calls

Siri requires a Wi-Fi or cellular Internet connection and can be slow to respond to your request — at times up to 30 seconds — depending on the type of Internet connection you have and because your request is sent to Apple's server, which processes the request and then instructs Siri how to respond. If you use Siri only for making phone calls, Voice Control will probably be faster and more accurate.

Voice Control

If you disable Siri, Voice Control is automatically active. Press and hold the Home button to activate Voice Control. Say "Call" or "Dial," followed by the name of the person or phone number you want to call. A slightly robotic voice repeats your request aloud and then places your call for you.

Voice Control may respond to your request in the following ways:

- **No Match Found:** That's what the Voice Control robot says (followed by three tone sounds) if it can't find a phone number in Contacts that matches the name you said or if it can't understand the phone number you gave it to dial for you. Either way, you can try again by immediately repeating the name or number (perhaps more slowly this time).

- **Multiple Numbers:** If a contact you're calling has more than one phone number, the Voice Calling robot says the contact's name aloud, and then rattles off the different phone numbers it finds for that contact, such as "home, mobile, or work." After listening to the choices, you can repeat the label or say, "the first number" or "the second one," and your call is placed to the correct number.

- **Multiple Matches Found:** That's what Voice Control tells you if it finds multiple numbers for a name you say, such as "Call Joe." Voice Control lists the names of contacts with the same name so you can pick one, or it asks you to be more specific.

Calling tips

Add relations to your card in Contacts so you can say "Call Dad" or "Call my sister" or to other contact cards, so you can request things like "Call Skip Johnson's brother" when you have a hard time remembering a name. Whether you're talking to Siri or Voice Control, when saying a person's name, you can differentiate between people who have the same first name by adding their last name, as well as say the specific phone number you want to call if you have more than one phone number for the person:

- Say "Call" or "Dial," and then say
  - "Joe Smith"
  - "Joe Smith at work"
  - "Joe Hutsko, mobile"

- Speak each number clearly and separately; for instance, if you want to call 555-6666, you would say "Call five five five, six six six six."

- If you're calling an 800 number, you can say "eight hundred," followed by the rest of the number you're calling.

The Voice Control and Siri features work even if your iPhone is locked, which is a handy feature — unless you misplace or lose your iPhone and someone picks it up and starts making international calls. To turn off the ability to make Voice Control calls when your iPhone is locked, open the Settings app and then tap Touch ID & Passcode. Enter your passcode and then turn off the Voice Dial option. (It will only be active if you've set up a Passcode.) When the Voice Dial feature is off, you can still use Voice Control or Siri when your iPhone is locked to do things like play or pause music or say "What time is it?" to hear the local time. If you say "Call Joe Hutsko," however, the ever-watchful genie that lives inside your iPhone politely responds, "Voice dialing is disabled."

Answering Calls

When you receive a call, your iPhone displays one of the incoming call screens shown in Figure 1-11, depending on whether your iPhone is locked (left) or awake (right). You'll hear your chosen ringtone and, if your iPhone is on your person — depending on how sensitive you are — you may feel it vibrating. If the information of the person calling you is saved in Contacts, you'll see the person's name (and photo, if you assigned a photo to that person's contact card). If the caller isn't one of your contacts, you either see the caller's phone number and name, or "Unknown" or "Blocked" if the caller has chosen to block her Caller ID from appearing when she places calls.

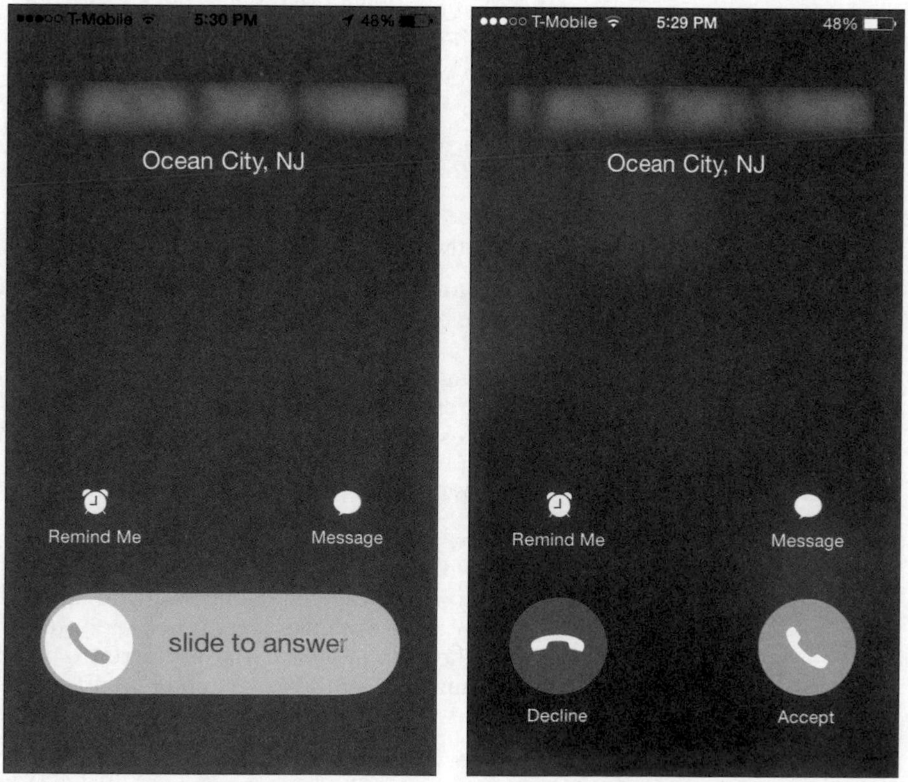

Figure 1-11: Two incoming call screens: one locked (left), the other not (right).

To answer an incoming call, do one of the following:

✓ Drag the Slide to Answer button to the right (if your iPhone is locked).

✓ Tap Answer (if your iPhone is unlocked).

TIP

To instantly quiet your iPhone's ringtone when you receive an incoming call, flip the Silent/Ring switch to the silent position, tap either volume button once, or press the Sleep/Wake button once. You can still answer the call, but the ringing is muted. When you answer an incoming call, the active call screen appears. We give you the full 411 on your options in the section "Managing Calls" a little further along in this chapter.

Declining Calls

Sometimes, you just can't respond to a call or don't want to talk to the caller. There are several ways to decline phone calls and two ways to respond, other than answering: You have the option of declining a call but sending a message to the caller that reads "I'll call you later" or something to that effect, or you can opt to be reminded in an hour to call the person back. Here are your call-declining options:

✓ **Press the Sleep/Wake button twice (which sends the call to voicemail).**

✓ **Tap the Decline button (if your iPhone is awake).**

✓ **Ignore iPhone's pleas to get your attention.** After a few moments, the call is automatically declined.

✓ **Tap either the Remind Me or Message button on the incoming call screen, and then tap one of the choices:**

• **Reply with Message:** Choose one of the options or tap Custom to create a specific response for that call. Open the Settings app, tap Phone, and tap Respond with Text to create different default replies. Tap in the field of the reply you want to replace and type your own reply, as shown in Figure 1-12.

• **Remind Me Later:** Tap one of the options: In One Hour or When I Leave. If you tap In One Hour, you'll receive a notification in an hour to call the person whose call you declined. If you tap When I Leave, you're given a few more options: Current Location (to be reminded when you leave the current location), Get Home (to be reminded when you get home), or Get to Work (to be reminded when you get to work). Choose whichever option you prefer.

Note: Location Services must be turned on and a My Info card must be set in Contacts (Book III, Chapter 1) for the When I Leave feature to appear and function.

Answering or declining calls while using your iPhone's stereo headphones is merely a matter of working the remote button as follows:

✔ Press the center button once to answer a call, or twice to decline a call.

✔ Put a call on hold to answer another incoming call by pressing the center button; press again to return to the caller you left on hold.

✔ Answer an incoming call but hang up on the current call by pressing and holding the center button for a couple seconds; two low beeps let you know you ended the first call.

✔ Press the volume + or – buttons to adjust the volume level.

When you decline a call in any of the preceding ways, the caller hears your voicemail greeting, followed by the option to leave you a voicemail message. Ditto if someone tries calling you when your iPhone is turned off, Airplane Mode is turned on, or Do Not Disturb is activated. (See Book I, Chapter 4 for more details.)

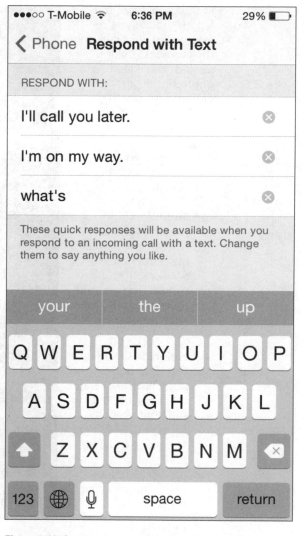

Figure 1-12: Create your own default replies to calls you decline.

Book II
Chapter 1

Managing Phone
and FaceTime Calls

Managing Calls

When you make or answer a call, the active call screen appears, as shown in Figure 1-13. The Active Call screen displays information about the person or business you're speaking with such as the phone number or name (if saved in Contacts), and the length of time you're engaged in your call from the moment you connected. You'll also see a photo of the person if you saved a photo with his contact card in Contacts.

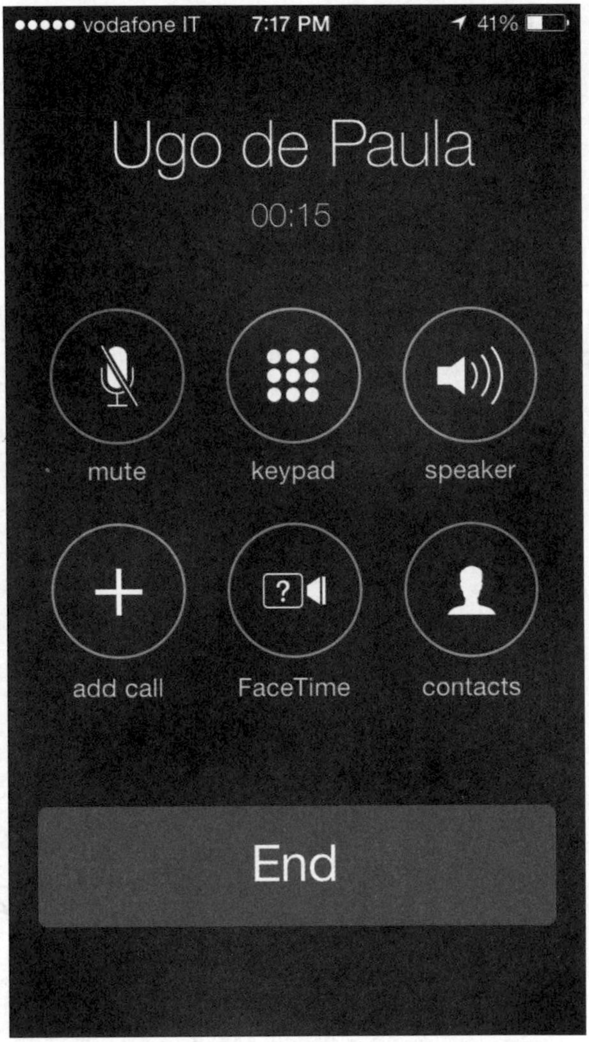

The buttons you see have the following functions:

Ugo de Paula

00:15

mute   keypad   speaker

add call   FaceTime   contacts

End

Figure 1-13: The Active Call screen.

✔ **Mute:** Tap Mute to prevent your caller from hearing sound on your end of the conversation, even though you can still hear your caller; tap again to turn off Mute.

 ✔ **Hold:** Press and hold the Mute button; the mute button changes into the Hold button; tap Hold again to turn off Hold. When you place a call on hold, neither you nor the person on the other end can hear the other.

✔ **Keypad:** Tap Keypad to display the keypad, and then tap any numbers or the * and # buttons to do things like respond to options when calling automated customer service phone numbers, or check your work voicemail inbox.

✔ **Speaker:** Tap the Speaker icon to hear your caller's voice through iPhone's built-in loudspeaker.

✔ **Audio Source:** You see this button in place of the Speaker button when you have a Bluetooth headset or Bluetooth calling in your car paired with your iPhone, which we explain in the section "Using Bluetooth connections."

✓ **Add Call:** Tap Add Call to put one person on hold and call another and also to set up a conference call. We explain this in detail in the section "Making dual and conference calls."

 ✓ **Use FaceTime:** Tap FaceTime to switch your current cellular call to a FaceTime Audio or video call, which uses a Wi-Fi or cellular data connection. Refer to the section "Making a FaceTime call," later in this chapter.

✓ **Contacts:** Tap Contacts to browse your contact cards to do things like find and share a phone number with the person you're currently speaking with, or choose another contact's phone number that you want to call while engaged in your current call.

Using Bluetooth connections

When you make a call while you're connected to a Bluetooth device (such as a headset, your car's audio system, or a speaker that offers speaker-phone functions) that you paired with your iPhone, the Audio Sources screen shown in Figure 1-14 appears while your call is being connected. Tap iPhone or Speaker if you want to switch to either of those audio sources instead of your Bluetooth device; or tap Hide to display the active call screen, which automatically appears after your call is connected. (We tell you how to set up and manage Bluetooth devices in Book I, Chapter 2.) To change the audio source, tap the Audio Source button on the active call screen to display the

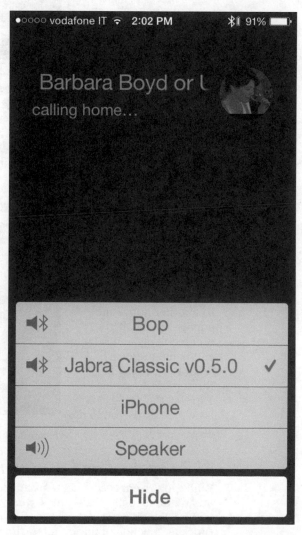

Figure 1-14: Choosing your preferred audio source while making or managing a call.

Audio Sources menu, tap the audio source choice you want to switch to, and then tap Hide to return to the active call screen.

Press iPhone's volume up and down buttons to increase or decrease the volume level of your call. If you're using headphones or a Bluetooth headset, you can also press the volume + and – buttons on those listening devices to adjust the call volume.

Multitasking while on a call

When you're engaged in an active call, you can click the Home button and then tap another app on the Home screen or double-click the Home button to see the App Switcher and tap an open app to do other things, like reading an e-book while you're stuck on hold. When you switch to another app while engaged in a call, the green pulsing active call banner shown in Figure 1-15 appears at the top of the screen. Tapping the active call banner returns you to the active call display.

Figure 1-15: The active call banner.

Making dual and conference calls

While you're engaged in an active call, you can make a second call, or you can answer an incoming call (unless you've turned off your iPhone's call-waiting feature, which we explain in the "Call Forwarding, Call Waiting, and Caller ID Blocking" section of this chapter). If you have a GSM-model iPhone, you can also initiate a conference call that lets you speak with up to five people at once; CDMA models are limited to two callers.

Making a second call

While on an active call, you can make a second call by doing the following:

1. **Tap Add Call to display your iPhone Contacts.**

2. **Scroll to find and tap to choose the contact you want to call.**

   You can tap the Favorites, Recents, and Keypad buttons at the bottom of the screen to use any of those options to add your second call.

   When your second call is established, the active multiple calls screen appears (refer to Figure 1-16).

3. **On a GSM phone, switch between your callers to speak privately with one or the other by tapping the caller's name at the top of the screen.**

Figure 1-16: The multiple calls screen.

See the section "Activating Your iPhone" in Book I, Chapter 2 to determine which type of phone you have if you're not sure.

CDMA phones only allow you to switch between calls if the second call was incoming.

4. **Tap End Call to hang up on the caller you're currently speaking with. Your other caller becomes your active call, and you can press End Call when you're finished conversing with that caller.**

Answering a second incoming call

If a second call comes in while you're engaged in another call, you see the screen shown in Figure 1-17. Respond to the incoming call screen by doing one of the following:

- **Tap Hold & Accept** to put your current call on hold and answer your second incoming call. When you choose this option, the active multiple calls screen appears.

- On GSM iPhones, **tap End & Accept** to disconnect with your current call and answer your second incoming call. On CDMA iPhones, **tap End Call,** and when the second call rings again, tap Answer.

- **Tap Send to Voicemail** to send the call directly to voicemail and remain on your current call.

Making a conference call

Figure 1-17: Options for responding to a second incoming phone call.

You initiate a conference call by making or answering a second call as described previously. After your second call is established, the multiple active calls screen appears (refer to Figure 1-16).

To turn your two calls into a conference call, and even add more callers to your two calls and turn those calls into a conference call, do the following:

1. **Tap Add Call to add a second person to a call you initiated and then choose the person you want to add from Contacts, Favorites, or Recents.**

   Or tap Hold & Accept to add an incoming call.

2. **On a GSM phone, you may have up to five people on your conference call. Repeat Step 1 to add the third through fifth people to your current group call.**

3. **Tap Merge Calls to combine your two (or more) calls into a single Conference Call in which everyone can speak and hear everyone else.**

   To merge calls on a CDMA phone, you must place the second call in order to merge with the first one.

   The names of the people on the conference call scroll across the top of the screen.

Book II
Chapter 1

Managing Phone
and FaceTime Calls

Managing a conference call

When a conference call is underway, you can use the conference call screen to manage your conference call by doing the following:

✔ Tap the Info button at the top of the screen to display a list of the people on the call, as shown in Figure 1-18.

✔ Tap the End button under a caller's name or number to disconnect that caller from the conference call.

Figure 1-18: Juggle individual callers during a conference call.

✔ To speak privately with one caller in your conference call, tap the Private button under the caller's name to speak with that caller; your other callers are put on hold while you speak privately with a single caller.

✔ Tap the Back button to return to the Conference call screen.

Visiting Voicemail

We recently heard that Voicemail has gone the way of the dinosaurs — rather than leave a recording, the caller will send a text message. Nonetheless, some people will still want to leave a voicemail message and you want to know how to set up your voicemail greeting, and listen to and manage voicemail messages, all of which we explain in this section.

Open the Phone app and then tap Voicemail to display the Voicemail screen, as shown in Figure 1-19.

Recording and changing your greeting

If this is the first time you're visiting the Voicemail screen, iPhone prompts you to create a password and record your voicemail greeting. Repeating the same steps is how you change your voicemail greeting message whenever you want.

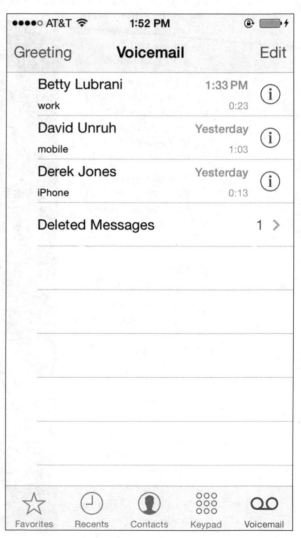

Figure 1-19: The Voicemail screen lists your voicemail messages.

Visual voicemail: Seen and heard

Visual voicemail is called that because you actually see your voice messages listed in a nice and neat list just like your email messages, whereas typical "nonvisual" voicemail only appears, well, nowhere, because only visual voicemail messages can be seen and heard. If you've never had voicemail, you may be unfamiliar with what it's like to retrieve your voicemail messages the "old-fashioned way" by dialing into your voicemail mailbox and then pressing buttons on the keypad to skip, fast forward, rewind, and delete those messages as they rattle off one after the other — all of which visual voicemail lets you do with your fingertips. You can select the messages you want to hear and listen to them in the order you want. Better yet, ask Siri to read your list of visual voicemail messages to you.

Unfortunately, visual voicemail isn't a feature you find on every iPhone. In some cases, you may have to pay an extra monthly fee for the feature. In other cases, the visual voicemail feature may not be offered by all carriers.

Tap Greeting to display the Voicemail Greeting screen and then choose one of the following options:

- **Default:** Tap Default if you want callers to hear your cellular provider's generic voicemail message (which says something like, "The person you are trying to reach at" — your phone number — "is not available," followed by instructions on how to leave a message, yada yada yada).

- **Custom:** Tap Custom if you want to record (or change) a personal greeting message in your own words, and then tap Record to record your greeting; tap Play to listen to your greeting.

- **Save:** Tap Save when you're happy with your choice, or tap Cancel if you've changed your mind and you want to keep the existing greeting.

Open the Settings app, tap Sounds, and then tap New Voicemail to designate the sound and vibration pattern you want to hear when you have a new voicemail message.

Listening to and managing voicemail messages

When you tap a voicemail message in the voicemail list, the selection expands to reveal the playback controls along with a couple other message management buttons, as shown in Figure 1-20.

- To listen to and control playback of a voicemail message

   • Tap the Play button to listen to the message. A Pause button replaces the Play button. You can juggle between the two to play and pause playback.

- Drag the playhead in the scrubber bar to move to any location in the voicemail message.

- Tap the Speaker button to hear messages out loud through iPhone's speaker (instead of holding iPhone to your ear or listening through headphones).

✔ Tap Call Back to call the person who left you the selected message.

✔ To display more information about the caller, tap the Info button on the right side of the names in the Voicemail list to display the Info screen.

✔ Tap Delete to delete the selected voicemail message. When you delete a voicemail message, the message is removed from the Voicemail list screen and is saved in the Deleted Messages list, which is automatically created if it isn't already displayed.

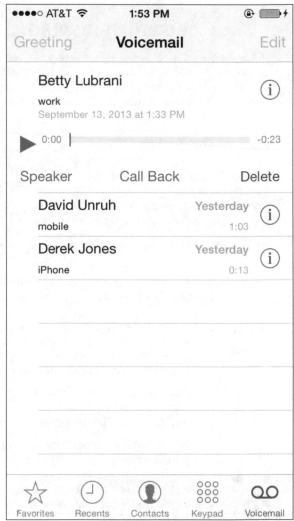

Figure 1-20: Listening to a voicemail message with the speakerphone turned on.

Messages you've listened to remain in your voicemail inbox until your cellular carrier deletes those messages. This means that even if you delete a message, it may pop back into the Inbox at a later date. How long messages you've listened to remain in your voicemail box varies; check with your carrier.

When viewing the Deleted screen, you can

✔ Tap a voicemail message to open it, and then

- Tap Play to listen to the message

- Tap Undelete to move the message out of the Deleted Messages list and back to the Voicemail messages list

✔ Tap Clear All to remove all deleted messages from the Deleted Messages list and back to the Voicemail messages screen.

If you want to keep prying ears from listening to your messages, open the Settings app, tap Phone, tap Change Voicemail Password, and tap in a four-digit code, which you then enter when you try to listen to your voicemail messages.

Taking Note of Phone Notifications

Using the Phone app puts you in control of placing and answering calls and voicemail messages when you want. iPhone works behind the scenes as your personal answering service, alerting you to missed calls or voicemail messages by displaying notifications and badges. Read more about notifications in Book I, Chapter 4.

The different notification messages iPhone displays when you miss (or decline) calls or receive new voicemail messages include the following:

✔ **Missed Call:** Displays the phone number, or name of one of your contacts, whose call went unanswered.

✔ **Voicemail:** Displays the phone number or name of one of your contacts who has left you a voicemail message.

✔ **Missed Call and Voicemail:** Combines both types of notifications.

The different notification badges iPhone displays when you miss (or decline) calls or receive new voicemail messages are as follows:

✔ **Phone App Icon:** A red badge indicates the combined number of missed calls and/or new voicemail messages.

✔ **Reminder:** If you declined an incoming call by tapping Remind Me Later, a reminder notification shows up on your phone per the instruction you tapped: an hour after you declined the call or when you leave or get home.

If your iPhone is unable to receive calls because it's in Airplane Mode, it's out of your cellular network range, or it's powered off, notifications messages, badges, and sounds for any missed calls or voicemail messages won't appear until your iPhone is able to receive calls again. When Do Not Disturb is on, a silent notification lets you know someone called.

Perusing Phone Settings

From the moment your iPhone is activated, you can use the Phone app to make, receive, and manage calls, and to listen to voicemail messages — all without ever needing to adjust (or even know about) any of your iPhone's many phone-related settings options.

We show you how to change a few phone-related settings throughout this chapter on a "need to know" basis; however, we encourage you to take a moment to get acquainted with the full spectrum of those settings.

By touring iPhone's phone-related settings options, you can maximize your awareness of every call-related feature, and potentially minimize the risk of incurring unexpected charges on your monthly phone bill by acquainting yourself with certain options that can cost you an arm and a leg if you happen to turn them on without realizing the implications.

You find various Phone settings in the Settings app. For details on the General settings, which gives you options for usage tracking and accessibility, and the Notifications settings, which let you choose how you'll be notified of missed calls, see Book I, Chapter 4.

Sounds

Open the Settings app and tap Sounds to choose your vibration, ringtone, and volume options, as shown in Figure 1-21. Choose when you want your phone to vibrate, if at all, by tapping Vibrate on Ring and Vibrate on Silent to the On or Off position. Tap Change with Buttons On so you can adjust the ringer volume with your iPhone's volume buttons. Tap Ringtone to choose the sound you want to hear for incoming calls. On the Ringtone screen, you can also select or create a vibration pattern. Remember to choose a sound for your New Voicemail, too.

See Book III, Chapter 1 to assign special ringtones to specific contacts. Open the Settings app and tap Phone to adjust the following information, as shown in Figure 1-22:

- **My Number:** Displays your personal phone number. Although it's set automatically, you can tap the disclosure triangle and change it.

- **Contact Photos in Favorites:** When on, the photo you assigned to a person in Contacts appears next to the name in the Favorites list.

- **Wi-Fi Calls (T-Mobile only at time of writing):** When enabled, you can make phone calls using a Wi-Fi connection instead of your carrier service or roaming. Tap this item and then, on the next screen, tap the toggle switch to the On position. You may have to contact your carrier to enable Wi-Fi calling.

✔ **Respond with Text:** Change the default replies for calls you decline with this option. Refer to the section "Declining Calls."

✔ **Call Forwarding, Call Waiting, Show My Caller ID (GSM models):** Turns those features on or off. See the next section to learn how to activate these features.

✔ **Blocked:** Shows a list of people whose attempts to call or send you a message are blocked. Add other names to the list by tapping this item and then tapping Add New. Contacts opens and you can choose who you want to block.

✔ **Change Voicemail Password:** To change your numeric voicemail password.

✔ **Dial Assist:** To have iPhone automatically add proper prefix number when calling the United States from abroad.

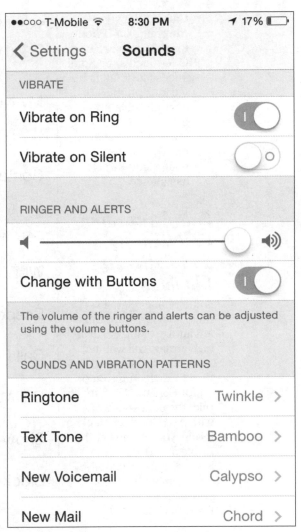

Figure 1-21: Change the Phone app settings to suit you.

✔ **SIM PIN (GSM models):** To turn on, choose, and change the secret code you can use to lock your iPhone's SIM card; when activated, you must type in the PIN code whenever you turn iPhone off then on again.

After three failed attempts to unlock the SIM code, you may need to type in a Personal Unlocking Key (PUK) code in order to unlock your iPhone; if so, contact your cellular carrier's customer service to find out your iPhone's PUK code.

✔ **Carrier Services (depends on iPhone model and carrier):** One-touch speed-dial access for dialing up various phone account–related information like your current bill balance, data and minutes usage, and directory assistance.

Call Forwarding, Call Waiting, and Caller ID Blocking

Some phone-related settings you may want to take advantage of include call forwarding, call waiting, and caller ID blocking. To turn those features on or off for GSM-model iPhones (like the ones that work with AT&T or the unlocked model you can buy at the Apple Store), open the Settings app, tap Phone, and then tap the setting you want to turn on or off. Refer to Figure 1-22.

You have to have cellular service when you turn Call Forwarding on,

Figure 1-22: Change the Phone app settings to suit you.

which means activate Call Forwarding before you go off into the wilderness with your iPhone. If you turn on Call Forwarding, a prompt appears so you can type in the phone number you want your calls forwarded to.

The call forwarding icon appears in the Status Bar when you turn on the Call Forwarding feature on GSM-model iPhones.

Don't forget to turn Call Forwarding off when you no longer want your calls sent to another number; otherwise, you'll be wondering why your iPhone doesn't ring anymore.

Caller ID blocking only works for phone calls; your ID still appears when you make a FaceTime call.

To turn these functions on or off for CMDA-model iPhones like the ones that work with Verizon, use the Phone app's keypad to type in the appropriate special code below for the particular feature you want to manage:

✔ **Call Forwarding on:** Type ***72** followed by the phone number you want your calls forwarded to, and then tap Call.

✔ **Call Forwarding off:** Type ***73**, and then tap Call.

✔ **Call Waiting off for a call you are about to make:** Type ***70**, and then type the number you want to call and tap Call.

✔ **Block Caller ID for a call you're about to make:** Type ***67**, and then dial the number you want to call and tap Call.

On CMDA-model iPhones, you can only turn off call waiting and caller ID blocking on a per-call basis, but you can't turn either feature off for all calls the way you can with GSM-model iPhones.

Doing FaceTime Calls

With FaceTime you can make video calls as well as audio one-to-one or conference calls. FaceTime connects to other iPhones with the phone number or email address, but uses an email address to call FaceTime-enabled Macs, iPod touches, or iPads. And if one of those devices is calling your iPhone, they use the email address associated with your FaceTime ID. Refer to "Adjusting FaceTime settings" later in this section.

Using FaceTime on the cellular network — instead of Wi-Fi — cuts into your data transfer allowance. If you have a cap on your data allowance, you'll want to keep track of how much you're consuming so you don't go over your monthly limit and incur additional charges. A 45-minute FaceTime call consumes roughly 65 megabytes (MB).

Making a FaceTime call

To use FaceTime, both parties need to be connected to a Wi-Fi network (iPhone 5 and later model users can also use FaceTime with a cellular data connection by opening the Settings app, tapping Cellular, and then scrolling down to the section Use Cellular Data For and tapping FaceTime to the On position) and meet one of the following requirements:

✔ You and the person you want to FaceTime with are both using iPhone models that offer the FaceTime feature, and that feature is turned on in the Settings app under FaceTime.

✔ Your iPhone meets the preceding requirement, and the person you want to connect with is using another FaceTime-capable device, such as an iPad 2 or later or a fourth-generation iPod touch or later, or a Mac with FaceTime.

Tap the FaceTime icon on the Home screen and then do one of the following:

✔ Enter a name, email, or mobile phone number in the field at the top of the FaceTime screen. If you type letters that match any names in Contacts, a list of matches appears.

✔ Tap the Contacts button in the upper right and search for the person you want to call in the same way you would to make a phone call.

When you find the person you want, tap the name of the person you want to initiate a FaceTime call with, and then tap the FaceTime audio or video button, whichever type of call you want to place. (If neither button is active, that contact doesn't meet the FaceTime calling requirements.) You see the outgoing call screen and when the person responds, you hear his voice, and see his face if you initiated a video call.

Making FaceTime audio calls

FaceTime audio calls have the same features and functions, such as call waiting and conferencing, as calls made with the Phone app, but you make calls to other iOS devices or Macs over Wi-Fi or cellular data.

Tap the Audio button next to the name of the person you want to call to initiate the call, and when the person responds you see the screen as in Figure 1-23. Tap the buttons to do the following:

✔ **Mute:** Tap to silence your voice.

✔ **Speaker:** Tap to put your caller on speaker.

✔ **Add Call:** Tap to add another person to your call. Contacts opens and you can add someone in the same way you choose a name or type in a number or email to initiate the first call.

✔ **FaceTime:** Tap to switch from a FaceTime audio call to a FaceTime video call.

✔ **Contacts:** Tap to open Contacts and add another person to your call.

Managing a FaceTime video call

When you're engaged in a FaceTime video chat call — that you initiate or accept — the active FaceTime call screen appears, as shown in Figure 1-24. The person you're connected with fills up most of iPhone's screen, while your own mug appears in a tiny window that you can drag to whichever corner you want.

During an active FaceTime video call, you can do a bunch of neat things, including the following:

- ✔ **Changing to Landscape view:** Rotate your iPhone sideways to view your caller in Landscape mode.

- ✔ **Switching cameras:** Tap the Switch Cameras button to switch your live video feed from iPhone's front-facing camera to the higher-resolution rear-facing camera. You can use this feature to show off things around you, like the snoozing kitty in your lap or the snowstorm coming down outside your office window. Tap the Switch Cameras button again to switch back to iPhone's front-facing camera and its focus on you.

- ✔ **Muting your sound:** Tap the Mute icon to squelch the mic on your end of the video

Figure 1-23: Manage FaceTime audio calls as you do calls made with the Phone app.

chat conversation. When you mute your mic, you can still hear sound from the person on the other end of your chat, and they can still see your video. Tap Mute again to allow yourself to be heard again.

- ✔ **Pausing your video:** Tapping Home and switching to another app puts your FaceTime video on hold; the person on the other end will still hear you, but you won't see each other while you're away from the FaceTime screen. Tap the banner that appears at the top of iPhone's screen (as you would in a regular phone call) to return to your FaceTime call, where you'll be both seen and heard once more.

✔ **Capturing a Screenshot:** Press Home and Sleep/Wake at the same time to capture a screenshot of your FaceTime chat; iPhone saves your screenshot in the Photo app's Camera Roll album. (You can capture a screenshot this way in other apps, too, not just in FaceTime.)

Some things to consider when making FaceTime calls:

✔ **During a call:** Tap the FaceTime button in the active call screen to switch a call made with the Phone app to a FaceTime audio or video call.

✔ **Using Siri (or Voice Control):** Press and hold the Home button and then say "FaceTime" followed by the name or number of the person to call.

✔ **Caller ID block:** Your phone number appears when you make a FaceTime call even if you have activated your iPhone's Caller ID Block feature (which we write about in the section "Call Forwarding, Call Waiting, and Caller ID Blocking," earlier in this chapter).

Figure 1-24: The active FaceTime call screen, live and in person (virtually speaking).

The "FaceTime Failed" message appears if a person you try to call isn't using a FaceTime-capable device or FaceTime is turned off on that device.

Accepting a FaceTime call

The FaceTime incoming call screen appears when you receive an incoming FaceTime call invitation, as shown in Figure 1-25. If you're chatting in a FaceTime video or audio call and someone else tries to contact you in FaceTime, you can put the current call on hold and respond to the new incoming call. You can then merge two FaceTime audio calls into a conference call — maybe we'll see FaceTime video conferencing in iOS 9.

Tap Accept or Decline to answer or decline the FaceTime invitation. You can also tap either the Remind Me or Message button to use those features as explained in the section "Declining Calls."

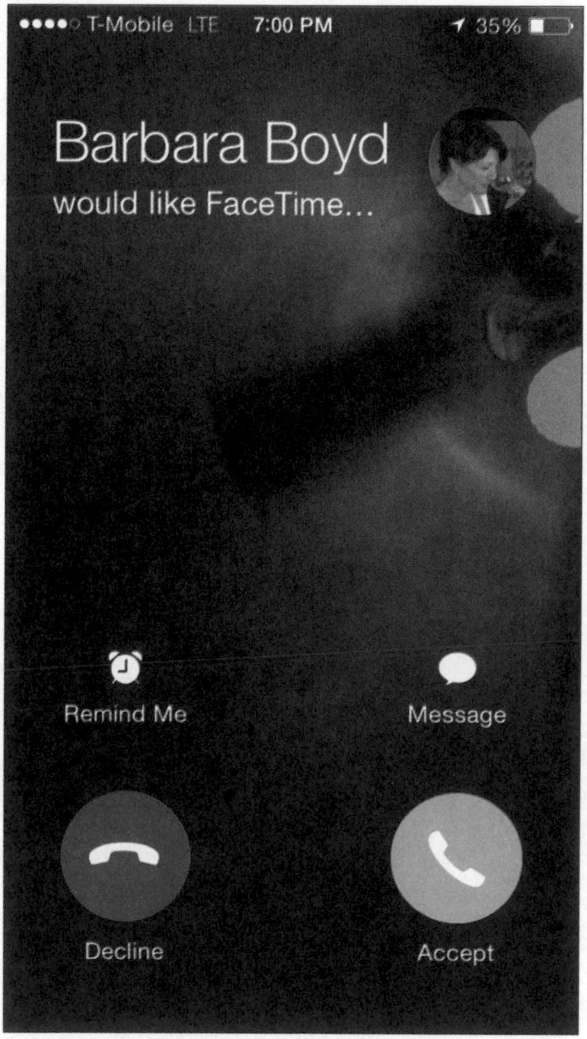

Adjusting FaceTime settings

Just like Phone and most of the other apps on your iPhone, FaceTime has a few settings that you can adjust to your liking. Open the Settings app and tap FaceTime to see the screen shown in Figure 1-26. There, you can do the following:

Figure 1-25: An incoming FaceTime call invitation.

✔ Tap the toggle switch to turn FaceTime Off or On. *Note:* You must be signed in for FaceTime to work. If you try to tap FaceTime On and it doesn't work, tap your Apple ID, enter your password on the screen that follows, and then confirm the phone number and email address where you can be reached via FaceTime.

When you're signed in to your Apple ID account, the following choices appear:

- **Change Location**
- **View Account**
- **Sign Out:** If you sign out, you'll have to sign in again to use FaceTime.

✔ Tap iPhone Cellular Calls on to allow FaceTime to make and receive calls using your cellular data connection; when off, FaceTime only works when you have a Wi-Fi connection.

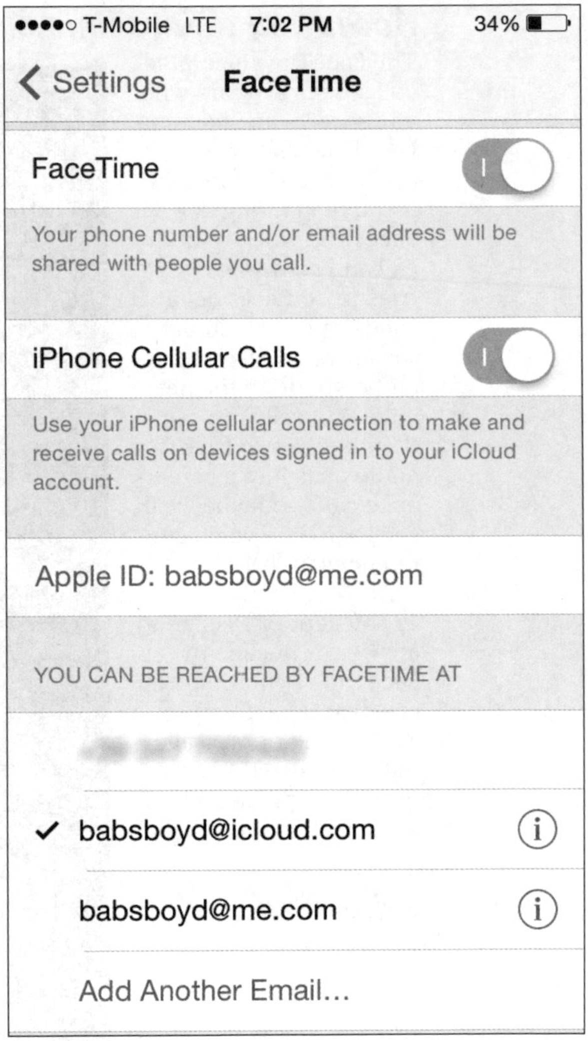

✔ Add email addresses that FaceTime can use to contact you. Under You Can Be Reached by FaceTime At, your cellular phone number is automatically filled in and uneditable. Tap the email address or addresses in the list that you want to use to receive FaceTime requests; a checkmark means that address is used by FaceTime. Tap the Info button to the right to remove the email completely from the list. Tap Add Another Email to do that.

●●●●○ T-Mobile LTE   7:02 PM   34% 🔋
‹ Settings   FaceTime
FaceTime ⬤
Your phone number and/or email address will be shared with people you call.
iPhone Cellular Calls ⬤
Use your iPhone cellular connection to make and receive calls on devices signed in to your iCloud account.
Apple ID: babsboyd@me.com
YOU CAN BE REACHED BY FACETIME AT
▓▓▓▓▓▓▓
✔ babsboyd@icloud.com ⓘ
babsboyd@me.com ⓘ
Add Another Email...

Figure 1-26: Choose the email others can use to reach you via FaceTime.

✔ Tap the phone number or email address you want FaceTime to use as your Caller ID; the identification will appear on the device of the person you're calling when you initiate a FaceTime call.

✔ Tap Blocked to see the list of callers you've blocked from contacting you with Phone, FaceTime, or Messages.

International Calling Options

Using your iPhone to make calls when traveling overseas is typically a very costly proposition. You can make and receive phone calls and send and receive text messages, although often with a roaming surcharge above and beyond your regular phone plan cost. For example, Barbara sends SMS for 10 cents per message when at home and 75 cents per message when overseas, so she tries to limit her text messaging when traveling. Your best plan is to contact your provider before you leave home.

Because data charges are often accidentally activated — and the most exorbitant — we recommend turning off the data roaming feature. Open the Settings app, tap Cellular, and tap Cellular Data to disable that feature and only use Wi-Fi, when available, for your data functions. If your carrier offers Wi-Fi calling, you can call home without paying roaming fees.

Book II
Chapter 1

Managing Phone and FaceTime Calls

Chapter 2: Sending and Receiving Text and Multimedia Messages

In This Chapter

✏ **Setting up for SMS and iMessage messages**

✏ **Using iMessage to text iOS devices and Macs**

✏ **Sending and receiving messages**

✏ **Exchanging media**

✏ **Having group conversations**

Some market research studies say phone calls, voicemail, and email are all being replaced by text messaging. We don't know if that's true, but we do know the Messages app on your iPhone is a powerful communications tool — you can use it to send text messages, images, video, even voice recordings to one person at a time or groups of friends or colleagues.

In this chapter, we show you the different ways you can send messages — traditional Short Message Service (SMS) and Multimedia Message Service (MMS), using Messages, the app that came with your iPhone, as well as iMessage messages, Apple's messaging service, which you exchange with your iDevice — and Mac — user friends. With iMessage, you can begin an exchange (called a *conversation* in Messages lingo) on one device (say, your iPhone) while you're at the bus stop, and then continue it on another (such as your Mac or iPad) when you get home — Apple calls this *continuity.* You can set up groups and set up the next staff meeting or wedding shower. Because messaging has moved beyond text, we show you how to add photos, videos, voice memos, and links to your messages. With all this communicating, we close the chapter with how to manage the messages you've been sending and receiving.

Before all that, however, we give you a quick run-through of the settings for the Messages app.

1:50 PM

New Message

To: Lindsay Konick

Reviewing Messages Features and Adjusting Settings

To understand the Messages features and settings, you should familiarize yourself with the parts of a message, as shown in Figure 2-1. Some of these fields appear only when the feature is turned on in Settings or when you use iMessage.

Figure 2-1: The features of a new message.

- **To field:** Enter names of people you have in Contacts (see Book III, Chapter 1), phone numbers, or email addresses (for iMessage) of whomever you want to send messages to.

- **Contacts:** Tap the plus sign, to the right of the To field, to open and choose recipients from Contacts.

- **Text and Subject fields:** Type your message here; the Subject field within the Text field is a feature you can turn on or off in the Settings app by tapping Messages.

- **Camera button:** Tapping the Camera button lets you add photos or videos to your messages. When sending an iMessage, holding the Camera button lets you instantly record and send a video without opening the Camera app.

- **Microphone button (iMessage only):** Holding this button to the right of the Text field instantly records and sends a voice message.

- **Character count:** This keeps track of how many characters your message contains. Again, this is a feature you can switch on or off in the Settings app. Some service providers limit the length of text messages (SMS or MMS, but not iMessage); if yours does, this option helps you write messages within the limit.

Setting up Messages settings

By now, you're probably familiar with the Settings app. It's where you turn the features for the other iPhone apps on or off. The settings for Messages let you turn iMessage on or off and offer some options that help when composing messages.

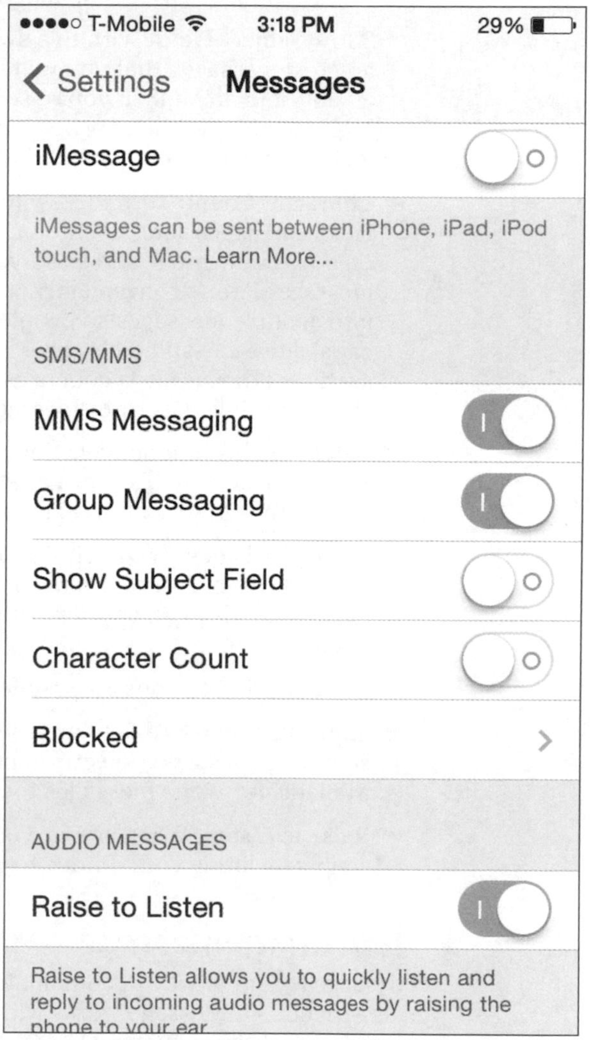

To open Settings for messages, open the Settings app and tap Messages. You'll have to scroll down because Messages is a little way down the list, after iCloud. You see the following options (shown in Figure 2-2):

✔ **iMessage:** Tap this toggle switch on to activate the iMessage service. We explain this service in the "Activating iMessage" section of this chapter.

✔ **MMS Messaging:** With this feature on, you can send and receive photos, video, and voice memos and insert a subject line in the text field. You may

●●●●○ T-Mobile 🛜   3:18 PM   29% 🔋

‹ Settings   Messages

iMessage   ⚪

iMessages can be sent between iPhone, iPad, iPod touch, and Mac. Learn More...

SMS/MMS

MMS Messaging   ⚫

Group Messaging   ⚫

Show Subject Field   ⚪

Character Count   ⚪

Blocked   ›

AUDIO MESSAGES

Raise to Listen   ⚫

Raise to Listen allows you to quickly listen and reply to incoming audio messages by raising the phone to your ear.

Figure 2-2: The Messages Settings screen.

have to enter information from your cellular service provider by opening the Settings app, tapping Cellular, tapping Cellular Data Network, and then going to the MMS section. There may be an additional charge to send MMS messages.

✔ **Group Messaging:** If you turn this on, you send one SMS/MMS message to several people and everyone in the group sees all the responses. With group messaging off, you can still address and send an SMS/MMS to many people but the responses will return only to you, not to the entire group. This option isn't available in all areas. This is different from creating an iMessage group, explained in the next section.

✔ **Show Subject Field:** With this switched on, a subject line appears before any text messages that you write — just like email. However, this turns an SMS into an MMS. If you're sending to someone who doesn't have MMS capabilities, he may not receive your message. If you leave the subject field blank, it remains an SMS, or you can just keep this setting off.

✔ **Character Count:** Turn this switch on in conjunction with Show Subject Field, and a character counter appears to the right of the text-entry field on the New Message screen so you can keep an eye on the length of your message. iPhone conveniently splits messages longer than 160 characters into multiple messages so people with phones that have limited text capabilities can still receive messages from you. The kicker is that each section of the message counts as one message, meaning one three-part message is billed as three messages.

✔ **Blocked:** This function lets you enter phone numbers you don't want to receive calls, messages, or FaceTime from. If you block numbers from Phone, FaceTime, or Contacts, they appear here as well.

✔ **Message History:** Tap to choose how long you want your message threads saved: 30 days, 1 year, or forever. Messages are saved to iCloud, which makes it available to any current or future devices signed in to the same iCloud account.

The following options are visible when iMessage is active:

✔ **Expire:** Choose to delete or save incoming and outgoing audio messages sent with iMessage. Select 2 minutes or never. The same function is available for video messages too.

✔ **Raise to Listen:** When active, you can listen and reply to audio iMessages simply by lifting your iPhone to your ear.

Activating iMessage

iMessage is a great way to communicate with your iDevice-toting and Mac-using friends — iMessage works with iPhones, iPads, iPod touches, and Macs (at least those running OS X 10.8 or later). iMessage automatically enters your phone number; you should also associate your Apple ID with iMessage, which lets your other devices and Macs receive and respond to regular SMS messages sent to your cellular number, too.

To set up iMessage, follow these steps:

1. **Open the Settings app, tap Messages, and tap the switch next to iMessage to turn it on.**

    If the left half of the switch is green, iMessage is already on.

2. **When prompted, enter the password associated with the Apple ID you use on your iPhone and tap OK.**

   If you don't see a password prompt, tap Use Your Apple ID for iMessage, type your password, and then tap Sign In.

   Your Apple ID is verified, and you're signed in to iMessage.

When iMessage is on, you have the following additional Messages Settings options:

- ✔ **Send Read Receipts:** When turned on, people who send you messages will be notified when you read their sent message.

- ✔ **Send As SMS:** If iMessage is unavailable, your message is sent as an SMS message. Your cellular service plan may charge an extra fee for SMS.

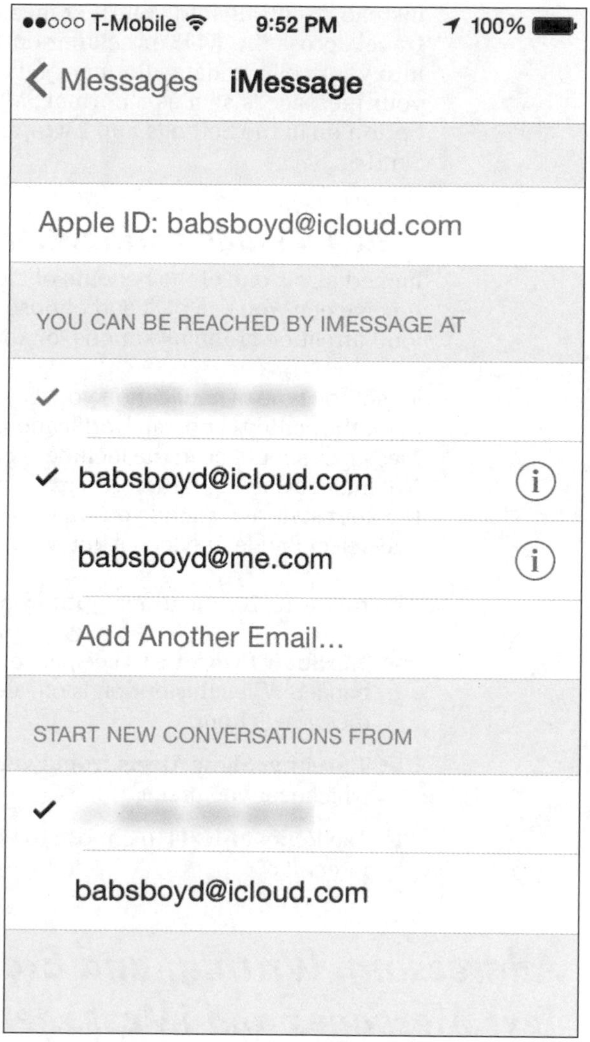

- ✔ **Send & Receive:** Add additional email addresses where you want to receive iMessages (in addition to your mobile phone number and Apple ID). When you tap Send & Receive, the iMessage screen opens, as shown in Figure 2-3. To add another email address, tap Add Another Email.

●●○○○ T-Mobile 🛜   9:52 PM   ⚡ 100% 🔋

❮ Messages   **iMessage**

Apple ID: babsboyd@icloud.com

YOU CAN BE REACHED BY IMESSAGE AT

✔ ▓▓▓▓▓▓▓

✔ babsboyd@icloud.com   ⓘ

babsboyd@me.com   ⓘ

Add Another Email…

START NEW CONVERSATIONS FROM

✔ ▓▓▓▓▓▓▓

babsboyd@icloud.com

Figure 2-3: Send unlimited iMessages to other iOS devices and Macs — for free!

After iMessage is activated, your iPhone takes care of everything for you. It immediately recognizes phone numbers and email addresses associated with iOS devices or Macs used by people in your Contacts. When available, Messages uses iMessage rather than traditional SMS or MMS. You know you have an iMessage connection because when you type a contact's name or phone number, it shows up blue.

Instead of cutting into your text message allotment, iMessage messages travel across the Wi-Fi or cellular data airwaves (with the latter it does cut into your cellular data allotment). If an Internet connection isn't available, your message is sent as a normal SMS or MMS, as long as you turned that option on in the Settings app by tapping Messages and then turning on Send as SMS.

New message notification and alert

Immediacy is one of the benefits of messages, so you'll want to know when you receive one. You can pick and choose between silent visual notifications and loud attention-grabbing sounds, or some combination and variation of both.

To set the type of notification you want to receive when a new message arrives, open the Settings app, tap Notifications, and then tap Messages. By default, Messages should be in the Include section; if you don't see it, scroll down to Do Not Include and tap it there. As explained in detail in Book I, Chapter 4, choose the alert style and sound you want to see and hear when a new message arrives and select Badge App Icon if you want that type of notification as well.

The following Notifications options are specific to Messages:

- Tap **Show Previews** to see part of the incoming message on the alert or banner. When this option is off, alerts show the name or phone number the message is from.

- Tap either **Show Alerts from Everyone** or **Show Alerts from My Contacts,** whichever you prefer.

- Tap **Repeat Alerts** to choose to hear the alert up to ten times at two-minute intervals.

Addressing, Writing, and Exchanging Text Messages and iMessages

Now that you're set up, you're ready to send a text message. It's not so different from sending an email, if you're familiar with that form of communication. You address your message, type it, and send it. Here are the steps:

1. **Tap the Messages icon on the Home screen.**

2. **Tap the Compose button in the upper-right corner. It's the one that looks like a pencil and a piece of paper.**

   A New Message screen opens.

3. **Address and write your message as explained in the following section.**

4. **Tap the Send button.**

Addressing your message

When you open a New Message screen by tapping the Compose button, the keyboard is active and the cursor is in the To field, where you fill in the name, number, or iMessage-enabled email address of the person you want to send your message to. Do one of the following to address your message:

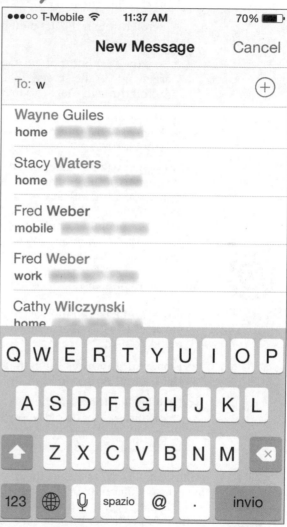

- ✔ Tap the 123 button in the lower-left corner of the keyboard to change the top row of letters to numbers. Type the phone number.

- ✔ If the person you want to send the message to is stored in Contacts, begin typing the recipient's name in the To field. Names of people or companies in Contacts that contain the typed letters show up as a list from which you can choose. Your choices narrow as you type more letters (see Figure 2-4). The phone number is listed under the con-

Figure 2-4: Begin typing the first letters of your recipient's name; Messages searches Contacts to find matches.

tact's name and if a contact has more than one phone number, his name is listed with each phone number. You can see that Fred Weber has two phone numbers. Blue phone numbers or email addresses indicate an iMessage-enabled contact.

✔ Tap the Contacts (+) button in the upper-right corner, which opens Contacts. Find the name you want by doing one of the following:

- Scroll through the list until you find the name of the person you want to send a message to.

- Tap the first letter of the name in the alphabet that runs down the right side of the screen to jump to names beginning with that letter. Scroll through that section to find the person you're searching for.

- Tap in the Search field. Type the name of the person you're looking for. Matches pop up when you type the first letter and diminish as you narrow your search by typing more letters.

After you've found it, tap the name of the person you want to send a message to. If the contact has just one phone number, when you tap the name, you automatically return to the New Message screen and the name of the recipient will be in the To field. If the contact has more than one phone number or also has an email address, the contact information opens. Tap the number you want to send the message to, and you'll bounce back to the New Message screen.

You can send messages from other apps or the App Switcher, too:

✔ From Contacts, tap the Text Message button next to a phone number or email address to open a New Message screen with your chosen contact in the To field.

✔ From your Favorites list in the Phone app, tap the Info button on the right, and then scroll down and tap the Text Message button.

✔ Double-click the Home button to open the App Switcher, which shows icons across the top of the screen for people in your Favorites and Recents lists. Tap the person you want to send the message to, and then tap the Text Message button.

A blue email address means the message can be sent via iMessage and travels over the cellular data or Wi-Fi network. Tapping a gray email address creates an MMS message, which may cost more than an SMS. If you only have that option, you're better off sending a message from the Mail app, as explained in Book II, Chapter IV.

If you want to send your message to more than one person, type in a phone number or name or tap the plus sign (+) button, and repeat the steps you used to add the first person. (See the section "Working in Groups," later in this chapter, for more information.)

Writing your message

After you've entered the names of the message recipients, tap Return. The cursor moves to the Text field:

1. **Type your message.**

   To ask Siri to write and send your message, tap the Dictation button to the left of the spacebar and speak your message instead of typing it. (Refer to Book I, Chapter 3.)

   Any features you activated for the keyboard in the Settings app, such as Auto-Correction or Enable Caps Lock, are active in Messages, as are specific language keyboards. Tap the globe button to switch between keyboard languages. If you haven't added any languages, you see an Emoji smiley-face icon. Tap either the globe or Emoji icon to switch to a different language or add emoticons to your message.

   If you need to edit your message, the Text field has the same functions for typing as other apps, as explained in Book I, Chapter 3.

2. **When you've finished typing your message, tap the Send button and it's on its way.**

   You'll see a progress bar at the top of the screen and hear a whooping sound when the message has been sent.

Receiving and replying to Messages

Ding-ding! You've got a message. Or your iPhone may only vibrate and you may or may not see a banner or alert on the screen, depending on the notification and alert settings you choose.

After you've received a message, you'll want to read it and maybe respond. Here's how to read your messages:

1. **If you set up a banner to appear on your Lock screen, swipe across it to open the incoming message, or tap Messages on the Home screen.**

   An unread message has a blue dot next to it. Threads you mark as Do Not Disturb have a quarter moon next to them.

   In the Messages list (refer to Figure 2-5), you'll see the name or number of the person or entity who sent the message, when it was sent, and the first two lines of the message.

   After an exchange begins, you see the last message exchanged regardless of who sent it, so if you sent a response to someone, you see the first two lines of your response next to the name of the sender.

2. **Tap the message and a message screen opens, displaying the whole message.**

   The text of an incoming iMessage is in a blue bubble; that of an SMS is in a green bubble.

3. **Tap once in the Text field.**

   The keyboard opens.

4. **Type your message.**

5. **Tap Send.**

As with a message you initiated, you see a Sending progress bar and you hear a sound indicating that the message has been sent — unless you have those sounds turned off.

If you choose Banner as the alert style in the Notifications section of the Settings app, a banner appears at the top of your iPhone screen when a message arrives while you're working in another app. You can ignore the banner, and it will disappear in a few seconds or swipe the banner down to send a quick response without leaving the app you're in. A text field and keyboard appear on top of the active app; type your reply and tap Send. Your reply is sent and you return to what you were doing.

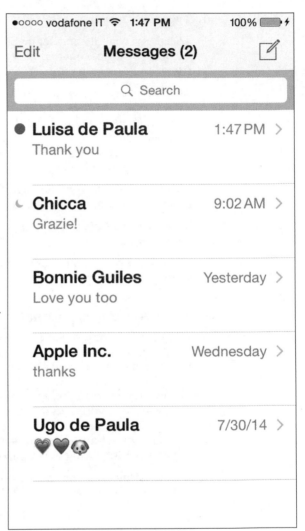

Instead of responding with a message, you can choose to place a voice or FaceTime call to the

Figure 2-5: The Messages list shows read and unread messages you've sent and received.

person. Tap Details in the upper-right corner of an open message and do one of the following:

- ✔ To call, tap the Call button at the top of the screen and then choose Voice Call or FaceTime Audio.

- ✔ To communicate via FaceTime, tap the FaceTime button. We explain FaceTime in Book II, Chapter 1.

✔ Tap the Info (i) button to call a number different from the one used for the message exchange or view and edit the person's information in Contacts.

✔ If you want to check out of the conversation for a while, tap the switch next to Do Not Disturb. The messages will arrive but you won't hear or see alerts. You can then read the messages when you want to.

If you're writing a message and you need to refer to something in the incoming message, or earlier in the conversation, you can scroll through the conversation. To free up more of the screen, touch the background (a non-message part of the screen) just above the text field and flick down to hide the keyboard, giving you more viewing room to scroll through the conversation. Tap in the Text field to bring the keyboard back.

When your iPhone is unable to receive incoming calls, it's also unable to send or receive SMS and MMS messages. Whether it's in Airplane mode, out of range of your carrier's cellular network, or powered off, notifications, badges, and sounds for any new SMS or MMS messages won't appear until your iPhone is able to receive calls — and messages — again. If you try to send a message and it doesn't reach its destination, an alert badge that looks like an exclamation point appears on the Messages icon on the Home screen. (iMessage and FaceTime still work if you have Wi-Fi service.)

A received message has information about a person or company that you can store in Contacts. To add a new name and phone number or new information to an existing contact, tap the message to open it, and then tap the Details button. Tap the Info (i) button and then choose Create New Contact or Add Existing Contact. Contacts opens and you can do either of those tasks as explained in Book III, Chapter 1.

Most people have MMS-enabled cellphones these days, but some people can't receive MMS messages, either because of the type of phone hardware or because of their cellular service contract. They'll still receive the message, but not the media, and they may receive a link to open the media in a web browser.

Adding media to your message

You can take stunning photos and video with your iPhone, but what fun is it to keep them to yourself? You can share your artistic expression and memories with the folks you know with MMS or iMessage messages. Here's how:

1. **Tap Messages on the Home screen, and then tap the Compose button.**

2. **Fill in the To field as described in the previous section.**

   If your recipient uses iOS 5 or later, your MMS may be sent with iMessage if the iMessage requirements are met.

3. **Tap the Camera button.**

Thumbnail images of recent photos appear along with three buttons — Photo Library, Take Photo or Video, and Cancel (see Figure 2-6).

4. **Do one of the following to include a photo or video with your message:**

- Tap the thumbnail of one or more photos or videos you want to send, and then tap one of the buttons that appear to either send the photo(s) or add a comment, after which you tap Send to send the message.

- Tap Photo Library to open the Photos app. Scroll through your images, tap the one you want to send, and then tap Choose.

- Tap Take Photo or Video to open the camera and then tap the Camera

●●●●○ T-Mobile 🛜	1:33 PM	62% ◼️◻️

New Message   Cancel

To: Marvi Nargi,   ⊕

Photo Library

Take Photo or Video

Cancel

Figure 2-6: Tap Take Photo or Video to insert a new image.

button at the bottom of the screen. The photo or video is taken and a Preview screen opens. You have the option of retaking the photo or video by tapping Retake in the lower-left corner, or using the photo or video by tapping Use Photo/Video in the lower-right corner. If you don't like the photo or video, tap Retake and try again, and again, and again until you have a photo or video you like.

5. **After you choose a photo from the library or take a photo or video, Messages opens and your photo or video appears in the Text field and the cursor blinks next to the image, as shown in Figure 2-7.**

6. **Type your message and tap Send.**

   You see a Sending progress bar and you hear the sound that lets you know the message has been sent.

If the Camera button is grayed and inactive, make sure MMS Messaging is On in Messages Settings. You can still send photos and videos with iMessage when MMS Messaging is Off.

To learn about sending photos and videos directly from the Photos app, go to Book IV, Chapter 1.

Figure 2-7: Include comments with the images you send.

Book II
Chapter 2

Sending and Receiving Text and Multimedia Messages

As with most things, you have to pay a price for messaging. Depending on the phone plan you have, you may pay a per-message fee (usually around 20 cents) for sending and receiving SMS or MMS, or you can opt for a bundled flat fee for a limited, or sometimes unlimited, number of messages per month. One message to 25 recipients doesn't count as one message but 25 messages, so keep your plan in mind when doing group sends to avoid unpleasant end-of-the-month invoice surprises. And remember iMessage messages don't count toward text messaging limits because they go through Apple.

Sending and receiving map locations, web page links, and more

The Share Sheet (refer to Figure 2-10) opens when you tap the Share button in many iPhone apps. You find it in Maps, Safari, Notes, and Photos. Likewise, to spread the word about a great new find from the iTunes Store or an interesting interview from Podcasts, tap the Share button. Tapping Messages on the Share Sheet opens a new message that contains the link to whatever it is you want to share. Address the message and tap Send.

Receiving links to locations or websites is just as easy as sending them. If you receive messages that have URLs embedded in them, the links are active, which means you can just tap them, right in the message, and Safari opens to the linked page, Maps opens to the location, iTunes opens to the album, and so on.

To rearrange the icons you see on the Share Sheet, scroll horizontally on the apps or services until you see the More button. Tap More. On the next screen, tap and hold the rearrange button to the right of the app or service you want to move, and then drag the app or service up or down the list. Tap Done when the items are in the order you want, and the Share Sheet will reflect the changes you made.

You can also share your location with a person or group by tapping the conversation to open it and then tapping the Details button. Tap Send My Current Location to send a map showing where you are as a message or tap Share My Location to send a map that will change as your location changes. You can share your location for an hour, until the end of the day, or indefinitely. After sharing, tap Stop Sharing My Location if you don't want the person to know where you are.

Sending audio and video iMessages

When you tap the dictation button on the Messages keyboard, you dictate your message but it's sent as a written text message. With iOS 8, you can send recorded voice and video messages to your iMessage-enabled contacts with the following steps:

1. **Touch and hold the Voice Message button (the microphone next to the text field) and begin speaking, as shown in Figure 2-8.**

   If you want to cancel your message before sending it, lift your finger, and then tap the X to the left.

   To send an instant video, touch and hold the Camera button to the left of the text field. Tap the Record button (the red circle) and begin recording. Tap the Stop button (the red square) to end recording.

2. **(Optional.) Tap the Play button to hear or see what you recorded before sending it.**

3. **Tap or swipe up to the Send button (the upward pointing arrow) to deliver your message.**

4. **The recording appears as an outgoing message in the conversation.**

If you receive an audio message, raise your iPhone to your ear or tap the Play button to listen to it.

Choose to delete your instant recordings after two minutes or never in the Messages Settings.

Saving media you receive

If someone sends you an image or video, you might want to save it outside Messages. Tap the conversation in the Messages list that holds the image you want to save and

Figure 2-8: Send audio recordings.

Book II
Chapter 2

Sending and Receiving Text and Multimedia Messages

then do one of the following to add the image or video to the Photos app on your iPhone:

✔ Tap the Details button in the upper-right corner of the message. All the images and videos that have been exchanged with that person appear in the Attachments section at the bottom of the screen, as shown in Figure 2-9. Scroll through to find the image you want and tap it once to open it in full-screen view. Tap it again to activate the Share button or swipe through all the attachments. Tap the Share button for the image you want, and then tap Save Image on the Share Sheet.

✔ Tap the image in the speech bubble, and then tap the Share button in the upper right and choose Save Image on the Share Sheet, as shown in Figure 2-10.

Working in Groups

As mentioned when we explained how to address messages, you can send the same text message to more than one person. With an SMS you communicate with all the recipients, but they don't communicate with each other — unless you turn on Group Messaging in the Messages settings. With Group Messaging, sent and received messages, along with any attached media, are seen by all group members.

If you create a group with your iMessage friends (those who have an iDevice or Mac), you have additional options. Tap the conversation in the message list, and then tap the Details button to do the following, as shown in Figure 2-11:

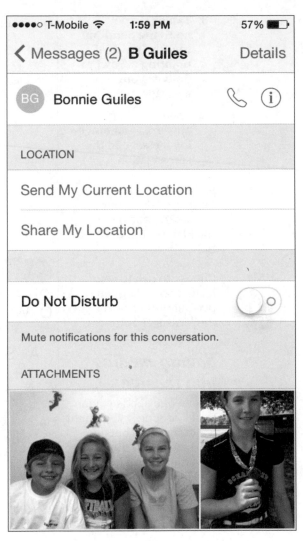

Figure 2-9: Details show all the attachments exchanged with that person.

- ✓ **Name the group:** Tap the Subject field, and then type a name for the conversation so you can easily find it in the Messages list.

- ✓ **Add people to the group:** Tap Add Contact to open a list of people you've exchanged messages with, and then tap the name of the person you want to add to the group.

- ✓ **Delete members:** Swipe across the name of the person you want to remove, and then tap the Delete button that appears.

✔ **Leave the conversation:** Tap the Leave This Conversation button to exit from the group.

 Text messaging can be overwhelming if you're trying to accomplish anything. The message comes through, you respond, they respond, you respond, and pretty soon it's lunchtime. If you want to keep your iPhone active but drop out of a conversation for a while, tap the Details button while viewing that conversation and then tap Do Not Disturb to the On position. The messages will arrive but alerts will be silent.

Figure 2-10: The Share Sheet lets you add images and videos to Photos.

Saving and Deleting Messages

As you send and receive messages, they stack up in reverse chronological order within the Messages app — what we've been referring to as the Messages list (refer to Figure 2-5).

Ongoing conversations

Incoming and outgoing messages exchanged with the same person are called *conversations* — notice that the icon for Messages is a conversation bubble. You see the name of the person you've exchanged messages with in the Messages list. Tap that name and you see all the messages you've exchanged with that person. Received messages are shown in grayed conversation bubbles on the left. Sent messages are on the right in green or blue conversation bubbles. If you're in the middle of an iMessage exchange, an ellipsis indicates that the other person is writing.

TIP

Drag your finger to the left to reveal timestamps for each message of the exchange.

TECHNICAL STUFF

SMS, MMS, and iMessage messages are all listed in Messages, and sometimes all three types appear in a conversation with the same person. This happens when you send a message to someone who has iMessage capabilities but the outgoing or incoming message was sent or received as an SMS because of technical difficulties, which could be one of the following: the data connection was substandard (2G or E) and the option to use SMS when iMessage isn't available was enabled in Settings or the phone number used wasn't associated with the iCloud account.

Only the most recent message is shown in the Messages list, whereas the most recent 50 messages are shown in the conversation. You can download older messages by scrolling up (dragging your finger down)

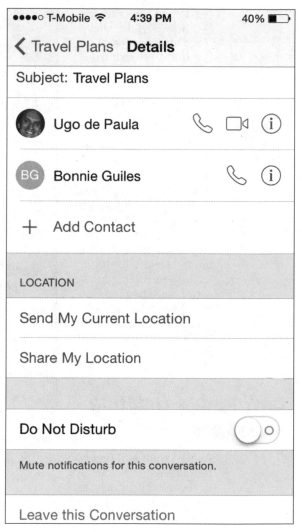

Figure 2-11: Create interactive group conversations with iMessage.

through the previous messages. The newest message is displayed at the bottom — Messages opens to show this message — so if you scroll to the top of the screen, you can read from top to bottom and follow the conversation as it occurred.

Deleting messages

Text messages often contain information of fleeting importance, so you probably don't want to keep them and clutter up your Messages list. You can delete messages that are part of the conversation or the entire conversation with all its exchanges.

To delete only parts of the conversation, press and hold the message you want to delete until you see two tabs above it: Copy and More. Tap More. A check mark appears next to the selected message and empty circles appear to the left of all the other messages of the conversation. Tap others if you want to delete more than one message, and then tap the Delete button (the trash can) at the bottom left of the screen. All the messages with a check mark next to them are deleted. If you tap Delete All in the upper left, the entire conversation is deleted, whether you select single messages or not. A blank message remains in the Messages list so you can quickly send a message and begin a new conversation with that person.

**Book II
Chapter 2**

**Sending and Receiving
Text and Multimedia
Messages**

Select messages in the same way to forward them to someone else, but tap the Forward button in the lower-right corner instead of the Delete button and then address the message to the person to whom you want to forward it.

There are two ways to delete complete conversations: You can use either a two-step method or a three-step method. After a message is deleted, it's gone, so if you want an extra step to think about what you're about to delete, use the three-step method:

- ✔ Tap Edit and red circles with hyphens appear next to each message. Tap the circle next to the message you want to delete. The circle rotates 90 degrees and a Delete button appears to the right of the message. Tap the Delete button and poof! The message is gone.

- ✔ If, on the other hand, you don't worry about deleting something by mistake, use the two-step method. Swipe across the entry for the message you want to delete. A Delete button appears next to that message. Tap the button and the message is deleted.

You can search for text within messages in the Messages list by using the Search box at the very top of the list. Just type the specific word or phrase you're searching for and tap the Search button on the keyboard.

Messages can be automatically deleted after 30 days or 1 year by selecting either option when you tap Settings, then tap Messages, then tap Keep Messages.

Chapter 3: Surfing the Web with Safari

In This Chapter

⤙ **Touring Safari's features**

⤙ **Opening and viewing web pages**

⤙ **Filling out forms**

⤙ **Managing bookmarks**

⤙ **Adding web apps and clips to your Home screen**

⤙ **Adjusting general and security settings**

One of the reasons you bought an iPhone was probably its online capabilities, namely surfing the web and accessing email. In this chapter, we talk about using Safari, your iPhone's browser app. We begin with a guided tour, pointing out basic features and ways you use Safari to browse web pages. Then we walk you through opening and viewing pages, showing you neat things along the way to make viewing web pages easier.

We show you the ins and outs of using Safari's Search feature to find web pages you're looking for — and to find things on those web pages. And finally, we conclude this chapter by giving you a rundown of Safari settings you may want to adjust to make your web surfing experience smoother — and safer.

If web browsing is old hat to you, you may want to skip ahead to the "Playing Favorites with Bookmarks" and "Accessing Websites from the Home Screen" sections, which explain some nifty features you may not be familiar with.

Surfin' Safari Tour

Websites comprise web pages. On your iPhone, when you open a web page (which we explain in an upcoming section), it opens in a new tab. As you tap links on that web page, you remain on the same tab, but if you open a new web page, a new tab opens.

After you tap the Safari button on the Home screen, you see the Safari screen divided into three zones: the title bar, the web page, and the toolbar. Refer to Figure 3-1 for the following explanations:

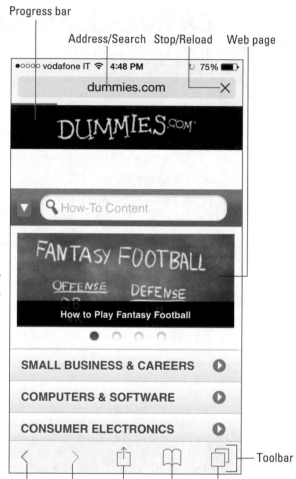

Figure 3-1: The Safari web browser screen displaying a web page.

↝ **Address/Search field:** Tap here to make the keyboard appear, so you can type a URL or type a few words that describe what you're searching for, such as a restaurant, a fact, or a person. (URL stands for Uniform Resource Locator and is the electronic address for a web page.)

Google is the default search engine that Safari uses to find things you search for using the Search field, but if you prefer Yahoo!, Bing, or DuckDuckGo, open the Settings app, tap Safari, tap Search Engine, and pick your preferred search engine.

You can ask Siri to search for you: Press and hold the Home button until you hear Siri ask how it can help you, and then speak your request or question.

↝ **Stop/Reload button:** A dual-purpose button you can tap to stop a web page from loading, or to reload an already loaded web page to see any new information that may have been updated on that web page.

As soon as you begin scrolling through a web page, the toolbar disappears and the address becomes a miniscule line beneath the Status bar. Just tap the Status bar at the top of iPhone's screen or lightly swipe down the screen to make the toolbar and Address/Search field reappear.

✔ **Web page:** Below the Address/Search field, you see the bulk of the web page content.

Across the bottom of the screen, you find the toolbar that displays buttons for the following functions:

✔ **Previous/Next (arrows):** Previous goes back to the previous web page you viewed in this tab; Next moves you Forward to the web page you just left when you tapped Previous. One or both buttons may be dim until you navigate away from the current web page you're viewing. Previous will be dim when you haven't visited a URL earlier on this tab or you've tapped your way back to the first URL visited. Next is dim if you haven't tapped Previous. Pressing and holding either button reveals the viewing history for the tab; you can tap to return to the page you want to see.

✔ **Share:** Opens the Share Sheet and displays options for sharing or doing something with the current web page you're viewing. See the section "Tapping into Web Page Links" later in this chapter for a full explanation.

✔ **Bookmarks:** Displays the Bookmarks screen, which holds a list of links that give you quick access to web pages you want to revisit. Reading List, (viewing) History, and Shared Links are listed in Bookmarks, too. We dedicate a whole section to bookmarks later in this chapter.

✔ **Tabs:** Lets you scroll through open web pages and move quickly from one to another.

Opening web pages

There are many ways to open a web page, and we go through each one here. Your iPhone needs to be connected to a Wi-Fi network or your cellular provider's data network in order to follow along with all the Safari goodness contained within these pages. Start with these steps:

1. **Tap Safari on the Home screen.**

   The Safari screen appears, and you see either the Favorites screen with a few pre-established favorite bookmarks or the last website you viewed the last time you used Safari.

2. **Do one of the following:**

   Tap the Address/Search field: The keyboard appears as shown in Figure 3-2; type the web address of a web page you want to view, or type whatever you're searching for, and then tap Go. As soon as you begin typing, Safari displays a list of potential matches for either a URL or a search criterion. If you see what you want in the list, you can tap that instead of tapping Go. Safari then displays the web page or search results for the text you typed in.

   Tap a Favorite button: The bookmarks you've nominated as Favorites appear when you tap the Address/Search field. The first four as shown in Figure 3-2 are pre-established (and we show you how to delete, add, and rearrange them in the section "Playing Favorites with Bookmarks").

Tap the Bookmarks button: Tap a web page bookmark you want to open. Safari displays the web page for the bookmark you tapped.

3. **Interact with the web page by scrolling through it, tapping links or buttons, or typing in fields.**

   We explain more things to do on a web page in the section "Navigating Web Pages," or you can repeat Step 2 to go to another web page.

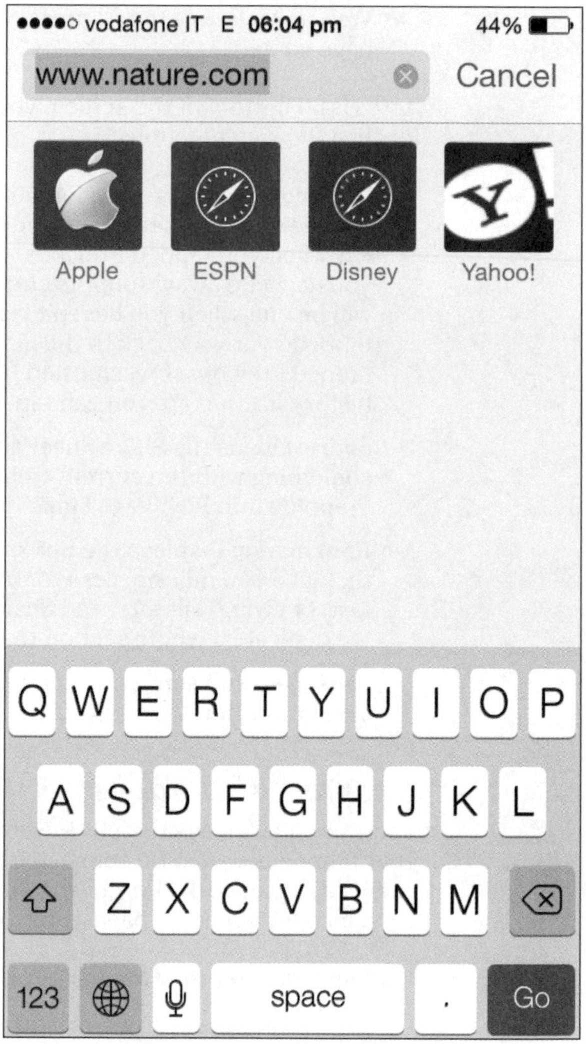

Safari keyboard tips and tricks

Typing in and editing the Safari Address/Search field is the same as typing in any other app on your iPhone, such as Notes or Calendar: Type as you

Figure 3-2: Type a URL or search criteria or tap a Favorite to open a web page.

would on any keyboard, tap and hold in the field to bring up the loupe and move the cursor within the text, release your finger to bring up editing commands such as Cut, Copy, and Paste, and tap the X on the right side of the field to erase the text within.

Here are a few other tips and tricks that can help you maximize your Safari keyboard experience, while minimizing how much typing you actually have to do:

✔ **Skip the www.** If you know the URL, type it without the "www" in the Address field and Safari presents a list of potential matches. Same goes for the ".com" suffix.

✔ **Press to complete.** Tap and hold the dot (".") button to display a list of domain extensions (.net, .edu, .org, .com, or one of the other choices), and then drag your finger to the one you want and let go to fill in that choice.

✔ **Use the landscape keyboard.** Rotate your iPhone sideways to display the wider-reaching landscape keyboard for easier, more accurate typing.

✔ **Call on Siri.** Tap the Dictation button (the microphone) on the keyboard and tell Siri the URL you want to visit or a word or two about the topic you want to search.

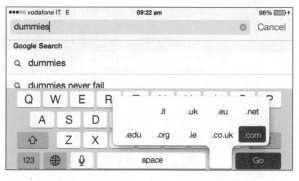

✔ **Use AutoFill.** Use Safari's AutoFill feature to automatically fill in common fields such as name, address, and phone number fields, email address fields, and username and password fields. We tell you about AutoFill later in this chapter.

You don't need to tap the erase button to clear the Address field before you type the web page address you want to open. Tap the Address field and begin typing the web address you want to open; the field is automatically erased. (Don't tap and hold, which inserts a blinking cursor allowing you to edit the existing URL.)

Stopping and reloading web pages

Whichever way you choose to open a web page, after Safari actually begins loading the web page, a trio of visual cues appears to let you know Safari is processing your request. Those cues include a blue progress bar in the Address field, the Reload button changing to the Stop button, and the twirling network activity icon in the Status bar.

You can stop or reload a web page by doing one of the following:

✔ Tap the Stop button if you want to immediately stop loading a web page.

✔ Tap the Reload button if you lose your network connection and Safari stops loading the page.

✔ Tap the Reload button to reload the web page and display any new information that may have been added to the web page since you began viewing it (such as the latest-breaking news on a news web page).

Viewing Web Pages

When the web page appears, you're free to move about the cabin — er, we mean view the web page — in any number of free-ranging ways.

Using full-screen and portrait views

When it comes to viewing web pages, Safari lets you use the entire real estate of your iPhone screen. As mentioned at the beginning of the chapter, as soon as you begin scrolling through a web page, the Address/Search field and toolbar go into hiding. You may want to change your point of view depending on the page you're viewing: Hold your iPhone upright for portrait orientation view (taller than it is wide) and turn it 90 degrees to use landscape orientation view (wider than it is tall), as shown in Figure 3-3.

Landscape view is particularly useful when you want to watch video on a web page.

Figure 3-3: Rotating iPhone sideways displays the landscape view, here in its full-screen glory.

 If you see the Portrait Orientation Lock icon in the top-right corner of the Status bar, turning your iPhone on its side won't switch your web page to the wide-screen landscape view. To turn the Portrait Orientation Lock feature off or on, drag up from the bottom of the screen to open the Control Center, and then tap the Portrait Orientation Lock icon to toggle that feature on or off.

Viewing desktop versions

Many websites have both full and mobile versions, so what you're used to seeing on your computer, beyond being smaller, may look completely different on your iPhone.

The notion behind "mobile" web pages is that they minimize graphics and much of the other extraneous "stuff" that normally appears on the desktop version of the web page, so as to make it easier for you to navigate those web pages on your mobile device — in this case, your iPhone. If a website has a mobile version, it will gauge whether the web browser you're using is a desktop browser or a mobile browser and automatically present the version that's right for you. After you arrive on the site, you may be given a choice to switch to the other version of the site — you usually find this at the bottom of the page with a toggle switch or a link to the mobile or full version.

If the mobile version opens automatically but you want to view the desktop version, Safari has a feature that lets you choose. Tap the Address field at the top of the screen and then swipe down from the middle of the screen. Two choices appear: Add to Favorites or Request Desktop Site, as shown in Figure 3-4. Tap Request Desktop Site.

Using Reader

If you see a Reader button (four horizontal lines in the left end of the Address field), you can view the article in Reader. Reader displays the text of the article on a plain white page without any of the ambient noise that surrounds it on the web page itself, as shown in Figure 3-5. Tap the small or large "A" at the top left of the article to change the type size. Tap the Reader button again to return to the regular web page view.

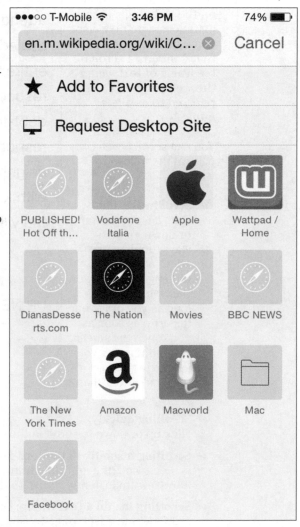

Figure 3-4: Switch to a website's desktop version.

Scrolling web pages

One thing you do a lot of when you're viewing a web page is scrolling — up, down, and sometimes all around — to see all the information on the web page. In rare instances, you may also come across a web page that contains a scrollable frame of text *within* the web page — which is referred to as a *text frame*.

You can scroll a web page in the following ways:

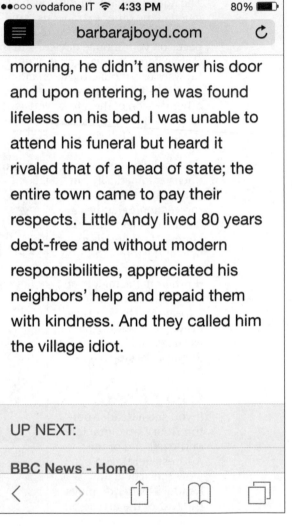

Figure 3-5: Reader makes reading web articles easier.

✔ **Scrolling carefully:** Drag a web page up or down, or sideways; don't worry about accidentally tapping something on the web page — as long as you drag your fingertip as soon as you touch the screen, Safari interprets your gesture as a scroll (or flick) rather than a tap.

✔ **Scrolling quickly:** Flick up or down to scroll in those directions more quickly.

✔ **Scrolling instantly to the top:** Tap the Status bar at the top of iPhone's screen twice (the first time brings the toolbar and Address/Search field into view) to instantly return to the top of a web page.

✔ **Scrolling inside a text frame:** Drag two fingers up or down in a text frame within a web page to scroll just the text in that frame up or down.

Zooming web pages

Using Safari's zoom view features can make scrolling web pages (and text frames within web pages) easier on your eyes — and fingertips. Safari's zoom in and out features make it easy to narrow your focus on just the section that you want to view.

You can zoom in and out of web pages by doing the following:

- ✔ **Double-tap zooming:** Double-tap on a web page to zoom in or out. The cool thing is, Safari understands what you tapped and zooms appropriately. For example, double-tap text and the text zooms only as large as the width of your iPhone so you don't have to scroll left to right to read, whereas double-tap an image and it zooms in to the maximum width of the screen. For a wider view, turn your iPhone to landscape position. Double-tap again to zoom out.

- ✔ **Spread and pinch zooming:** Spread two fingers apart or pinch together to zoom out or in to a web page.

Double-tapping only works after the web page is fully loaded, but spread and pinch works even while the page is loading. If you have a Wi-Fi or 4G/LTE connection, this doesn't really matter, but if you have a slower connection, it can explain why double-tapping isn't working.

Although you can always zoom in and out of any full-size web page on iPhone's screen, not all mobile versions of certain websites allow zooming.

Navigating Web Pages

When you open and view a web page, more often than not, you don't stay on that one web page. Web pages contain links, which can be words or buttons or graphics, that you tap to open other web pages that contain more links, and all those links weave a web of pages that seems infinite. One tap leads to another tap, and pretty soon you've spent your whole morning learning about the habits and habitats of the wild boar that decimated your neighbor's wheat field the previous evening. Barbara refers to it as the Internet vortex, but Safari's navigation features can help you stay the course as you wind your way from web page to web page, as we explain in the following subtopics.

Moving from page to page

It's important to distinguish between the terms *website* and *web page*. A website comprises web pages. Web pages can contain links to other sections of the same web page, to other web pages within the same website, or to other websites, which have their own sets of web pages. Safari acts differently depending on which type of link you tap.

When you tap a link to a web page within the website you're viewing or on a list of search results, the Previous and Next buttons are activated. You can backtrack one or two or ten or more steps to return to whatever web page you started on before you wound up getting inadvertently lost (or [un]intentionally sidetracked). And, you can repeat your steps forward to the farthest web page you visited before you backtracked *away* from that farthest point. Safari gives you two ways to move backward and forward along your web page trail:

✔ Swipe right to go to the web page you viewed previously and swipe left to go forward to a page you were viewing before you swiped to go to the previous page.

✔ Tap the Previous or Next button in the toolbar to move from one web page to another.

When you tap a link to a different website, Safari moves your current screen to the tabs screen and opens the just-tapped link. You can view only one screen at a time, but the open web pages reside on tabs like you have in the browser on your computer. To move from one website, or tab, to another, tap the Tab button, and all the open web pages are displayed, as shown in Figure 3-6.

Things you can do when viewing the Tabs screen include the following:

The New Tab button

Figure 3-6: The Tabs screen.

✔ **Open a new web page:** Tap the New Tab button to open a new Safari web page.

✔ **Switch between web pages:** Scroll up and down to see tabs of other open web pages, and then tap the web page you want to view to open that web page. Scroll to the very bottom to see tabs you have open in Safari on other devices signed in to the same iCloud account (refer to Figure 3-6).

✔ **Reorder the tabs:** Tap and hold the tab, and then drag it to a new position above or below where it was.

✔ **Close a web page:** Tap the X button in the upper-left corner of a tab to close that web page or swipe left.

Tap and hold the New Tab button to see a list of recently closed tabs, and then tap the one you want to re-open.

✔ **Open iCloud tabs:** Scroll to the bottom of the tabs to see shared tabs from other devices.

✔ **Close the Tabs screen:** Tap Done to close the Tabs screen.

If you tap and hold a link on a web page, a menu appears, as shown in Figure 3-7. Consider the first two options (we discuss the others in a bit):

✔ **Open:** Opens the web page in the same manner as if you tapped the link.

✔ **Open in New Tab:** The linked page opens in a new tab, even if it's on the same website.

Book II
Chapter 3

Surfing the Web with Safari

Figure 3-7: Tap and hold a link to see more opening (and sharing) choices.

OR

✔ **Open in Background:** This option, which you activate in the Settings app by tapping Safari and then Open Links, opens a new tab for the linked site but adds it to the tab screen. The page you're viewing remains on the screen.

We prefer this option. If you just tap a link to another website, a new tab opens on top of the one you were viewing, but tap and hold and a tab is opened in the background to be viewed later. You don't lose the link but you also don't interrupt what you're doing — for example, you're reading an article and there's a link that you want to open but you'd like to finish reading the article before going to the linked page.

When you see words or phrases underlined or in a different color within the text of an article, those (usually) are links that open another web page related to the word or phrase you tapped.

Revisiting history with History

Sometimes you want to go back in time to a web page you viewed a few hours ago or even a few days or weeks ago. Thanks to Safari's History feature, you can do just that.

Opening previously viewed web pages

To view your Safari browsing history, tap Bookmarks, and then tap History to view your web history activity, as shown in Figure 3-8. Safari lists the web pages you've

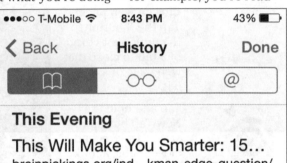

Figure 3-8: Revisit web pages you previously viewed in the History folder.

visited in chronological order, with the most recent at the top of the list. Subheadings indicate the time period, such as This Afternoon, This Morning, Monday Evening, and so on. This can help you find the web page you want to revisit — book reviews, hmm must have been Sunday morning, or that sort of mnemonic trigger. Scroll through and then tap a listed item to revisit that web page.

If you don't see the History folder shown in Figure 3-8, that means you previously navigated to another Bookmarks folder; tap the Bookmarks button in the upper-left corner, or swipe right, to back your way out of whatever folder you're in until you see the History folder, and then tap the History folder to view your Safari web history. Or you may be in Reading List, in which case, tap the Bookmarks button at the top of the screen.

**Book II
Chapter 3**

To see your most immediate viewing history, tap and hold the previous button.

**Surfing the Web
with Safari**

Erasing your web history

Safari lets you erase history, well, your browsing history. You can be selective about what Safari forgets or wipe out the memory of your browsing escapades completely. Choose one of the following methods:

- ✓ **One by one:** Swipe right to left across the web page you want to delete in the History list, and then tap the Delete button that appears.

- ✓ **Short-term memory:** Tap the Clear button and then choose one of the time spans to delete your browsing history: The Last Hour, Today, or Today and Yesterday.

- ✓ **Wipe out:** To erase your entire Safari web page viewing history, tap Clear, and then tap All Time. Open pages in tabs and bookmarks remain, but your history is wiped out.

Keeping your browsing private

You can also cancel history before it happens. If you don't want Safari to keep track of your web browsing history, tap the Tabs button, and then tap the Private button in the lower left. When you tap this button, tabs are pushed out of view until you tap the Private button again. If you tap the Bookmarks button, your bookmarks are active and you can see the history of web pages visited before you tapped the Private button.

You know Private Browsing is turned on because the Address/Search field and toolbar background is dark gray and when you tap the Tabs button, the Private button in the lower-left corner is highlighted. While you're in Private Browsing mode, you can open multiple tabs and use the Previous and Next button to move between web pages, but after you close a tab, Safari develops amnesia about sites and pages you visited.

To turn Private Browsing off, tap the tabs button and then tap the Private button again. If you have open tabs, you're asked to choose either Close Private Tabs, which eliminates them, or Keep Private Tabs, which saves them so you can see those tabs the next time you activate Private Browsing.

Tapping into Web Page Links

When a web designer creates a site, she can use almost any element as a link; when you click that link, an action takes place. In this section, we tell you about interacting with the different types of links you may encounter, such as phone numbers, email addresses, and location addresses. We tell you how to view and do things with content-rich web links, such as saving photos or graphics to your iPhone's Photos app, or opening other apps to view the contents of a link, like Word files or PDFs, or a presentation. In addition to opening other web pages, web links can initiate the following actions:

- Display a graphic or photo or a photo slideshow you can tap through to view a series of photos.

- Open a PDF document file.

- Display a form with fields you can fill in with information, such as your shipping address on a shopping site, or your email address, so you can receive a weekly newsletter from a museum you're fond of.

- Play an audio file, such as a news story, a podcast, or a song.

- Play a video file — say, a movie trailer or a friend's dog catching a Frisbee.

- Open another app, which you must exit (by double-clicking the Home button) to return to Safari.

Working with basic links and forms

You can open a link with a quick tap or access more options with the tap-and-hold gesture. The web page link's full URL appears at the top of the dialog, and below the web address are buttons you can tap:

- **Open:** Opens the web page link.

- **Open in New Tab or Open in Background:** Explained in "Moving from page to page" and Figure 3-7 earlier in this chapter.

- **Add to Reading List:** Places the entire text in your Reading List so you can come back later and read whatever it is that interests you on this web page. Open your Reading List by tapping the Bookmarks button.

- **Save Image:** Only appears when you tap and hold an image; selecting it saves the image to your Photos library.

✔ **Copy:** Copies the web page address to the Clipboard so you can paste the web address elsewhere, like in a note in the Note app or in a text message in the Messages app.

✔ **Cancel:** Closes the web page information and options screen.

Filling in forms and fields

When it comes to filling in forms, Safari serves up some useful helpers to make tapping out type and numbers using the keyboard as easy as possible.

Tap a field and begin typing. If you're having trouble seeing the field you're typing in, you can zoom in and out of the web page even while the keyboard is displayed. Turning your iPhone to landscape view makes the keyboard slightly larger.

When you open a field that offers a pop-up menu of choices such as size, color, or state, a rotor appears at the bottom of the screen, as shown in Figure 3-9. Scroll to your choice, tap to highlight it, and then tap Done.

Tap the arrows to move the cursor to the next or previous field in the form. Tapping either of those two buttons repeatedly quickly moves you from field to field. You can also scroll down to tap into any other fields you need to complete.

Tap Done when you finish filling in the form fields.

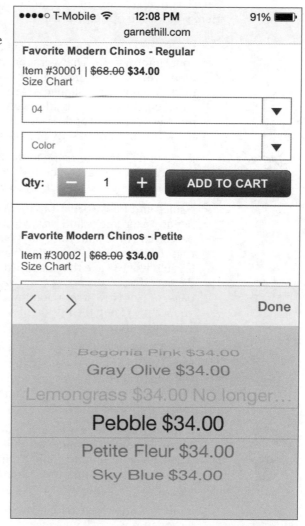

Figure 3-9: When filling out forms, Safari helps you "tab" between fields with the Next and Previous arrow buttons.

Using AutoFill to do the typing for you

For information about you that remains constant (such as your name and address), Safari's AutoFill feature automatically fills in your personal information with a single tap instead of requiring you to fill in those fields individually. Safari can also keep track of usernames and passwords and credit card information. What's more, when you create a new account on a website, Safari asks if you want it to generate and memorize a password for you.

To turn on Safari's AutoFill feature and options, open the Settings app, tap Safari, and tap Passwords & AutoFill to display the AutoFill settings screen. Here's how each option works:

- **Use Contact Info:** Tap On and Safari fills in online forms with your personal information. That personal information is pulled from your information in Contacts. You should see your own name in the My Info option field. When you're filling in a form, tap AutoFill on the keyboard and Safari copies the information you've saved in the name, address, phone number, and email address fields of your own Contacts card and pastes those bits of information into the appropriate fields.

  If you don't see your name in the My Info option field, tap that field to display your Contacts, and then locate and tap your own Contacts card name to select it as the card you want to use for the My Info option.

- **Names and Passwords:** Tap the option On if you want Safari to remember any usernames and passwords you type to access certain web pages. The first time you type your name and password on a web page that requires that information, Safari displays a pop-up message, asking if you'd like to save the password. Tap Yes if you would, Never for This Website if you never-ever-ever want to save the password for the web page, or Not Now, if you don't want to save the password right now, but you want to keep the option of saving the password the next time you visit the web page.

- **Saved Passwords:** Tap to see a list of websites for which you have a saved name and password. Tap the disclosure arrow to the right of the website to see the username and password spelled out. To delete any of the websites, swipe right to left across the website, and then tap the red Delete button that appears.

If you turn off Passcode Lock, a dialog asks if you want to continue using AutoFill in Safari because without the security of a Passcode, anyone who uses your iPhone could access any AutoFill information you keep in Safari, including your stored credit card information. Use AutoFill without a Passcode only if you keep your iPhone chained to your body.

Some websites have a Remember Me option for usernames and passwords that works if you accept cookies, in which case Safari doesn't ask if you want it to remember because the website takes care of that. (See the section "Adjusting General and Security Settings" at the end of this chapter to learn about cookies.)

✔ **Credit Cards:** If you shop frequently online, this feature can be a real time-saver. Tap on and then tap Saved Credit Cards and Add Credit Card to add your cardholder information to Safari. You can type the information in the appropriate fields or tap the Use Camera option. Place your credit card on a flat surface and hold your iPhone over it until the card fills the outline, as shown in Figure 3-10. When the number comes into focus, your iPhone automatically captures the number and expiration date. Type in the Cardholder name and a Description if you want, and then tap Done.

When you purchase something online, tap in the credit card field and then tap AutoFill Credit Card. Safari will automatically fill in the credit

Figure 3-10: Capture your credit card information with the iPhone camera.

card information. If you have information for more than one credit card saved, a list shows the last four digits of the card and any description you added (see Figure 3-11). Tap the card you want to pay with or tap Use Camera and capture a different card with the camera as explained previously. If you don't have any credit card AutoFill information saved, instead of AutoFill Credit Card you see Scan Credit Card.

If you sync Safari with iCloud, all your AutoFill information is available on all devices and computers that sync with iCloud.

Opening app web links

Sometimes a web link you tap closes the Safari screen and opens another app to display the contents of the link you tapped. For instance, you might be viewing the website for your favorite store and find they have a special iPhone app; when you tap that link, the App Store opens so you can download the app.

Safari automatically re-opens when you finish working with the app you switched to. Here are some ways Safari links to other iPhone apps:

✔ **Phone:** Tap a phone number link you want to dial, and then tap Call in the pop-up screen that appears. The Safari screen closes and the active call screen appears as your iPhone places your call.

✔ **Mail:** Tap an email address you want to use to send an email message, and a new message appears with the address already filled in the To field. Complete your new email message and then tap Send. The email message screen closes and returns to Safari.

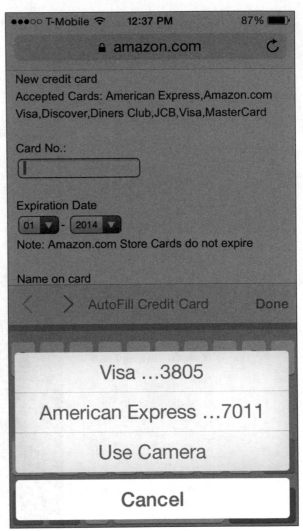

Figure 3-11: Store credit card information for quick online purchases.

To do other things with a phone number or email address link, press and hold on the phone number or email address to display the link options screen, and then choose one of the following options (options vary for phone number or email):

- **Call:** Dials the phone number.

- **Text Message:** Opens a new text message and pastes the phone number into the To field.

- **New Message:** Creates a new email message with the email address you tapped already filled in the To field.

- **Add to Contacts:** Opens an Info screen in Contacts where you can choose Create a New Contact or Add to an Existing Contact.

- **Copy:** Copies the phone number or email address to the Clipboard so you can paste it into another app such as Notes or Messages.

✔ **Photos:** Press and hold on a photo or other kind of image file to display the Safari options screen, and then tap Save Image to save that image file to the camera roll in the Photos app or Copy to place the image in the Clipboard and then paste it in another app. If the image you tap is actually a link, you'll see more options, such as Open, Open in New Page, Add to Reading List, and Copy.

A bit of copyright "fine print" you ought to keep in mind: Although it's generally acceptable to save any photo or other kind of image file for your own viewing pleasure, you're generally not permitted to use those photos or other image files to share with others — on your own website, or in a magazine you write for, for instance — without the express consent/permission of the person or organization who owns the rights to those image files you may have saved to your iPhone.

✔ **Videos:** When you tap a streaming video or audio link on a web page, Safari opens and begins playing the link with its built-in video or audio player feature. The player displays all the controls you need for starting, pausing, stopping, rewinding, fast-forwarding, and adjusting the volume of the content you're watching or listening to.

When you're watching video content, those controls typically disappear after a few moments, so you can enjoy the video without having those distracting controls blocking your view.

Here are a few things you can do when you're watching video content:

- Tap the screen to make the video controls reappear after they disappear.

- Double-tap the screen when you're watching a video in portrait mode to zoom in or out.

- Rotate your iPhone sideways to watch a video in landscape, full-screen mode to enjoy the fullest possible view.

Sometimes instead of seeing a thumbnail of a video on a web page, you may see a message informing you that your web browser requires Adobe Flash to view the video. Unfortunately, viewing Flash videos with Safari isn't possible because of Apple's choice to not support Flash on iPhone.

Your iPhone can play videos embedded in web pages if they are in either the popular MPEG-4 (MP4) format or Apple's own QuickTime format. Safari can't play other video format such as Flash Video (.flv). These days, most websites use MPEG-4 or QuickTime for their videos.

✔ **Quick Look:** This isn't an app you'll find on your Home screen, but it does open certain document files you may encounter on your web adventures. Tapping on a document link on a web page you're viewing prompts Safari to try to open the document file using its built-in Quick Look feature. The Quick Look feature can display a number of popular document file types, including Microsoft Word and PDF documents.

✔ **Other Apps:** Sometimes you may want to open a document you're viewing using another app you have installed on your iPhone. To open a document using another app, tap the Open In *<appname>* button on the right to use the default app displayed on that button, or tap the Open In button on the left to display other apps on your iPhone that you can use to open the app. Tap the button that corresponds to the app you want to use to open the document.

Sharing Web Page Links

The Share button in the toolbar at the bottom of the Safari screen lets you do many things with the web page you're viewing. Say you want to send someone an email with a link to a web page you want them to look at or you want to post a link to Facebook. Or maybe you want to copy a web page link so you can paste it in another program such as Notes. You can do all those things and more directly from the web page you're browsing. Follow these steps:

1. **While viewing a web page in normal or Reader mode that you want to share, print, or copy, tap the Share button at the bottom of the screen.**

   The Share Sheet (shown in Figure 3-12) appears.

2. **Tap your sharing method of choice from the following (scroll horizontally in each section to see all the options):**

   • **AirDrop (iPhone 5 or later):** Share the web page link with other AirDrop users near you. iOS 8 users can share with Macs using OS X 10.10 Yosemite via AirDrop.

   • **Message:** A new text message, which may be SMS or iMessage depending on the recipient, appears with the web page address pasted into the body of the message; complete the message as usual and then tap Send.

   • **Mail:** A new message appears with the web page address pasted into the body of the message; complete the message as usual and then tap Send.

      If you share an article from Reader, the entire article will be pasted into the Mail message.

- **Twitter:** Write something to accompany your link, and then tap Send.

- **Facebook:** Write something to accompany your link, and then tap Post.

- **Pinterest:** Tap Board to select the board you want to pin an image to; then scroll through the images that are available from the web page. When you see the image you want to pin, tap the PinIt button to pin the image to your selected board.

- **LinkedIn:** Choose who you want to share the link with, write something to accompany the link, and then tap Post.

- **Add Bookmark:** Adds the URL to your bookmarks. Learn more about this function in the next section, "Playing Favorites with Bookmarks."

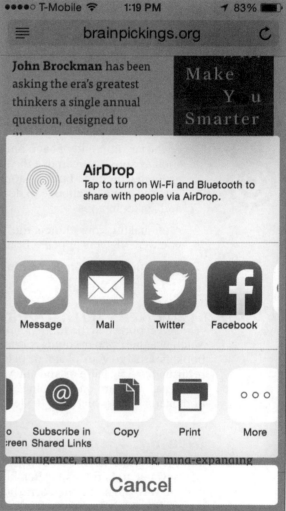

Figure 3-12: Tap the Share button to see your sharing options and more.

- **Add to Reading List:** Adds the web page to your Reading List so you can view it later.

- **Add to Home Screen:** Places an icon on the Home screen that, when tapped, opens directly to the web page.

- **Subscribe in Shared Links:** Similar to an RSS feed, tap this button to automatically receive updates from pages. Learn more in the section "Playing Favorites with Bookmarks."

- **Copy:** The web address is copied to the Clipboard so you can paste it to another app. Return to the Home screen or the multitasking bar to open another app and paste the link. Double-click the Home button to open the multitasking bar and tap Safari to return to the web page you were viewing.

- **Print:** Select a printer if your printer isn't selected, tap the plus sign to print more than one copy, and then tap Print. Anything iPhone's Quick Look feature can open and display on the screen, you can print to an AirPrint-enabled printer.

At the far right end of each horizontal list, tap More to see other options such as apps that can use the link. From here you can also rearrange the order in which the buttons appear by dragging them up and down the list. You can also choose to deactivate the Twitter, Facebook, Pinterest, and LinkedIn apps.

After making your choice, the Share Sheet disappears and the web page you were viewing appears front and center once more.

3. **Continue what you were doing in Safari.**

Playing Favorites with Bookmarks

Much like their paper counterparts save your place in a book, electronic bookmarks save your place, or places, on the web — it's a way of easily returning to a website or specific web page whenever you want. Even better, as long as you turn on Safari in iCloud on all your devices, you find the same bookmarks from whichever device you access the web.

Viewing, opening, and creating bookmarks

Tap the Bookmarks button in the toolbar to open the Bookmarks screen, where you also find tabs for Reading List and Shared Links. To view a bookmarked web page, tap the corresponding bookmark. Your iPhone comes with some pre-installed bookmarks — a few are in Favorites — to get you started. You see the list as shown in Figure 3-13 when the Bookmarks tab is selected:

- **Favorites:** In the Settings app, tap Safari and then tap Favorites. Here, you can choose which folder you want to head up the Bookmarks list. The Favorites folder is the default, but you can choose News or Entertainment or another folder you create. It will appear at the top of the Bookmarks list. You see buttons for the bookmarks within the Favorites folder when you tap the Address/Search field.

- **History:** Tap to see a list of web pages you viewed on your iPhone.

- **Bookmarks Menu, Folders, and (single) Bookmarks:** You can create any of these on your iPhone and, if Safari is on in iCloud, you sync with any bookmarks you have in these places on your computer or other devices.

You may need to scroll down your list or tap a folder stored in the Bookmarks list to find the bookmark you want to open.

To access tabs open on other devices with which you share your iCloud account, tap the Tabs button from the Safari screen and scroll to the very bottom to see a list of devices and open tabs.

Adding bookmarks

To create a new bookmark for a web page you're viewing, do the following:

1. **Tap the Share button to display the Share Sheet, and then tap Add Bookmark to display the Add Bookmark screen.**

   The keyboard appears, and the blinking cursor is positioned at the end of the web page name.

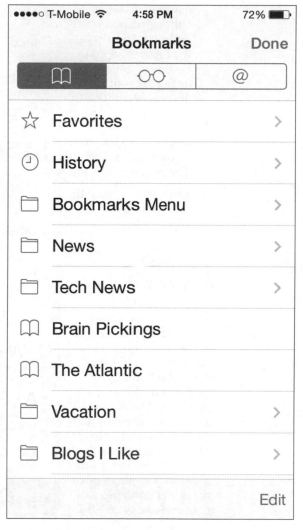

Figure 3-13: Bookmarks mark your favorite web pages so you can return in a tap.

2. **(Optional) Edit the name of the website if you don't like the name that's automatically created for the bookmark, as shown in Figure 3-14.**

   You may want to use something more descriptive or shorter so the whole name appears in the Bookmarks list.

3. **(Optional) Tap Location to choose where to store the bookmark, and then tap the Back button.**

   A list that contains Favorites and all your folders appears. Tap the location where you want to store the bookmark. Choose Bookmarks to store it at the top level, although if you store many bookmarks at the top level it can become a long, confusing list so it's often a better idea to group similar bookmarks in appropriately named folders, as we explain in the next section.

4. **Tap Done or Save to save your new bookmark.**

Organizing bookmarks

The number of bookmarks you have can get out of hand quickly if you want to remember and revisit many web pages. Placing bookmarks for similar web pages together in folders makes your browsing easier and saves you from scrolling through hundreds of bookmarks to find the one you want. Deleting bookmarks you don't use anymore is also a good idea.

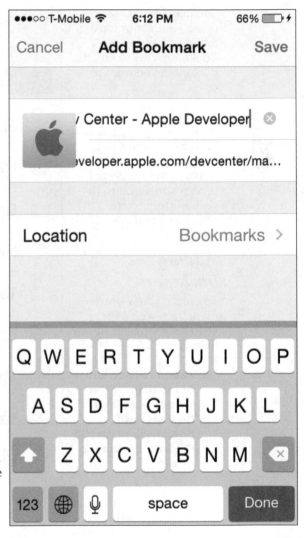

Figure 3-14: The Add Bookmarks screen.

You create new folders and delete or rearrange folders and bookmarks using the Bookmarks edit feature. Tap the Bookmarks button on the toolbar of the Safari screen, tap the Bookmarks tab, and then tap Edit to display the Bookmarks edit screen. You can do the following:

- **Rearrange your bookmarks and folders:** Tap the Rearrange button to the right of a bookmark or folder, and then drag the bookmark up or down the list and release your finger to drop the bookmark in its new location.

- **Delete a bookmark or folder:** Tap the red – (minus sign) to the left of a bookmark or folder you want to eliminate, and then tap the Delete button. The bookmark or folder (and the bookmarks within) disappears.

✔ **Create a new bookmark folder:**

1. **Tap New Folder, and then type a name for your new bookmark folder in the Title field that appears.**

   The folder lands in the top level of the Bookmarks list. To place a folder inside another folder, on the Bookmarks Bar, or Bookmarks Menu, tap Location, and then tap where you want it to go. A check mark lets you know where that folder will be placed.

2. **Swipe right to return to the previous screens.**

✔ **Rename an existing bookmark or folder:** Tap the bookmark or folder, and then type a new name in the name field.

✔ **Move an existing bookmark or folder:** Tap it, tap Location, and then tap the desired position.

Tap Done when you're finished editing the Bookmarks list, and Safari returns you to the web page you were viewing before you started tweaking your bookmarks.

Book II
Chapter 3

Surfing the Web with Safari

Saving to read later

So much of our news and research reading takes place on the web these days. The Reading List function of Safari stores articles or web pages you want to read later. To save an article or web page to your reading list, while you're on the page, tap the Share button and then tap Add to Reading List.

To view an article in the Reading List, tap the Bookmarks button on the toolbar and then tap Reading List (if you don't see Reading List, tap the Bookmarks button in the upper-left corner to return to the main Bookmarks screen). The title, source, and the first two lines of the article appear in the list, as shown in Figure 3-15. Tap the Show All or Show Unread button in the bottom-right corner to expand or limit the articles you see.

Tap an article and it opens in Safari. Scroll down to the bottom and the next article on your reading list is ready to be opened under an Up Next heading. Just scroll up to see it, and likewise for the article after that.

You can read articles in your Reading List offline and, like bookmarks, Reading List items sync between devices so if you put something on your Reading List on your iPhone, you find it on your iPad and computer (in the Safari browser) — how great is that? Articles remain in Reading List until you remove them by swiping across and then tapping the Delete button (refer to Figure 3-15).

Accessing Shared Links

Shared Links creates an actively updated newsfeed for sites you frequent and lists links shared from people you follow on Twitter or other social media. To add a site to Shared Links do the following:

1. **Open the site in Safari — for example, a newspaper, magazine, or blog — and let the site finish loading.**

2. **Tap the Bookmarks button on the toolbar.**

3. **Tap the Shared Links tab.**

4. **Tap Subscriptions in the lower right.**

5. **Tap Add Current Site.**

6. **(Optional) Tap the on/off toggle to activate or deactivate your Twitter feed and see links shared by people you follow.**

7. **Tap Shared Links to see your newsfeed or tap Done to return to the website.**

To remove a site from your shared links, repeat steps 2 through 4 and then tap the Delete button (the red circle) next to the site you want to remove.

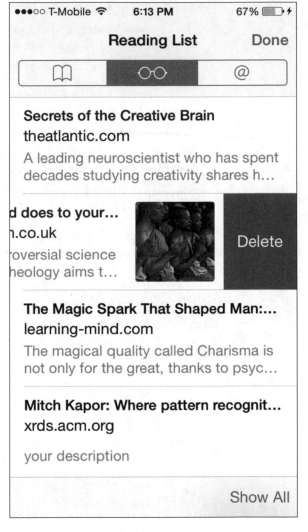

Figure 3-15: Reading List puts articles and web pages you want to read later all in one place.

Accessing Websites from the Home Screen

Instead of bookmarking sites you visit frequently, you can have a button on your Home screen that taps in directly to the website or web page. There are two ways to go about this: web apps and Web Clips. Here we explain both.

Web apps

When you visit a website, your iPhone automatically checks to see if a site-specific app is available on your device or in the App Store. For example, type "American Express" in the Address/Search field and the Amex Mobile app in the App Store appears at the top of the list, above the search engine choices. When you tap that link, the App Store opens and gives you the opportunity to download an app for that site. (See Book IV, Chapter 5 to learn about downloading and installing apps.) Alternatively, tap a search engine choice and then tap one of the resulting web pages from the list of search results. When the page opens, a banner appears across the top of your screen with the app icon, a description, and one of two options: View, which opens the app in the App Store so you can download it, or Open, when you already have the app installed on your iPhone. You can tap either of those options or tap the X to the left to close the banner and proceed with the website in Safari.

When you use the web app, you see the content of the website, but you usually see other functions as well that help you navigate and interact with the information that website provides. Or you may have a streamlined version of the main service that website offers. Like apps in general, there's no hard and fast rule for how and what they present, so the best thing to do is explore.

Web Clips

If you visit a particular web page often and no web app is available, you can create a Home screen icon, called a Web Clip, for that web page. Tapping the Web Clip automatically opens the web page. If you want Safari to open to a specific Home page, create a Web Clip for that page.

To create a Web Clip:

1. **Open the web page for which you want to create a Web Clip.**

2. **Tap the Share button to display the Share Sheet, and then tap Add to Home Screen.**

    The Add to Home screen appears, displaying a name and icon for the Web Clip you want to add to the Home screen.

3. **Edit or type a new name for your Web Clip — nine letters is optimal if you want to see the whole name under the icon.**

4. **Tap Add.**

    Safari closes and ushers you to the Home screen where your new Web Clip has been added.

Adjusting General and Security Settings

In the sections before this one, we occasionally ask you to check out or adjust a particular Safari setting, like turning on the AutoFill feature, for instance. In this section, we give you a rundown of Safari's settings and feature options that we haven't mentioned elsewhere.

Open the Settings app and tap Safari to display the Safari Settings screen.

Here's the 411 on Safari's settings:

- **Search Engine:** Tap and choose your preferred search provider.

- **Search Engine Suggestions and Spotlight Suggestions:** Enable to allow Safari and Spotlight, respectively, to suggest matches to your search criteria based on what you type.

- **Quick Website Search:** Tap the item, and then tap the switch on the following screen to quickly search within a website by typing the name of the website as part of your search criteria.

- **Preload Top Hit:** Begins loading a web page in the background when a match is determined based on your bookmarks and browsing history.

- **Block Pop-ups:** When on, Safari does its best to block pop-up ads or solicitations.

- **Do Not Track:** When on, Safari asks websites that track data about you (ostensibly, to offer you more tailored information when you visit their sites) not to track your activity. It's a request, not a demand, so it's up to the website to respect your request (or not).

- **Block Cookies:** *Cookies* are bits of information certain websites store so those websites can know and remember certain things about you. Tap and choose whether you want to receive cookies Always, Not from Current Website, Not From Previously Visited, or Never. Not from Previously Visited is the choice we recommend so that websites you go to can remember things like your ZIP code for giving you the weather forecast and so on. Choosing Never may result in some websites not functioning properly, and choosing Always also allows sites you didn't visit but that appeared via pop-ups to grab and store information about your Internet activity.

- **Fraudulent Website Warning:** Turn this on if you want Safari to warn you if what seems like a legitimate website you want to open may, in fact, be a potentially harmful site.

- **Clear History and Website Data:** Tapping this option wipes out Safari's memory of any websites you visited and clears cookies and data including any crumbs of cookie information you may have typed in to certain websites, like your ZIP code.

- **Use Cellular Data:** Downloads articles to Reading List using your cellular data connection (when Wi-Fi isn't available) so you can read them offline.

If you're concerned about your cellular data limits and consumption, turn this option off.

✔ **Advanced:** Opens the following three choices:

- **Website Data:** Tap to view any databases that are automatically created by certain websites so those websites can speed up your web browsing experience when you use them. You may see databases for `mail.google.com` for instance, if you use Safari to read your email. The list also displays how much space that database is taking up on your iPhone. Tapping Edit allows you to delete items one by one from the list, whereas tapping Remove All Website Data at the bottom of the screen clears the list completely.

- **JavaScript:** Turned on, this feature allows websites to present information and options in fancy ways, with things like pop-up buttons, swirling graphics, and interactive features that won't appear or work if you turn this feature off.

- **Web Inspector:** Website developers turn on this feature to help them troubleshoot problems the web pages they create may run into. Average Joes like you and us can keep this option turned off.

If you want to keep advertisers' snooping eyes from gathering information about your web habits (to then offer you things they think you should buy from them), in the Settings app, tap Privacy, tap Advertising, and then turn on Limit Ad Tracking.

**Book II
Chapter 3**

**Surfing the Web
with Safari**

Chapter 4: Emailing Every Which Way You Can

Although you can send text messages with Messages or through Facebook, LinkedIn, Twitter, and the myriad other social networks, good ol' email is still a viable choice. It's an efficient way to send and request information, make reservations, and, yes, keep in touch with family and friends, especially when you want to keep your communication a bit more private.

With your iPhone, you have email at your fingertips. In this chapter, we show you how to configure your iCloud email account, as well as that of any other email service providers you work with. Then, we explain the ins and outs of Mail — writing and sending a new message, receiving and replying to a message, and saving and deleting messages. We give you tips for managing your messages. New messages can be generated from other apps such as Notes, Maps, and Photos, so we review that, too. Then we take a look at the account settings you can change.

Configuring Your Email Account

The first step to using Mail is setting up an account. If you established the iCloud account while setting up your iPhone, you already have a configured email account — although iCloud may not be your only email account.

You configure your email account directly on your iPhone with a series of taps. Apple has been kind enough to insert the technical stuff needed to access some of the most used email services. For the following email services, you need to have your email address and password handy:

 ✔ AOL

 ✔ iCloud

 ✔ Google Mail

 ✔ Microsoft Exchange

 ✔ Outlook.com

 ✔ Yahoo!

Setting up an iCloud account

If you set up an iCloud email account when you created your Apple ID, you have an `@icloud.com` address. If you're a long-time Apple user, you may have an address that ends with `@me.com` or `@mac.com`, both of which work transparently with iCloud.com. You may have already turned on your iCloud account when you set up iCloud syncing (refer to Book I, Chapter 5). If not, we explain it here.

Follow these steps to set up your iCloud email on your iPhone:

1. **Tap Settings on the Home screen, and then tap Mail, Contacts, Calendars.**

   You have to scroll down.

2. **If you have no email account, the Add Account screen opens directly, as shown in Figure 4-1.**

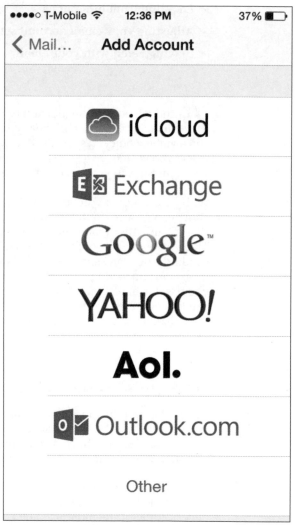

Figure 4-1: The Add Account screen.

If you see iCloud in the Accounts list and Mail is listed beneath it, as in Figure 4-2, you can skip ahead to the "Using Mail" section.

If you see iCloud but Mail isn't listed or you don't see iCloud at all but you want to add it, tap Add Account and go to Step 3.

3. **Tap iCloud.**

   iCloud recognizes the @icloud.com, @me.com, or @mac.com email address domains as iCloud accounts.

4. **Type in the email address and password associated with your Apple ID and then tap the Next button.**

   If you don't have an Apple ID, tap Get a Free Apple ID and follow the onscreen instructions to set one up.

   Your account is verified.

5. **The iCloud screen opens.**

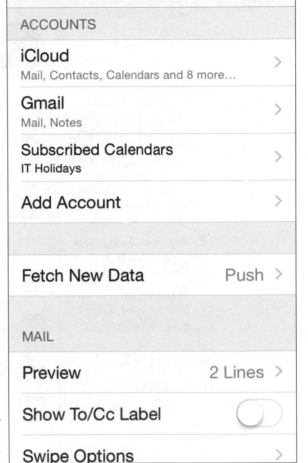

Figure 4-2: The Mail, Contacts, Calendars screen shows which accounts you have set up on your iPhone.

A message asks if you want iCloud to use the Location of Your iPhone. We suggest you tap OK. Find My iPhone is explained in Book I, Chapter 4.

On the screen shown in Figure 4-3, you have a series of options and toggle switches that turn those options on. Turning an option on means that the information in that app — for example, your contact information in the Contacts app — is accessed by your iPhone from iCloud. Any other devices you access iCloud with, such as an iPad, Mac, or Windows

PC, can access the same information. You can, however, enable different options on different devices — say you want Contacts active on your iPhone and computer but not on your iPad. Any time you make changes to one of them on one device, the changes go up to the iCloud and rain down on the other devices. We explain each option fully in Book I, Chapter 5.

6. **Tap or slide the toggle Mail switch to the on position.**

   Turn this on and you receive your iCloud mail on your iPhone.

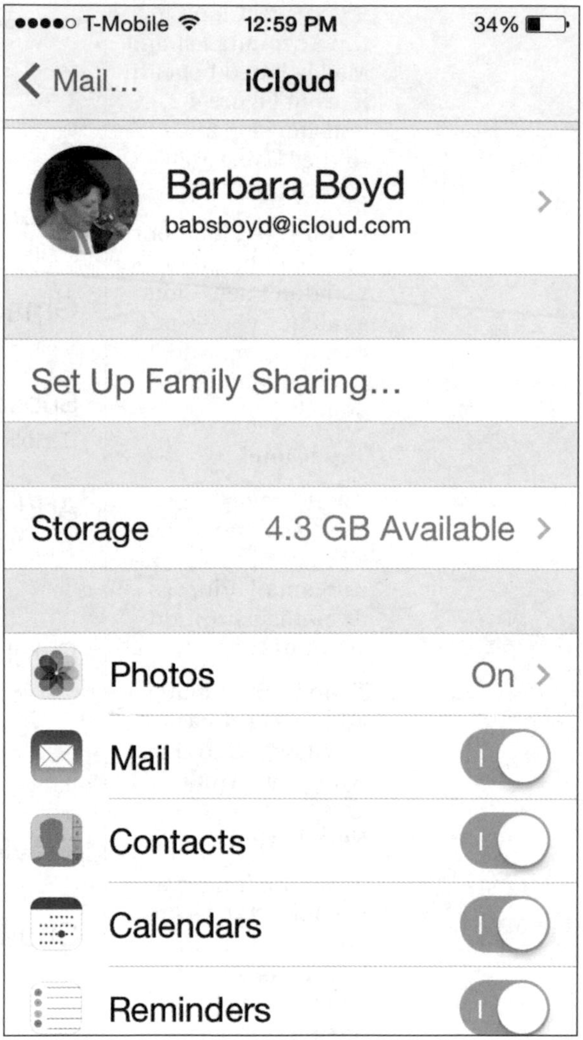

Gmail, Yahoo!, AOL, and Outlook.com accounts

Apple has already put the incoming and outgoing server information for the most popular email providers on iPhone. If you use Gmail, Yahoo!, AOL, or Outlook.com, do the following:

Figure 4-3: Tap the Mail switch on to send and receive email on your iPhone with your iCloud account.

1. **Tap Settings on the Home screen, and then tap Mail, Contacts, Calendars.**

2. **Tap Add Account.**

3. **The Add Account screen opens (refer to Figure 4-1).**

4. **Tap the name of the account you use; for example, Google Mail, also known as Gmail.**

5. **The Google Mail (or Yahoo! or AOL or Outlook.com) screen opens, as shown in Figure 4-4.**

   Filling in the Name field is optional (Windows Live Hotmail doesn't even have one). Type your email address in the Address field and your password in the Password field.

6. **Tap the Next button in the upper-right corner.**

   Your account is verified.

   The Google Mail (or one of the others) screen opens. You have a few options to consider turning on or off, depending on the services you use. For our purposes, turn on Mail.

   This connects you to your email account so that messages download to your iPhone in the Mail app and you can send messages from your email account in Mail.

7. **Tap Save.**

   Your account is added to the Accounts list of Mail, Contacts, Calendars settings.

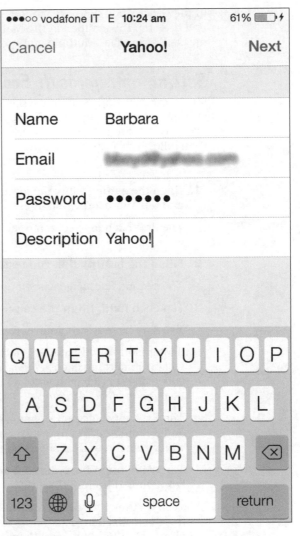

Figure 4-4: Type your name, email address, and password in the designated fields.

The Description field is automatically filled in with Exchange, Google Mail, Yahoo!, AOL, or Outlook.com, but if you tap there, you can change it. For example, we set up two Gmail accounts: one for personal email exchanges and another for newsletter subscriptions. This way, we don't have to weed through a dozen or more daily newsletters to find more important messages.

In the Description field, we named one Friends and the other Subscriptions, and then tap the mailbox in the Mailboxes list to view only those types of messages. See the "Multiple mailboxes" section for more information.

Setting up Microsoft Exchange

Microsoft Exchange is often used in a corporate setting where a company-specific server manages the employees' email. If you use Microsoft Exchange, you may need to ask your network administrator for the server name, and then follow these steps to set up a Microsoft Exchange account on your iPhone:

1. **Open the Settings app; tap Mail, Contacts, Calendars; tap Add Account; and tap Microsoft Exchange.**

   The first Exchange screen opens and requests your email address, password, and a description, which is optional.

2. **Fill in the information requested and tap Next.**

   The second Exchange screen opens.

3. **Tap each field, fill in the requested information, and tap Next.**

   You may have to ask your network administrator for some of the details.

   If Microsoft Auto Discovery didn't fill in the server address, type it in. It will be something like *exchange.company.com*. If you use Microsoft's Office 365 service instead of an Exchange server at your company, it will be *outlook.office365.com*.

   The Exchange account opens with options for Mail, Contacts, Calendars, and Reminders. You may also have an option for Notes, depending on which version of Exchange you use.

4. **Turn Mail on to have email from your Exchange account accessible from your iPhone.**

   Turn on the other options as well if you want to access that information from your Exchange account. See Book III, Chapters 1 and 2 to learn more about Contacts and Calendars.

Setting up other IMAP and POP accounts

If you or your company uses another email provider, it's probably an IMAP (Internet Message Access Protocol) or POP (Post Office Protocol) account. iOS 8 is pretty clever at finding the account and setting it up based on just your email address and password, which we explain here:

1. **Open the Settings app; tap Mail, Contacts, Calendars; tap Add Account; tap Other; and tap Add Mail Account.**

   A New Account screen opens.

2. **Fill in your name, email address, password, and a description (if you want something different from what is automatically entered), and tap Next.**

   Mail looks for your account and verifies it.

   Your iPhone automatically recognizes if it's an IMAP or POP account and presents the appropriate choices.

3. **Turn the options for Mail, Notes, and so on to the On position to have that data accessible from your iPhone, and tap Save.**

   The account is added and appears in the list of accounts in the Settings app under Mail, Contacts, Calendars.

Depending on the type of service, you may be asked for other information during the setup — for example, Host Name, which is usually something like *mail.providername.com,* the User Name, which is the name you gave when you signed up for this email service and is often the part of your email address before the @ (at symbol), your password, and the Outgoing Mail Server Host Name. You can find this information on the website of the provider on the page that references iPhone or smartphone setup, or ask the tech support person or the network administrator at your office.

IMAP services keep your messages on the email or Internet service provider (ISP) server, for a specified period of time, even after you've read them, whereas POP services only store your messages until you download them to your device, after which they're no longer on the server. Although most web-based email service providers use IMAP, if yours uses POP, you can configure both your computer and iPhone to leave the messages on the server after you've downloaded them so you can access them from the other device at a later time. We explain in this chapter under "Incoming Settings."

Using Mail

iPhone's Mail app works like most email programs. Terms we're familiar with for printed material (what's that?) delivered to our homes and offices — mail, inbox, carbon copy — are used to describe electronic material that is delivered to our homes and offices via computers, iPhones, and other devices. We start by explaining how to create and send a message, and follow up with replying to, forwarding, filing, and deleting messages. We also go through the ways you can view and organize messages.

Creating and sending email messages

To create and send an email message, just follow these steps:

1. **Open the Mail app.**

   The Mailboxes screen opens, as shown in Figure 4-5.

Notice that we added an Unread mailbox — see the section "Multiple mailboxes" to learn how to do it.

2. **Tap the inbox for the account you want to send the message from.**

3. **Tap the Compose button in the lower-right corner of the screen.**

A New Message screen opens. The cursor is blinking in the To field.

You can tap the Compose button in the lower-right corner of the Mailboxes screen. The message will be sent from the default mailbox you establish in the Settings app under Mail. We show you how to change the outgoing email address from within the message in Step 5.

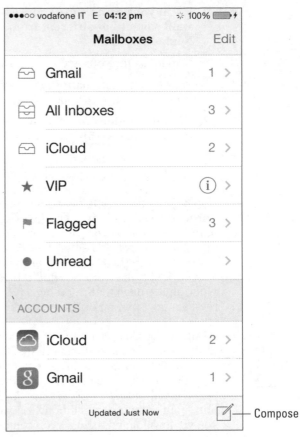

Figure 4-5: The Mailboxes screen lists the inboxes and accounts on your iPhone.

4. **In the To field, type the email address of the person you want to send the message to.**

As you begin typing the recipient's name in the To field, names of people in Contacts or people with whom you recently (or not so recently) exchanged email that contain the same letters show up as a list from which you can choose. Recently used email addresses that aren't in Contacts have an information button (i) next to them; tap it to add the address to a new or existing contact or remove the address from the Recents list. Your choices narrow as you type more letters.

Referring to Figure 4-6, the email address is listed under the contact's name and the type of address appears to the left. If a contact has more than one email address, his name is listed with each address. If you addressed and sent an email to several people, you see a listing that has those names grouped together.

When you find the name you want, tap it. If you want to add another recipient, repeat the previous step.

To open Contacts and choose the recipients from there, tap the plus sign button on the right of the To field. Contacts opens. Scroll through the list and tap the names of the desired recipients. You can access all your contacts or address a specific group by tapping the Groups button.

5. **If you want to send a Cc (carbon copy), or Bcc (blind carbon copy), to other recipients, tap the Cc/Bcc field.**

The field expands into three fields: Cc, Bcc, and From. Fill in the Cc and/or Bcc fields the same way you fill in the To field.

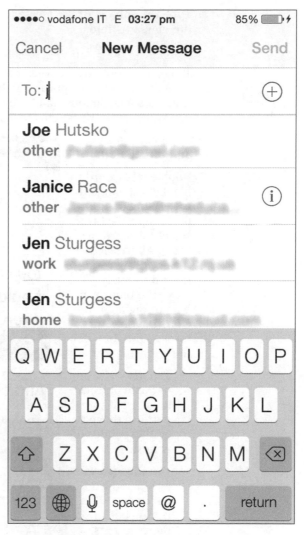

Figure 4-6: Type the first letters of the name of the person you want to send a message to in order to find the email address in Contacts.

If you want to change the address from which the message is sent, tap the From field and choose the account you want the message to be sent from.

6. **When you finish addressing the message, tap Return.**

The cursor moves to the Subject field.

You can move names from one address field to another, such as from To to Bcc, by touching and dragging them where you want.

7. Type the subject of the message, and then tap Return or tap directly in the message field.

The cursor moves to the Message field.

To receive a notification when the recipient replies, tap the Subject field; an outlined bell icon appears on the right of the field. Tap again and the Notify Me menu opens. Tap Notify Me. The bell icon is filled in, which lets you know Notify Me is activated for this message thread. (See Figure 4-7.)

8. Type your message and then edit it.

Double-tap a word to highlight it and activate selection grabbers. Tap Select to select the word or Select All to select the entire text and then, optionally, move the blue grabbers to highlight the word(s) you want to format, and then do the following:

- Tap the Cut, Copy, or Paste buttons if you want to perform those editing actions on your text.

- Tap the arrows on the right or left ends of the button bar to see more options.

- Select just one word, and tap Replace to see a list of alternate spelling corrections or tap Define to see a definition.

- Tap **B**/<u>U</u> to open a button bar with bold, italic, and underline options, which you tap to format the selected text.

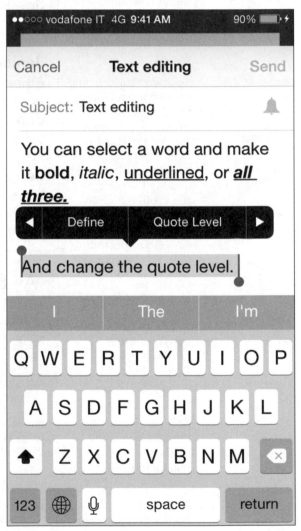

Figure 4-7: Format text with in-message editing buttons.

- Tap Quote Level to open a button bar that offers an increase (indent) or decrease (outdent) option. Tap the one you want to use.

- Tap Insert Photo or Video to open the Photos app and choose an image or video to attach to your message.

Repeat the process to apply more than one formatting option to the same text or to remove the format. (Refer to Figure 4-7.)

Tap and hold the emoji (a globe if you add additional keyboards) button to activate (or deactivate) predictive typing, as explained in Book I, Chapter 3.

9. **Tap the Send button.**

The word *Sending* appears at the bottom of the screen, and then a blue sending progress bar opens. If you've turned on the Sent Mail alert in the Settings app under Sounds, the sound you chose confirms your message has been sent.

If you're composing a message and have to stop midway, you can do two things:

- **Save it as a draft.** Use this if you're going to leave Mail for a while. Tap Cancel in the upper-left corner, and then tap Save Draft from the buttons that appear onscreen. The message goes into your Drafts inbox to be opened later and modified. Tap Delete Draft if you want to eliminate the message or Cancel to return to the message and continue writing. Tap and hold the New Message button to see a list of Drafts waiting to be completed.

- **Switch to an existing message.** Use this if you want to read or copy something from an existing message. Drag the message down and it conveniently drops out of sight, so you can look through your other inboxes and messages. Tap New Message at the bottom of the screen (as shown in Figure 4-8) to return to the message you're writing.

Siri is happy to read as well as compose and send email messages (as long as you have an adequately robust Internet connection). Press and hold the Home button and tell Siri whom you want to send a message to, and then start dictating. See Book I, Chapter 3 to learn more about Siri.

Sending messages from other apps

One of the great things about the Mail app is its flexibility and bandwidth. It's the backbone for sending so much more than just email messages. You can access Photos directly from the message you're composing, which makes inserting photos and videos super easy. You can send a note directly from Notes, an address or web page link from Maps or Safari, and new media or apps you like from the iTunes and App Stores. The process for each type of object is the same, as we outline here. We mention the pre-installed apps that came with your iPhone, but other apps often have a Share button that allows you to send information from Mail.

1. **Open the app you want from the Home screen.**

2. **Write the note or go to the address, web page, song, or app.**

   In Photos, for example, open the Collection or Album you want, tap Select in the upper-right corner, and then tap the photo(s) you want to send.

3. **Tap the Share button at the bottom of the page.**

   The Share Sheet opens.

4. **Tap the Mail button.**

   A new message opens with the cursor blinking in the To field.

5. **Address the message as explained previously.**

   Type a subject and write something in the Message field, if you want.

6. **Tap Send.**

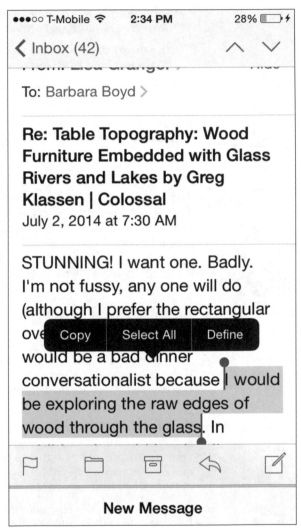

Figure 4-8: Tap New Message to switch from an existing message to one you're composing.

Size matters: Your cellular service provider may have a limit on the file size that you can send across the cellular data network. Likewise, your recipient's email server may restrict the size of incoming messages (usually 5MB) and your media won't reach its destination.

Giving VIP status

If you send and receive a lot of email, there may be communications with very important people who you don't want to get lost in the electronic slush pile. Mail lets you put people and companies on a VIP list so any incoming and out-going messages exchanged with those VIPs go to a special VIP mailbox. Those messages will still be in the mailbox they were sent to and you'll see a star next to the VIP's name. You can also select a special alert that lets you know when a message has arrived from one of your VIPs. To give someone VIP status:

1. **Tap a message that you sent to or received from the person or business you want to give VIP status to.**

2. **Tap the name in the To or From address field.**

   The screen that opens gives you at least three options: Add to VIP, Create New Contact, and Add to Existing Contact. If the person is in your Contacts, the related info screen appears with the various Contacts options (see Book III, Chapter 1).

3. **Tap Add to VIP.**

4. **Tap Message in the upper-left corner to return to the originating message.**

5. **Tap the back button in the upper-left corner or swipe right several times to return to the Mailboxes screen.**

6. **Tap the Info button to the right of the VIP inbox.**

   A list of your VIPs appears.

   If you eventually want to delete a VIP, tap Edit and then tap the red and white minus sign followed by the Delete button, or swipe the person and tap Delete. Tap Done when you finish removing VIPs.

7. **Tap VIP Alerts to set the alert style, sound, and notification you want to receive when a VIP sends a message to you.**

8. **Double-tap the Home button and then tap Mail to return to the Mail app.**

To add VIPs directly from Contacts, tap Add VIP on the VIP List screen. Contacts opens and those with email addresses are bold in the list. Tap the name you want to add.

Noticing you've got mail

iPhone has several ways of letting you know you've received a message. You choose which you want in the Settings app by tapping Notifications and then tapping Mail. Tap Allow Notifications to the on position to activate one or more of the following alerts or leave it off to receive no new mail notifications.

If you have multiple email accounts, you can choose distinct notifications for each email account you use. You can also choose the type of notifications you receive for messages from VIP contacts and/or Thread Notifications (from threads to which you assigned the Notify Me option). Tap the account name, such as iCloud or Gmail, or VIP or Thread Notifications, and set the following:

- ✓ **Show in Notification Center:** When enabled, messages show up in the Notification Center, accessed when you pull down from the top of the iPhone screen.

- ✓ **Notification Sound:** Tap to choose the audible alert you want to hear when you receive new messages. Choose a vibration, too.

- ✓ **Badge App Icon:** When enabled, the Mail app icon on the Home screen wears a badge showing the number of unread messages.

- ✓ **Show on Lock Screen:** When enabled, alerts appear on the Lock screen.

See Book I, Chapter 4 to learn more about Notification Center settings.

Replying to, forwarding, filing, printing, and deleting messages

One way or another — a badge, banner, or audible alert — you notice that you received a message. To read your messages, open the Mail app. The Mailboxes screen opens. To see incoming messages from all your accounts, tap All Inboxes; to see those from just one account, tap the name of the inbox you want to view. If you have only one email account on your iPhone, this is the only inbox you'll see.

To refresh your inboxes, drag down from the top of the screen (just below the Status bar or you'll open the Notification Center). A spinning gear lets you know Mail is working for you. Mail checks for any new messages. (Refer to the end of the chapter to learn how to adjust the Push and Fetch settings.)

When you tap the inbox, a list of the messages opens, as shown in Figure 4-9. Here's how to interpret the icons:

- ✓ Unread messages have a blue dot next to them.

- ✓ The gray To label indicates that Barbara was a direct recipient of the message.

- ✓ The gray Cc means Barbara received a copy of the message. We explain how to activate this feature in the section, "Adjusting Email Account Settings."

✔ A flag indicates messages you've flagged.

✔ A double arrow lets you know this message is the most recent in a thread.

✔ The paper clip means the message has attachments. Mail can open PDF files; images files (such as JPEGs, TIFFs, PNGs, and GIFs); iWork files; and Microsoft Word, Excel, and PowerPoint files. Tap an attachment to download and open it on your iPhone. Tap and hold an image attachment, and then tap Save Image to save it to your Camera Roll.

✔ A star indicates the person is in your VIP list.

✔ A bell means you activated Notify Me and you'll be notified as soon as another message in this thread comes in.

An email exchange you have with the same subject line, whether with the same person or not, is called a *thread*. A thread is created when you have three or more exchanges of sending and receiving messages. Turning this feature on in the Settings app under Mail (which we get to a bit later in this chapter) puts related messages, the so-called thread, together. In the main message list (refer to Figure 4-9), you see the most recent message of the thread — a double arrow indicates a thread. Tap that message and you see the thread of messages. The subject and number of items in the thread is above the message list; a curved arrow to the left of a message means you responded to that message.

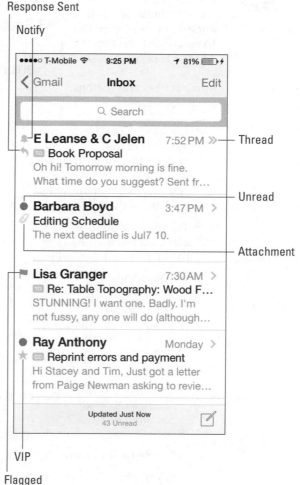

Figure 4-9: Messages are listed in reverse chronological order within a mailbox.

Tap on the message you want to read in either a mailbox or thread, and it opens (as shown in Figure 4-10).

REMEMBER

Turn iPhone 6 Plus to landscape orientation to view Mail in a split screen; the message list runs down the left side and the message you tap to read opens on the right side of the screen.

You have several options from the message screen:

- ✔ Tap the up and down triangles in the upper-right corner to read the next or previous message in the mail list or thread.

- ✔ Tap the Flag button, and then tap one of the following:

  - • **Flag:** Add a colored flag to the message so it stands out in the Inbox message list (refer to Figure 4-9).

  - • **Mark as Unread:** Mark a message as unread, in which case the blue dot reappears next to the message in the list.

  - • **Move to Junk:** Move it to the Junk file.

  - • **Notify Me:** As soon as a response to the thread is received, you receive a notification. To remove the notification from the thread, tap the flag button again and select Stop Notifying.

Figure 4-10: A received message.

TECHNICAL STUFF

Mail tucks away information about messages you move to the Junk folder and little by little learns who the offenders are and automatically puts messages into that folder. If you're expecting an email, but it doesn't show up in your inbox, check the Junk folder — it may have been errone-ously sent there. In the message list, swipe to the left over the message, tap More, and then tap Not Junk. If you accidentally place a message in the Junk folder, when you swipe and then tap More, the option you should choose is Move Message, which lets you move the message back to its original location.

✔ Tap the File button, and a screen opens as shown in Figure 4-11. Tap the folder where you want the message to reside. To file the message in a different mailbox, tap Accounts, and then tap the folder to which you want to move the message. If you change your mind, tap Cancel.

✔ Tap the trashcan but-ton to delete your message. Tap one of the two buttons that appear: a Delete Message button and a black Cancel button.

✔ If Archive Messages is on, you won't see a trashcan button. Tap and hold the button for an option to Archive or Trash the message. Archived messages are removed from your inbox but held in a storage file, whereas Deleted messages will be erased. To enable or disable the Archive Messages feature, open the

Book II
Chapter 4

Emailing Every
Which Way You Can

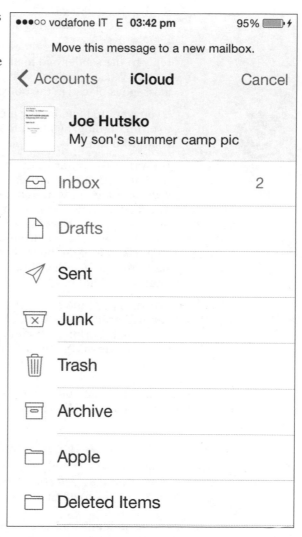

Figure 4-11: Choose the folder where you'd like to file the message.

Settings app; tap Mail, Contacts, Calendar; and tap *Account Name;* then for iCloud accounts, tap Mail in the Advanced section, tap Advanced, and then tap Archive Mailbox or Deleted Mailbox, or for other types of accounts, tap Account, tap Advanced, and then tap Archive Mailbox or Deleted Mailbox as the destination for discarded messages.

✔ Tap the Forward button, and then tap one of the following options:

- **Reply:** Tap to reply to the sender of the message. When you finish writing your message, tap Send.

- **Reply All (if there are other recipients besides you):** To send a reply to the sender and to all addresses in the To or Cc list, tap this button. When you finish writing your message, tap Send. The entire message is placed in the body of your reply.

  If you want to include only a portion of the message you're replying to or forwarding, highlight that portion before tapping the Reply or Forward button.

- **Forward:** To forward a copy of the message to someone else, tap the Forward button. If there are attachments, Mail asks you if you want to include the attachments. After you make this choice, the message window opens with the cursor blinking in the To field. Address the message as explained previously. Write something in the Message field, and then tap Send. The Re in the subject field changes to Fwd so the recipient knows this is a forwarded message. You can forward any kind of attachment, even those you can't open with iPhone.

- **Print:** To print the message, you must have access to an AirPrint-enabled printer. Tap Print, and then tap Select Printer. iPhone looks for available printers. When one is found, you return to the Printer Options screen. Tap the + (plus sign) to print more than one copy, and then tap Print.

✔ **Compose:** The last button on the right is the Compose button, which takes you to a New Message screen to write a new message.

Working with multiple messages

You may want to delete multiple messages, move several from the inbox to another folder, or flag a selection of messages or mark them as unread, all at once. Here's the way to do that:

1. **Open the Mail app and tap All Inboxes or one of the account-specific inboxes.**

2. **Tap the Edit button in the upper-right corner.**

   Empty circles appear to the left of each message.

Swiping Away Your Messages

Swiping lets you quickly replay, flag, or trash a message from the message list. A soft swipe, more like a flick, reveals one or more options that you tap to activate; a hard swipe, that is swiping decisively from one side to the other of the screen, makes the action take place without tapping. Here are the default swipe settings:

- Soft swipe left to right to reveal the Mark as Unread/Read button. (If the message is Read, you have the Unread option and vice versa.)

- Hard swipe left to right to automatically mark the message as Unread or Read, whichever is the opposite of its current status.

- Soft swipe right to left to reveal the More button, which gives you all the options listed above, as shown in the following figure, as well as the Flag/Unflag and Archive (or Trash) buttons. Flag/Unflag reflects the message's status and Archive or Trash reflect the account settings.

  If you soft swipe a thread, the additional Show Related Messages option appears, which opens the thread. Actions taken on a swiped thread affect all messages in the thread. If you want to act on a single message within a thread, tap the thread, and then swipe only the message you want to work with.

- Hard swipe right to left to Archive (or Trash) the message. If you do this by mistake, shake your iPhone to Undo the action.

To change your swipe options, open the Settings app; tap Mail, Contacts, Calendars; tap Swipe Options. Tap Swipe Left and Swipe Right to make changes.

3. **Tap the circle next to the messages you want to delete, move, or mark.**

A white check mark in a blue circle appears and the number of messages selected is indicated at the top.

Notice in Figure 4-12 that although it *appears* only two messages have been selected, the first one is a thread, so there are actually six messages selected because all the messages in the thread are selected. Whatever action you take will affect all the messages in the thread.

If you want to mark all the messages in the mailbox or folder, tap the Mark All button and then tap Mark as Unread or Flag.

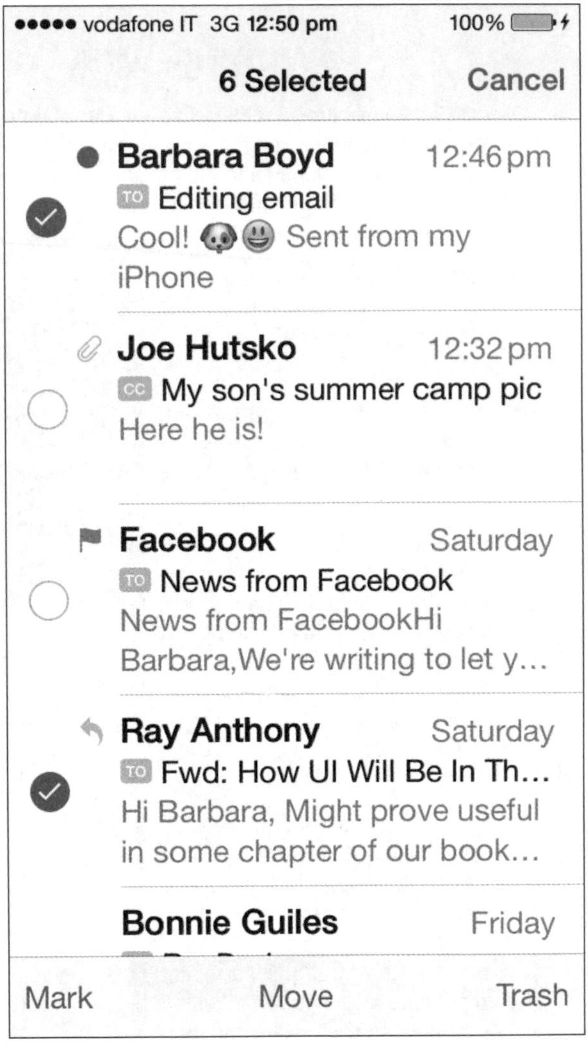

4. **After you've selected all the messages you want, tap the appropriate button: Mark, Move, or Trash (may be Archive depending on your settings), as shown in Figure 4-12.**

Tapping Mark lets you flag the messages, in which case a little flag waves next to the message in the message list, or mark them as *unread,* which reinstates the blue dot next to the message that indicates unread messages. Repeat the steps to Unflag or Mark as Read messages that are flagged or marked as unread. Tapping Move opens the filing options. Tapping Trash, well, that eliminates the selected messages.

WARNING!

●●●●● vodafone IT 3G **12:50 pm**   100% ▭ ⚡

6 Selected   Cancel

✓   ● **Barbara Boyd**   12:46 pm
      🅣🅞 Editing email
      Cool! 💀😃 Sent from my
      iPhone

◯   📎 **Joe Hutsko**   12:32 pm
      🅒🅒 My son's summer camp pic
      Here he is!

◯   🚩 **Facebook**   Saturday
      🅣🅞 News from Facebook
      News from FacebookHi
      Barbara,We're writing to let y…

✓   ↩ **Ray Anthony**   Saturday
      🅣🅞 Fwd: How UI Will Be In Th…
      Hi Barbara, Might prove useful
      in some chapter of our book…

      Bonnie Guiles   Friday

Mark   Move   Trash

Figure 4-12: Tap Mark, Move, or Trash when managing messages.

If you select no messages, Mark becomes Mark All, tap that to apply an action to all the messages in the selected inbox or folder.

The thing is, just because you tapped Trash, your messages still aren't really deleted — they've just been moved to the trash. To truly take out the trash or delete your messages from your iPhone, follow these steps:

1. **Tap the button in the upper-left corner or swipe right to return to the Mailboxes list (refer to Figure 4-13).**

2. **Tap the name of the account you want to work with in the Accounts list, not the Inboxes list.**

3. **Tap the Trash button, which looks like a trashcan.**

   If Archiving is on, instead of the trashcan, you see an archival box icon.

4. **Tap Edit.**

   The Delete All button at the bottom of the screen is activated.

5. **Tap Delete All.**

   Your messages are truly deleted.

Likewise, you should tap into the Junk folder every now and then, tap Edit and then tap Delete All.

**Book II
Chapter 4**

**Emailing Every
Which Way You Can**

Tapping into in-message links

An incoming message contains much more than just the written message. Take a look at these features (refer to Figure 4-10):

✔ Tap the name of the sender or one of the other recipients of the message. A screen opens that gives you an option of adding the contact to the VIP list, creating a new contact, or adding this email address to an existing contact.

✔ Phone numbers, email addresses, and website addresses that appear blue and underlined are active links. Tap the phone number, and an option of calling that number appears. Tap the email address, and a New Message screen opens. Tap a website address to open the page in Safari.

✔ Tap Hide/More, next to the sender's name, to hide or show the recipients of the message. When there are a lot of recipients, it's helpful to tap Hide so you can see more of the message in the opening screen.

✔ If you receive an invitation from a calendar app that uses the iCalendar format (.ics files), tap on the file and the Event Details open. Tap the Add to Calendar button at the bottom of the screen and then choose the calendar where the event should be inserted. For more details about sending and receiving event invitations, see Book III, Chapter 2.

✔ Zoom in on the message by spreading two fingers on the screen.

Multiple mailboxes

Even if you have only one email account, you may want to see more than what the default Mailboxes list shows you.

When you open the Mail app, the first screen that opens shows a list of inboxes and a list of accounts. Each account contains more than just the inbox. Within the account, you find folders for Drafts, Sent Messages, and even Junk mail. By default, you have to tap the Account on the Mailboxes list to see those other folders, but you can add them to the Mailboxes list, create other folders to group your messages by Unread or Attachments, and rearrange the order you see the mailboxes. Tap the button in the upper-left corner until you reach the Mailboxes list and do the following:

1. **Tap Edit.**

   A screen like the one shown in Figure 4-13 appears. Blue circles with white check marks indicate the mailboxes that you see.

2. **Tap an empty circle, such as the one next to Unread, to add that mailbox to the Mailboxes list.**

3. **Tap and drag the rearrange button to move a mailbox higher or lower on the list.**

4. **Scroll down to the Add Mailbox option and tap it.**

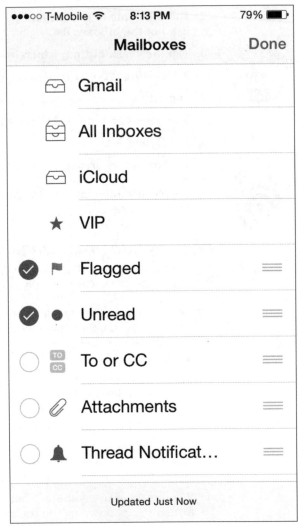

Figure 4-13: Edit the Mailboxes list to see more mailboxes or reorder the list.

If you have multiple accounts, you see a list of your accounts; tap the one you want to work with.

The list of mailboxes for that account appears.

5. **Tap the mailbox you'd like to see added to the Mailboxes list — Drafts, for example.**

6. **Tap Done.**

You now see that additional mailbox in the list with a check mark next to it.

Searching messages

There are times when you know who sent you an email, you know it arrived sometime between last Thursday and Friday, you know the subject was something about a train, but you can't find the message. Thankfully, there's Spotlight, iPhone's searching tool that works with Mail, as well as many other apps such as Contacts, Reminders, and Messages. To use Spotlight, follow these steps:

1. **From within a mailbox — it can be All Inboxes, a specific mailbox, or even the Trash box — tap the Status bar at the top of the iPhone screen or scroll up until you see the Search field.**

2. **Tap in the Search field.**

3. **Type the word or phrase you're searching for.**

   Mail searches the address and subject fields as well as content of messages within that mailbox, including the Trash and Junk files.

4. **Tap the message(s) you want to read from the list that appears.**

When you search from the Home screen, Mail messages that meet your search criteria are included in the results.

Adjusting Email Account Settings

When you set up your email account on iPhone, you've pretty much set up everything you need with regard to the technical information about the account. As with most things iPhone, however, there are many adjustments you can make in Settings to improve and personalize your Mail experience.

First, we go through the settings that are specific to the Mail app and affect how your inboxes and messages appear and behave. Then we go through the more technical aspects of managing your email account.

Settings for message presentation

These options have to do with the local management of your messages. Open the Settings app; tap Mail, Contacts, Calendars; and scroll to see the Mail settings, as shown in Figure 4-14. We explain each one in the following list:

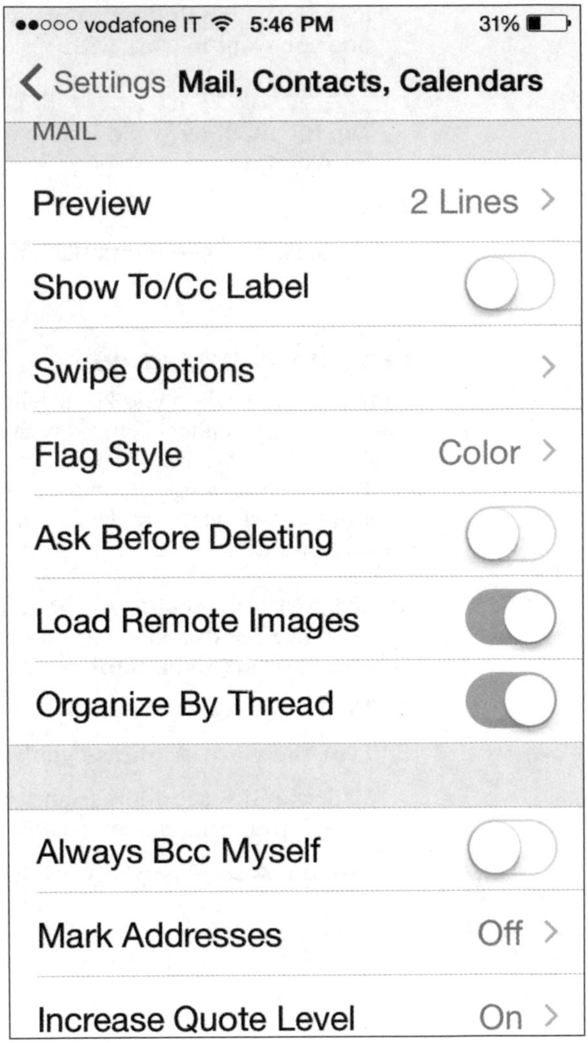

- **Preview:** Tap to choose how many lines of a message you want to see in the list of messages. You may choose from zero (None) to five lines.

- **Show To/Cc Label:** This puts a small label next to the subject line in the list of messages in your inbox. *To* means that the message was sent directly to you; *Cc* means you were sent a copy of the message whose primary recipient was someone else.

- **Swipe Options:** Select what options appear and which actions take place when you swipe across messages.

- **Flag Style:** Tap to choose between a flag icon or a colored dot.

- **Ask Before Deleting:** If you're prone to accidentally tapping the trash-can button when you don't want to, turn this on so that iPhone asks if you want to delete a message before it's actually deleted.

- **Load Remote Images:** Remote images reference an image on a web page that Mail would have to access, which gives the hosting site an

Figure 4-14: The Mail settings section of the Mail, Contacts, Calendars screen.

••○○○ vodafone IT 📶 5:46 PM	31% ▮
‹ Settings **Mail, Contacts, Calendars**	

MAIL

Preview	2 Lines ›
Show To/Cc Label	⚪
Swipe Options	›
Flag Style	Color ›
Ask Before Deleting	⚪
Load Remote Images	🔵
Organize By Thread	🔵
Always Bcc Myself	⚪
Mark Addresses	Off ›
Increase Quote Level	On ›

opportunity to log your activity. You can save cellular time, and increase your privacy, by turning this off, which leaves you the option to manually open the images.

✔ **Organize by Thread:** This turns *threading* (the grouping of messages with the same subject) on or off.

✔ **Always Bcc Myself:** A Bcc is a blind carbon copy, meaning the recipients of your message don't see this name on the list of recipients, but the person who receives the Bcc sees all the (non-Bcc) recipients. If you turn this switch on, you receive a Bcc of every message you write.

✔ **Mark Addresses:** Any email addresses that don't have the suffix you type in this field will show up in red when you address a message.

✔ **Increase Quote Level:** Tap this option on and when you respond to a message, the original message will be indented. In an exchange, each time a response is sent, the text is indented more. You can select the text and use the quote level editing tool to manually shift it.

✔ **Signature:** This is the line (or lines) that appears at the end of email messages you write. The default is *Sent from my iPhone.* Tap the button, and a screen opens where you can type a new signature line. Tap Per Account to customize the signature line for each email account you use, as shown in Figure 4-15.

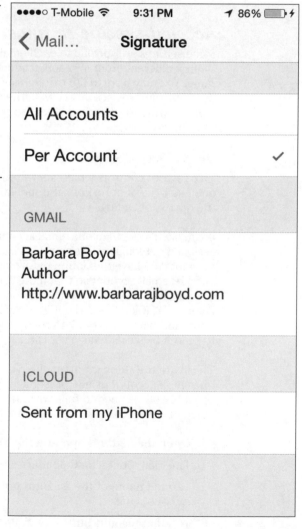

Figure 4-15: Write a custom signature line for your outgoing email messages using the Signature feature.

You can't type an active link to your web page, but you can copy one from Safari and then paste it to your signature so people who receive messages from you can access your website directly from your email message.

✔ **Default Account:** The default account is used to send messages from other apps, like Maps or Safari. This is also the account your messages will go from if you tap the Compose button on the main Mailboxes screen and don't change the From field in outgoing messages. If you have multiple e-mail accounts, tap this button and choose the account you want to be the default account.

Account-specific settings

Some settings are specific to each email account and are represented in a slightly different order for each account, but the titles and functions are the same. You may have to tap through several screens to reach your final destination. Any time you see an arrow in the right end of a field, you can tap it to see more information. Here are what the settings you find mean and how you may want to use them.

Outgoing Mail Server

This feature controls which server your mail is sent from. If you have only one email account on your iPhone, leave this alone. You can skip down to the next subheading.

If you have more than one email account on your phone, each one has an assigned outgoing mail server. This is called the Primary Server for that account. You have the option of turning on the outgoing server associated with another email account so that if the primary outgoing mail server of one email account doesn't work, iPhone tries one of the other servers. If you look at Figure 4-16, iCloud uses the iCloud SMTP server to send mail. If that server is down and Barbara's trying to send a message, iPhone uses `smtp.gmail.com` to send it because that server is turned on in the list of Other SMTP servers.

These are the steps for managing your outgoing mail servers. If you have just one email account or use preset accounts such as iCloud or Gmail, you'll probably never need to fuss with these settings. If you have more than one account set up under Other, take a look to see how it works:

1. **Open the Settings app and tap Mail, Contacts, Calendars.**

   The Mail, Contacts, Calendars screen opens.

2. **Tap the name of the account you want to work on under the Accounts list.**

3. **Tap the Account button or Mail for iCloud accounts.**

4. **Tap the SMTP button under Outgoing Mail Server.**

The SMTP screen opens, and you see which outgoing servers are used for sending your mail (refer to Figure 4-16).

5. **Tap Add Server at the bottom of the list of servers.**

   An Add Server screen opens.

6. **Type in the Host Name (for example,** smpt.verizon.com), **and then type in your username and password.**

7. **Tap Save.**

Figure 4-16: If your primary server is down, iPhone attempts to send messages with a secondary server.

WARNING!

The From address on your email is the one associated with the server that sends the message. For example, if your work server is down and you've set your personal Gmail account as the secondary server, the email is sent from your Gmail account. Your colleagues, clients, or CEO see the email as coming from hotdiggitydog@gmail.com rather than johnsmith@ab4.org.

Mailbox Behaviors

This setting controls where your draft and sent messages are stored, either on iPhone or on the mail server. Depending on your email service provider, you may also have the option of when the deleted items are ultimately deleted (for example, immediately, a week after they've been removed, or once a month). In iCloud, you have four options for deleting messages from the server:

✔ **Never:** Messages remain on the server after you've deleted them manually. This means you may access them on another device.

✔ **After One Day/Week/Month:** Messages are deleted from the server after one day, one week, or one month, whether you've read them or not.

Gmail only lets you choose where drafts are stored — it doesn't let you choose when deleted messages are removed. Other accounts may or may not give you the same choices — you have to poke around in the deeper levels of the Settings screens.

Even if your provider lets you manage different mailboxes, the process is the same:

1. **Open the Settings app and tap Mail, Contacts, Calendars.**

   The Mail, Contacts, Calendars screen opens.

2. **Tap the name of the account you want to work on.**

3. **Tap the Account button or Mail for iCloud accounts.**

4. **Tap the Advanced button.**

   The Advanced screen opens; it's similar to Figure 4-17. There may be fewer (or more) options depending on your service provider.

5. **Tap Drafts Mailbox.**

   This setting controls where your draft messages are kept.

6. **Tap Drafts under On My iPhone if you want to keep your draft messages on your iPhone.**

   A check mark appears next to Drafts.

7. **Tap Drafts (or another folder if you want) in the list under On the Server if you want your draft messages to be stored on the server.**

   If you have large draft files, perhaps with multimedia attachments, it may be more convenient to store them on the server so as not to deplete the memory on your iPhone.

8. **Repeat Step 7 for Sent Mailbox and Deleted Mailbox.**

9. **(Optional) Tap Remove under Deleted Messages to set how soon messages are removed from the server after you delete them.**

10. **Tap the button in the upper-left corner to return to the previous level. Continue tapping the upper-left button until you reach the Settings screen. Tap Done if you see it along the way and have made changes. Press the Home button to go to the Home screen.**

The S/MIME option, which you may see, lets you add certificates for signing and encrypting outgoing messages. To install certificates, you need a profile from your network administrator or from a certificate issuer's website on Safari or sent to you in an email. If you want to send encrypted email without going through the certificate process, you can download an app like iPGMail in the App Store.

Configure your computer email program to leave messages on the server as well. Go to its Preferences or Tools menu and follow the instructions for your particular email program.

Incoming Settings

The Incoming Settings section (refer to Figure 4-17) gives you limited options for encrypting incoming email and changing the path it comes in on. You probably shouldn't change these settings unless instructed to do so by a technical support person from your cellular provider or a network administrator at your place of employment. In fact, iCloud doesn't even give you the option of changing them because they're preset by Apple. Here, we go through the settings briefly, but remember: You probably don't want to change them.

**Book II
Chapter 4**

Emailing Every
Which Way You Can

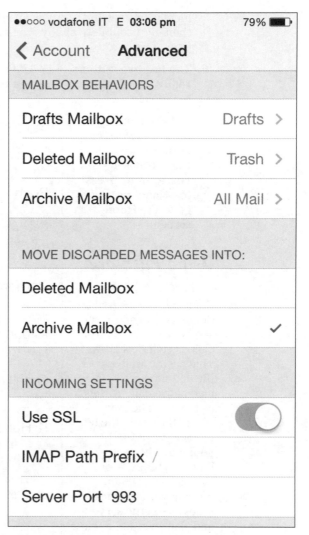

Figure 4-17: The Advanced features allow you to manage where your draft and deleted messages are stored and adjust the pathway for incoming mail.

1. **Open the Settings app and tap Mail, Contacts, Calendars.**

2. **Tap the name of the account you want to work on.**

3. **Tap the Account button.**

4. **Tap the Advanced button.**

5. **Turn Use SSL (Secure Sockets Layer) on or off.**

Ideally, this setting is on because it encrypts incoming messages, making them unreadable to shady types who want to "eavesdrop" on your email conversations.

6. **The last two options — IMAP Path Prefix and Server Port — should really be left alone unless you're instructed to change them by a technician.**

7. **Tap the back buttons in the top-left corner to return to the Settings screen you want or press the Home button to go to the Home screen.**

Using Push and Fetch

Going back to the Mail, Contacts, Calendars screen, you see a button called Fetch New Data. Think of the Mail app as the dog and your incoming email messages as the ball. The mail server throws — the terminology is *pushes* — your messages and iPhone catches — or downloads — them. Alternatively, the messages are on the server and Mail goes and fetches them when told. Once again, you have the option of turning Fetch and Push on or off.

Here's how to activate or deactivate Fetch:

1. **Open the Settings app; tap Mail, Contacts, Calendars; and tap Fetch New Data.**

The Fetch New Data screen opens, as shown in Figure 4-18.

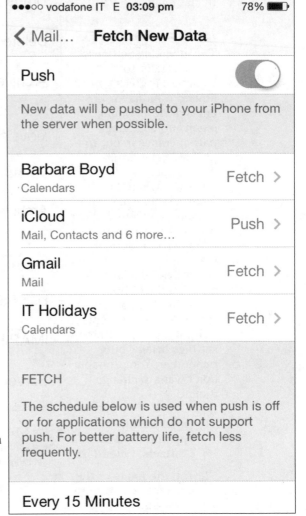

Figure 4-18: Fetch New Data lets your iPhone play catch with incoming email messages.

2. **Turn Push on and new data is pushed to your iPhone from the server.**

   Whether Mail is open or not, messages arrive in real-time in your mailbox and you hear an audible alert as they arrive, if you've established one.

3. **Set Push or Fetch for each account. Tap the name of an account.**

   A screen opens with the schedule options available. iCloud also lets you assign Push to specific mailboxes, such as Inbox or Drafts and the others remain Fetch.

4. **Tap the option you want:**

   - **Push:** To automatically retrieve new messages as they arrive in your inbox on the server

   - **Fetch:** To check for messages at the interval you previously established

   - **Manual:** To check for messages only when you open the Mail app or when you drag down below the Status bar to refresh your inbox

5. **Choose a frequency for Fetch. (Scroll down to see your options.)**

   If you turn Push off or use an application that doesn't support Push, your iPhone automatically downloads messages at the frequency you chose.

6. **Tap the back buttons in the top-left corner or swipe right to return to the Settings screen you want or press the Home button to go to the Home screen.**

Book III
Making iPhone Your Personal Assistant

●●●●○ vodafone IT E   **13:54**   93% ▰▮

🔍   +

| 29 30 | 27 28 29 30 31 | 24 25 26 27 28 29 30 |

JUL | **AUG** | **SEP**

1 2 3 4 5 6 7	1 2 3 4	1
8 9 10 11 12 13 14	5 6 7 8 9 10 11	2 3 4 5 6 7 8
15 16 17 18 19 20 21	12 13 14 15 16 17 18	9 10 11 12 13 14 15
22 23 24 25 26 27 28	19 20 21 22 23 24 ㉕	16 17 18 19 20 21 22
29 30 31	26 27 28 29 30 31	23 24 25 26 27 28 29
		30

OCT | **NOV** | **DEC**

1 2 3 4 5 6	1 2	1
7 8 9 10 11 12 13	3 4 5 6 7 8 9	2 3 4 5 6 7 8
14 15 16 17 18 19 20	10 11 12 13 14 15 16	9 10 11 12 13 14 15
21 22 23 24 25 26 27	17 18 19 20 21 22 23	16 17 18 19 20 21 22
28 29 30 31	24 25 26 27 28 29 30	23 24 25 26 27 28 29
		30 31

2014

JAN | **FEB** | **MAR**

1 2 3 4 5	1 2	1 2
6 7 8 9 10 11 12	3 4 5 6 7 8 9	3 4 5 6 7 8 9
13 14 15 16 17 18 19	10 11 12 13 14 15 16	10 11 12 13 14 15 16
20 21 22 23 24 25 26	17 18 19 20 21 22 23	17 18 19 20 21 22 23
27 28 29 30 31	24 25 26 27 28	24 25 26 27 28 29 30
		31

APR | **MAY** | **JUN**

1 2 3 4 5 6	1 2 3 4	1
7 8 9 10 11 12 13	5 6 7 8 9 10 11	2 3 4 5 6 7 8
14 15 16 17 18 19 20	12 13 14 15 16 17 18	9 10 11 12 13 14 15
21 22 23 24 25 26 27	19 20 21 22 23 24 25	16 17 18 19 20 21 22

Today   Calendars   Inbox

Visit www.dummies.com/extras/iphoneaio to discover how to use your
iPhone as a slide show remote control.

Contents at a Glance

Chapter 1: Perfecting Your People Skills with Contacts

In This Chapter

↳ **Adding existing Contacts**

↳ **Accessing friends from social networks**

↳ **Creating new Contacts**

↳ **Viewing Contacts**

↳ **Searching Contacts**

↳ **Contacting a Contact**

*E*ven if your iPhone is your only device, Contacts is a sort of hub for your iPhone activities. Many of the apps on your iPhone retrieve data from Contacts to perform their functions: Phone accesses Contacts to call a stored phone number or FaceTime address, while Messages and Mail rely on Contacts to send messages to stored mobile phone numbers and email addresses. Contacts use isn't limited to communication apps; for example, both Calendar and Reminders access Contacts for information about people or places with whom you have appointments. Third-party apps may use the information in Contacts, too — if you give them permission.

If you already have an iPhone-compatible electronic address book, one of the first things you'll want to do is transfer the data to your iPhone by syncing your iPhone and your computer. We begin this chapter by explaining how to sync your existing electronic address book with Contacts on your iPhone. We discuss syncing in Book I, Chapter 5, but we go through the specifics for Contacts here. We then explain the editing procedures for a single contact: adding a new contact, making changes, even deleting a contact. We show you how to search for a contact, too. We conclude this chapter with the interactive aspects of Contacts, including adding your Twitter and Facebook friends to Contacts, sharing your contacts with someone else, and communicating with your contacts via phone, FaceTime, email, and text messages.

11:24 AM

ettings   iCloud

Barbara Boyd
babsboyd@icloud.com

et Up Family Sharing…

Adding Existing Contacts

You probably have some form of electronic address book on your computer or another device such as a tablet; you may also access a company directory through Microsoft Exchange or IBM Lotus Notes. (If you don't — or if you prefer to keep contacts on your iPhone separate — skip this section and go directly to the section "Creating New Contacts," in which case you create your address book in the Contacts app on your iPhone.) Your existing contacts could be in one or more of the following places:

- On your Mac in Contacts, Address Book, Entourage, or Outlook
- On your PC in Microsoft Outlook, Windows Address Book, or Windows Contacts
- Online in Microsoft Exchange, Yahoo!, Google, or a social network such as Facebook or LinkedIn
- On the SIM card of a previous cellphone (refer to the sidebar at the end of this section)

To transfer your contacts from an old iPhone to a new iPhone, simply sign in to your iCloud, Gmail, Yahoo!, or Exchange account on the new iPhone. With the exception of iCloud, this holds true if you're migrating from another smartphone that uses Android. Your new iPhone accesses anything you've already saved to any of those accounts automatically.

In this section, we explain how to sign in to these different applications on your iPhone. We also give specific steps for imports from Microsoft Exchange, Google, Yahoo!, LDAP or CardDAV formatted data, and a SIM card. At the end of this chapter, we explain adding contact information from incoming phone calls, voicemail messages, SMS messages, and vCards attached to email.

If you use IBM Lotus, you can use IBM Sametime, Lotus Notes Traveler, or a third-party contact management app such as DejaOffice (www.dejaoffice.com) to sync your contacts to your iPhone. Consult with your network administrator for the necessary passcodes.

If you use Windows, you can sync with just one application. On a Macintosh, you can sync with multiple applications.

Accessing your contacts from iCloud

We explain how to set up an iCloud account in Book I, Chapter 5. Essentially, iCloud stores your data, including contacts, on a remote server called a *cloud*. When you add or make changes to data on one device associated with your iCloud account, the new information is pushed to all your other devices connected to iCloud.

If your contacts reside only on your computer, activate iCloud on your computer first and click the Contacts switch to the on position. Your contacts will sync to iCloud, and then when you turn on iCloud on your iPhone, the contacts will sync there, too.

To sync Contacts on your iPhone with your computer and other iOS devices via iCloud, do the following:

1. **Open the Settings app and tap iCloud.**

2. **Tap the Contacts switch on, as shown in Figure 1-1.**

   If your screen doesn't look like Figure 1-1, go to Book I, Chapter 5 to set up an iCloud account.

If you want to use iCloud with your Windows PC, download the iCloud Control Panel for Windows app from Apple (www.apple.com/icloud/setup/pc.html).

Figure 1-1: Turn Contacts On in iCloud to automatically sync Contacts on your iPhone with other devices using iCloud.

Book III Chapter 1

Perfecting Your People Skills with Contacts

Adding and syncing Microsoft Exchange contacts

Particularly in a corporate setting, some of your contacts, such as the company directory, may be in Microsoft Exchange or Microsoft Office 365. As long as the technical support folks in your office will give you the access information, you can sync the contacts from Microsoft Exchange with your iPhone.

Follow these steps to set up the account on your iPhone:

1. **Open the Settings app, and tap Mail, Contacts, Calendars.**

   The Mail, Contacts, Calendars screen appears.

2. **Do one of the following:**

   1. If you set up a Microsoft Exchange account when you first set up your iPhone or when you set up email as explained in Book II, Chapter 4, tap the name of that account in the list that appears.

   2. **Tap the Contacts switch on** in the account screen.

   Or

   1. Tap Add Account to set up a new account.

   2. Tap Exchange.

   3. Fill in the requested information.

   4. Tap Next.

      After the information you entered is verified, you'll be asked to turn on a series of switches to establish which types of things you want to sync. Turn on Contacts. (Turn on the others such as Mail, Calendars, or Reminders, if you want to sync those with Exchange.)

   You now see Microsoft Exchange in the list of accounts on the Mail, Contacts, Calendars settings screen.

3. **Tap the Save button in the upper-right corner.**

   You return to the Mail, Contacts, Calendars settings screen.

4. **Tap Fetch New Data.**

5. **Tap Push On.**

   Anytime changes are made to the contacts on the server now associated with your Microsoft Exchange account, those changes are pushed to your iPhone.

6. **If your server doesn't support push, or you want to conserve battery power, select a default fetch interval — every 15 or 30 minutes, or hourly.**

   Your iPhone contacts the server for new data at the interval you select.

Importing Google, Yahoo!, AOL, and Outlook contacts

Apple has made importing your contacts from the most frequently used email service providers simple. By configuring your iPhone to recognize your account from one or more of these providers, you can access the contact information you store with them. And you can have more than one account. For example, if you use Google for your personal contacts but Outlook for work, you can have both on your iPhone. Later in this chapter we explain how to manage several accounts in Contacts.

To set up an account for one of these providers on your iPhone, follow these steps:

1. **Open the Settings app, and then tap Mail, Contacts, Calendars.**

2. **Tap Add Account.**

    The Add Account screen appears.

3. **Tap the name of the service provider you use — Google, Yahoo!, AOL, or Outlook.com.**

    If your service provider is not one of those listed, for example Comcast or Verizon, tap Other, and then tap Add Mail Account. A New Account screen appears where you can type in your email address and password, and then tap Next. Your iPhone will search the Internet for that service provider and set up an account for you. It's almost like magic!

4. **The Add Account screen opens.**

    Filling in the Name field is optional. Type your email address in the Address field and your password in the Password field. An identifier is automatically entered in the Description field; however, you can tap and hold on the text to replace it with something that helps you remember the account, such as "work" or "golf team."

5. **Tap the Next button in the upper-right corner.**

    The next screen shows a list of available services.

6. **Tap the Contacts switch On.**

Some services, such as Yahoo!, store your address book on a remote server, so you have to have an Internet connection to access it.

Configuring LDAP or CardDAV contacts accounts

LDAP and CardDAV are Internet protocols that allow access to data on a remote server. Multiple users can access the same information, so they're often used in business and organization settings. The difference between the two is that LDAP data remains on the server — you access it from your iPhone via an Internet connection, but it isn't synced to your iPhone. CardDAV data is synced over the air (and copied) to your iPhone, and, depending on the way the server is set up, you may be able to search the server for contact information.

If your employer uses a contacts program that uses the LDAP or CardDAV protocols (methods for data exchange), which you want to access or sync with your iPhone, you can add an LDAP or CardDAV account. You'll need some account information from your IT department or network support person:

- **Server:** This has your company or organization information.

- **Username:** This is your identification. (Optional for LDAP.)

- **Password:** A password is required. (Optional for LDAP.)

- **Description:** Although optional, this name helps you identify the account in the accounts list on the Mail, Contacts, Calendars settings screen.

After you've gathered the necessary information, set up the account on your iPhone by following these steps:

1. **Open the Settings app and tap Mail, Contacts, Calendars.**

2. **Tap Add Account.**

3. **Tap Other.**

4. **In the Contacts section, tap Add LDAP or Add CardDAV Account, whichever is indicated.**

5. **Type the information requested.**

6. **Tap the Next button in the upper-right corner.**

   After your account information is verified, make sure Contacts is turned on, and the contacts data are added to your iPhone.

7. **Tap the Save button in the upper-right corner.**

   You return to the Mail, Contacts, Calendars settings screen. When you open Contacts, your contacts are automatically synced.

8. **Tap Fetch New Data.**

   The Fetch New Data screen opens.

9. **If your server supports push notifications, tap Push on.**

   Anytime changes are made on the server where the contacts reside, that change is pushed to your iPhone, and vice versa.

10. **If your server doesn't support push or you want to conserve battery power, select a default fetch interval — every 15 minutes, every 30 minutes, or hourly.**

    Your iPhone contacts the server for new data at the interval you select.

Copying SIM card contacts the SIM-ple and not-so-SIM-ple way

Although your iPhone doesn't store information on the SIM card, if you're transferring to iPhone from another cellphone, you may have contact information on the old SIM card that you want to transfer.

If your old device is an Android or other non-iPhone smartphone that uses a nano-SIM card, you can typically pop out the nano-SIM in your new iPhone and pop in your old one to copy those contacts to your new iPhone. (Open the Settings app; tap Mail, Contacts, Calendars; and tap Import SIM Contacts.)

If your old phone's SIM card isn't the same type of SIM card as the one in your new iPhone — regardless of iPhone model — you

may still be able to copy any contacts from your old smartphone by connecting it to your computer and using special data export software that may come with your old phone or is available to download from the phone manufacturer's website, or by using a third-party smartphone data transfer program. Check your smartphone's manual or search the manufacturer's support site to see if they offer a software application you can download to export your contacts from your old phone so you can copy them to your new iPhone.

If your contacts are in another program, you can try exporting them as vCards (the file will have a `.vcf` suffix) and then importing them into Address Book (OS X 10.7 or earlier), Contacts (OS X 10.8 or later), or Entourage or Outlook 2011 on the Mac or Outlook or Windows Address Book on a Windows PC. Follow the previously outlined procedure for syncing with iCloud or Outlook to sync the contacts with your iPhone.

Adding your social network contacts

You often find contact information from social networks and with just a few taps, you can import the information to Contacts directly from any of these social networks. Follow these steps:

1. **Open the Settings app and then tap Twitter, Facebook, Flickr, or Vimeo.**

   The appropriate settings screen opens.

   If you don't have the app installed, tap the Install button to download it from the iTunes Store.

2. **Tap in the User Name field and type your username.**

3. **Tap in the Password field and type your password.**

4. **Tap Sign In.**

   A disclaimer appears that explains what happens on your iPhone when you sign in to the social network. Essentially, information about your friends will be downloaded to Contacts; events will sync to your Calendar; you can post status updates and images directly from the Photos app; and apps enabled to work with your account have your permission to do so.

5. **Tap Sign In again to accept these conditions.**

   You can change the settings after you sign in if you don't want these things to happen.

6. **The settings screen reappears with Calendar and Contacts options, as shown in Figure 1-2.**

   The apps enabled to work with your account are listed as well, and you can tap the switch to turn access on or off (refer to Figure 1-2).

7. **Tap Contacts On.**

8. **Tap Update (All) Contacts to provide the social network with information from your Contacts, which allows it to update matching contacts.**

   You may want to repeat Step 8 periodically, especially if you add new contacts to Contacts.

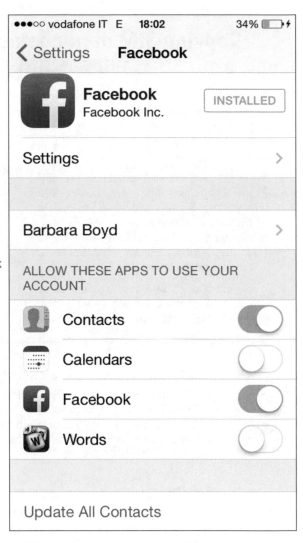

Figure 1-2: Turn Contacts on in Facebook settings to see your Facebook friends in Contacts.

Unifying contacts

When you import or access contacts from different sources, you may find you have more than one information record for the same contact. Contacts links contacts that have the same name, and creates a unified contact. A unified contact doesn't merge the information but does display all the information for one person on one record. If the names aren't exactly the same, two records appear, but you can manually link contacts and change which one is the top unified contact by doing the following:

1. **Tap a contact that has more than one record, and then tap Edit.**

2. **Tap the Link Contacts field at the bottom of the Info screen.**

   Your list of contacts opens.

3. **Tap the name of the contact you want to link to the first contact.**

4. **Tap the Link button in the upper-right corner.**

5. **Tap Done.**

6. **To unlink contacts, tap Edit, and then tap the minus sign next to the source you want to unlink.**

You can link two or more contacts with the same name or with different names, such as a personal card and a company card or two partners at the same business, but when you link two or more contacts, only the primary contact appears in the Contacts list and the linked contacts are listed on the contact they've been linked to. To use a different name for the unified card, tap the contact you want to change in Contacts and then tap Edit. Scroll to the bottom of the contacts card to see a list of linked contacts. Tap the disclosure triangle to the right of the name you want to see in the Contacts list, and then tap the button that reads Use This Name for Unified Card. The names on the individual contact records don't change but the unified card shows the name you selected.

If you make changes to one record, that information syncs with the source it came from, but doesn't change on records from other sources. This means if you change the email on a contact in Google, the information is updated on the Google server and on your devices that access the Google server, but it isn't changed on the record that comes from Facebook.

Creating New Contacts

When you meet new people, chances are, you'll want to add them to Contacts on your iPhone. If you use iCloud, the new information syncs automatically to your computer and other iOS devices you use with iCloud. Contacts stores much more than names, addresses, and phone numbers. You can add a photo of the person, a birthday or anniversary (which nicely links to Calendar), email addresses, websites, and whatever kind of field you want to invent, like favorite color or namesake holiday date. In this section, we show you how to create new contacts, fill in the contact info with everything you know about the person, make changes, and, well, delete them if things go bad in the relationship, for whatever reason.

Filling in name, address, phone number, and more

Follow these steps to fill in basic information about your contacts:

1. **Tap the Contacts app icon on the Home screen or tap the Contacts button at the bottom of the Phone app.**

   If you want the contact to be part of a group, follow these steps:

   1. Tap the Group button at the top of the screen.

      If you added contacts from your social networks or other services like Gmail but don't have groups, you still see the Groups button.

   2. Tap Hide All Contacts, and then tap the group you want to display.

      You can only add a contact to a group that resides on your iPhone not a remote group such as Facebook.

      A check mark indicates which group is active. Even if you add a contact to a group, it's part of All Contacts.

   3. Tap Done.

   Despite the outcry of many Contacts users, Apple has still not added a create groups function within the iOS Contacts app. Groups you create in other contact management apps that you access from Contacts are reflected. If you use iCloud, you can sign in to www.icloud.com from a computer, sign in to your account, click Contacts, and create groups there. If you use a Mac, you can do so from the Contacts app directly.

2. **Tap the plus sign in the upper-right corner.**

   A New Contact screen opens.

3. **Tap in the field that reads First.**

   The cursor appears in that field and the keyboard opens.

4. **Type the first name of your new contact.**

   Not all contacts have first and last names and you aren't obligated to fill in any field that you don't have information for. If you just have the name and phone number of a company, you can fill in only those fields.

5. **Tap Return to move from one field to the next.**

   Continue typing the information you have for your contact.

If you have contacts from more than one account — for example, a Microsoft Exchange account as well as contacts on your iPhone — select the default account where new contacts will be saved by opening the Settings app; tapping Mail, Contacts, Calendar; and then tapping Default Account in the Contacts section. Tap the account you want to use or On My iPhone to automatically place new contacts on your iPhone.

The following sections describe fields that have specific functions.

Phone, E-mail, and URL fields

The Phone, E-mail, and URL fields behave the same way, but their behavior may seem a bit peculiar at first. Here we give you a few tips to help you understand them:

✔ As soon as you begin typing in the first field, say, phone number, a minus sign appears to the left and a new field is added beneath it. You can type a second phone number in this new field. As soon as you begin typing in the second phone number field, a third one appears. This happens with the Phone, E-mail, and URL fields. Don't worry: Those empty fields won't clutter up the final view of your contact's info screen. You only see the blank field in Create or Edit mode.

✔ Notice that there's a line between the field name and the empty field for Phone, E-mail, and URL. You can change the field name of these fields by tapping on the field name to the left of the line. A Label list opens. Tap the label you want to associate with the phone number, email, or URL that you type in the adjacent field.

✔ Scroll down to the bottom of the Label list and you see Add Custom Label. Tap this and you can enter a label of your own for the field.

Ringtone, Vibration, and Text Tone fields

You can assign a special sound or vibration so that when a contact calls or sends a text message, you know by the sound who is calling or who the message is from:

✔ **Tap Ringtone or Text Tone.** A list opens from which you choose the ringtone you want to hear when that contact calls or the Text Tone you want to hear when that contact sends you a text message. Tap Buy More Tones to access the ringtone section of the iTunes Store and download tones that can be used for ringtones or text tones.

✔ **Tap Vibration.** A list gives you options for the vibration you want associated with a text message that arrives from that contact. Tap Create New Vibration to record your own custom vibration.

Add Address

Scroll down to find this rarely used option. To add an address, tap the plus sign to the left of the field or in the blank field. The field expands as shown in Figure 1-3. Type the address.

Here, too, as soon as you begin typing, a second field opens, so you can add a second address. And by tapping on the field name to the left, you can change the field name so it reflects which address it's associated with, like work or home or even a custom field, like cabin or boat slip.

Tap an address in Contacts, and Maps opens to show the location. See Book III, Chapter 3 for more information about Maps.

Birthday and Date fields

The neat thing about Contacts is that it not only manages information about *how* or *where* to contact someone but also information *about* the person, like a birthday or other important date. If you link your Facebook friends to Contacts, information from their profiles flows into Contacts. This information can also be accessed by Calendar so you don't forget to call, or send a dozen roses, on the important date.

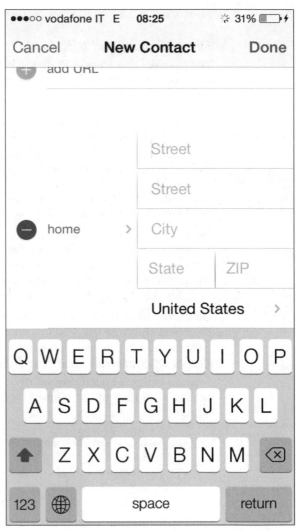

Figure 1-3: The Add Address field expands so you can type in the street address, city, state, ZIP, and country.

✔ **Birthday:** Tap Birthday and a rotor opens, as shown in Figure 1-4, so you can choose the month, day, and year of the contact's birth date. A birthday that is added to a contact appears in Calendar if you activate the Birthday calendar. Read more about Calendar in Book III, Chapter 2. And notice that second Birthday option? That's for entering a birthday using a Chinese, Hebrew, or Islamic calendar. Tap the field name to choose which you want to include.

✔ **Date:** The first field name that comes up is Anniversary for this field, after which you can add as many other important dates related to this contact as you want. Use the rotor to put in the date you want. Like the Phone, E-mail, URL, and Address fields, as soon as you add this field, a blank one appears beneath it. You can also edit the name of the field by tapping on it and choosing Other or adding a custom label.

Add Related Name

If you remember people by association, you're gonna love this feature. To add people who are related to the Contact (such as a parent, spouse, sibling, partner, assistant, or manager), tap Add Related Name, and then tap the Info button on the right. The Contacts list opens; tap the name you want to add as a relation, and you return to the contact information screen. Tap the field label to reveal a list of choices for the type of relation, and tap the appropriate one.

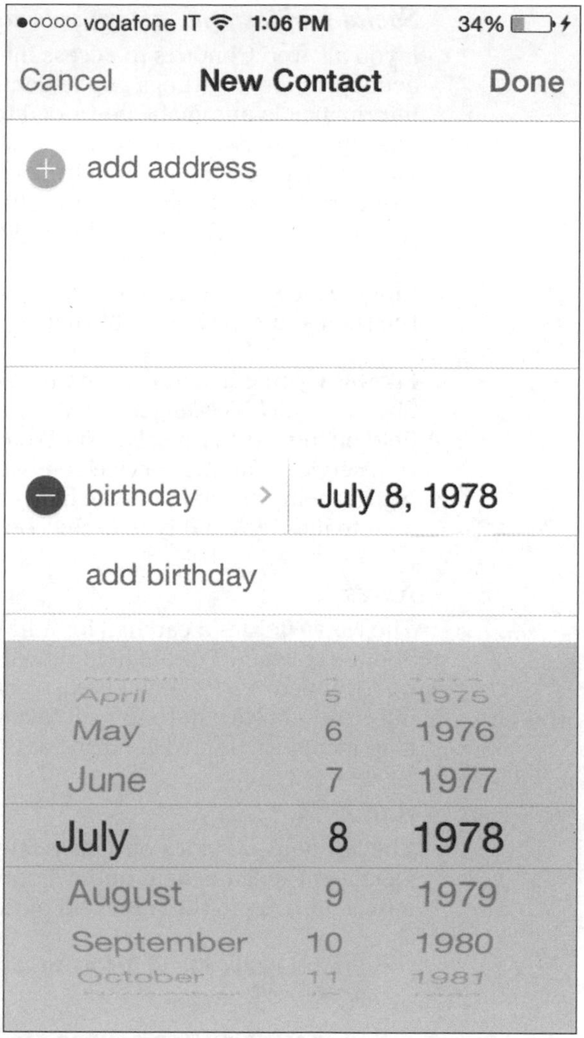

The relations are one-sided: If you add Jack to Jill's card, you see Jack's name on Jill's card, but you don't see Jill's name on Jack's card. And it's not an active link, which means seeing Jack's name on Jill's card can jog your memory but tapping Jack's name does nothing.

●○○○○ vodafone IT 🛜 1:06 PM		34% 🔋⚡
Cancel	**New Contact**	Done

➕ add address

➖ birthday > July 8, 1978

add birthday

April	5	1975
May	6	1976
June	7	1977
July	**8**	**1978**
August	9	1979
September	10	1980
October	11	1981

Figure 1-4: Use the rotor to set your contact's birthday.

If you want to cancel the relation — say Jack and Jill split up — tap Edit in the upper-right corner. Tap the minus sign that appears to the left of the relation, and then tap Delete, which appears on the right. This action only deletes the relation between the two contacts; it doesn't delete any contacts.

Related Names are not the same thing as Linked Contacts. Refer to the earlier sidebar, "Unifying contacts" to understand how contacts from different sources appear on one screen.

Social profiles and instant message addresses

If you allowed Contacts to access information from your social network accounts (in the Settings app under Twitter, Facebook, Flickr, or Vimeo), this information is automatically added to Contacts. If you want to limit promiscuous sharing between Contacts and your social networks or your friends don't share this information publicly, you can manually add multiple social network profile usernames to each contact. Tap Add Social Profile, and then tap the field label to the left to choose which social network you want: Twitter, Facebook, Flickr, LinkedIn, Myspace, Sina Weibo, or a custom service. After tapping the service, the Info screen re-opens. Tap the Social Profile field to the right and type the profile name.

Likewise, you can enter instant message addresses for services such as Skype or MSN Messenger. Tap Add Instant Message, and then tap the service field on the left to reveal a list of ten IM services plus an option to add a custom service. Tap the service you use to instant message with this contact. After tapping the service, the Info screen re-opens. Tap the Instant Message field to the right and type in the contact's IM address.

Notes

The Notes field is a catchall for additional information you want to keep about a contact. Tap the field (you don't have to tap Edit first), and the keyboard appears so you can type, or dictate if you use Siri. We use this field for information relevant to the contact such as business hours, club membership numbers, or favorite dishes at restaurants.

Add Field

The last field provides options related to the name of the contact. Tap Add Field and the list of field options opens. After one of the options is used, it no longer appears in the Add Field options list.

- **Prefix:** Adds a field before first name where you can type in a title such as Mr. or Princess.

- **Phonetic First Name, Phonetic Middle Name, and Phonetic Last Name:** Are inserted immediately after the First, Middle (if added), or Last name fields so you can type in a phonetic spelling of the names that are pronounced differently than they're spelled.

- **Middle:** Adds a field between the First and Last for a middle name.

- **Suffix:** To add common suffixes like MD or Jr.

- **Nickname:** Comes right before company.

- **Job Title and Department:** Are inserted before Company.

Create a New Contact for yourself including your own related people and then specify which is your card in the Settings app by tapping Mail, Contacts, Calendars, and then tapping My Info, which opens Contacts.

Choose the contact you created for yourself. The My Info card is used by Siri, Reminders, and other apps to understand commands like "Remind me upon arriving home" or "Call my sister." Specify the My Info card for Siri by opening the Settings app, tapping General, tapping Siri, and tapping My Info.

Each time you add a custom label, that label is added to the list beneath whatever options Contacts gives you for that field. If you add a lot of custom labels, the Add Custom Label button is all the way at the bottom — just scroll down to find it. You can delete custom labels from the list by tapping the Edit button. Tap the minus sign that appears next to the label you want to delete, and then tap the Delete button. If the custom label was being used on a contact, it will be replaced by a generic label.

Adding photos

The first thing you see on the New Contact screen is a field in the upper-left corner called Add Photo. This lets you add a photo of the contact, and when a call comes in from any of the phone numbers of that contact, the photo appears on your Home screen. You have three ways to add photos:

- **From Social Networks:** If you give Facebook, Twitter, or one of the other social networks access to contacts, the profile photo for your contact is automatically added to the contact info. You can edit or replace this photo if you want.

- **Tap Add Photo:** A dialog appears, which gives you the option to take a photo or choose an existing photo.

  - **Tap Take Photo:** The Camera app opens. Book IV, Chapter 1 talks all about the Camera, but here's a quick rundown.

  1. Aim the camera at the subject you want to photograph, and tap the Switch Camera button if you see yourself instead of your subject. When you're satisfied, tap the white camera button.

  2. If you like the shot, you can resize it by pinching or spreading your fingers on the image and drag to move it to a pleasing position.

  3. If it's just not right, tap Retake, and try again (refer to Figure 1-5).

  4. When you like the result, tap Use Photo.

     You see the photo you took in the photo field on the Contact Info screen.

  Or

  - **Tap Choose Photo.**

    The Photos app opens.

1. Tap the album where the photo you want to use is stored.

2. Tap the photo you want to use.

3. Move and scale as explained in Step 2 previously.

4. When you like the photo, tap Choose.

   The photo is saved to the New Contact screen.

The data in Contacts in the Phone app is the same data as in the Contacts app — just two ways to reach the same information.

Adding contacts from phone calls and messages

If you receive or initiate a phone call, text message, or email from a number or address that isn't in Contacts, you may want to add that information to an existing contact or create a new contact. Here's how:

Figure 1-5: Take a photo of your contact and adjust it until it's just right.

1. **After you finish a conversation, open the Phone app and go to the Recents screen.**

   A list of recent incoming and outgoing calls appears.

2. **Tap the Info button to the right of the number you want to add.**

   It can be from a call you received or one you initiated.

   An Info screen opens.

3. **Tap Create New Contact.**

   A New Contact screen opens. Type in the information you have and select a special ringtone if you want.

   Or

   Tap Add to Existing Contact.

   The Contacts screen opens.

4. **Search for the contact you want to add the number to and add the number in the appropriate field.**

5. **Tap Done.**

To create a new contact or add a number to an existing contact from the keypad, when you call a new number:

1. **Open the Phone app and go to the Keypad screen.**

2. **Enter the number you want to call, but don't tap Call.**

3. **Tap + Add to Contacts at the top of the screen just under the number.**

   A dialog gives you three choices:

   • Create New Contact

   • Add to Existing Contact

   • Cancel

4. **Tap the button for the action you want to take.**

5. **Follow the procedure for creating a new contact or adding a number to an existing contact.**

6. **Tap Done.**

To create a new contact or add a number to an existing contact from a received message:

1. **Open the Messages app.**

2. **Tap the message that came from an unidentified number.**

3. **Tap Contact, and then tap the Info button.**

4. **Follow Steps 3 through 6 as outlined previously.**

To create a new contact or add a number to an existing contact from an email:

1. **Open the Mail app.**

2. **Tap the message that has the email address you want to add and do one of the following:**

- In the address fields, tap the sender's or recipient's address and then choose Create New Contact or Add to Existing Contact on the screen that appears.

- On an address within a message, tap and hold the address, choose Add to Contacts, and then choose Create New Contact or Add to Existing Contact on the screen that appears.

3. **Follow Steps 3 through 6 as outlined previously.**

Editing and Deleting Contacts

People move, change jobs, change phone numbers, and change names, and you want to keep Contacts current with the state of affairs. The point of departure for editing and deleting contacts is the same:

1. **Open the Contacts app or tap Contacts in the Phone app.**

2. **Tap the name of the contact you want to edit or delete.**

3. **Tap the Edit button in the upper-right corner.**

4. **Tap in the field you want to edit.**

   The keyboard opens so you can make your change.

   Scroll to the next field you want to edit and make any other changes.

   If no photo is present, tap Add Photo and proceed as described in the section "Adding Photos." To change an existing photo, tap Edit under the photo and then tap one of the options in the pop-up menu: Take Photo, Choose Photo, Edit Photo, or Delete Photo. The first two options let you replace the existing photo with a new photo, the third option lets you move or zoom the existing photo, and the last option removes the photo.

5. **To delete a field, tap the red and white minus sign to the left of the field, and then tap Delete, which appears to the right.**

   If you want to delete a field that you added from the Add Field selections, tap that field, tap the X that appears to the right, and then tap Done. When the field is empty, it will no longer appear on the Contact Info screen.

6. **To add an additional phone, email, website, or address, tap in the blank field below the last filled-in field.**

7. **To add a field, tap the Add Field field at the bottom of the screen and proceed as explained previously in the "Creating New Contacts" section.**

8. **Tap Done in the upper-right corner.**

   The corrected Contact Info screen appears.

To delete a contact, tap the name of the contact, tap Edit, and then tap the Delete Contact button at the bottom of the Edit screen.

Changes, additions, and deletions you make are automatically pushed to your computer and other devices logged in to the services you use such as iCloud or Google.

Sorting and Displaying Contacts

You can adjust the sort order and the display options in the Settings app by tapping Mail, Contacts, Calendars, and going to the Contacts section (refer to Figure 1-6). The settings apply to groups and All Contacts. You can mix and match the options in four different ways; for example, you can sort by last name and then display by first name — whatever makes the most sense to you.

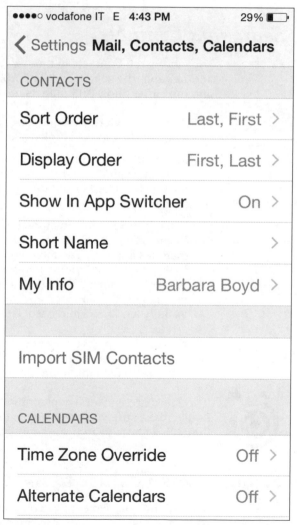

Figure 1-6: Sort and display contacts in the order you want.

- ✔ **Sort Order:** Tap to open options for choosing to sort your contacts by first name and then last name, or vice versa.

- ✔ **Display Order:** Tap to open options for viewing your contacts by first name followed by last name, or vice versa.

- ✔ **Show In App Switcher:** When the switch next to this feature is on, you see your Favorite and Recent contacts at the top of the App Switcher screen.

(Double-click the Home button to open it.) The Recents include people you contacted with the Phone or Messages app.

- **Short Name:** Tap to open the screen that gives the option to turn on and define how you want names to appear when there isn't enough space to display the whole first and last name of a contact. The choices are first name and last initial, first initial and last name, first name only, or last name only. From this screen you can also turn on the Prefer Nicknames option. Contacts will display the nickname and you can use it with Siri and Voice Control.

Searching Contacts

You can search Contacts in three ways. Each time you open Contacts from another app, the search and find process is the same. Open the Contacts app and tap either Show All Contacts or the group you want to search in:

- Scroll through the list until you see the name you want. If you scroll very fast, tap to stop the scrolling, and then tap on the name you want.

- In the index that runs down the right side of the screen, tap the letter that corresponds to the initial letter of the name of the person you're looking for. Then scroll through that section of the alphabet to find the person.

- Tap in the Search field at the top of the screen to open the keyboard. Begin typing the name of the person you want to find. A list of possible matches appears. The more you type, the fewer the choices. Contacts looks at the first letters of first names, last names, and words that are part of a company name. If you type "Jo," first names like **Jo**e come up, last names, like **Jo**hnson appear, and companies or organizations such as **Jo**lly Ice Cream and Association of **Jo**urnalists show up as well.

Whichever way you choose to search, when you find the name you're looking for, tap the name to either open the Contacts Info screen or to add that name to the To field in the program you're sending from.

If you're searching for a contact that you know is in Contacts but you can't find it, make sure you're looking in the right group or switch to the All Contacts view to search your entire address book.

Sending One Contact to Another

Say a friend compliments you on your new haircut and asks for your stylist's name and phone number. You can dictate the name and number or write it down, or you can send the information directly from Contacts:

1. **Open the contact you want to share.**

2. **Tap Share Contact at the bottom of the screen.**

3. **Tap one of the choices to send the information:**

   - **AirDrop:** Share with other iDevices that have AirDrop turned on and are on the same Wi-Fi network or close enough for a Bluetooth connection.

   - **Message or Mail:** Fill in the address and tap Send. The information is sent in vcf or vCard, which is a file format for electronic business cards.

Calling and Messaging from Contacts

Although you use Contacts to manage information, you can also generate communications directly from a Contact Info screen. Tap the contact you want to connect with and then do one of the following:

- Tap a phone number to call the person.

- Tap an email address to open a pre-addressed New Message in Mail. Type a subject and a message, and tap Send.

- Tap FaceTime to initiate a FaceTime video chat.

- When a phone number or email address can be used by more than one service, buttons appear to the right, as shown in Figure 1-7. Tap the Messages or Phone button to send a text message or call a mobile number; tap the video or phone button to make either type of FaceTime call; tap the Messages or Mail button to send an iMessage or email to an address.

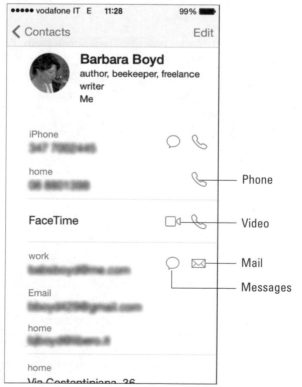

Figure 1-7: When more than one option is available, appropriate buttons appear.

✔ Tap Send Message at the bottom of the Contact Info screen, and then choose the correct phone number or email address if sending to a device with iMessage to send a message. A New Message in Messages opens, addressed to the contact. Type your message and tap Send.

You can access Contacts from communication apps that use the information in Contacts — Phone, FaceTime, Mail, and Messages. Contacts also appears when you want to send things from non-communication apps like Photos and Safari. We take you through the process for each one in their respective chapters, but after you learn to send things to a contact from one app, you pretty much know how to send them in any app. Ah, the beauty of iPhone!

Chapter 2: Managing Your Time with Calendar, Reminders, and Clock

In This Chapter

✔ Adding and syncing existing Calendars

✔ Viewing and hiding Calendars

✔ Creating, changing, and deleting Calendar events

✔ Sharing Calendar through iCloud

✔ Remembering with Reminders

✔ Using Clock to help pass the time

These days, we all have a lot to remember and the three apps explained in this chapter can help.

The Calendar app on your iPhone helps you keep track of appointments, birthdays, and deadlines along with fun things like parties and vacations. Calendar syncs with calendars on your computer and other iOS devices, as well as remote calendars you subscribe to. When you receive invitations, Calendar inserts the event on the right date and time. We begin this chapter by explaining how to add your existing electronic calendars to your iPhone. Then we show you Calendar's different views and settings. Next we look at creating and editing events on your iPhone, how to respond and send event invitations, and how to search for an event.

The second app we explain is Reminders, the list-making, automatic reminding app that's great for simple shopping lists, as well as projects that have tasks with deadlines. Both Calendar and Reminders work with Notifications, which means your events and time commitments are viewable when you open the Notification Center (see Book I, Chapter 4). While we're on the subject of time, we explain the Clock app, too. You learn that it's not just your ordinary clock but a world clock, alarm, stopwatch, and timer.

Adding and Syncing Existing Calendars

The Calendar app consists of one or more calendars and events on those calendars. You can create blank calendars on your iPhone and then fill in the events as you schedule them or sync with calendars kept on other services, such as Google, Yahoo!, Facebook, and Microsoft Exchange. First we explain how to create a calendar on your iPhone, and then, in case you use one or more other calendar services, we explain how to access calendars from your iPhone and keep all your calendars synced in the future.

Adding a calendar on your iPhone

You probably have your iPhone with you almost all the time, so it makes sense to use Calendar as your time management system. You can create one calendar that has everything or, as we recommend, create a separate calendar for each area of your life, which could be as simple as work and play, or a more complex setup with separate calendars for doctor appointments, sporting events, entertainment, and deadlines.

Calendar lets you view one, some, or all of your calendars; for example, you could view all of them when setting up a new appointment, but then view just one calendar to see how many times you went to the dentist in the last year.

To create a calendar, follow these steps:

1. **Open the Calendar app.**

2. **Tap the Calendars button at the bottom of the screen.**

   A list of your local and remote calendars appears.

3. **Tap Edit in the upper-left corner.**

4. **Tap Add Calendar.**

   If you turned the Calendar option on in iCloud, you find this in the iCloud section; otherwise, it's under the On My iPhone heading.

   The Add Calendar screen opens.

5. **Type a name for the calendar and then tap a color you want to use to identify events in this calendar, as shown in Figure 2-1.**

6. **Tap Done.**

   The Edit Calendars screen appears and you see your new calendar in the list.

7. **Tap Done in the upper-left corner to return to the main Calendars list.**

8. **Tap Done — once more — in the upper-right corner to view your events.**

Using Calendar with iCloud

We explain how to set up an iCloud account in Book I, Chapter 5. iCloud stores your data on a remote server that syncs data updates between your computers or iOS devices. Even if you only use Calendar on your iPhone, it makes sense to use iCloud so you have a remote copy of your Calendar in the unfortunate event that something happens to your iPhone.

To turn on iCloud, open the Settings app, tap iCloud, and tap the Calendars switch on.

Any changes you make in Calendar on your iPhone or on other devices associated with iCloud, such as your computer, iPad, or iPod touch, are automatically pushed to all devices.

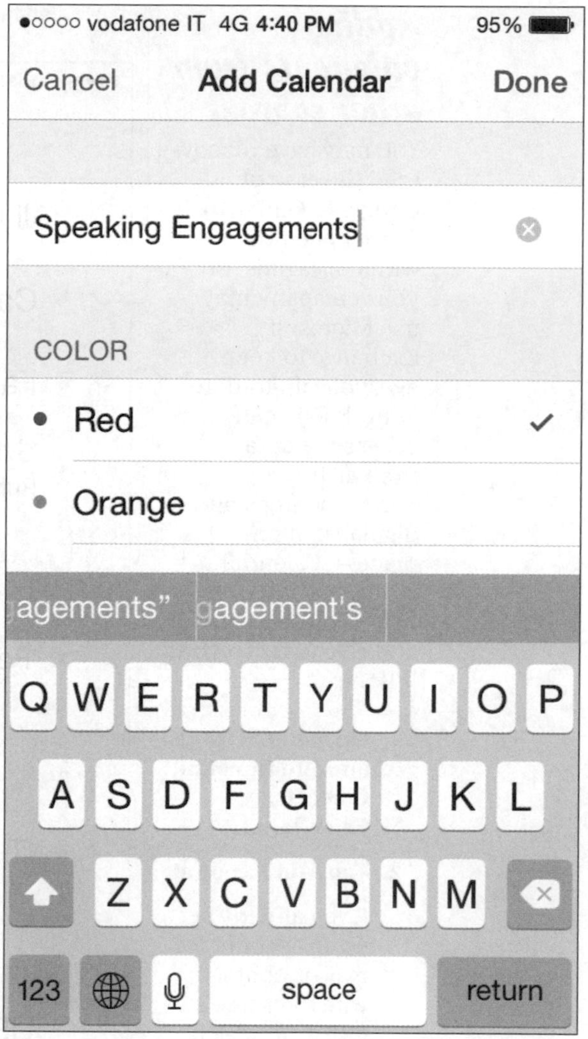

You can edit the name and color and delete iCloud calendars on your iPhone. Open the Calendar app and then tap Calendars at the bottom of the screen

Figure 2-1: Create new calendars directly on your iPhone in the Calendar app.

Book III
Chapter 2

Managing Your
Time with Calendar,
Reminders, and
Clock

to see the calendar list, as shown in Figure 2-2. Tap the red info button to the right of the calendar, do one of the following, and then tap Done:

✔ Edit the name of the calendar by tapping in the first field, selecting the text, and typing a new name.

✔ Edit the color of the calendar by tapping the color you want to associate with that calendar's events.

✔ Delete a calendar by scrolling to the bottom of the screen and tapping the Delete Calendar button.

Adding calendars from other sources

You may have discovered the ease of Google Calendar to share appointments with colleagues, or your company may use Microsoft Exchange to keep everyone up-to-date. Your iPhone can access the data from all these remote sources and display it in one place — Calendar.

Follow these steps to add calendars to your iPhone:

1. **Open the Settings app and tap Mail, Contacts, Calendars.**

2. **Tap Add Account.**

   If you already set up an account for mail or contacts with the same service from which you want to add Calendar, tap the name of the account in the list and go to Step 6.

Active calendar   Info

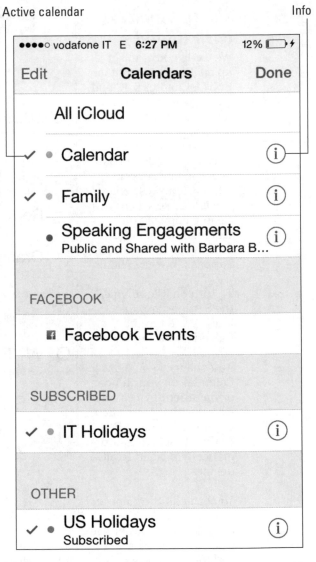

Figure 2-2: The Calendar list shows the calendars you sync with and those you subscribe to.

3. **Tap the service you use: Exchange, Google, Yahoo!, or Outlook.com.**

   The Add Account screen opens.

4. **Filling in the Name field is optional. Type in your email address in the Address field and your password in the Password field.**

   An identity is automatically entered in the Description field, but you can tap and hold on the text to replace it with something you prefer.

5. **Tap the Next button in the upper-right corner.**

   After your account is verified, a screen opens showing a list of available services.

6. **Tap the Calendars switch on.**

   When you return to the Calendar app, any accounts that have the Calendar switch on will appear in the calendar list (refer to Figure 2-2).

7. **Swipe back to the first Mail, Contacts, Calendars settings screen and you now see the added account in the Accounts list and the activated services under each account name.**

If you want to use iCloud with your Windows PC, download the iCloud Control Panel for Windows app from Apple (`www.apple.com/icloud/setup/pc.html`).

You have to sign in on your iPhone with the same account information you use on your computer to have the same information in both places.

Configuring CalDAV calendar accounts

CalDAV is an Internet standard that allows access to data in the iCalendar format on a remote server. Multiple users can access the same information, so it's often used in business and organization settings. If your employer uses a CalDAV-supported calendar program and you want to access that calendar from your iPhone, you can add a CalDAV account. You'll need some account information from your IT department or network support person:

- ✔ **Server:** This has your company or organization information.
- ✔ **Username:** This is your identification.
- ✔ **Password:** A password is required.
- ✔ **Description:** This name shows up on the list of accounts on the Mail, Contacts, Calendars settings screen.

Set up the account on your iPhone by following these steps:

1. **Open the Settings app and tap Mail, Contacts, Calendars.**
2. **Tap Add Account.**
3. **Tap Other.**
4. **Tap Add CalDAV Account in the Calendars section.**
5. **Type the information requested.**
6. **Tap the Next button in the upper-right corner.**

   After your account information is verified, the calendar data is added to your iPhone.

Book III
Chapter 2

Managing Your
Time with Calendar,
Reminders, and
Clock

7. **Tap the Save button in the upper-right corner.**

   You return to the Mail, Contacts, Calendars settings screen.

8. **Tap Fetch New Data.**

9. **If your server supports push notifications — and you want to use it — tap the Push switch on.**

   Anytime you make a change to the calendar on your computer that's associated with your iCloud or Microsoft Exchange account, that change is pushed to your iPhone, and vice versa.

10. **If your server doesn't support push (or you want to conserve battery power — push is power hungry), select a default fetch interval — every 15 minutes, every 30 minutes, or hourly.**

    Your iPhone contacts the server for new data at the interval you select.

Adding Facebook events to Calendar

Linking Facebook to Calendar can be an easy way to keep track of friends' birthdays and other events posted on Facebook such as class reunions and store promotions. This is optional, so follow these steps to activate this feature, or not:

1. **Open the Settings app and tap Facebook.**

   The Facebook settings screen opens.

   If you don't have the Facebook app installed, tap the Install button to download it from the iTunes Store.

2. **Tap in the User Name field and type your username.**

3. **Tap in the Password field and type your password.**

4. **Tap Sign In.**

   A disclaimer appears that explains what happens on your iPhone when you sign in to Facebook. Essentially, information about your Facebook friends is downloaded to Contacts; Facebook events sync to your Calendar; you can post status updates and images directly from the Photos app; and Facebook-enabled apps work with your permission.

5. **Tap Sign In again to accept these conditions.**

   You can change the settings after you sign in if you don't want these things to happen.

   The Facebook setting screen reappears with Calendar and Contacts options.

   You may see other apps that access Facebook information listed as well.

6. **Tap the Calendar switch on.**

Facebook now appears in the calendar list (refer to Figure 2-2).

Even if you turn this feature on, you can hide the Facebook Events calendar, as explained in the later section, "Viewing and Hiding Calendars."

Subscribing to iCalendar (.ics) calendars

One of the strong points of Calendar is the ability to access calendars created by other people and see those events on your iPhone. You may learn about these events through electronic invitations sent via email or from a public calendar site where you can search for published calendars.

An iCalendar or .ics file is the standard file type for exchanging calendar information. Calendar, Outlook, and Google Calendar support the .ics standard.

If you receive an email with an invitation to an event attached, the invitation probably has the `.ics` suffix. You simply tap that attachment, either from the email message or in the inbox in the Calendar app on your iPhone, and then choose one of the following responses:

- ✔ **Accept** the invitation, and the event is automatically added to your calendar. The event syncs to any other devices signed in to the same calendar account.

- ✔ **Decline** to refuse the invitation.

- ✔ **Maybe** to postpone your decision to attend the event or not.

The person who invited you receives a message with your decision.

If you receive a list of events in Mail — say, upcoming staff meetings — tap the calendar file in the message. When the list of events appears, tap Add All. Choose the calendar where you want to add the events, and then tap Done.

Others may also want to share their calendars with you. If you receive an invitation to a calendar, you can choose to Decline or Join Calendar; either way, an email informs the sender of your decision. If you join, the calendar is added as one of your calendars in Calendar. You can choose to view or hide that calendar's events by selecting or deselecting it in the calendars list.

To subscribe to published, public calendars, you can search a site like www. icalshare.com or Google Calendars and subscribe to the calendars that interest you. Some organizations post a subscription link on their website so you can automatically receive notifications of their events. To add a calendar subscription on your iPhone, do one of the following procedures:

1. **Open the Safari app.**

2. **Type the URL for the calendar sharing site you want to use, for example,** icalshare.com.

**Book III
Chapter 2**

Managing Your
Time with Calendar,
Reminders, and
Clock

3. **Find the calendar you want to add, and then tap the Subscribe to Calendar button.**

4. **Tap the appropriate response, such as Open, Subscribe, or Add Calendar, in the dialogs that appear.**

5. **The calendar is automatically added to Calendar and appears on the calendar list.**

If the calendar you want to add isn't part of a service like iCalShare, have the URL of the shared calendar handy, or open the calendar in Safari on your iPhone and copy the URL, and then follow these steps:

1. **Open the Settings app and tap Mail, Contacts, Calendar.**

2. **Tap Add Account.**

3. **Tap Other.**

4. **Tap Add Subscribed Calendar (near the bottom of the screen).**

5. **Type (or paste) the server address for the calendar on the Subscription screen.**

6. **Tap Next.**

   The server address is verified and a Subscription screen appears. You may have to enter a username and password to have access to the calendar. Some calendar providers ask you to use secure socket layer (SSL) for security reasons. See Book II, Chapter 4 to learn how to turn on SSL in Mail.

7. **The calendar appears on the calendar list in the Calendar app.**

 You can make changes to the event in a subscribed calendar in Calendar, but the changes are not reflected on the source calendar (such as Google Calendars), which is stored on a remote server and accessed on the Internet.

Deleting calendars

There are different ways to delete calendars, depending on the source:

- **iCloud calendars:** Open the Calendars app, tap the Info button to the right of the calendar you want to delete, and then tap Delete Calendar at the bottom of the screen. If you only have one iCloud calendar, this option doesn't appear because you have to have at least one iCloud calendar.

- **Third-party calendars (Google, Microsoft Exchange, and so on):** Open the Settings app; tap Mail, Contacts, Calendars; tap Account; and turn off the Calendars option.

- **Subscribed calendars:** If you want to delete a calendar you subscribe to, open the Settings app; tap Mail, Contacts, Calendars; and tap Subscribed Calendars. Tap the calendar you want to delete, and then tap Delete Account.

Viewing and Hiding Calendars

You now have one or multiple calendars on your iPhone. Use the calendar list to choose which calendars you want to see:

1. **Open the Calendar app.**

2. **Tap the Calendars button at the bottom of the screen.**

   A list of your calendars appears.

3. **Tap the name of the calendar you want to see or hide.**

   If there's a check mark next to the name of the calendar, events in that calendar show up in the four views. Note that the Calendars are color-coded. Events shown in List and Day views are color-coded to respond to the calendar they come from.

4. **Tap Show All Calendars if you want to see all events; tap the Status bar if you don't see it.**

5. **Tap Done.**

   Calendar opens to the view you most recently used.

Calendar views

Calendar neatly presents the data in four formats, as shown in the upcoming figures: in portrait (vertical) position, Calendar displays a year-at-a-glance, a month-at-a-glance, a day-at-a-glance (which displays the dates of the associated week across the top of the screen and a scrollable list of your events and appointments). Turn your iPhone to the landscape (horizontal) position to see several days at-a-glance.

When you open Calendar from the Home screen, you see the screen you were viewing when you last closed Calendar. The buttons on the screen, from top to bottom, work as follows:

✔ **Year/Month:** Think of Calendar as being arranged hierarchically: the top view shows the entire year; tap a month and you move down a layer to see the entire month; tap a date to see the detail of a day's appointments. Tap in the upper-left corner to move back to a higher level: the month's name to move from Day view to Month view; the year to move from Month view to Year view.

When in Year or Month view, scroll up and down to move to the past or future month or year. In Figure 2-3, you can see the end of 2013 and the beginning of 2014.

To reach Day view, tap a date in Month view. When in Day view, tap a date in the week displayed at the top to move to that date; scroll up and down in the day to move between morning to evening hours and scroll left and right to move backward and forward in time to select a different

**Book III
Chapter 2**

Managing Your
Time with Calendar,
Reminders, and
Clock

day. All-day events are displayed between the week and hour sections, as shown in Figure 2-4. Notice the current day is in red (July 7) and the birthday is indicated by a gift icon.

To view several days of your calendar together, rotate your iPhone to landscape position and you see a multiday calendar. Swipe left and right to scroll to previous and upcoming days. Swipe up and down to scroll from morning to evening. All-day events are posted at the top of the day. Multiday events are highlighted across all the days of the event.

Multiday view doesn't work when you have the orientation lock turned on. To permit Week view, drag up from the bottom of the screen to open the Control Center and tap the Orientation Lock switch off. Drag down to close the Control Center and Week view appears when you turn your iPhone to the horizontal position.

Figure 2-3: Scroll up and down to move from one year to the next in year view.

↙ **Events:** When tapped from the Day view, the List view opens as shown in Figure 2-5. You see five or six events. If you have a busy day, you may see only one day. If you have just one or two things each day, you see more days. The colored line to the left of the event corresponds to the calendar it comes from. You can scroll up and down this list to see what you did or what's coming up.

When tapped from Month view, you see the selected day's events listed below the month calendar.

Tap the List view button again to return to the Day or Month view.

✓ **Search (the magnifying glass icon):** Tap to open the Search field at the top to look for an event. Calendar searches in the Title, Location, Notes, and Invitees fields of calendars that are active; if you don't find an event, tap Calendars at the bottom of the screen, tap Show All Calendars, and then try your search again.

✓ **Plus Sign:** Tap this button to add an event to your calendar. We explain that in detail in the next section.

✓ **Today:** Tap this button at the bottom of the page in any of the views, and today is highlighted (refer to Figure 2-3) in that view.

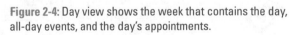

●●○○○ vodafone IT 4G 6:06 PM					77% ▬▭

‹ July   ☰ 🔍 +

S	M	T	W	T	F	S
6	7	**8**	9	10	11	12

Tuesday July 8, 2014

all-day 🎁 **Lucy Cane's 2nd Birthday**

6 PM

7 PM

8 PM

Dinner with Simona

9 PM

10 PM

11 PM

Today   Calendars   Inbox

Figure 2-4: Day view shows the week that contains the day, all-day events, and the day's appointments.

✓ **Calendars:** Takes you to the list of your calendars.

✓ **Inbox:** Shows invitations you've received from other calendars. The number in parentheses indicates how many invitations you've received. Tap the button and a list of invitations opens. We talk about responding to invitations in the "Responding to meeting invitations" section later in this chapter.

Book III
Chapter 2

Managing Your
Time with Calendar,
Reminders, and
Clock

Showing birthdays

If you use Contacts, you probably know that you can include a birthday as part of the contact information (refer to Book III, Chapter 1). Calendar links to Contacts and can display the birthdays on your calendar.

Scroll to the bottom of the Calendars list screen. You find the Other section and Birthdays. A check mark indicates that Birthdays is selected; tap Birthdays if it isn't selected. Tap Done. Birthdays are automatically inserted as all-day events.

You now see birthdays in the Day, Week, and List views and a dot on the date in Month view. The gift icon is next to the event so you know it's a birthday.

You can set a default alert time for birthdays in the Settings app. Tap Mail, Contacts, Calendars; tap Default Alert Times; tap Birthdays; and choose when you want to receive an alert that someone's birthday is near (from a week before to the day of).

If you use birthdays from Contacts and add the birthday as an event, it shows up twice on your calendar.

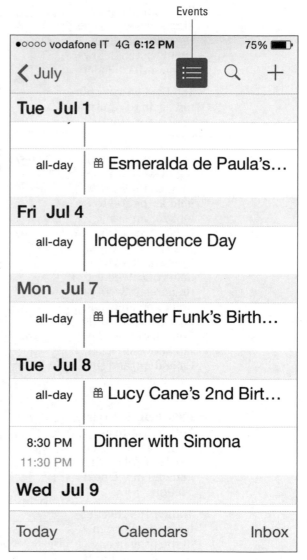

Events

●○○○○ vodafone IT 4G 6:12 PM		75%
‹ July		☰ Q +

Tue Jul 1

all-day	🎁 Esmeralda de Paula's…

Fri Jul 4

all-day	Independence Day

Mon Jul 7

all-day	🎁 Heather Funk's Birth…

Tue Jul 8

all-day	🎁 Lucy Cane's 2nd Birt…
8:30 PM 11:30 PM	Dinner with Simona

Wed Jul 9

Today	Calendars	Inbox

Figure 2-5: Tap the Events button to see a list of your appointments and events.

Creating, Changing, and Deleting Calendar Events

If you're frequently away from your computer, you may add appointments to your iPhone more often than on any other device. (Of course, every entry is synced to your computer and devices with iCloud.) In this section, we show you how to create new events and change or delete existing ones. We explain setting up repeating events and alerts so you don't miss any important scheduled encounters, and we discuss how to send and respond to invitations.

Filling in who, what, where, and when

If you're familiar with Calendar on a Mac (iCal in OS X 10.7, and earlier), creating events in Calendar will be a breeze. Even if you use Outlook or another calendar program, Calendar is pretty straightforward. Here's how to add an appointment or event:

1. **Open the Calendar app.**

2. **From Day, Month, or Year view, tap the plus sign button in the upper-right corner to open the Add Event screen.**

   In Day or Week view, press and hold the time at which you want to add an event until an Add Event screen appears.

3. **Tap the first field, where you see Title.**

   The keyboard appears.

4. **Type the name of the event or appointment in the Title field.**

5. **Tap Return, and then type a Location or something else pertinent to the appointment.**

   This field is optional.

6. **Tap the Starts field.**

   The time and date rotor opens, as shown in Figure 2-6.

7. **Using the rotor, set the date and time the appointment begins.**

8. **The ending time is automatically set for one hour later. To change it, tap the Ends field. Set the date and time the appointment ends.**

   Tap the Ends field again to close the rotor.

9. **If it's an all-day event such as a meeting or anniversary, tap the All-Day switch on.**

   The rotors change and show only the month, day, and year. If the event is more than one day — say, a conference or vacation — choose the beginning and ending dates.

   The advantage to using the all-day feature instead of setting the beginning time to 8 a.m. and the ending time to 8 p.m. is that in Day view, the event shows up at the beginning of the day rather than as a highlighted

**Book III
Chapter 2**

Managing Your
Time with Calendar,
Reminders, and
Clock

event over the course of the whole day. This way, you can add specific appointments during the course of the all-day event. In List view, All-Day appears next to the event title.

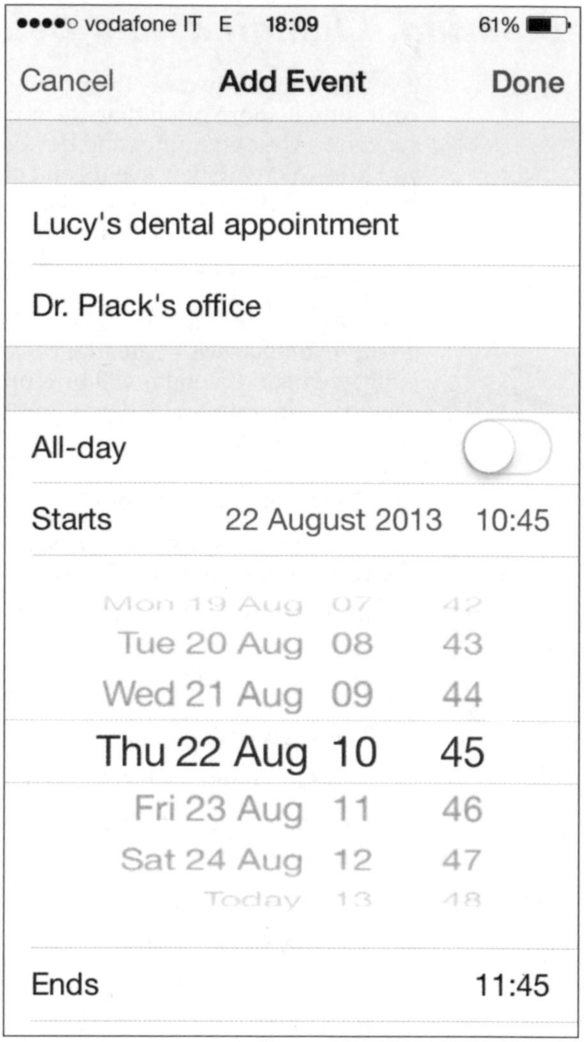

10. **Tap the Time Zone field if you want to set the event in a time zone other than your own.**

    A field opens where you type in the name of a large city that resides in the time zone you want to use. Tap the city from the list when a match appears. You return to the Add Event screen.

11. **(Optional.) Tap Travel Time.**

    Tap the toggle switch on and then tap the amount of travel time you want to allow prior to the event.

Your iPhone keeps track of your movements and places you frequently visit, as long as Frequent Locations is turned on in the Settings app (tap Privacy, tap Location Services, tap System Services, and tap Frequent Locations). iPhone uses your location history to calculate travel time to your appointments and then adds that information to the Today view of the Notification Center.

12. **Tap the Calendar field.**

    The Calendar screen opens.

●●●●○ vodafone IT E   18:09   61% ▮▬▷

Cancel   **Add Event**   Done

Lucy's dental appointment

Dr. Plack's office

All-day   ⬭

Starts   22 August 2013   10:45

Mon 19 Aug   07   42
Tue 20 Aug   08   43
Wed 21 Aug   09   44
Thu 22 Aug 10   45
Fri 23 Aug   11   46
Sat 24 Aug   12   47
Today   13   48

Ends   11:45

Figure 2-6: Use the rotor to set the starting and ending date and times for your event.

13. **Tap the calendar you want to put this event on if it's different from what is shown in the field.**

    You choose the calendar under Settings, which we explain in the section "Adjusting iPhone's Calendar Settings.".

14. **Tap Done.**

You can stop here or you can add some more details to your event with the remaining fields: Repeat, Alert, and Notes. If you use an over-the-air service like iCloud or Microsoft Exchange, you also have the options of indicating if you're busy or free during the event and of inviting people to your event.

If you receive text or email messages with time and date references — even things like "Meet me at 6" or "Dinner next Thursday" — the reference is highlighted and underlined and tapping it opens a pop-up menu that lets you create an event or show the time or date in Calendar.

Setting up a repeating event

The default repetition setting for a new event is Never. If your event is one-time only, skip this. For recurring events like an anniversary or weekly tennis lessons, the repeat function is handy. You only have to enter the information once, and Calendar takes care of the rest. Here's how:

1. **Tap Repeat on the event you created.**

    If it's an event that you created previously, open that event and tap Edit in the upper-right corner.

2. **Choose the frequency with which you want the event to repeat.**

    Tap Custom to create events that repeat at intervals that need more definition, for example, every Monday and Wednesday, the third Thursday or the 15th of every month. Tap Frequency and then tap Daily, Weekly, Monthly or Yearly. Tap Every and select the date or day that the event should occur, as shown in Figure 2-7.

    If you tap a preset interval, you return to the Add Event screen, but another field — the End Repeat field — is added under Repeat.

    If you tap Custom, swipe right to return to the New (or Edit) Event screen or tap the buttons in the upper left corner until you reach it.

3. **Never is the default for the End Repeat field. To change it, tap the End Repeat field and then tap On Date.**

4. **Use the rotor to choose the date the event ends.**

5. **Tap Add Event or Edit in the upper-left corner to return to the event screen.**

6. **Tap Done.**

Book III
Chapter 2

Managing Your
Time with Calendar,
Reminders, and
Clock

Adding Alerts

If you have a lot on your plate — and who doesn't? — alerts can be a big help. Your iPhone beeps (or vibrates if the Ring/Silent switch is set to Silent) and sends a notification message at the interval you select. You can set alerts for a specific event when you create a new event or by editing an existing event. You select the type of alert you want to receive from within Notifications in the Settings app. Refer to the section "Adjusting iPhone's Calendar Settings" for details.

Set two alerts so you can be reminded of your dear Aunt Sybil's retirement dinner two days before the event, giving you time to get a gift, and then again, the day of the dinner. Add one or two alerts to a specific event by doing the following:

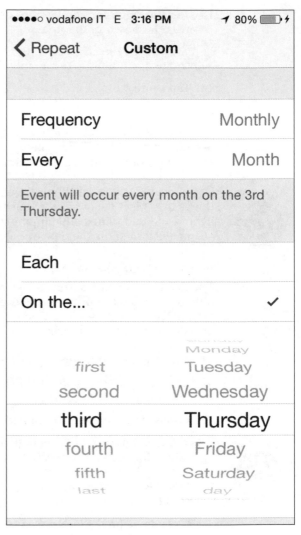

Figure 2-7: Use Custom to specify intervals for repeating events.

1. **Tap Alert on the New Event screen or the Edit screen, if you want to add an alert to an existing event.**

2. **Tap how long before the event you want to receive an alert.**

   You can receive alerts for all day events one week before, two days before, one day before, or the day of the event, whereas for events scheduled for a specific time block, you can also choose to receive an alert one or two hours before, or 5, 15, or 30 minutes before, or at the time of the event.

3. **(Optional.) Tap Second Alert and repeat Step 2 if you want an additional alert.**

4. **Tap Done.**

If you always want to be alerted for birthdays, events, or all-day events, set default alert times, as explained in the section "Adjusting iPhone's Calendar Settings." You receive an alert for all those happenings, so if you have a lot of events, default alerts for events or all-day events may be more a cause of confusion than a reminder. In that case, you may want to only assign individual alerts to your most important events. Personally, the default alerts for birthdays have saved us from several social gaffes!

When your iPhone is locked, you hear the beep, or whatever sound you choose for Calendar alerts, and the notification appears. For alerts, slide the notification to view the event, for banners, pull down from the banner or do nothing and it will disappear in a few seconds. When you sync your calendars, alerts sync to the corresponding calendar on your computer, and vice versa.

If you have an alert scheduled during a time that Do Not Disturb with the Always option is turned on, you won't receive the alert, although it will be in the Notification Center, if you activated that option.

Adding Notes

Adding a URL and a note to an event is a great way to remember things associated with that event. For example, if you're scheduling a video conference or a webinar attendance, adding the URL for the call gives you instant access at the scheduled time and adds any other useful information about the appointment in the Notes field, such as the phone number of the person you're going to meet or the confirmation number for a flight. To add a URL and/or note:

1. **Tap URL on the Add Event screen or the Edit screen (if you want to add to an event you already created).**

2. **Type the URL or copy it from Safari and then tap and hold the field to paste it in the event.**

3. **Tap Notes.**

4. **Type in the information you want or double-click the Home button to switch to another app, copy the information you want, and then switch back to Calendar to paste the information in the event.**

5. **Tap Done.**

Indicating your availability

If you post an event to an over-the-air calendar such as one in iCloud, Google Calendar, or Microsoft Exchange, you can indicate that you're free, or busy, during the event that you post by tapping Show As on the Add Event (or Edit) screen, and then tapping Busy or Free, as appropriate.

Inviting people to your event

If you activate iCloud for Calendar or use a Microsoft Exchange calendar, you can invite people to your event directly from Calendar. Make sure you

Book III
Chapter 2

Managing Your
Time with Calendar,
Reminders, and
Clock

accurately complete the details of your event before sending it to the invitees. Then follow these steps:

1. **Tap Invitees.**

   The Add Invitees screen opens.

2. **Type the email addresses of the people you want to invite or tap the plus sign on the right.**

   Contacts opens; cards that contain email addresses are bold, and those without email addresses are dimmed. Scroll the list or tap the letters down the right side or use the Search function to find the name you're looking for.

3. **Tap the name of the person you want to invite.**

   You return to the Add Invitees screen and the name appears in the space at the top.

4. **Repeat Steps 2 and 3 to add more people.**

5. **Tap Done in the upper-right corner.**

   An event invitation is automatically sent to your invitees.

Figure 2-8 shows a completed Add Event screen. You see the response to the invitation. If you want to see when someone declines your invitation, open the Settings app; tap Mail, Contacts, Calendars; and tap the Show Invitee Declines switch on.

●●●●○ vodafone IT E 19:04	92% 🔋⚡
Cancel **Add Event** Done	
Lucy's birthday party	
Bow Meow Chow	
All-day	⬭
Starts 30 August 2013 16:00	
Ends 19:00	
Time Zone New York >	
Repeat Yearly >	
End Repeat Never >	
Invitees 3 >	

Figure 2-8: A completely filled-in Add Event screen.

Of course, one of the easiest ways to add an event is to call on Siri. Press and hold the Home button until Siri appears and then speak the details of your event, such as "Set up a meeting with Joe on Thursday at 3 p.m." or "Create a repeating event every Tuesday from 10:15 to noon." Siri asks the necessary questions to send invitations, add locations, and even edit events at a later date.

Editing and deleting events

Meetings get canceled, appointment times and dates get changed, and in the old pen-and-paper calendar world, we used a lot of correction fluid. You can swiftly edit or delete appointments and events on your iPhone without inhaling those nasty fumes.

1. **Open the Calendar app.**

2. **Locate the event you want to change or delete from one of the views.**

3. **Tap the event you want to work on.**

   An Event Details screen opens, as shown in Figure 2-9.

4. **Tap Edit in the upper-right corner.**

   The Edit screen opens, which looks like the Add Event screen except it's filled in.

5. **Tap in the field you want to change.**

6. **Make changes using the same techniques you use to enter data in a new event.**

7. **Tap Done.**

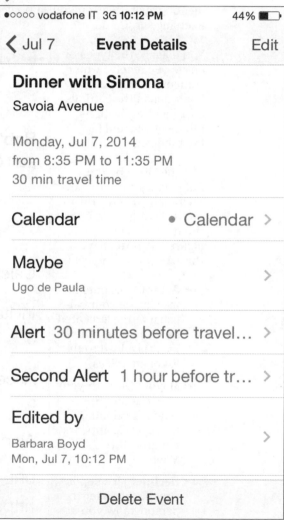

Figure 2-9: The Event Details screen shows information about events you created.

Book III
Chapter 2

Managing Your
Time with Calendar,
Reminders, and
Clock

If you want to delete the event, instead of editing as in Step 5, tap the red Delete Event button at the bottom of the screen. Two buttons pop up, Delete Event and Cancel. Tap the appropriate one.

Responding to meeting invitations

Once upon a time, we used the phone to invite people to meetings, but email and electronic calendars have changed that. You can receive and respond to meeting invitations on your iPhone if you've enabled calendars on Microsoft Exchange or iCloud.

You manage the types of alerts you receive when someone sends you an invitation in the Settings app. Tap Notifications, tap Calendar, and tap Invitations.

Tap the inbox on the Calendars screen to view invitations received. Tap on the invitation to open the details (see Figure 2-10). You have three response choices:

- **Accept:** This puts the meeting on your calendar at the indicated date and time. Your name is added to the list of attendees.

- **Maybe:** On both your calendar and the sender's calendar, the meeting appears tentative if you select Maybe.

- **Decline:** This sends a response to let the person know you won't be attending. Nothing is added to your calendar. The invitation is deleted from your iPhone unless you switch on

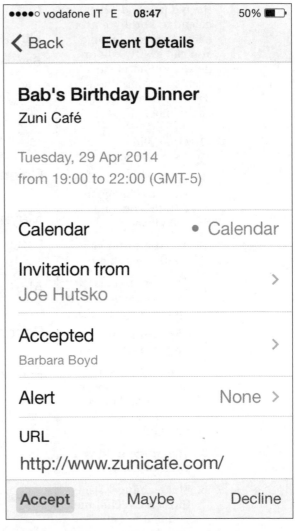

Figure 2-10: You can Accept or Decline an invitation, or choose Maybe while you think about it.

the Show Declined Events option on the Calendars screen. This is a good option because you can go back and accept an invitation if you change your mind.

If you receive an invitation in an email, it shows up as an attachment with an `.ics` suffix, which indicates the iCalendar standard. Tap the attachment and the Event Info screen opens. You can then add the event to your calendar and respond.

Sharing Calendars

Just as you can subscribe to other calendars on servers like iCalshare.com, you can share calendars you create on iCloud with other people. Private calendars can only be seen by people who have an iCloud account, whereas Public calendars can be shared with anyone with an Internet connection and browser. Sharing calendars lets others know what you're up to and in some cases gives others the possibility to post events on your calendar.

Follow these steps to activate sharing:

1. **Open the Calendar app.**
2. **Tap the Calendars button at the bottom.**
3. **Tap the red Info button to the right of the calendar you want to share. (It must be an iCloud or Microsoft Exchange calendar.)**

   Tap Edit and then tap Add Calendar if you want to create a new calendar. Then tap Done.
4. **To share the calendar with one or more specific persons, tap Add Person.**

   An Add Person message screen opens; it looks like an email message.
5. **Type the name of the person you want to share the calendar with or tap the plus sign to choose someone from your Contacts list.**

   Add as many names as you want.
6. **Tap Add.**

   The Edit Calendar screen appears and the name or names of the people you're sharing with appear in the Shared With list.
7. **Tap View and Edit to grant or remove calendar editing privileges to the person.**
8. **Tap Edit Calendar to return to the previous screen.**
9. **Scroll to the bottom of the screen to find the Public Calendar option.**
10. **Tap On to allow anyone to subscribe to a read-only version of your calendar.**

11. **Tap Share Link to open the Share Sheet and send an email or message to people you want to invite to subscribe to this calendar.**

    Alternatively, copy the link to post it elsewhere such as Twitter, Facebook, or your blog.

12. **Tap Done.**

If you set up Family Sharing (see Book IV, Chapter 2), a family calendar is automatically created and appears in the calendars list. Each family member can view and edit the family calendar.

Adjusting iPhone's Calendar Settings

Although we explain notifications in Book I, Chapter 4, Calendar offers app-specific options. Open the Settings app from the Home screen, tap Notifications and tap Calendar, then tap the Allow Notifications switch to the on position, as shown in Figure 2-11. Tap Show in Notification Center and choose how many events you want to appear in the Notification Center: 1, 5, or 10 and you receive alerts when your iPhone is locked or sleeping.

In addition, you can assign different notifications and alerts (or none) to four types of Calendar activities: Upcoming Events, Invitations, Invitee Responses, and Shared Calendar Changes (refer to Figure 2-11). Tap each item and then choose the notification and alert items as for other apps — Notification Sound, Badge App Icon, Banners or Alerts. (See Book I, Chapter 4 for more details about notifications.)

If you want to see, or remove, your events or reminders in the Notification Center, swipe down from the top of the screen to open the Notification Center, tap the Today tab and scroll to the bottom of the screen. Tap the Edit button and tap the Remove (minus sign) button next to Calendar or Reminders to remove it from the Notification Center, or tap the Add (plus sign) button to include it in the Notification Center.

While you change alert sounds and styles in the Notifications settings, you open the Settings app, and then tap Mail, Contacts, Calendars to change Calendar settings. Scroll down to the bottom of the screen. The Calendars settings are in the last section. You can adjust eight items:

- **Time Zone Override:** When Time Zone Override is on, events and alerts you enter in Calendar maintain the time of the time zone you choose, regardless of what time zone you're actually in. When off, events display according to the time zone of your current location.

  To change your time zone, tap Time Zone Override on the Mail, Contacts, Calendar Settings screen. The Time Zone Override screen opens. Tap the switch On and then tap Time Zone. The Time Zone screen opens with a keyboard. Begin typing the initial letters of the city or country of the time zone you want to use. A list of potential cities appears and the results narrow as you type more letters. Tap a city that's in the time zone you want. You return to the Time Zone Support screen. Tap the Mail button in the upper-left corner to return to the Settings screen.

Turn Time Zone Override off, and your events reflect the local time of your current location. The times for events you already created change. For example, an event at 9:30 a.m. in London changes to 2:30 a.m. when you land in Atlanta.

✓ **Alternate Calendars:** Tap to open three additional calendar options: Chinese, Hebrew, Islamic. You can choose one to add to Calendar.

✓ **Week Numbers:** When on, the week number appears in Calendar's Month view.

✓ **Show Invitee Declines:** When on, you'll be notified when someone declines your invitation, as well as when they accept or respond with maybe.

✓ **Sync:** Choose how much event history you want to include when you sync your events. Tap to open the Sync screen and choose 2 Weeks Back; 1, 3, or 6 Months Back; or All Events.

✓ **Default Alert Times:** Set alerts for all birthdays, all events, or all all-day events. Tap the type of event you want an alert for — Birthdays, Events, or All-Day

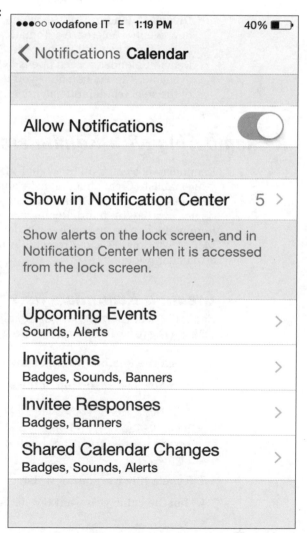

Book III
Chapter 2

Managing Your
Time with Calendar,
Reminders, and
Clock

Figure 2-11: Designate specific alerts for different types of Calendar activities.

Events — and then, from the list that opens, choose when you want to be alerted to the event.

Time To Leave (found when you tap Default Alert Times): Tap to the on position and Calendar will automatically calculate, and tell you, the time it will take to get from your current location to your next appointment. Travel time appears on the Notification Centers.

✔ **Start Week On:** Tap to choose which day you want Calendar to display as the first day of the week.

✔ **Default Calendar:** Choose which calendar you want as the default. Any new events you create automatically are placed on the default calendar, unless you change it on the Add Event screen. Tap Default Calendar. The Default Calendar screen opens, which displays the calendars that are available. Tap the calendar you want. A check mark appears to the right of the selected default calendar.

Remembering with Reminders

Reminders is a catch-all for your To Do lists, neatly divided into categories you establish. Create lists of tasks and then have Reminders send you an alert based on a time or location. So you never forget a task regardless of the device you have at hand, Reminders automatically syncs via iCloud with the Reminders app on your other iOS devices or Mac and with Outlook on your Mac or Windows PC. Just remember to turn Reminders on in the Settings app under iCloud.

Creating Reminders lists

Reminders comes with one list: Reminders. You add other lists and then add tasks to the lists. To add a list, follow these steps:

1. **Open the Reminders app, shown in Figure 2-12.**

2. **Tap New List at the top of the screen.**

   A New List appears with the keyboard at the bottom of the screen.

   If you see an open reminder, tap the white strip at the bottom of the screen to open the list of reminders and the New List option (refer to Figure 2-12).

3. **Type a title for your new list.**

4. **Tap the color you want the list to be.**

5. **Tap Done.**

Reorder your lists by touching and dragging them up and down the screen until they're displayed in the order you like.

Tap a list and then tap the Edit button in the upper right to do the following:

- ✔ **Rename the list:** Tap and hold to select the name and then type a new one.

- ✔ **Change the list color:** Tap Color and choose a new hue.

- ✔ **Share the list:** Tap Sharing and then tap Add Person. Type an email address or tap the plus (+) button to open contacts and choose the person(s) you want to share your Reminders list with. Each name appears in a list. Tap Done when you finish adding names of people.

  If you want to stop sharing your list, tap Sharing, tap the person you want to remove, and then scroll to the bottom of the screen to tap Stop Sharing.

  When Family Sharing is activated a Family reminder list is automatically created and shared by family members.

- ✔ **Rearrange the order of items in your list:** Tap and drag the rearrange button to the right of each item to move it up or down in the list.

- ✔ **Delete the list:** Tap Delete List at the bottom of the screen.

Search in Reminders by tapping the Search field (tap the Status bar if you don't see the Search field). Type a few words of the task you're looking for in the Search field or use Spotlight Search from the Home screen. Or just ask Siri to find a reminder for you.

Figure 2-12: Reminders shows your lists like neatly stacked index cards.

Book III
Chapter 2

Managing Your
Time with Calendar,
Reminders, and
Clock

To see a list of your scheduled tasks, tap the alarm clock to the right of the Search field. To hide the Search field and alarm clock when you finish, push the list up.

Creating new Reminders tasks

We prefer to ask Siri to add new tasks to our Reminders lists (see Book I, Chapter 3), but if you don't have an Internet connection or your connection is slow, you can create them by yourself. Here's how to "manually" create new Reminders:

1. **Open the Reminders app.**

   The first time you open Reminders, you see a blank list.

2. **Tap the lined piece of "paper."**

   The keyboard appears.

3. **Type the task you want to remember.**

   The task appears in the list with a radio button to the left — which you tap to indicate a task has been completed — and an Info button to the right.

4. **Tap the Info button to open the Details screen.**

5. **Tap each item to specify how you want Reminders to help you remember this task.**

   - *Remind Me on a Day:* Tap On and tap the date to open a rotor that allows you to specify the date and time.

     When you tap Remind Me on a Day, the Repeat and End Repeat options appear. Tap Repeat and then tap a set interval, such as Every Week, or tap Custom to choose a frequency for the reminder, such as every three months. Refer to the previous section, "Setting Up a Repeating Event" and Figure 2-7 for details.

     Repeating reminders appear once on your list. When you indicate a task is complete, the reminder is updated with the next due date and a new incomplete item appears. (The completed item appears at the bottom of the list when you tap Show Completed.) If you assign an alert to the repeating reminder, the alert will occur at the interval you established in relation to the new due date.

   - *Remind Me at a Location:* Tap On and then tap Location. Tap one of the choices that appear: Current Location or Home, or tap in the Search field to enter a specific street address or the name of a person or business that you've stored in Contacts. Tap the address you want to use; a map showing the address appears in the bottom half of the screen. A pin indicates the address and a circle indicates the *geofence* (the distance from your address at which the Reminder will be activated); drag to increase or decrease the geofence. Tap either When

I Leave or When I Arrive to hear an alert when one of these actions occurs. Tap Details in the upper-left corner, as shown in Figure 2-13. The Location option only works with iPhone 5 or later and doesn't sync with Outlook or Exchange calendars. It works better if you use a street address, and you do need a GPS connection when you're at the location for location-based Reminders to work.

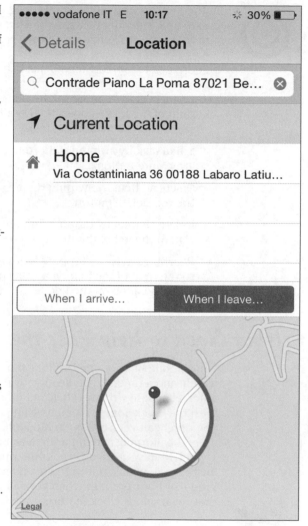

Figure 2-13: Choose when and where Reminders should prod you to your task.

Open the Settings app, tap Notifications, and tap Reminders to choose the alert tone and style you want Reminders to use.

- *Priority:* Tap the exclamation points to set the task's level of importance.

- *List:* Tap to choose which list you want to keep the reminder. See the previous section, "Creating Reminders lists."

- *Notes:* Tap to type in any additional details about the reminder.

6. Tap Done to return to the list.

When you complete a task, tap the circle to the left of the task on the list (refer to Figure 2-12). You can hide or view completed tasks for a specific list by tapping Hide Completed or Show Completed at the bottom of the list.

**Book III
Chapter 2**

Managing Your Time with Calendar, Reminders, and Clock

In the Settings app under Reminders, choose the Default List so when you create new reminders outside of a list (for example, in Outlook or another app that syncs to Reminders), they're added to the chosen list.

To edit, delete, or rearrange tasks in a list do the following:

- ✓ Edit a task by tapping the item and then tapping the Info button to the right of the task to open the Details screen. Edit the task following the steps you use to create a task.

- ✓ Edit a task by swiping right to left across the task and then tapping the gray More button.

- ✓ Delete an item by swiping right to left across the task and then tapping the red Delete button.

- ✓ Delete an item by tapping Edit and then tapping the red and white minus sign to the left of the item, and then tapping Delete.

- ✓ Rearrange a list by tapping Edit and then holding the rearrange button to the right of the item you want to move and dragging it up or down to a new position on the list.

Using Clock to Help Pass the Time

Your iPhone has not one but four time tools: a world clock, an alarm, a stopwatch, and a timer. If you keep your iPhone by your side, you can pretty much eliminate wristwatches and most clock-like gadgets in your home. With the Clock app, you can do things like use the world clock to make sure you don't call your cousin in Mongolia at 2 a.m. Or set an alarm to wake you up in the morning and separate alarms to wake your children in time for school. Help your friend track trial times for the 100-meter dash. Set a timer for the cake you've put in the oven and to turn off your iPhone's Music, Video, or Podcasts app when you fall asleep. We take you through each of these marvelous clock features, one by one.

Take a close look at the Clock app icon on the Home screen — yup, it shows the actual time and the red second hand moves continuously.

Adding clocks from around the world

When you tap the Home button to wake your iPhone, you see the time on the screen. You set that time on the World Clock function of your iPhone's Clock app. You can also set up clocks from other time zones to keep you informed of what time it is in your overseas office or in the country where your sister is studying.

You see four or more clocks at a time (depending on your iPhone model), but you can scroll down the list and have as many clocks as there are time zones.

Follow these steps:

1. **Open the Clock app or swipe up from the Lock, Home, or an app screen to open the Control Center and tap Clock there.**

2. **Tap the World Clock button in the bottom-left corner.**

3. **Tap the plus sign in the upper-right corner.**

   A Search field and a list of cities appear.

4. **Scroll through the list of cities or begin typing the name of the city or country that you want to add a clock for.**

   If we type **S**, both Scotland and San Rafael come up, as does Detroit, U.S.A. The more letters you type, the narrower your search results.

5. **Tap the city you want to add.**

   If you don't see the exact city you were searching for, tap one that's in the same time zone.

6. **The World Clock screen returns, as shown in Figure 2-14.**

   You see the city you chose added to the list. In Figure 2-14 the time for each city is shown. Tap the time to reveal analog-style clocks instead of a digital readout. The clock has a white face if it's daytime in that city and a black face if it's night.

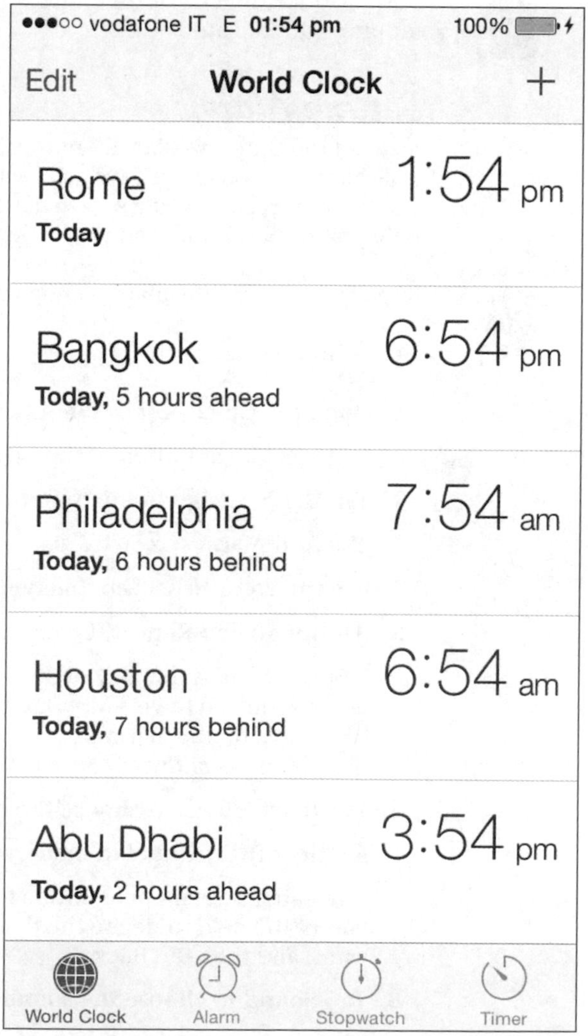

●●●○○ vodafone IT E **01:54 pm**   100% ▭ ⚡

Edit   **World Clock**   +

Rome   1:54 pm
Today

Bangkok   6:54 pm
Today, 5 hours ahead

Philadelphia   7:54 am
Today, 6 hours behind

Houston   6:54 am
Today, 7 hours behind

Abu Dhabi   3:54 pm
Today, 2 hours ahead

World Clock   Alarm   Stopwatch   Timer

Figure 2-14: World Clock shows clocks from multiple time zones.

Book III
Chapter 2

Managing Your
Time with Calendar,
Reminders, and
Clock

7. **Tap the Edit button in the upper-left corner to do one or both of the following:**

- *Rearrange the list order:* Tap and hold the rearrange button on the right, and then drag the clock to the position you want.

- *Delete a clock:* Tap the red button on the left and then tap the Delete button that appears to the right.

8. **Tap Done after you finish.**

Turn 24-hour time on or off in the Settings app by tapping General and then tapping Date & Time.

Setting Alarms

Some of the things we like about the Alarm function are that you can have multiple alarms, choose the days an alarm should repeat, select the sound you want it to have, and add a snooze function. If you want the alarm to vibrate only, leave your iPhone in Ring mode but turn the volume completely down.

Keep in mind that the alarm sounds even when your iPhone is in Silent mode.

Here's how to set alarms:

1. **Open the Clock app or tap it in the Control Center.**

2. **Tap the Alarm button at the bottom of the screen.**

3. **Tap the plus sign in the upper-right corner.**

The Add Alarm screen opens.

4. **Use the rotor to set the time you want the alarm to sound.**

5. **(Optional) Tap Repeat if you want to create a repeating alarm.**

You can choose any day of the week or a combination of days, which means you can have a Monday-through-Friday alarm, which is labeled Weekdays on the alarm list, whereas a Saturday/Sunday alarm is labeled Weekends, as shown in Figure 2-15.

6. **Tap Back after you choose the days you want the alarm to repeat.**

7. **(Optional) Tap Label to name your alarm.**

The Label screen opens with a field and keyboard. Tap the X on the right end of the field to delete the default Alarm label, type the name you want, and then tap Back.

8. **Tap Sound to choose the sound you want for your alarm.**

Choose a sound from the list — scroll down to see all the options, which include ringtones you purchased or created. You can buy more tones by tapping the button at the top of the list, which takes you to the iTunes Store.

To use a song for an alarm sound, tap Pick a Song and then tap the song you want from the music collection on your iPhone. You can add more than one song and assign a different song to different alarms.

9. Tap Snooze on or off.

Snooze lets you tap the alarm off when it sounds. After ten minutes, it sounds again.

10. Tap Save.

The alarm is added to the list of alarms on the Alarm screen. Use the switch on the right to turn the alarm on or off so you don't have to add and delete alarms you use frequently.

11. When the alarm goes off, just tap the screen to turn it off.

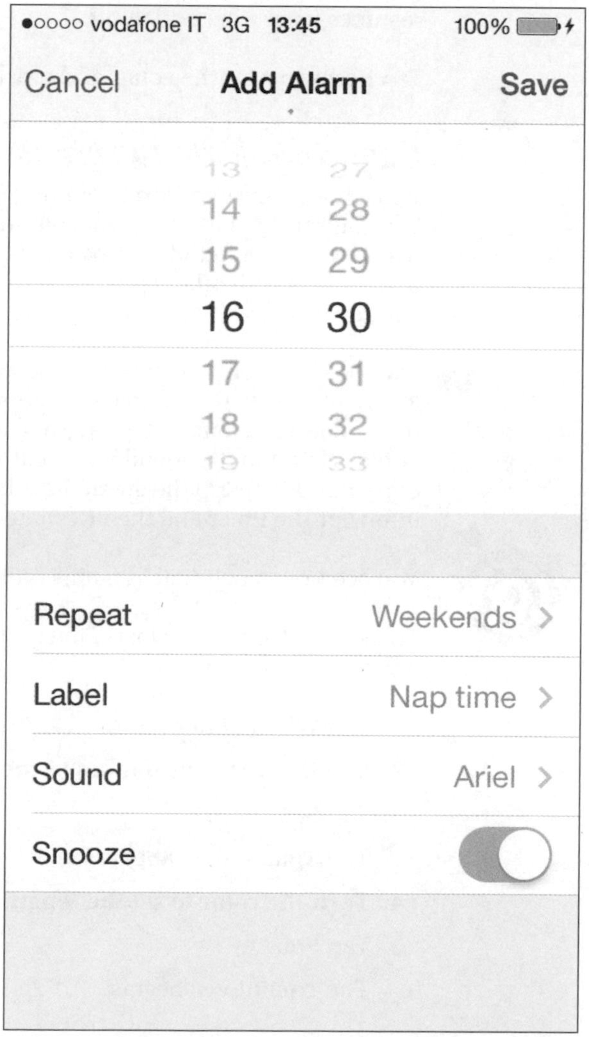

To make changes to an existing alarm, tap the Edit button on the top left of the screen, and then tap the name of the alarm you want to change. The Edit Alarm screen opens, which is the same as the Add Alarm screen but has the information of the selected alarm.

To delete an existing alarm, tap the Edit button. Tap the red button to the left of the alarm time, and then tap the Delete button that appears on the right. Tap Done after you finish.

When you set an alarm, the alarm icon, which looks like a clock, appears in the Status bar at the top of your iPhone's screen.

Figure 2-15: Set a repeating alarm for selected days of the week.

Book III
Chapter 2

Managing Your
Time with Calendar,
Reminders, and
Clock

Timing events with Stopwatch

You can use the Stopwatch to time single events such as a speech or laps. Tap Start to start counting.

To time one thing, let it run until the action stops, and then tap Stop.

To time laps, tap Lap each time the runner rounds the bend or the swimmer touches the end of the pool. The large numbers continue giving a cumulative time; the smaller numbers above show the lap's duration. When you tap Lap, the laps are listed with each lap's time. If you tap Start again, the count resumes from where it left off.

Tap Reset to zero the count and erase the lap times.

Counting down to zero with Timer

While the Stopwatch starts counting from zero, the timer counts down to zero. You can set the timer from one minute up to 23 hours and 59 minutes, after which, you're better off setting an alarm. After you set the timer, you can go on to do things with other apps, even press the Sleep/Wake button. The timer continues to count down in the background and sounds when the time's up.

Tap the Timer button on the Clock app and then tap the rotor to set the length of time you want to pass before the timer sounds. Choose the "time's up" sound you want by tapping When Timer Ends and then scroll through the choices and tap the sound you want. Tap the Set button in the upper-right corner and then tap the green Start button on the Timer screen. Tap Pause to interrupt the timer and then Resume to restart or Cancel to turn it off.

You see how much time remains on the Lock Screen.

To use the Timer as a Sleep Timer while you're listening to audio or watching a video:

1. **Tap When Timer Ends.**
2. **Scroll to the very bottom of the screen and tap Stop Playing.**
3. **Tap Set.**

   The Time screen appears.
4. **Turn the rotor to set the length of time you want to enjoy your media.**
5. **Tap Start.**

   The countdown begins.

6. Press the Home button.

7. Tap Music, Podcasts, or Videos depending on the type of media you want to listen to or watch.

8. Tap your selection.

9. Tap the Play button to begin playback.

10. Whatever you're listening to or watching is turned off when the timer stops.

Book III
Chapter 2

Managing Your
Time with Calendar,
Reminders, and
Clock

Chapter 3: Tapping into Maps, Compass, and Weather

In This Chapter

- ✔ Adjusting iPhone's location settings and services
- ✔ Seeking, finding, and sharing points of interest
- ✔ Getting the traffic report
- ✔ Asking for directions
- ✔ Talking about the Weather
- ✔ Staying on course with Compass
- ✔ Keeping things on the Level

The apps in this chapter help you navigate to a destination, find out ahead of time how to dress for where you're going, and get your bearings once you get there. What are we talking about? Maps, Weather, and Compass.

In Maps, just type in beginning and ending points and a mapped out route appears, turning your iPhone into a GPS navigator that guides you to your destination. The Weather app can help you decide whether you should wear a raincoat or apply sunscreen. The Compass app can be a handy ally when you want to know which way is north by northwest, and the flip side of Compass is a level that shows the inclination of surfaces where you rest your iPhone.

Adjusting iPhone's Location Settings and Services

Location Services is auxiliary to a lot of apps — Camera uses it to geotag photos, that is to add information about where the photo was taken in addition to putting a time and date stamp on it, and Reminders uses it to alert you to a task when you arrive at or leave a specified address. For Maps and Compass, however, Location Services is essential in order to get the most out of the app. Without Location Services, Maps can give you directions from one address to another and the Compass can give you magnetic north. If you want to know where you are, or you want true north, you have to turn on Location Services in Settings. We give you a simple explanation about the difference between true north and magnetic north when we talk about Compass.

The first time an app wants to use Location Services, a notification message appears asking if you want to allow the app to use your location. You can choose yes or no. For example, if you don't want the Camera to put your location on your photos, just tap no when Camera asks to use your Location. You can change these settings at any time, as explained in the third step here:

1. **Open the Settings app.**

2. **Tap Privacy, tap Location Services, and then tap the toggle switch on.**

   The Location Services list opens and displays all apps that can use your location in one way or another.

   When Location Services is being accessed by an app, its icon appears in the Status bar.

3. **Turn Location Services on or off for each app.**

   The Location Services icon next to apps indicate the following:

   - *Purple icon:* The app has recently used your location.

   - *Gray icon:* The app has used your location in the last 24 hours.

   - *Purple outlined icon:* The app uses a geofence, which is a limit to the location and is used by apps like Reminders to alert you when you leave or arrive at a specified address.

Location Services must be on for Find My iPhone to work. This should be a strong incentive to use a passcode to lock your iPhone. Otherwise, whoever "finds" your iPhone could just turn off Location Services and render Find My iPhone useless.

Getting There from Here with Maps

With Maps, you can do normal things that maps do — like find out where you are, if you're curious (or lost); or find directions to where you want to go. Maps becomes particularly useful when used to chart a course to an appointment because it provides the travel time and alternate routes. If you use Maps to plan leisurely jaunts, you can find rest stops, outlet malls, historic sites, and hotels along the way.

In this section, we tell you how to find your present location and locate a known address. Then we show you how to find a nearby service, such as a restaurant or bookstore. We talk about how to get directions from one place to another, and how to share or save the locations and directions you use.

Finding yourself

With Location Services on, Maps can tell you where you are. Tap Maps on the Home screen to open Maps, and then tap the Tracking button in the lower-left corner. If you have Location Services turned off, a notification message gives you the option of turning it on so Maps can find you.

Your exact location is the blue dot on the map, like you see in Figure 3-1. If there is a pulsing circle around the blue dot, your location is approximate; the smaller the circle, the more precise your location. If you're walking or driving, the blue dot moves along the map as you move along the road (or hiking trail or beach surf — you follow our point).

Change the orientation, size, and view of the map by doing the following:

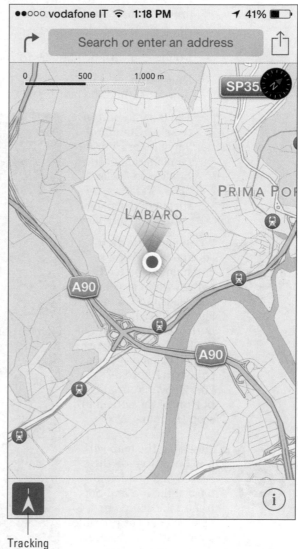

Tracking

Figure 3-1: The blue dot indicates your present location and follows your every move.

✔ Double-tap the Tracking button and a flashlight beam shines from the blue dot, lighting the way your iPhone is oriented. The Tracking button at the bottom of the screen changes from an arrow pointing to the right to a solid arrow pointing up. A compass appears in the upper-right corner to show the direction you're facing (refer to Figure 3-1).

✔ Use the spread and pinch gestures with your thumb and forefinger (or the two fingers that are comfortable for you) to zoom in and out of the

Book III
Chapter 3

Tapping into Maps,
Compass, and
Weather

map. When your fingers are on the screen, a scale appears in the upper-left corner (refer to Figure 3-1) to help you understand distances; it disappears when you lift your fingers.

✔ Double-tap with one finger to zoom in.

✔ Double-tap with two fingers to zoom out.

✔ Drag two fingers up the screen to switch to 3D mode; drag two fingers down to flatten the map again.

✔ Tap the Info button to select Standard, Satellite, or Hybrid (a combination of the first two) view and 2D or 3D for any of them — especially cool in satellite view.

Figure 3-2: City Flyover Tour takes you over the rooftops of cities worldwide.

 When in Hybrid view, zoom out until you see city names. Tap a city name written in yellow. A flag reads *City Name* Flyover City. Tap the Tour button on the left end of the flag, and a 3D flyover video begins playing, as shown in Figure 3-2. Tap End Flyover Tour at the bottom of the screen to stop the tour.

 Single-tap the map with one finger to hide the search and command bars at the top and bottom of the screen to see as much map as possible; single-tap again to bring them back into view.

The following gestures cancel Tracking if you're using it, although the zooming and 3D gestures work with or without Tracking:

✔ Use two fingers to rotate the map.

✔ Tap the Compass button that appears in the upper-right corner to return to a north-facing orientation.

✔ Drag one finger around the screen to move the map up, down, or sideways.

TECHNICAL STUFF

Maps combines the GPS, Wi-Fi, and cellular network data to determine your location and then uses TomTom and other mapping services to display locations and calculate r

Av jams

Eve yo inf tr miss im ments. We find Maps real-time traffic report to be an accurate tool for avoiding bumper-to-bumper conditions. Tap the Info button, and then tap Show Traffic. The roads on the map show you traffic conditions, as shown in Figure 3-3:

Figure 3-3: Show Traffic can let you know when you're better off choosing a different route.

✔ **Red dashes** show where traffic is heavy and stop and go.

✔ **Orange dots** mean traffic is moving slowly.

✔ **Road Closed icons** mean what they show — road closed.

✔ **Men At Work icons** indicate road work.

Service icons show gas stations, train stations, hospitals, airports, parks, shopping, and cafes. Tap the Tracking button and then tap the icon for a service to bring up its flag. Tap the Quick Driving Directions button to get instructions to reach the service from your current location.

Seeking and finding locations

Instead of finding a street name on a list, and then flipping a large unwieldy piece of thin, easily ripped paper, otherwise known as a map, to look for quadrant K-5, Maps lets you type in the address you seek. As fast as your Internet connection allows, the equivalent of quadrant K-5 appears on your iPhone screen. You can also find addresses from Contacts and from book-marks that you set up in Maps. Follow these steps to map-folding freedom:

1. **Open the Maps app.**

2. **Tap the Search field at the top of the screen. (Tap the screen once if you don't see the Search field.)**

   The keyboard opens and a list shows your recent searches and any addresses that were mentioned in recent messages or emails.

3. **If the address you seek is in the list, tap it to open a map showing that location.**

   Or

   Type one of the following in the search field (if an address is already in the search field, tap the X at the right end of the field to delete the text):

   • *An address* in the form of a street name and number or an intersection, with the city and state or just the name of a city or town.

   • *A neighborhood or landmark.*

   • *The name* of a person or business that's stored in your Contacts.

   A list of potential matches from Contacts and the Maps database appears; if you see the address you seek in the list, tap it to open a map showing that location.

4. **If there's no match, tap the blue Search button in the bottom-right corner of the keyboard.**

   A red pin on the map indicates the address you seek. The address is written on a flag attached to the pin. If the location is near your current location, you also see the travel time under the driving button.

If you want to keep the found address for future use, tap the Share button in the upper right, and then tap Add to Favorites. To add the address to Contacts, tap the flag, and then tap Create New Contact or Add to Existing Contact to store the address and associated information in Contacts.

To view and use an address you've recently used, tagged as a Favorite, or from your Contacts list, do the following:

1. **Open the Maps app.**

2. **Tap the Search field.**

3. **Tap the Favorites button at the top of the list.**

   A list of favorite locations opens.

   Or

   Tap the Recents button at the bottom center of the screen to use an address you've recently accessed.

   A list of recently used addresses opens.

   Or

   Tap the Contacts button at the bottom right of the screen to choose a person or business from Contacts.

   Your All Contacts list appears. Scroll through the list to open the Info screen that contains the address you seek.

4. **Tap the address you want to use.**

   A map opens and a red pin indicates the address or location you're looking for.

TIP

If you want a clean slate, you can clear your Favorites by opening the list and tapping Edit, and then tap the red and white minus sign followed by the Delete button, or simply swipe across the favorite address and tap Delete. Although Favorites can be removed singly, removing recent locations is an all-or-nothing deal: Tap Recents and then tap the Clear button and the list is emptied. If you want to save a Recents address, open it, and then save it as a Favorite or an addition to Contacts.

You can blunder around an unfamiliar city looking for a place to eat until you stumble upon an appealing restaurant, or you can rely on Maps, which uses Yelp! to make suggestions for eateries and the like. Follow these steps to find sites and services quickly and easily:

1. **Open the Maps app.**

2. **Tap the Tracking button to find something near your current location; otherwise, Maps searches for something near the last location you worked with.**

3. **Tap the Search field at the top of the screen.**

   The keyboard opens so you can type what you're looking for, say, *books* or *museums Prague*.

4. **Type your criteria in the Search field.**

   As you begin typing, Spotlight lists potential matches of locations (which have a red pin next to them) and words (which have a magnifying glass icon next to them).

5. **If your desired search word appears before you finish typing, you can tap it. If not, finish typing and then tap the Search button in the bottom-right corner.**

   Red pins appear on the matches in your vicinity or in the city you specified.

6. **Tap one of the pins to see a flag with the name of the result, as shown in Figure 3-4.**

   Or

   Tap List Results at the bottom of the screen to see a list of names and addresses of all the results. Tap a result to see it on the map (or tap Done to return to the map).

7. **Tap the flag in Map view or tap the Info button in List view to see information about the location.**

A Location screen opens that shows the distance of the location from your current location (determined by Location Services), along with

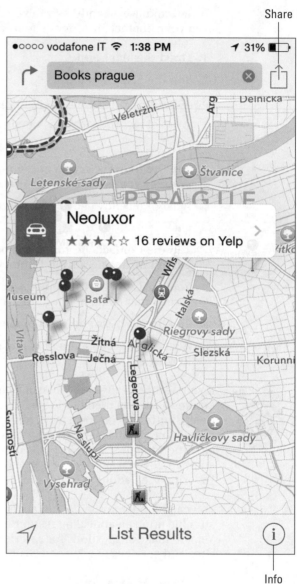

Share

Info

Figure 3-4: Use Maps to find services in a city or near a specific address.

information like the phone number and address of the selected site, the site's web address, or a link to Yelp!, as shown in Figure 3-5.

Tap the URL to open the related website or tap the phone number to call. If you search for an eating establishment, Maps also integrates with the OpenTable app (free to download at the App Store) to make reservations.

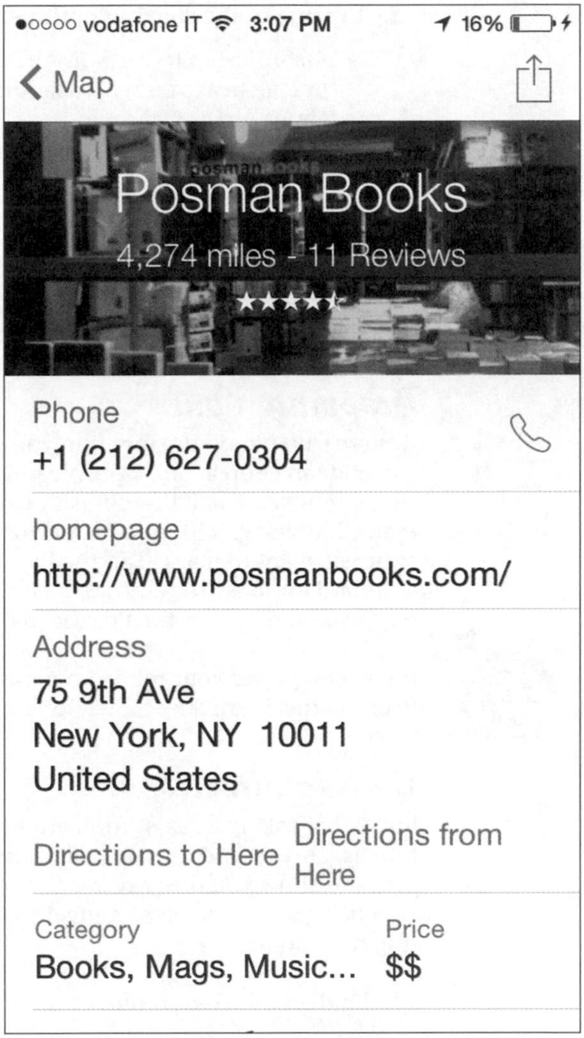

Scroll down the Location screen to see photos, reviews, and find the Create New Contact and Add to Existing Contact buttons to take those actions on the address you've found. Tap the Share button to add the location to your Favorites.

Sharing points of interest

When you find a great restaurant or want to share the address for a party, you can share it in several ways directly from Maps. Here's how to share locations:

●oooo vodafone IT 🛜 3:07 PM   ⌁ 16% 🔋 ⚡

‹ Map   ⬆️

Posman Books
4,274 miles - 11 Reviews
★★★★☆

Phone   📞
+1 (212) 627-0304

homepage
http://www.posmanbooks.com/

Address
75 9th Ave
New York, NY 10011
United States

Directions to Here   **Directions from Here**

Category   **Price**
Books, Mags, Music…   **$$**

Figure 3-5: The Location screen shows information about a location you select.

1. **Find the address you want to share with someone, either by searching or choosing one from Favorites, Recents, or Contacts.**

2. **Tap the Share button at the top right of the screen.**

   The Share Sheet opens.

3. **Tap one of the sharing options:**

   • *AirDrop:* Tap to turn on AirDrop and share the location with other people near you who use AirDrop. (See Book I, Chapter 4 to learn about AirDrop.)

   • *Message or Mail:* Tap to open an outgoing message that contains the location. Fill in the address for one or more recipients and then tap Send. (See Book II, Chapters 2 and 4 to learn about Message and Mail.)

   • *Twitter or Facebook:* Tap to post to either of these social networks. You must be logged in to your account.

Dropping a pin

If there's no pin on the location you want to save or share, tap the Info button and tap Drop a Pin. A purple pin shows up on the map with a flag that reads *Dropped Pin.* If the pin isn't exactly where you want it, zoom in on the map (double-tap with one finger), drag the pin, and then let go on the exact spot you want to mark. Tap the flag to display a Location screen with the standard options. To remove the pin, tap Remove Pin. That's exactly what happens when you return to the Map screen — out of sight, out of mind.

If you still prefer your maps on paper, tap the Share button and then tap Print on the Share Sheet. See Book I, Chapter 2 for details about printing.

Getting directions

Instead of asking a gas station attendant where the intersection of First and Pine is, only to find he said "left" when he should've said "right," you can ask Maps to show you the way. Maps provides voice-guided navigation just like a GPS navigator — one less gadget to cart around. Follow these steps for getting directions:

1. **Find an address in one of the three ways detailed previously.**

   The pin with the flag indicates the sought-after address.

2. **To get directions to the address from your current location, tap the Quick Driving Directions button (the car icon, refer to Figure 3-4) on the left end of the pin's flag or the Directions button to the left of the Search field in the upper left.**

   A route is immediately calculated; skip ahead to Step 5.

   Or

   Tap the flag and go to Step 3.

3. **You can obtain directions to and from this location by tapping one of the buttons:**

- *Directions to Here:* The Directions screen opens. Current Location is the default for the starting point.

- *Directions from Here:* The Directions screen opens; however, Current Location is the default ending point or destination.

To use an address different from your Current Location as a starting or ending point, tap the field that contains Current Location.

Current Location is highlighted.

1. Tap the circled X on the right end of the field to clear the field.

2. Type in the address you want to use.

3. Tap the Next button on the bottom right.

    The cursor moves to the other field, which has the previously established address. You can change it with the keyboard if you want.

    Swap the Start and End points of the Directions by tapping the Swap button.

4. **Tap the Route button in the upper-right corner or on the lower-right corner of the keyboard.**

    The screen displays a map showing the route from your starting point to your destination, or from your destination back to your starting point, if you prefer, as shown in Figure 3-6.

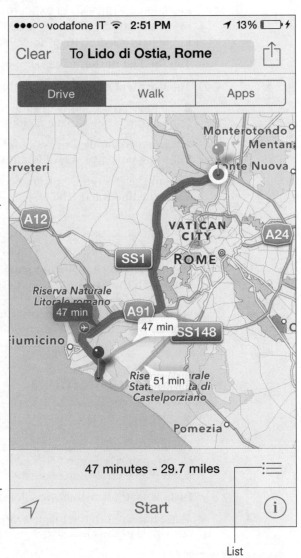

List

Figure 3-6: Choose your route and mode of transportation.

The distance and estimated travel time are displayed below the map. If more than one route is available, Maps displays alternate routes and shows the travel time for each. Tap the route you want to follow.

5. **(Optional) Tap Walk or Apps if you want to change your mode of transportation.**

   The Walk button provides directions and travel time for walking between destinations.

   The Apps button reveals a list of map and public transportation apps available for the area of your chosen directions. Installed apps are listed first, followed by apps that are available from the App Store. Tap the app in the list to switch to or download it.

6. **Tap the List button to see step-by-step directions.**

7. **Tap the Start button at the bottom of the screen.**

   If you have an iPhone 4s or later and an active Internet connection, point-to-point directions are dictated to you as you move along the route.

   A white arrow indicates an intersection or road change at each step. The following taps give you different views along the way:

   • Tap the Overview button to see the entire route from starting point to destination on the map; tap Resume to return to the point-to-point instructions.

   • Tap List Steps at the bottom of the screen to see a list of the point-to-point directions.

8. **If you want to change your starting point or destination or the whole route, tap the End button in the upper-left corner and start over.**

When you're looking for directions during the dark hours of the day, Maps automatically switches to Night mode, which shows light text on a dark background.

Setting Maps' settings

You have a few choices of how Maps gives you directions. Open the Settings app, tap Maps, and then tap your choices for the following:

✔ **Navigation Voice Volume:** Choose from No Voice and three volume levels. Unfortunately, you can't choose the voice itself, only how loudly you hear it. The same choices appear when you tap the Speaker button in Maps.

✔ **Distances:** Choose miles or kilometers.

✔ **Map Labels:** Turn the toggle switch on to see labels in English or off to see labels in the local language.

TIP

If you get lost using Maps because of wrong information, tap the Info button and then tap Report a Problem. This lets you help Apple improve the Maps app. Choose from four problems: Information Is Incorrect, Pin Is at Incorrect Location, Place Does Not Exist, or My Problem Isn't Listed. Tap the one you want, and then tap Next. Answer the questions on the subsequent screen, and then tap Send.

Talking about the Weather

Fresh air is good for your physical and mental health, but it's nice to know how to dress for the occasion, and for that you have Weather on your iPhone. Brought to you by the Weather Channel, iPhone's Weather app is updated hourly and gives you the current temperature and conditions and a ten-day forecast for cities across the country and around the world.

Adding, removing, and reorganizing cities

Weather uses Location Services to provide the forecast for your current location, but you may want to add other cities and locales too. Say you have to go on a multicity book tour and want to know what the weather will be like in each city. You can add the cities you'll be going to and then quickly flip through each day to see whether to expect sunny skies in your upcoming stop. Follow these steps:

1. **Open the Weather app.**
2. **Tap the List button in the bottom-right corner.**

   A screen similar to that in Figure 3-7 opens.

3. **Tap the F or C button if you want to switch between Fahrenheit and Celsius temperature readings.**

4. **Tap the plus sign to add locations where you want to track the weather.**

   A screen opens with a search field and keyboard.

5. **Type in the name, ZIP code, or airport code of the city or town you want to add.**

   A list opens with possible matches.

6. **Tap the name of the city you want to add.**

   The city now appears in your list.

To delete a city from your list:

1. **Open the Weather app.**
2. **Tap the List button in the bottom-right corner.**

3. **Swipe left across the city you want to delete.**

   A Delete button appears to the right of the name (refer to Figure 3-7).

4. **Tap the Delete button.**

   The city disappears from the list.

   If you swiped by mistake, tap anywhere but the Delete button to cancel.

5. **Tap a city in the list to return to the weather screen.**

To rearrange the order of the cities in the list, which in turn affects the order they're displayed on the weather screen, touch and hold a city, and then drag it to the position you want on the list. Drag the names of the cities around until they're in the order you like.

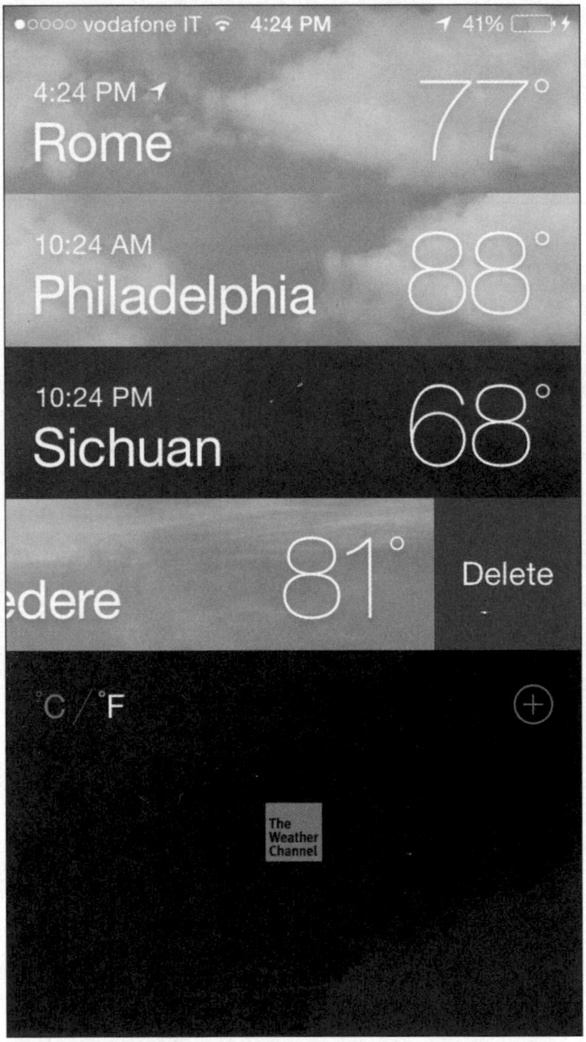

Viewing current and upcoming conditions

After you've added and organized the cities, tap a city to return to the weather screen, as shown in Figure 3-8. Each city on your list has its own weather forecast screen.

Figure 3-7: Add, delete, and reorder the cities you want Weather forecasts for.

Flick left or right to move between screens. If you have Location Services on for the Weather app (in the Settings app, tap Privacy, and tap Location Services), the first screen shows the forecast for your current location. The white dots at the bottom of the screen tell you how many cities you have forecasts for. Notice that the Location Services icon appears to the left of the dots.

The dynamic background reflects the current weather, so you may see the Milky Way with an occasional shooting star or cumulus clouds drifting across a blue sky. Under the city name you see the current temperature and conditions. The day's hourly forecast, including sunrise and sunset times, runs horizontally across the middle of the screen and below that a list of the next nine-days' forecast with the weather symbols you're used to: sunny, partly sunny, cloudy, thunderstorms, and so on. Scroll down to see weather values including humidity, wind, and a UV index, among others. Swipe the hourly forecast left to see the conditions for later in the day.

Figure 3-8: Weather gives you the current temperature and a five-day forecast.

Book III
Chapter 3

Tapping into Maps, Compass, and Weather

REMEMBER

When you pull down the Notification Center, you'll see the local forecast. Tap on the forecast in the Notification Center and the Weather app opens.

If you want more information, tap the Weather Channel button in the bottom-left corner. This opens www.weather.com in Safari and gives you more detailed weather information along with links to websites with news and other information about that city.

Staying on the Straight and Level with Compass

iPhone uses a built-in magnetic field sensor — a magnetometer — to give compass readings. The first thing we explain in this section is how to calibrate the Compass to cancel any interference and get Compass back on course. We show you how to read the Compass, and explain the difference between true and magnetic north and how to select one or the other.

Calibrating your iPhone for greater accuracy

When you first open the Compass app — it may be in the Utilities or Extras folder — a notification message appears indicating that you should calibrate your iPhone. Any time iPhone detects some interference, usually something with a magnetic field or an electronic device like a cellphone or stereo, you see a message asking you to calibrate your phone. As instructed onscreen, simply tilt your iPhone around until the circle is completely filled in and the Compass itself appears.

Getting your bearing

Whether to determine the direction you're facing — for example, to make sure your plants are on the east side of your house to get the morning sun — or find the direction you want to go, Compass is a great tool. After the Compass is calibrated, hold your iPhone (face up, of course) so the back of your hand is parallel to the ground.

Choosing between true north or magnetic north

Compass gives accurate readings of both true north and magnetic north, and both are valid indications. True north, which is a GPS bearing linked to the geographical location of the North Pole, works when Location Services is turned on.

Magnetic north, on the other hand, depends on the Earth's natural magnetism, which changes based on your physical location. It works when Location Services is both on and off. Because magnetic north changes at different latitudes, it can be a few to many degrees different than true north and even south of your latitude. This difference is called *declination.* In some places, declination is less than one degree so it barely alters your bearings. Keep in mind, however, if you're hiking in the wilderness on a trail with 10 degrees of declination, those seemingly minor ten degrees can result in you being miles off course after several hours of continuous hiking. Technically speaking, to achieve the most accurate results, you have to know the actual declination degrees you're traversing for your current location to calculate the difference between magnetic north and true north. Localized trekking maps often have declination degrees on them, so you can adjust the orientation of your map when using true north.

To turn on true north, open the Settings app, tap Compass, and then tap Use True North on.

The red arrow on the Compass points north; the direction your iPhone is pointing is written in white below the compass. Move around, and the compass rotates and the headings change. When you have Location Services turned on, your geographic coordinates and sometimes the town name are displayed below the compass, as shown in Figure 3-9.

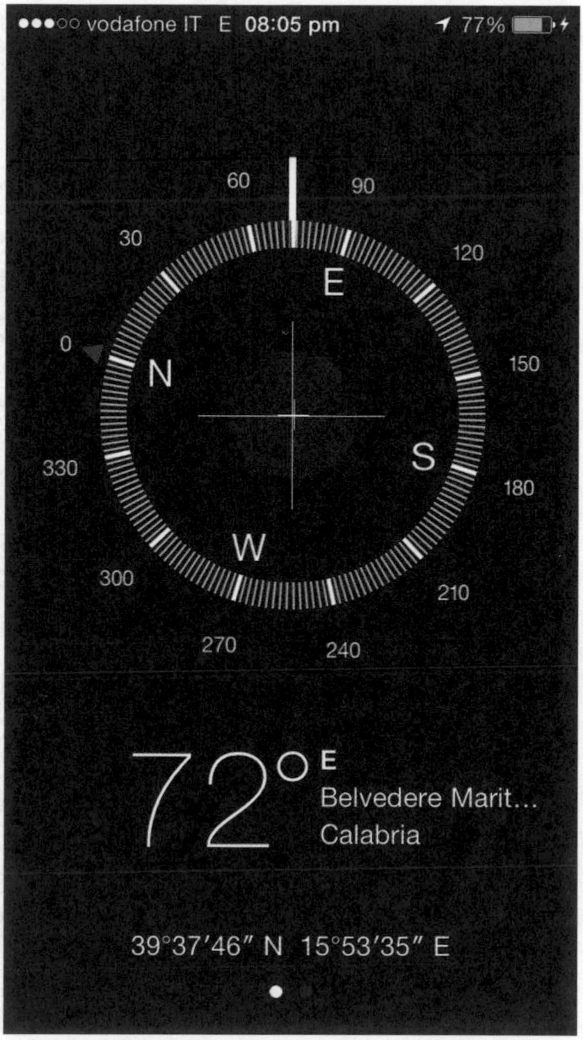

What's really helpful is that Compass links to Maps. If you want to see where you are on a map, tap the coordinates at the bottom of the screen. Maps opens and the tracking flashlight indicates your location and the direction you're facing. If you want to know the address, drop a pin and the address appears in the attached flag.

TIP

If you want to make sure you stay on an exact course, point the compass in the direction you want to go and then tap it. If you go off course, a red stripe indicates how many degrees off you've gone. Tap again to release the direction.

Figure 3-9: The Compass shows both the heading and the geographic coordinates for your location.

Book III
Chapter 3

Tapping into Maps, Compass, and Weather

Keeping things on the Level

The Compass is really two, two, two tools in one! (Anybody but us remember the old Certs commercial?) Swipe left from the Compass screen and you find an electronic spirit level. Instead of having an air bubble that must fall between two lines to indicate a level horizontal surface, two white bubbles, um, circles must line up when you place your iPhone on a horizontal surface. The degree of inclination appears in the circles, as shown in Figure 3-10, and when your iPhone is in a perfectly level position, the whole screen turns green and zero degrees show in the center circle. If you use the edges of your iPhone, instead of circles, you have a horizontal line across the center that divides the white top from the black bottom. When your iPhone is in a position of zero inclination, the black turns green.

Figure 3-10: Make sure your surfaces have the inclination you want with the Level.

Chapter 4: Figuring with Calculator, Stocks, and Numbers

In This Chapter

- ✔ Doing the math with Calculator
- ✔ Tracking investments with Stocks
- ✔ Summing it up in Numbers

This chapter is dedicated to number-crunching apps: Calculator, Stocks, and Numbers, Apple's spreadsheet app. Whether you want to tackle basic math problems or complicated scientific equations, Calculator helps you find the solutions. The Stocks app is a great tool for checking daily price quotes and tracking the historical performance of your investments. Numbers lets you build simple or complex spreadsheets and then share your calculations in colorful graphs and charts.

The apps we cover here are related yet stand-alone tools, so don't feel obliged to read this chapter from start to finish (although we're always happy if you do). We give you ins and outs, tips, and tricks so you get the most out of each app.

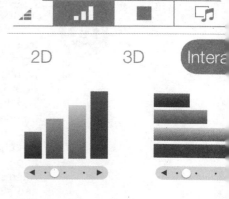

Doing the Math with Calculator

The Calculator app on your iPhone is really two calculators: a basic four-function calculator that you use for addition, subtraction, multiplication, and division, and a scientific calculator that is capable of performing trigonometric calculations, logarithms, square roots, and percentages.

Doing basic addition, subtraction, multiplication, and division

Even if you remember your times tables, there are times when you reach for a calculator and you don't have to reach any farther than your iPhone. The basic four-function calculator opens when you open the Calculator app. Follow these steps:

1. **Drag up from the Lock, Home, or an app screen to open the Control Center, and tap the Calculator button.**

   You can also open the Calculator on the Home screen, or you may find it in the Extras folder on the Home screen.

   The Calculator opens, as shown in Figure 4-1.

2. **Tap the numbers and operations you want to perform.**

   A white outline appears around the operation key you tap to remind you which operation is active.

You can copy and paste numbers from the Calculator results display to another app by pressing and holding on the results display until the Copy button appears. Tap the Copy button, double-click the Home button to open the App Switcher and open the app you want to paste

Figure 4-1: The four-function Calculator adds, subtracts, multiplies, divides, and calculates percentages.

the result in. Press and hold the location where you want to paste the result, and tap the Paste button that appears. You can also reverse the process and copy a number from another app, then paste it into the calculator display to use it in a calculation. See Book I, Chapter 3 to learn about editing functions and commands.

Switching to a scientific view

Most cellphones have calculators today, but iPhone offers a full-function scientific calculator, too. To open the scientific calculator, turn your iPhone to landscape view, as seen in Figure 4-2. (If you've locked your iPhone in portrait view, this won't work until you unlock it: Swipe up from the bottom of the screen to open the Control Center and tap the Portrait Orientation Lock button.)

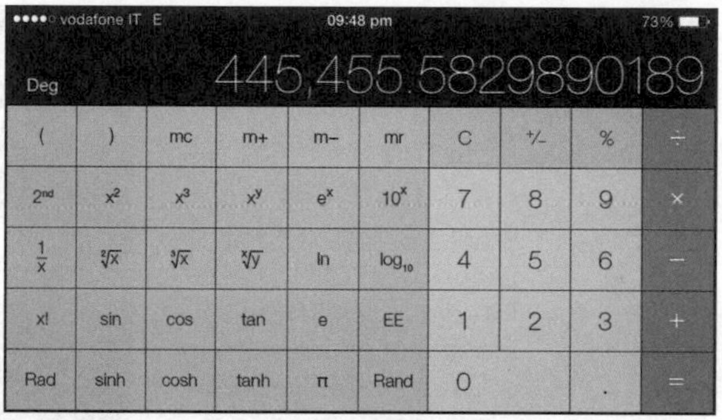

Here you'll find the memory commands:

Figure 4-2: Turning your iPhone to landscape view opens the scientific calculator.

- **mc** clears any numbers you have in memory.

- **m+** adds the number on the display to the number in memory.

- **m−** subtracts the number on the display from the number in memory.

- **mr (memory replace)** uses the number you put in memory in your current calculation. The button is outlined in black when a number is stored.

Two keys on the calculator toggle the other keys:

- **2nd:** Tap to change trigonometric (sin, cos, tan) and hyperbolic functions to the inverse. The button is outlined in black when active.

- **Rad/Deg:** Tap to switch between Radians and Degrees for trigonometric functions. Deg or Rad in the left corner of the number display tells you what mode you're in.

You find keys that calculate square, cube, and other roots; decimal and Naperian logarithms; and factorials; as well as generate random numbers.

Tracking Investments with Stocks

Whether you have a single mutual fund or a sizeable portfolio managed by a financial advisor, keeping an eye on your investments is usually a good idea. And that's exactly the idea behind iPhone's Stocks app, a simple yet powerful tool you can tap into to display and track activity for the stocks and funds you're interested in for the time interval you want. First we show you how to add the companies you want to watch and put them in an order that you like. Next we show you how to manage the viewing options Stocks offers.

Adding, deleting, and reordering stocks, funds, and indexes

Stocks comes with an assortment of U.S. and foreign index listings along with share activity of a few publicly traded companies already set up, as shown in Figure 4-3.

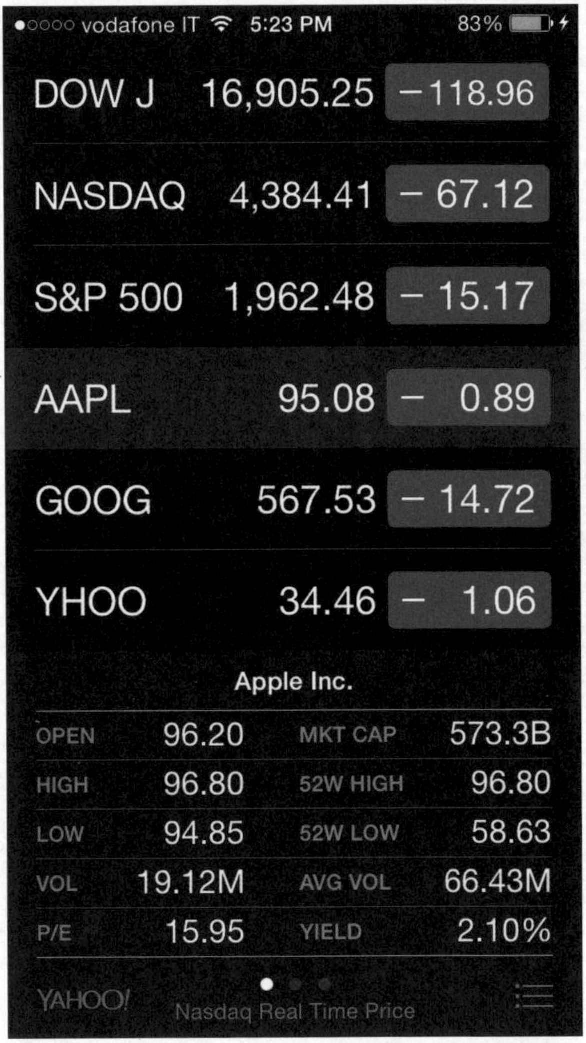

The first thing you want to do is add your personal stock or fund holdings or those that you're interested in watching for potential investments and delete any loaded ones that don't interest you. Here are the steps to follow:

1. **Open the Stocks app.**

   You might find it in the Extras folder.

2. **Tap the List button in the bottom-right corner.**

   The Stocks setup screen opens.

3. **Tap the plus sign button in the upper-left corner.**

   A search field opens with a keyboard.

4. **Type a company name or a stock identification code.**

   Stocks searches and a list of possible matches appears.

5. **Tap the stock you want to add to your list.**

   The screen returns to the list. The stock or fund you chose is added to the bottom of the list.

●○○○○ vodafone IT 🛜 5:23 PM		83% 🔋⚡

DOW J	16,905.25	−118.96
NASDAQ	4,384.41	− 67.12
S&P 500	1,962.48	− 15.17
AAPL	95.08	− 0.89
GOOG	567.53	− 14.72
YHOO	34.46	− 1.06

Apple Inc.

OPEN	96.20	MKT CAP	573.3B
HIGH	96.80	52W HIGH	96.80
LOW	94.85	52W LOW	58.63
VOL	19.12M	AVG VOL	66.43M
P/E	15.95	YIELD	2.10%

YAHOO! Nasdaq Real Time Price

Figure 4-3: Stocks shows market activity for U.S. and foreign indexes, as well as individual corporate share prices.

6. **Repeat Steps 3, 4, and 5 to add as many stocks as you want.**

7. **Delete a stock or index by tapping the minus sign to the left of the name, and then tapping the Delete button that appears.**

   If you tapped the minus sign by mistake, tap it again to cancel.

8. **Tap the Done button in the upper-right corner.**

   The current price screen returns.

You can arrange the stocks and indices in any order you want, such as putting those you're most interested in at the top.

Touch and hold the rearrange button, and then drag the stock to the position on the list. Drag the names of the stocks around until they're in the order you like.

The three buttons at the bottom of the Stocks setup screen let you choose how you view market fluctuations: by percentage changes, by price changes, or by market capitalization.

The market fluctuations appear on a green background if there's been a price increase and on red if there's been a decrease. The information lags about 20 minutes behind actual market activity.

Scrolling through views and news

After you establish the stocks and indices you want to follow, you may want to look at some historic data or see what the press has said about that company today.

Referring to Figure 4-3, the screen is divided into two zones: The top holds the list of stocks and indices you follow (six appear at a time, but you can scroll to see the other companies on your list).

The lower zone shows information about whichever stock or index you select from the upper zone. This zone scrolls left to right. After the price activity section, there's a graph that shows historic activity from one day up to two years. Scroll to the next screen to see a vertically scrollable list of news stories related to the stock or index highlighted in the upper zone — tap a news headline to open the complete article in Safari or tap and hold to add the article to Reading List. At the very bottom of the screen, you see the market quote status for the selected stock or index, such as Market Closed, Delayed Quote, or Nasdaq Real Time Price. That's one information-packed screen!

By default, Stocks appears in the Notification Center, which you see when you pull down from the top of the iPhone screen. To remove it, move to a more or less prominent position in the Notification Center lineup, drag down to open the Notification Center, scroll to the bottom and tap the Edit button.

If you don't want to see Stocks in the Notification Center, tap the Delete button (the red and white minus sign) and then tap Remove. Tap, hold, and drag the rearrange button next to Stocks to change its position.

Monitoring investment performance over time

But wait, there's more. Go back to the graph that shows historic activity. There are seven time intervals at the top. Tap any of those intervals and the graph expands or contracts to show price fluctuations from today back to the date that corresponds with the interval you chose.

To display a more detailed view, turn your iPhone to landscape view, as in Figure 4-4. The graph for the interval you were viewing in portrait view appears with the greater detail that increased landscape size allows. This screen is interactive. For example, tap the one-week view, and then touch and drag the blue line left and right. You see price fluctuations at intervals throughout the day. If you knew an announcement was made at a certain time on a certain day, you could see how soon after the announcement a change in the share price appeared.

Figure 4-4: Turn Stocks to landscape view and the share price fluctuation graph becomes interactive.

Press and hold on the screen to bring up the blue line, and then drag left and right to see the price for different days. In the three-month, six-month, and one-year views, the detail gives the daily closing price; in the two-year view, the daily closing price is given for every other day; in the five-year view, every year; and in the ten-year view, every other year.

If you put two fingers on the screen at once, two vertical, blue lines bracket a time interval and the share price change in that period is shown.

Move your fingers in and out to shorten and lengthen the time interval. In landscape view, when you flick from left to right, you see the graph for the same interval for each of the stocks and indexes on your personalized list.

Summing It Up with Numbers

Numbers could be a chapter, if not a mini-book of its own, but here we present a quick introduction. We take you through creating a simple spreadsheet with a few formulas, a graph, and several formatting tweaks. We encourage you to poke around the app to discover more features or review the in-app tutorial by tapping the Charting Basics template on the main Numbers screen.

If you purchased your iPhone after September 2013, you can download Numbers from the App Store for free. If you have an older iPhone, you can purchase Numbers for $9.99 at the App Store.

Numbers, and its iWork sibling apps Pages and Keynote, work with iCloud, which means that if you go to the Settings app, tap Numbers, and tap Use iCloud, your documents automatically sync with other iOS devices and Macs that use Numbers with the same iCloud account. You can also share your Numbers spreadsheet with other people through the iCloud.com website.

Creating a spreadsheet with formulas

Numbers comes with 30 templates and one blank, and these are the same templates as in the Mac version of Numbers. Even if you don't use a template, looking at them gives you a good idea of the power of Numbers — granted, it's unlikely you'll create a spreadsheet on your iPhone, especially if you want to get fancy; you'll probably create your spreadsheet on an iPad or a Mac, save it to iCloud, and use your iPhone to access your data, make minor corrections, or project it on a computer or monitor.

Here are the steps for creating and working with a blank spreadsheet:

1. **Open the Numbers app.**

   For our purposes, Numbers is turned on in iCloud so we can share the spreadsheet after it's created.

2. **If this is your first spreadsheet, tap the New Spreadsheet button (the plus sign on the top left) and then tap Create Spreadsheet.**

   If you already created a Numbers spreadsheet or you save Numbers spreadsheets to iCloud from another device or Mac, tap Create New. You can tap existing spreadsheets to open them. Likewise if you saved Excel documents in Numbers on your Mac; they have an "E" on them in the Numbers chooser until you open them and then you see a preview on the icon on the Numbers screen.

   If you receive a Numbers or Excel spreadsheet in an email or access one from a cloud storage service, such as Dropbox, or a link in Safari, tap the spreadsheet icon and then tap Numbers in the Open In options that appear. Numbers opens with the spreadsheet in view.

3. **Tap Blank.**

   A sheet, named — drumroll, please — Sheet 1, is created and contains one blank table.

4. Double-tap in any field to enter data. Tapping the buttons at the top changes the keyboard to reflect the type of data you want to enter:

- Tap the value button (42) to enter a number value. Tap the button on either side of the keypad to assign a value type, such as dollar or percent. Tap the star to create a ratings box or the check to create a check box.

- Tap the clock to enter a date or time. Tap the calendar or hourglass by the keypad to switch between months and numbers.

- Tap the text button (T) to enter text.

- Tap the formula button (=) to enter a formula, as shown in Figure 4-5. You can see the formula in the field at the top of the screen. To use a cell to create a formula, tap the cell and it appears in the field. Tap the operator you want to use and then tap another cell or a number. In the figure, you see the formula for cell C3 equals B3 + 30 percent. Tap the check mark on the right end of the field when you finish entering the value, date, text, or formula you want.

An easier way to enter a formula is to use Numbers' functions. Tap the

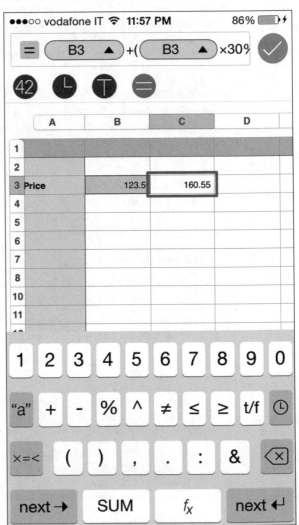

Figure 4-5: Type your own formulas cell by cell.

function key (next to the SUM key, refer to Figure 4-5) to open the list of function categories. Tap Categories at the bottom of the screen if it isn't selected, and then tap a category from the list. A list of functions in that category opens. Tap the Info button (i) to the right of a function to read a definition of the function and how it operates, as well as an example of how it's used. Tap the Back button in the upper-left corner to return to the function list and then tap the function you want to use. It's pasted into the cell you had selected. If you're only poking around the functions list, tap Categories to return to the main functions screen and then tap Done to return to your spreadsheet.

All keyboards have a Delete button. The value, clock, and formula keyboards have Tab buttons, which move the cursor one cell to the right, and Return buttons, which move the cursor to the beginning of the next line, whereas the text keyboard only has a Next button, which moves down one cell. The formula keyboard has a clock and text (A) button, which switches to those keyboards so you can insert those types of variables in your formulas; tapping Done takes you back to the formula keyboard. The formula keyboard also has a symbol shift key, which toggles between different mathematical symbols to give you more choices, much like the numbers and globe keys on the text keyboard toggle between different keyboard layouts and languages.

5. **Tap the Add Column button (the vertical equal sign) in the upper-right corner of the sheet to add a column or the Add Row button (the equal sign) in the lower-left corner of the sheet to add a row.**

6. **Tap the Add Sheet button (the plus sign next to the left of the Sheet 1 tab) to add another sheet to the spreadsheet.**

7. **Double-tap the name of a sheet to select it and type a more descriptive name.**

Formatting tables

The Format button (it looks like a paint brush) opens up the options to customize the parts of your sheet, as shown in Figure 4-6. Tap a cell or select a group of cells by tapping and dragging on the table, and then tap the Format button. Tap through the tabs to format the parts of your table:

✔ **Table:** Tap a table style to apply it to your table — for example, choosing a table with row and column headers and alternating row colors. Tap Table Options to see more choices, such as naming your table, selecting a font for the name, and defining where you want grid lines placed.

✔ **Headers:** Set from zero to the first five rows and/or columns as headers. Freeze them in position so they don't move when you scroll vertically or horizontally through the sheet.

✔ **Cells:** The options here affect all the selected cells, so you probably want to select the headers and format those cells and then select the data cells to format in a different way. The type can be formatted as bold or italic, and tapping Text Options lets you choose the font family, size, and color. Scrolling down, you also have choices for how to align the data within the cell and the option of adding a background (fill) color and cell border style.

✔ **Format:** A list of character types appears. Tap a type, such as Currency or Number, and then tap the Info (i) button to better define your choice — for example, currency format or the number of decimals. You can also designate a cell or group of cells as Checkboxes, Star Ratings, or a Pop-up Menu. If you choose Text, numeric characters don't have a numeric value.

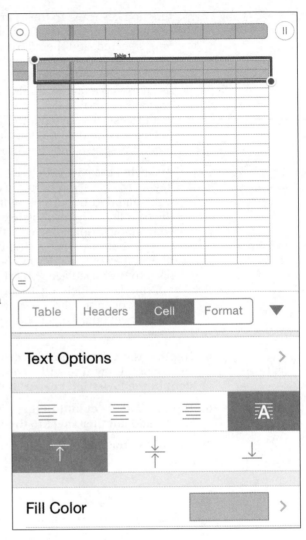

Figure 4-6: Make your table more attractive with the formatting tools.

Tap the triangle to close the formatting options.

Adding tables, charts, and media

Numbers doesn't just calculate and tabulate your data; it makes it meaningful and compelling with charts, images, or even songs. Use these steps to add elements to your sheet:

1. **Tap the Add Elements button (+).**

   A screen similar to Figure 4-7 appears.

2. **Tap the tab for the type of element you want to add:**

   - *Tables* offers a selection of table styles in color schemes that coordinate with the template theme you chose, if you're working with a template.

   - *Charts* takes data from a table and displays it as a graph or pie chart, 2D, 3D, or interactive. After you insert a chart, follow the onscreen instructions to select the data it will represent. As with Tables, the color scheme coordinates with the template theme, if you're using one.

   - *Shapes* gives you a choice of inserting text or simple line drawings that can be combined with text boxes to liven up your spreadsheet or highlight a specific point.

   - *Media* inserts photos, movies, and audio from the Photos and Music apps.

3. **Tap the element style you want to insert, such as a photo, a pie chart, text, or an arrow.**

   The element appears on your sheet.

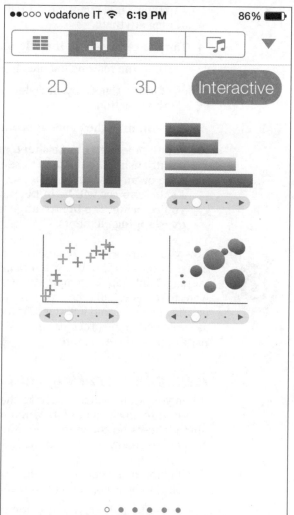

Figure 4-7: Add interest to your sheet with charts, shapes, and media.

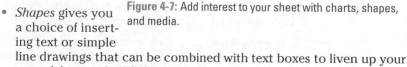

Book III
Chapter 4

Figuring with Calculator, Stocks, and Numbers

Tap the triangle on the right end of the tabs to leave this area without adding anything.

4. **Tap the element and then do one or more of the following:**

- Drag the resizing handles to shrink or enlarge photos or shapes.

- Tap the Cut, Copy, or Delete buttons in the pop-up menu to take those actions.

5. **Tap and drag the element around to place it where you want.**

6. **Tap the element on the sheet, and then tap the Format button (the paintbrush). Tap the tabs to see the options for changing the appearance or modifying the typeface family, size, and color of any text. Again, choices will be in keeping with the theme of any template you're using. Tap the Arrange tab to establish the hierarchy between overlapping elements.**

Now you know how to create a spreadsheet on your own, but admittedly, it's easier to select one of the 30 templates that come with Numbers. Instead of tapping Blank, tap the template you want to use. Tap the placeholder data you want to replace, and then type your data. The template calculates results using existing formulas and functions. You can reformat any of the template elements as explained in the previous steps. You also find more free and fee-based template apps in the App Store.

Renaming, sharing, and deleting spreadsheets

When you want to take an action that affects the whole spreadsheet, as opposed to an element of it, which we explain up until now, tap the Spreadsheets button in the upper-left corner to return to the opening Numbers screen. You can do the following:

✐ Tap the name under a spreadsheet on the Numbers screen to rename it. The keyboard opens, and you can give the spreadsheet a meaningful name.

✐ Tap edit, and then tap the document(s) you want to copy or delete. Tap the Copy button in the upper-left corner, and a copy is immediately added to the Numbers screen. Tap the Delete button (the trashcan), and then confirm that you want to delete the document(s).

✐ Tap the Share button and choose the action you want to take. When prompted to Select a Spreadsheet, tap the one you want to share and then proceed as follows for the option you chose:

- *Share Link via iCloud:* Sends only a URL link that will open the document on iCloud.com. After tapping the document you want to share, the Share Sheet opens. Tap the sharing method you want to use: AirDrop, Message, Mail, Twitter, Facebook, Pinterest, or LinkedIn. (If you don't see all the social network options, tap More to activate them.) A message or posting form opens; address the message, add a note and tap

Send or type a sentence to accompany your post and tap Post. The link is sent or posted. A green sharing icon appears on the upper-right corner of the document, reminding you that the document is shared; tap it to see the sharing settings and tap Permissions to change editing privileges. People with this kind of access can make changes to your document and it will sync on all your devices.

- *Send a Copy:* Sends a copy of the document. The Share Sheet opens with the usual options. Choose AirDrop, Message, or Mail, to send an actual document file or Facebook or Twitter to send a link. Tap iTunes to send the document file to iTunes. This lets you save your Numbers spreadsheet as a Numbers, Excel, PDF, or CSV file, after which you connect your iPhone to your computer and copy the file from your iPhone to your computer through iTunes. Tap WebDAV to send a copy to a WebDAV server. Type the server address, username, and password, tap Sign In and your spreadsheet is uploaded to the WebDAV server.

- *Open in Another App:* Lets you view your spreadsheet in a different app on your iPhone. Choose a format — Numbers, Excel, CSV, or PDF. Numbers saves your spreadsheet in the chosen format and then opens the Share Sheet with choices of apps that can read that format. Tap the app and your spreadsheet opens there. You can also upload to remote storage servers like Dropbox with this method.

**Book III
Chapter 4**

Figuring with Calculator, Stocks, and Numbers

Chapter 5: Creating Notes, Memos, Flyers, and Presentations

In This Chapter

✏ **Creating, viewing, managing, and sharing notes**

✏ **Adding accounts to Notes**

✏ **Recording, playing, managing, and sharing voice memos**

✏ **Syncing voice memos with iTunes**

✏ **Publishing with Pages**

✏ **Making your point with Keynote**

A re you the note-taking type who goes through multicolored sticky notes faster than a chimp in a peanut factory? Do ideas pop into your head that you don't remember later because those sticky notes and a pen aren't within reach? Do you like to share your great ideas in print and presentations?

If you answered yes to any or all of those questions, you're in good company. This chapter is all about recording and sharing your thoughts with a few of iPhone's most useful apps — Notes, Voice Memos, Pages, and Keynote. You can capture your every thought on the fly, as neatly typed out notes that you type or dictate to Siri, or as recorded audio files captured using your iPhone's built-in mic (or your stereo headphone's mic) and share them as is or in stylish printed pieces and colorful presentations.

Taking Note of Notes

Notes is a super-simple app you can use to make lists, jot down ideas, and record anything you'd normally scribble down on a sticky pad or cocktail napkin. Notes you create are stored on your iPhone and, optionally, synced with your computer and other iOS devices through iCloud, Gmail, or another IMAP account, or through Microsoft Exchange 2010 or later.

To get started, open the Notes app. The main Notes screen shows a list of any notes already saved in Notes, as shown in Figure 5-1.

You may see one or more notes listed even if you hadn't previously created a single note using the Notes app. That's because Notes can also come from email accounts set up on your iPhone for which you've turned on Notes. We write about syncing Notes and email accounts in the section "Setting up multiple Notes accounts," later in this chapter.

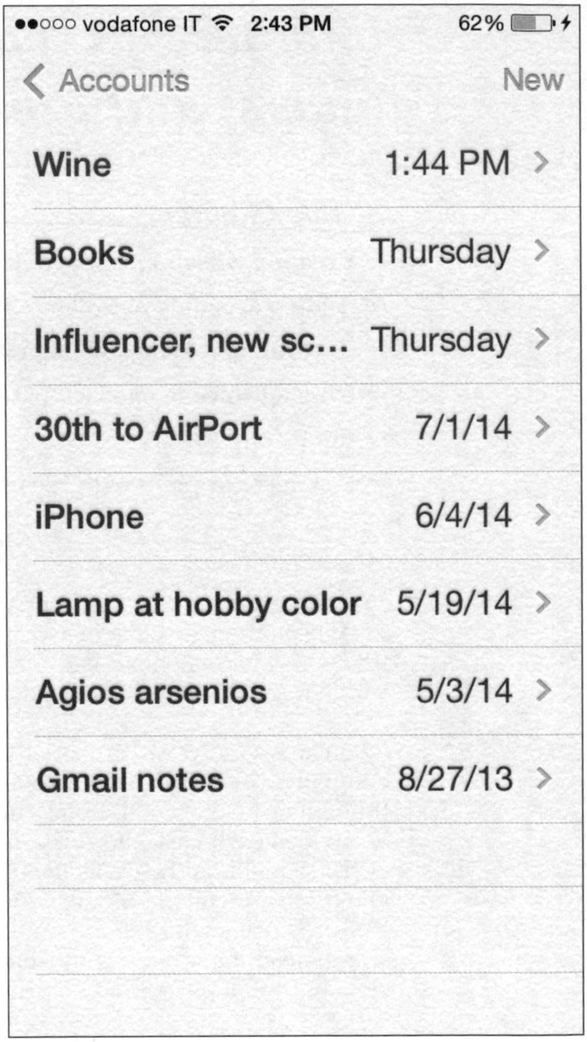
●●○○○ vodafone IT 2:43 PM 62%
Accounts
New
Wine 1:44 PM
Books Thursday
Influencer, new sc... Thursday
30th to AirPort 7/1/14
iPhone 6/4/14
Lamp at hobby color 5/19/14
Agios arsenios 5/3/14
Gmail notes 8/27/13

Figure 5-1: A list of notes you've saved in the Notes app.

Creating a new note

Tap the New button to create a new note. The keyboard appears, ready to capture your every thought or idea. Type the things you want to remember or tap the Dictate button and speak your mind. Tap Done to save your note and hide the keyboard. Tap Back to return to the Notes list.

Turning your iPhone sideways displays the landscape mode keyboard, which can help increase your typing speed and accuracy — although it does decrease the number of lines you see as you write your note. If the wider keyboard doesn't appear when you turn your iPhone sideways, flick up from the bottom of the screen to open the Control Center, and then tap the Portrait Orientation Lock button to unlock the Portrait Orientation Lock feature and flick down to close the Control Center.

Press and hold the Home button to activate Siri. When Siri is ready, just say, "Create a note," and when asked, dictate your note. If your iPhone is connected to a power source and you turned voice activation on in the General settings of the Settings app, you can also say "Hey, Siri" to get Siri's attention.

Searching and managing your Notes list

Notes are listed in chronological order, with the newest (or most recently edited) note appearing at the top of the list, and the least recently modified note relegated to the bottom of the list. Notes titles are automatically generated based on each note's first line; if you enter a return in the first line, only the word(s) before the return appear in the title — you see more of the note title in landscape view.

When viewing the Notes list, you can do the following:

✔ Swipe left across a note title to display the Delete button, and then tap Delete to delete the note. If you swipe by mistake, just tap Cancel at the top right of the screen.

✔ Tap a note to view, edit, share, or delete the note.

✔ When viewing a list of notes, tap the Status bar at the top of iPhone's screen or drag your finger down the list to reveal the Search field, and then type in the first few characters of whatever you're looking for. Note contents are searched and the titles of any notes containing matches to your search criteria are displayed; tap the note title to view that note.

If you've selected Notes in the Settings app by tapping General and then tapping Spotlight Search, any searches you perform from the Spotlight Search Home screen will search in Notes, too.

Browsing, editing, deleting, and emailing Notes

Notes you create can contain regular and accented letters, numbers, and symbols (in other words, any of the alphanumerical stuff you can type with the keyboard), as well as images you save in Photos.

When viewing a note, you can do the following:

✔ To add more text or edit a note, tap where you want to begin typing or editing; the keyboard appears and you can then type or edit to your heart's content.

✔ Tap a second time to see the formatting menu, as shown in Figure 5-2, and do the following:

   • Tap Select or Select All to highlight the text you want to edit. After you select text, the menu gives you editing options. (See Book I, Chapter 3 for editing tips.)

   • Tap Insert Photo to open Photos; tap the photo you want to insert in your Note, and then tap Choose. Notes reopens and you see the image in your note.

✔ Shake your iPhone to display the Undo message; tap Undo to, well, undo what you just did. Shake again to display the Redo option and tap Redo to redo what you undid.

✔ Tap Back at the top of the screen to return to the Notes list.

✔ Tap the Delete button (the trashcan) to delete your note (see Figure 5-3).

✔ Tap the Share button to open the Share Sheet, and then tap the method you want to use to share your note — AirDrop, Message, Mail, Copy, or Print.

✔ Tap the New Note button to create a new note.

Setting up multiple Notes accounts

You can keep your Notes notes on your iPhone only or sync

Figure 5-2: Edit and add photos to your note.

Notes with your computer and other devices from multiple sources, including iCloud or another Notes-enabled service such as Gmail, Exchange, or Yahoo!.

Notes will sync with IMAP email accounts but not POP email accounts.

Notes you choose to sync with iCloud appear on any computers or other iOS devices logged in to your iCloud account with the Notes option turned on.

Those you sync with your email accounts appear on both your iPhone and on your computer's email program (Outlook) or your web-based email service (Gmail or Yahoo!). If you're using a Mac OS prior to Mountain Lion, Notes will continue to sync with Mail. Activate syncing as follows:

- **iCloud:** Open the Settings app, tap iCloud, and tap the Notes switch on.

- **Other email accounts:** Open the Settings app; tap Mail, Contacts, Calendars; and then tap the account you want to sync Notes with. Tap the Notes switch on to automatically sync your notes over-the-air.

Tap Accounts in the upper-left corner of the Notes list (refer to Figure 5-1) to display any of the notes you sync with iCloud or email accounts for which you turned on the Notes sync setting in the Settings app under Mail, Contacts, Calendars. (If you only use iCloud, instead of Accounts, you see Folders.) When viewing the Accounts list, as shown in Figure 5-4, you can do the following:

- Tap All Notes to display a list of all your notes saved and synced with all your email accounts or on your iPhone.

Figure 5-3: Share or delete your Note.

Book III
Chapter 5

Creating Notes, Memos, Flyers, and Presentations

✔ Tap Notes under an email account name or On My iPhone to display only the notes stored and synced in that location. Under the iCloud section, you see top-level Notes but not the Notes stored in folders. Tap All iCloud to see all Notes stored on iCloud, including those in folders.

✔ Tap a folder in the iCloud section to see Notes in that folder. (This option is available if you use Notes on a Mac with iCloud.)

If you want to store some Notes only on your iPhone, create at least one note before turning Notes on in iCloud or an email account (or turn Notes off — in the Settings app under Mail, Contacts, Calendar — for each of those, create a note, and then turn Notes back on). You then see an On My iPhone section in the Accounts list (refer to Figure 5-4).

If you have multiple accounts, open the Settings app, tap Notes, and tap Default Account to choose the account you want new notes to be created in if you create a new note from the All Notes list. If you're viewing notes from one source, such as On My iPhone or Gmail, and you create a new note, the new note is stored in that source.

Figure 5-4: Accounts displays email accounts for which you have Notes turned on.

Speaking of Voice Memos

With iPhone's Voice Memos app, you can record, listen to, edit, and share out-loud sounds all with the tap of your finger. And so, because we're big believers in the adage "actions speak louder than words," instead of listening to lengthy introductory words by yours truly, why don't you act on recording and listening to *your* spoken words and other sounds with Voice Memos?

Open the Voice Memos app (it may be in the Utilities or Extras folder).

Recording voice memos

The recording function is handled by your iPhone's built-in mic, or by the mic built into the EarPods that came with your iPhone if you have those plugged in.

Other mic-enabled options for recording audio with Voice Memos include external mics designed to plug into your iPhone's Lightning or Dock Connector, and wireless Bluetooth headsets and headphones that let you cut the proverbial cord altogether (thus, freeing your hands for flailing, gesticulating, or whatever).

Center stage of the Voice Memos screen is the sound level meter. As you speak or record other sounds around you, the sound waves expand vertically to indicate the decibel level of your recording. The waves appear in response to any sounds the mic picks up, whether you're actually recording those sounds or not.

For optimal recording quality, Apple recommends a recording level between –3 and 0 decibels (dB). Translation: As you're speaking, move your iPhone (or headphone mic) closer or farther from your mouth, or lower or raise your voice, or use a combination of both, to try to keep the recording level in or as close to that optimal-quality sweet spot between –3 and 0 dB.

When you're ready, tap the red Record/Pause button and say "hello" to your iPhone or snap your fingers to see the meter in action.

When you begin recording, four things happen at once to let you know your live recording session is underway: A single-chime sound plays, the Record button changes to a Pause button, the timer starts, and the sound level meter flows to the right, as shown in Figure 5-5.

If you go to the Home screen or switch to another app while you're recording a voice memo (or you pause a memo you're recording), a red banner appears at the top of the screen so you don't forget about your recording. Tap the red banner to return to Voice Memos. If your iPhone locks while Voice Memos is recording or paused, when you press the Home button to unlock it, you see the sound level meter in action, even if you have another app open and Voice Memos is recording or paused in the background.

Figure 5-5: Live, from New York! (Or wherever are!)

 To pause recording, tap the Record/Pause button. If you switch to another app or go to the Home screen, the red banner pulses at the top of the screen but reads "paused."

To resume a paused recording, tap the Record/Pause button. Recording resumes; you can repeat this process of pausing and resuming your recording as many times as you want until you decide to tap Done, to end your recording session (refer to Figure 5-5).

To stop recording, tap the Record/Pause button to stop recording, and then tap Done. A double-chime plays, and a New Voice Memo dialog opens. Tap the Backspace key to delete the text, and then type a name for the voice memo. Tap Save. Your newly recorded voice memo appears in the list of recordings.

 You *shouldn't* hear the chime and double-chime sound effects that play when you start and stop recording a memo if iPhone's ring/silent switch is switched to silent mode. We say *shouldn't* because in some countries or regions, the recording sound effects play even when the ring/silent switch is set to silent.

Our guesstimate as to why those sound effects may still be heard even when iPhone is set to be quiet? To offer some kind of audible warning to anyone within earshot that you may be recording anything they say. However, we can only speculate.

Listening to voice memos

The voice memo list appears on the lower half of the screen and displays your voice memos in chronological order, from newest to oldest (see Figure 5-6). Below the title, you see the date the voice memo was made and the length of the recording. To listen to, pause, and control playback of a voice memo, tap it in the list and then do the following:

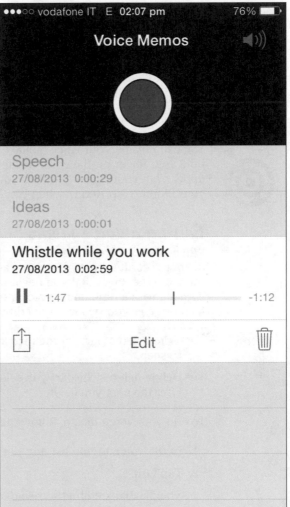

Figure 5-6: Pausing a voice memo.

✔ Tap — you guessed it — the Play button to hear your voice memo. When your voice memo begins playing, the Play button turns into a Pause button and the playhead moves forward on the scrubber bar.

✔ Tap the Pause button to pause listening to your voice memo, as shown in Figure 5-6, and then tap Play to resume.

✔ Drag the playhead left or right in the scrubber bar while the voice memo is playing or paused to move backward or forward.

Book III
Chapter 5

Creating Notes,
Memos, Flyers, and
Presentations

✔ Tap the Speaker button in the upper right of the screen if you want to hear your voice memos out loud through your iPhone's built-in speaker. (By default, voice memos play through your iPhone's receiver speaker, or through your headphones, if you have those plugged in.)

✔ To select another voice memo, tap the list to close the open voice memo and then tap the one you want to listen to. Use the Play, Pause, and scrubber playhead buttons as previously described to listen to your selected voice memo.

You can rename your voice memo when you tap it for playback. Press and hold your finger on the voice memo title until the editing loupe and keyboard appear. Lift your finger and then edit the title as you would any other text on your iPhone. Tap Return when you finish.

Editing a voice memo

When possible, we suggest leaving a bit of air time at the beginning and end of your recording to give you leeway for trimming your voice memo. Then there are the times that you begin recording something and forget and find yourself with a ten-minute voice memo of a three-minute conversation. Voice Memos gives you two ways to edit your recording:

✔ **Trim** deletes parts of the recording before and after the part you select to keep.

✔ **Delete** deletes the part you select, merging the recording before and after the part you delete.

To edit your voice memo, follow these steps:

1. **In the voice memo list, tap the voice memo you want to edit.**

2. **Tap Edit.**

    The playback editing screen displays the sound waves of your recording, as shown in Figure 5-7.

3. **Tap Play.**

    The blue line indicates the time of the playback and the recording flows behind it.

4. **Tap Pause when the playback is just past where you want to begin trimming or deleting.**

5. **Tap the Trim button (the blue square on the right) and you find the blue line where you positioned it in Step 4.**

    The red lines at the left and right sides of the recording are the trim grabbers (see Figure 5-8).

6. **Touch and hold the left red grabber and drag it toward the middle to shorten your recording, slightly before the blue line.**

   Refer to the timers to precisely position the grabber.

7. **Tap the Play button.**

   The blue line moves to the right as the recording plays so you can see the exact point at which you want to trim or delete.

8. **When the blue line is just past the point you want to end trimming or deleting, tap the Pause button.**

9. **Drag the right grabber to a few seconds after the position of the blue line.**

10. **When you're pleased with the position of the trim grabbers, tap the Trim button to save or tap Delete to eliminate the selected part (the recording between the grabbers). Tap Cancel if you change your mind and you don't want to trim your voice memo after all.**

Figure 5-7: Use the editing screen to find the exact place you want to trim your recording.

Book III
Chapter 5

Creating Notes, Memos, Flyers, and Presentations

Three choices appear:

- *Delete From/Trim Original:* Replaces the original recording with the edited recording.

- *Save As New Recording:* Creates a new edited voice memo. This choice is our recommendation — you can always delete the original later but you can't bring it back after it's replaced.

- *Cancel:* Returns to where you left off working.

 You can use a voice memo as a ringtone by trimming the file to shorter than 30 seconds, email it to yourself, and then, on your computer, change the file extension to .m4r and open it. The file imports into iTunes as a ringtone, which you can then sync to your iPhone. If you use a Mac, you can trim and edit the file in GarageBand and save it as a ringtone.

Sharing or deleting a voice memo

Some recordings are better left unsaid, or even deleted, and others you'll want to shout out to the world. Both actions are just a tap away in Voice Memos.

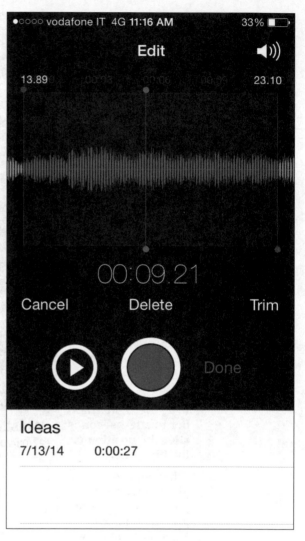

Figure 5-8: Editing a voice memo down in size.

To share a voice memo:

1. **Tap a voice memo to open it.**

    The screen appears as in Figure 5-6.

2. **Tap the Share button to open the Share Sheet, and then tap the method of sharing you want to use: AirDrop, Message, Mail, Twitter, Facebook, Flickr, Vimeo, or iCloud. Proceed as usual for sharing.**

    If you want, you can tap More to edit the sharing options for the Voice Memos app.

3. Tap another voice memo to return to the list.

If a message saying your voice memo file is too large to send appears, you need to trim your voice memo using the edit tool (see the previous section) before trying to send your message again.

To delete a voice memo, swipe left across the voice memo in the list and tap the Delete button that appears to the right, or tap the memo and then tap the Delete button (the trash can) — tap Cancel if you tapped Delete by mistake.

Syncing voice memos with iTunes

Deleting a voice memo instantly erases the voice memo from your iPhone. However, if you sync voice memos with iTunes, copies of your recorded voice memos are stored on your computer even if you later decide to delete those synced voice memos from your iPhone.

You probably want, or need, to keep some audio files but don't have to keep them on your iPhone, where they consume storage space you'd rather free up. Sync any voice memos you want to keep with iTunes on your computer, and those voice memos remain safe and sound, so to speak, until you want (or need) to hear them again.

We give you the full lowdown on how to pick and choose the kinds of information and files (including voice memos) you want to sync between your iPhone and your computer using iTunes in Book I, Chapter 5, so we won't repeat ourselves here. But we would be remiss if we didn't take a moment to at least mention a few points relative to syncing your voice memos with iTunes:

- ✔ iTunes automatically creates a playlist named — drum roll, please — Voice Memos on your computer, and that's where you can track down new, not-so-new, and downright ancient voice memos you recorded and synced with iTunes syncs.

- ✔ Voice memos you delete from your iPhone remain safely backed up in your iTunes library.

- ✔ If you delete a voice memo from iTunes that you have saved on your iPhone, that voice memo will be deleted from your iPhone the next time you sync with iTunes.

You can also email the voice memo to yourself and avoid iTunes syncing altogether.

Publishing with Pages

Pages is two apps in one: a powerful word processor for creating documents that can go on for, well, pages and pages, and a page layout app for creating mixed media documents such as newsletters, posters, flyers, invitations, and

**Book III
Chapter 5**

Creating Notes, Memos, Flyers, and Presentations

more. We give you the down and dirty here, but encourage you to get creative, have fun, and spread your words around.

You can download Pages from the App Store for free — if you purchased your iPhone after September 2013. If you have an older iPhone, Pages will cost you $9.99 in the App Store.

Creating a Pages document

Although it's most likely you'll use Pages to edit documents you keep on iCloud Drive or receive from others, in a pinch you may want to create a new document. Before you create your document, think about how you want to communicate. Will you use mostly words with a few images or a lot of images and some words to support them? Being clear about your purpose helps you choose the right template — you can create a Pages document from scratch, but templates make it easier and faster. Pages makes it pretty easy to choose because the templates are divided by document type.

After you create your document in one type of template, you can't change over to another without a bunch of copying and pasting — yuck!

Do the following to create a new document and start creating:

1. **Open the Pages app.**

   For our purposes, Pages is turned on in iCloud so we can share the document after it's created.

2. **If this is your first document, tap the New Document button (it's the plus sign on the top left) and then tap Create Document.**

   If you already created a Pages document or you save Pages documents to iCloud from another device or Mac, tap Create New. You can tap existing documents to open them. Likewise if you saved Word documents in Pages on your Mac; they have a *W* on them in the Pages chooser until you open them and then you see a preview on the icon on the Pages screen.

   If you receive a Pages or Word document in an email or access one from a cloud storage service, such as Dropbox, or a link in Safari, tap the spreadsheet icon and then tap Numbers in the Open In options that appear. Numbers opens with the spreadsheet in view.

3. **Scroll through the template categories and choose one that most closely matches the type of document you want to create.**

   You can also choose blank if you want to start from scratch and do everything yourself. We chose Modern Report for our example because it has both text and images.

Many third-party developers make templates for Pages and Keynote, too. Search the App Store to see them and go to Bonus Chapter 1 online to read about some of our favorites.

4. **Tap the template you want to use.**

   Your chosen template appears on the screen.

5. **Tap the placeholder text and begin typing your own words.**

   This is a situation where a Bluetooth keyboard would come in handy.

   Because this is a report, even if the text goes beyond the placeholder space, it flows onto successive pages.

   The word count appears onscreen as you type. If you select a portion of text, the word count reflects on the selected text. Tap the Tool button in the upper right, and then tap Settings to turn this feature off or on.

6. **Tap the Add Image button (the plus sign) on the first placeholder image.**

   Your Photos library opens. Tap through the Camera Roll and your other libraries and albums to find the photo you want to insert.

   If you have a lot of photos in Photos, it helps to go through and flag those you may want to use beforehand or even put them all in an album so you can quickly find the ones you want to place in your document. See Book IV, Chapter 1 to learn about working with Camera and Photos.

7. **Tap the image you want to insert.**

   It shows up in your Pages document, replacing the placeholder image. You can drag it around or resize it if you want, but that may cause some of the other parts of the document to shift around.

8. **Double-tap the image to bring up a slider so you can scale, pan, and crop the photo, as shown in Figure 5-9. Tap Done when you're happy with the size and position.**

9. **Repeat Steps 5 through 9 until your document is complete.**

Fine-tuning your text and images

Templates make creating documents quick and easy because the creative legwork is done for you — you only have to supply the content. You may find that you want to tweak some of the elements of your document, however. Tap the text or image you want to fine-tune, and then tap the Format button (the paintbrush). These are the options you have:

✓ **Text:** Three tabs let you alter the Style of the typeface and paragraph (as shown in Figure 5-10); scroll down to see the paragraph styles

**Book III
Chapter 5**

Creating Notes,
Memos, Flyers, and
Presentations

associated with the template. The List tab defines how bulleted or numbered lists are formatted, and the Layout tab lets you change the number of columns and increase or decrease the line spacing. Tap each tab and then play with the options. You see the changes immediately in the document. Tap on the document and then tap Undo or shake your iPhone and tap Undo if you don't like how it looks.

✓ **Image:** Here, the Style tab offers frames, borders, and shadow effects. Tap the Image button to edit or reset the original cropping (called a Mask) or use the Instant Alpha effect, which, when selected, makes areas of the same color that you drag your finger across transparent. Instant Alpha makes parts of your image stand out and works best when you have two or more contrasting colors. You can also tap Replace to

Figure 5-9: Scale, pan, and crop images to add the most impact to your document.

choose a different image to substitute the existing one. The third tab, Arrange, lets you flip the image horizontally or vertically and also moves it backward or forward in relation to other elements on the page. This is helpful when you layer several images or elements and one is larger than the other. The larger one should be moved backward so the smaller one can be seen on top.

Tap the triangle to the right of the tabs to exit the Format screen without making changes.

Adding other design elements

You can copy and paste elements and objects from other apps — for example, a chart you create in Numbers — or you can create the chart directly in Pages. The charts, tables, shapes, and text styles are in keeping with the style of the template you're working in, although you can edit them as just explained for text and images. Follow these steps to use the design elements in Pages:

1. **Tap the Add Element button (the plus sign).**

   A screen similar to Figure 5-11 appears.

2. **Tap the tab for the type of element you want to add:**

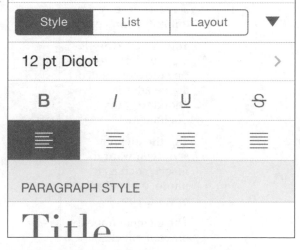

Figure 5-10: The Format tabs give you options for customizing the style of your text and images.

Book III
Chapter 5

Creating Notes,
Memos, Flyers, and
Presentations

   - *Tables* offers a selection of table styles in color schemes that coordinate with the template theme you chose.

   - *Charts* takes data from a table and displays it as a graph or pie chart, 2D, 3D, or interactive. After you insert a chart, follow the onscreen instructions to select the data it will represent. As with Tables, the color scheme coordinates with the template theme.

   - *Shapes* gives you a choice of inserting text or simple line drawings that can be combined with text boxes to liven up your spreadsheet or highlight a specific point. Scroll through to choose different colors.

- *Media* inserts photos, movies, and audio from the Photos and Music apps. Tap the type of media you want to insert and then scroll through the apps' libraries to find the piece you want.

3. **Flick through the screens to see different color choices.**

   You can edit the element with the formatting tools explained above after it's been added to your document.

4. **Tap the element style you want to insert, such as a photo, a pie chart, or an arrow.**

   The element appears on your sheet.

   Tap the triangle on the right end of the tabs to leave this area without adding anything.

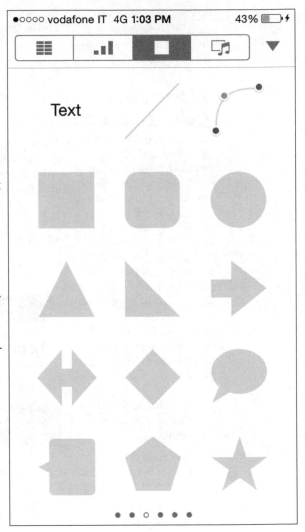

Figure 5-11: Spice up your document with charts, shapes, text, and media.

5. **Tap the element and then do one or more of the following:**

   - Drag the resizing handles to shrink or enlarge the inserted element.

   - Tap Edit Data in the pop-up menu of a chart. Tap in the fields, as shown in Figure 5-12, to type the data you want displayed in the chart, and then tap Done.

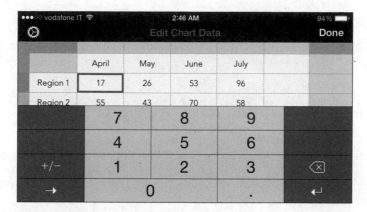

Figure 5-12: Substitute the placeholder data with your own.

- Double-tap a field in a table and type in the information you want.
- Tap the Cut, Copy, or Delete buttons in the pop-up menu to take those actions.

6. **Tap and drag the element around to place it where you want.**

7. **Tap the element on the sheet, and then tap the Format button (the paintbrush). Tap the tabs to see the options for changing the appearance or fill color, or modifying the typeface family, size, and color of any text.**

   Again, choices will be in keeping with the template theme.

   Tables have the same Table, Header, and Arrange options as they do in Numbers. Tap through here or see Book III, Chapter 4 for details.

   Charts give you options for labeling the *x*- and *y*-axes and stylizing the gridlines and tick marks.

Use the Arrange feature of the Formatting tabs to properly layer overlapping elements such as a text box on a shape.

Checking your spelling

In addition to the Auto-Correction and Check Spelling options you can find in the Settings by tapping General and then tapping Keyboard, Pages has a spelling option. Tap the Tools button in the upper-right corner of the document screen, and then tap Settings in the list of tools. In the Settings screen, tap the Check Spelling switch on. Although you adjust the settings within a specific document, they're applied across all the documents you work on in Pages.

TIP

If you share and work on your document with other people, turn on Comments and add your Author Name in Settings. Then turn Tracking on in the Tools menu so each contributor's comments and changes are easy to spot in the shared document.

Making Your Point with Keynote

Your iPhone may not seem like the ideal place to design a presentation — and it's probably not — but with a little patience (and maybe a pair of reading glasses), you can pull together a nice message and you can then project your presentation on a larger screen with Apple TV and AirPlay.

Creating a new presentation

Like the other iWork apps, Keynote can be downloaded in the App Store (free for iPhone's purchased after September 2013; $9.99 for those purchased prior). It comes with a bevy of themes that you use as the jumping-off point for the creation of your presentation. Each theme is applied to a dozen or so slide layouts. The steps are the same as for Pages. Open the Keynote app, and then do one of the following:

- Tap Create New, and then tap the theme that best reflects the style and tone you want your presentation to have.

- Double-tap text placeholders to type in your text — headers, bulleted lists, quotes, and so on.

- Tap the Add Media button (the plus sign) on the image placeholders to insert your own photos.

- Tap the Add Elements button to insert media, charts, text, and shapes, as explained in the previous section, "Adding other design elements."

- Tap the Add Slide button (the plus sign at the bottom left of the screen) to choose the slide layout you want to use for a new slide, as shown in Figure 5-13. Tap the layout, and it appears in the main part of the screen.

REMEMBER

Check out the online article "How to Use Your iPhone as a Slideshow Remote Control" found at www.dummies.com/extras/iphoneaio.

Adding transitions between slides

With Keynote, you can use transitions to jolt your audience when you move from one slide to the next. Keynote comes with many types of transitions, and you can experiment to find those that you like. To add transitions between slides, do the following:

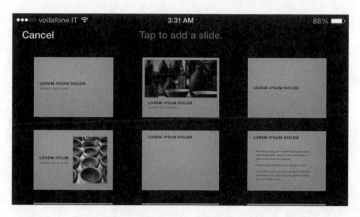

Figure 5-13: Tap the slide layout you want to use when you add a new slide.

1. **Tap the presentation you want to work on in the Keynote opening screen.**

2. **Tap the slide that will come before the transition.**

3. **Tap the Tools button, and then tap Transitions and Builds.**

   A flag appears, which points to the active slide.

4. **Tap the Add Effect button (the plus sign) on the flag.**

   The effects and options list opens, as shown in Figure 5-14.

5. **Tap the Effects tab at the top, and then tap the type of transition you want.**

   Magic Move moves an object from a location on one slide to a location on the next slide. Follow the onscreen instructions to create this effect.

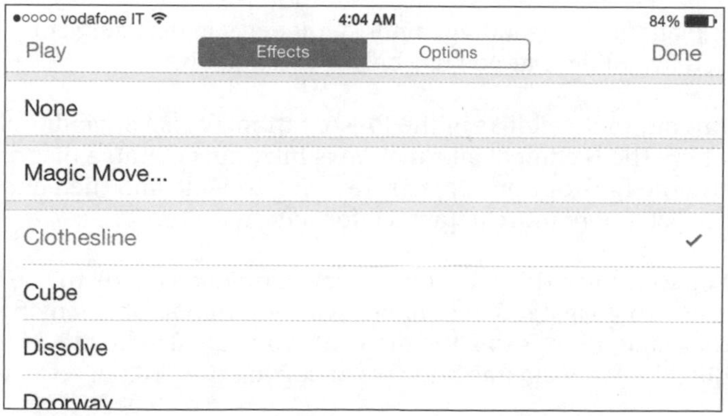

Play	Effects	Options	Done
None			
Magic Move...			
Clothesline			✓
Cube			
Dissolve			
Doorway			

Figure 5-14: Choose transitions from the list.

6. **Tap the Options tab, and then scroll through the tools to set the duration, direction, and delay of the transition and when you want it to begin.**

7. **Tap Play to see a preview, and then tap Done.**

8. **To create an animation, tap an object or element of the slide.**

   A flag with two options — Build In and Build Out — points to the object.

9. **Tap the left plus sign to add the first part, the build in, of the animation.**

   A list of possibilities opens.

10. **Tap the Effects and Options tabs to choose the type of animated effect you want.**

11. **Repeat Steps 8 and 9 for the second, build out (right side), part of the animation.**

12. **Tap the Order tab to rearrange the order in which the animated effects occur.**

13. **Tap Play to see a preview, and then tap Done.**

Tap an object or element, and then tap the Format button (the paintbrush) to see the editing options available for that object.

Using interactive links

Keynote has some nifty tools to help you put on a great show, like the transitions and animations we just outlined. We want to highlight one other. Tap the Tools button at the top of the presentation editing screen, and the list of tools opens. Tap Presentation Tools and then tap Interactive Links.

With the Interactive Links tool, you select an element of a slide and then link it to another slide or a web page or email message. For example, there are technical aspects of your presentation that may or may not need further explanation, depending on the audience's expertise. Set up a link to a more detailed slide that you use only if you need it.

Tap Interactive Links in the Presentation Tools list, and then tap the slide where the technical information is introduced. Tap a diagram on the slide and the Link options appear. Tap Link to Slide and then choose a slide from the list where more detailed information is stored.

You won't use this slide unless your audience needs to see it, but you have it ready to go instead of fumbling with your computer looking for the explanatory image and losing the moment. You can also link to a web page by tapping the Webpage tab and then inserting the URL, or to an email, which is a great tool for self-playing presentations that you share with others. When the viewer finishes watching, he taps the linked object and an email opens with your address filled in so the viewer can contact you. Tap Done after you assign the link. Tap the Tool button to add more.

Tap the Play button in the upper right of the screen to begin playback of your presentation. Tap and hold on a slide to open tools that let you write on the slide or use a pointer, as shown in Figure 5-15. Using a stylus can make these tasks easier and more precise.

Figure 5-15: Write on your slide or highlight items to make your point.

Renaming, sharing, and deleting documents

Document management is the same for both Pages and Keynote (for Numbers, too, so some of this may be repetitive if you read Book III, Chapter 4). You can do the following:

- Tap the name under a document on the opening Pages or Keynote screen to rename it. The keyboard opens and you can give the document a meaningful name.

- Pull or flick down in the upper third of the screen to see sort tabs: Date or Name. Tap one or the other to sort your documents by that criteria.

- Tap edit, and then tap the document(s) you want to copy or delete. Tap the Copy button in the upper-left corner, and a copy is immediately added to the screen. Tap the Delete button (the trashcan), and then confirm that you want to delete the document(s).

- Tap the Share button and choose the action you want to take:

- *Share Link via iCloud:* Sends only a URL link that will open the document on iCloud.com. You can give people view-only access or allow them to make changes to your document, which will then sync on all your devices. Tap the sharing method on the Share Sheet and proceed to send the link via Mail or Messages or post the link to a social network.

- *Send a Copy:* Sends or posts a copy of the document. The Share Sheet opens with the usual options. Choose AirDrop, Message, Mail, Twitter, Facebook, Flickr, Vimeo, or iCloud Photo Sharing. Choose the file format you want to send (Pages, PDF, Word, or ePub for Pages; Keynote, PDF, or PowerPoint for Keynote). Address or post the document, depending on the sharing method you chose. Select iTunes to send the document file to iTunes. This lets you save your document in the format you want, after which you connect your iPhone to your computer and copy the file from your iPhone to your computer through iTunes. Tap WebDAV to send a copy to a WebDAV server. Type the server address, username, and password; tap Sign In; and your spreadsheet is uploaded to the WebDAV server.

- *Open in Another App:* Lets you view your document in a different app on your iPhone. Choose a format. Pages or Keynote saves your document in the chosen format and then opens the Share Sheet with choices of apps that can read that format. Tap the app and your document opens there. You can also upload to remote storage servers like Dropbox with this method.

Chapter 6: Staying Healthy

In This Chapter

✔ **Creating a Medical ID**

✔ **Entering health and fitness data**

✔ **Counting your steps**

✔ **Working with other apps**

*W*ith the release of iOS 8, Apple introduced the Health app, a single repository that gathers data from third-party health and fitness apps along with data you enter yourself to give you — and your doctor — a global view of your state of health, from what you eat and how you sleep to the number of steps you take each day.

Although Health is in its nascent stage at the time of writing, this chapter introduces you to the concept and shows you how to add your own data. When apps and apparatus (including the long-anticipated iWatch) that push data to Health come to the fore, you'll be ready for them.

Preparing for Emergencies

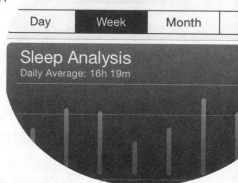

If you use Health for nothing but creating a Medical ID, it could save your life. The Medical ID puts all your critical health data, along with one or more emergency contacts, in one place. The lifesaving part is that it's accessible from your iPhone's Lock screen so if the ambulance shows up and you're unconscious, the EMT can tap the Emergency button on the Lock screen and pull up the name and phone number of your in case of emergency (ICE) contact and see that you're allergic to iodine and penicillin. Follow these steps to fill out your Medical ID:

1. **Open the Health app.**

2. **Tap Medical ID in the Browse bar at the bottom of the screen.**

3. **Tap Create Medical ID.**

   In the future, to make changes you'll tap the Edit button in the upper-right corner.

4. **Tap each field and type in your information (such as name, medical conditions or allergies, medications you take, blood type, and whether you're an organ donor).**

5. **Tap the Show When Locked switch on so this information can be accessed from your iPhone's Lock screen.**

6. **When you tap Add Emergency Contact, the Contacts app opens.**

   Scroll to and tap the name of your emergency contact and then tap the phone number you want to add. Tap the person's relation to you on the next screen, and then you automatically return to the Medical ID screen in Health.

7. **Tap Done and your Medical ID appears, as shown in Figure 6-1.**

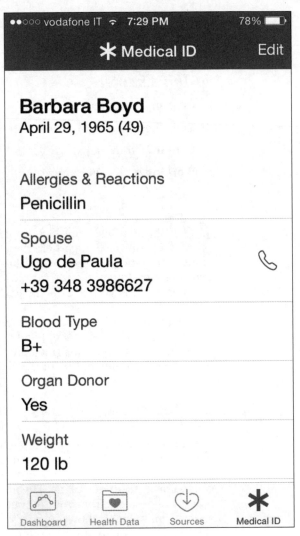

Figure 6-1: Your Medical ID provides vital information.

Keeping Track of Your Health

The real strength of the Health app comes with entering data points about your health and fitness. Health lets you track as much or as little information and builds a graph that helps you see how many steps you walked, if your resting heart rate is improving with increased exercise, and whether you're getting enough sleep.

Tap the Health Data button in the Browse bar, and a list of eight categories opens. At the very top of the list, you see an All button, which opens an alphabetical list showing all the items from each of the following lists:

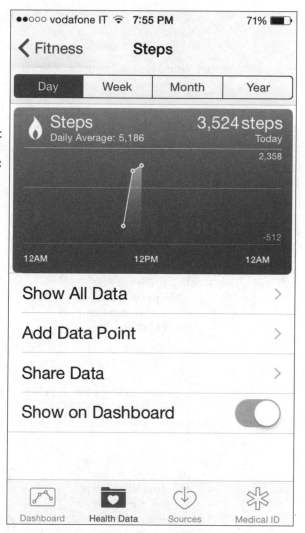

✔ **Body Measurements:** Record your height and weight along with your body mass, body fat, and lean body mass information.

✔ **Fitness:** Add your own data as well as data collected from other apps and devices such as active and resting calories consumed. Here you find a link to the NikeFuel app, which works in conjunction with the NikeFuel fitness bracelet. You also find Steps, which your iPhone 5s or later tracks automatically when your iPhone is on your person.

Figure 6-2: View and add data for each medical analysis or fitness statistic.

**Book III
Chapter 6**

Staying Healthy

✔ **Me:** Add your birthdate, biological sex, and blood type.

✔ **Nutrition:** Track your fat and sodium intake along with a couple dozen other nutrition points. You can enter the values yourself for now, although Health will probably gather data from apps that track what you're eating. Caffeine works with Jawbone's Up Coffee app.

✔ **Results:** Tracks measurements such as blood glucose, blood alcohol content, and inhaler use. We predict more items will appear in this category as apps are developed that connect to the measurement devices.

✔ **Sleep:** Tap into Health just before your head hits the pillow and again when you open your eyes to learn just how much shut eye you get each night or on a weekly or monthly basis.

✔ **Vital Signs:** Record your heart and respiratory rate, temperature, and other vital signs.

Recording your data manually

To record data for any of these items, do the following:

1. **Tap Health Data, and then tap the category you want to use (for example, Fitness).**

2. **Tap the item for which you want to enter a data point (for example, Steps).**

   The Steps data screen opens, as shown in Figure 6-2. The data screens for any of the analysis or statistics are the same.

3. **Tap one of the tabs at the top to view the data on a graph for the current day or for the past week, month, or year.**

4. **Tap Show All Data to see a list of data points gathered.**

5. **Tap Add Data Point to open the Add Data screen, as shown in Figure 6-3.**

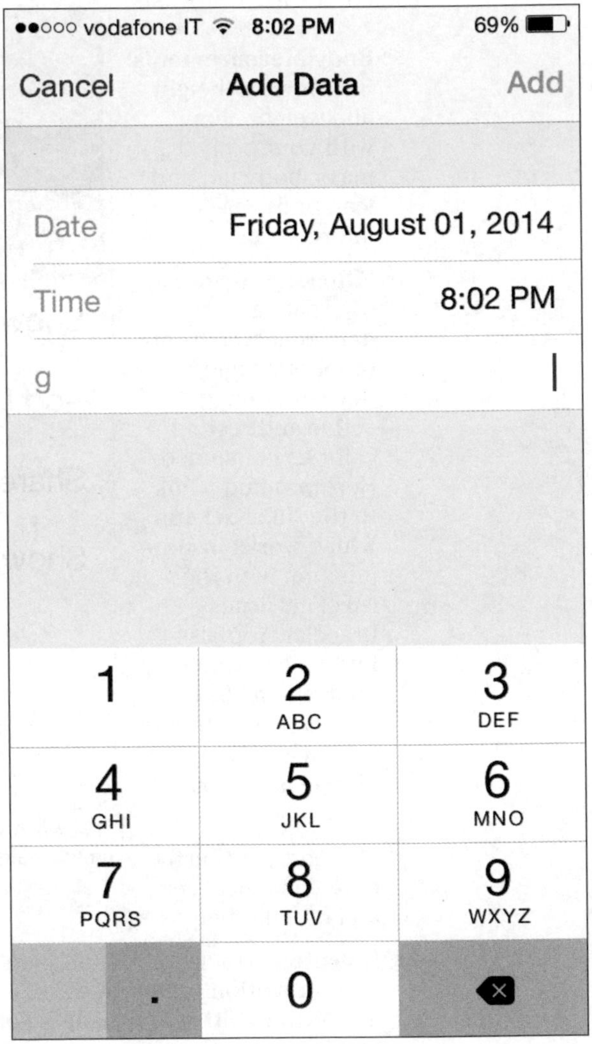

●●○○○ vodafone IT 🛜 8:02 PM		69% 🔋
Cancel	**Add Data**	Add
Date		Friday, August 01, 2014
Time		8:02 PM
g			

1	2 ABC	3 DEF
4 GHI	5 JKL	6 MNO
7 PQRS	8 TUV	9 WXYZ
	.	0	⌫

Figure 6-3: Add data points one by one.

Here, too, the Add Data screen has the same setup for each type of data. The current date and time are pre-imposed, but you can tap either to change them. Tap the data field to enter relative information, which could be your blood pressure or the grams of sodium you ate at lunch. The unit of measure appears on the left end of the field.

6. **Tap Share Data to specify apps you want to share data with and sources you want to record data from, as shown in Figure 6-4.**

   You can see that the data about the number of steps taken is recorded by the iPhone.

7. **Tap the Show on Dashboard switch on to see the graph of this item on the Dashboard.**

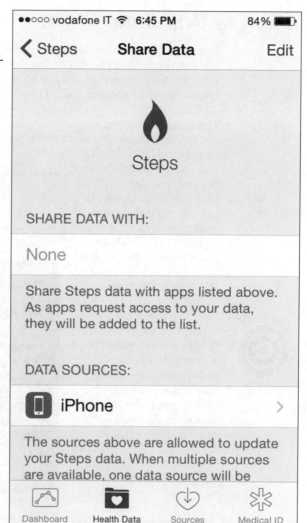

Book III Chapter 6

Staying Healthy

Figure 6-4: Identify apps to share with and sources for data.

Getting data from apps

As you download apps that track your health and are programmed to work with the Health app, you find them by tapping Sources in the Browse bar. Here you find a list of apps that want to push data to Health. Tap the app in the list and grant or deny it permission to post. If you tap the switch next to the app on, data from that app will automatically show up in the appropriate item in Health.

Viewing Your Data

The great thing about Health is having all your medical, fitness, and nutrition information in one place. The long-term idea is that you'll be able to send this information to your doctor so if something spikes, help can be on the way faster than you can call 911.

The graphs help you gauge your progress toward your fitness or dietary goals. Place items you want to keep a more constant eye on in the Dashboard. Tap Dashboard on the Browse bar and you see graphs for each item for which you selected Show on Dashboard, as shown in Figure 6-5. Choose the time interval you want to view by tapping one of the tabs at the top.

One app that's been with iPhone for several years is Nike + iPod, which works with special sensor-enhanced Nike shoes that sent information to your iPhone and was then viewable in the app. You can get the same Nike + iPod workout goodness, minus having to spend big bucks to buy the sensor and sneakers. Head over to iPhone's App Store and install the Nike+ Running app (free), which uses your iPhone's built-in GPS feature to track your location, pace, and distance instead of relying on the Nike+ sensor and shoe combo. Although math was always Joe's worst subject, the way he sees it, if $E = mc^2$, then Nike+ = Nike + iPod − $100 = :-).

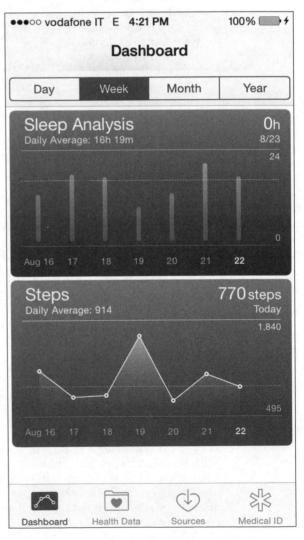

Figure 6-5: Health graphs your health and fitness progress.

Book IV

Letting iPhone Entertain You: Photos, Videos, Music, and More

Contents at a Glance

Chapter 1: Capturing, Editing, and Sharing Photos

In This Chapter

✔ Snapping a picture with Camera

✔ Taking in the panorama

✔ Focusing, flashing, and zooming

✔ Turning the lens on yourself

✔ Editing photos

✔ Storing and sharing with iCloud

Taking photos with your iPhone means you never miss a memorable moment and you have one less gadget — a camera — to tote around. The Camera app takes advantage of two objective lenses on your iPhone. On the back, the iSight camera is the still and video camera that takes regular photos and 240-degree panoramic photos plus high-definition (HD) videos. All iPhone models have an LED flash, but iPhone 5s or later models sport a True Tone flash, which combines two LED lights — one white and one amber — to produce natural skin tones as well as crisper photos in low-light conditions. The Camera app offers burst mode, which takes ten photos per second in rapid succession. iPhone 5s or later models capture slow-motion and time-lapse video.

On the front of your iPhone you find the FaceTime camera, a 1.2-megapixel still camera that also shoots 720p HD video so you can take self-portraits and use FaceTime, your iPhone's video and audio chat app. All the functions work in portrait and land-scape position.

In this chapter, we explain how to use the still cameras, front and back. (We explain the video functions along with the Videos app in Book IV, Chapter 4.) We talk about focusing, brightening your image, flashing — er, using the flash — and zooming in on your subject. You can also apply a filter to your photo before or after taking it (options vary among iPhone models). After you capture photos in the Camera app, you probably want to edit them, so we show you how to use the Photos app to enhance the photo quality, crop photos, and cure that terrible red-eye disease. At the end of the chapter, we give you all your options for storing and sharing your photos between your own devices with Photo Stream or iCloud Photo Library and with others via AirDrop and iCloud Photo Sharing, email, text messages, Twitter, YouTube, Flickr, and good old-fashioned slide shows and printing.

Camera Features and Controls

The first time you open Camera, a message appears asking if Camera can use your location. Tapping OK lets Camera geotag your location. A geotag uses GPS, Wi-Fi, and cellular access to add the longitude and latitude of the location of the photos and videos you shoot. (In some situations — say, if you're standing in a lead-walled bunker — your iPhone may not be able to activate geotagging.) Like the date and time, a *geotag* is a piece of information about your photo that's kept in the *metadata* (that is, data you don't see that describes your data). You can then sort and search for photos based on the location — more about that later in this chapter.

If at some point you want to turn geotagging off, open the Settings app, tap Privacy, and tap Location Services. You can turn off Location Services completely or turn off Location Services for specific apps (in this case, Camera).

Previewing through the viewfinder

We think the easiest way to learn about taking photos with your iPhone is to snap a few shots. The two basic "parts" of any camera that you need to know are the viewfinder and the shutter button. Like some digital cameras, your iPhone doesn't have a viewfinder. Instead, you point your iPhone at your subject and then look at the screen to see how it will be framed.

As for the shutter button, your iPhone actually has three:

- **Camera button:** Tap the button on the bottom of the screen in the center to snap a photo. The button is a red circle when you switch to video mode.

- **Volume buttons, either one:** Press one of the volume buttons on the left side of your iPhone to snap a photo or to start and stop video recording.

If your iPhone is locked, when you press the Home or the Sleep/Wake button, a Camera button appears in the bottom-right corner, as shown in Figure 1-1. Touch and drag the Camera button up (as if you want to push the Lock screen out of the way) to open the Camera app, and then take photos as explained next.

Taking photos with the iSight camera

The iSight camera is located on the back of your iPhone. Here's how to take a photo with it:

1. **Open the Camera app or, if your iPhone is locked, unlock it by pressing the Home button and then drag the Camera button up.**

   A shutter opens, revealing a screen as shown in Figure 1-2.

   The words above the onscreen shutter button indicate the type of photo you're going to take:

   • *Time-Lapse (iPhone 4s or later):* Records a scene for a length of time and then creates a time-lapse video

   • *Slo-Mo (iPhone 5s or later):* Takes slow-motion video

   • *Video:* Shoots video, which we discuss in Book IV, Chapter 4

   • *Photo:* Takes a standard rectangular photo

   • *Square:* Takes a square "Polaroid" or Instagram-style photo

   • *Pano:* Takes panoramic photos; we explain how to use this function in the next section

Figure 1-1: Access the Camera from the Lock screen by dragging the Camera button by the unlock slider.

2. **Flick across the middle of the screen to move from one photo style to another.**

   The one you choose is highlighted.

3. **Point your iPhone at whatever you want to photograph.**

4. **Tap the point on the screen that you want to be in focus to activate autofocus on that spot.**

   Camera automatically focuses on the center of the shot, but you can tap elsewhere to focus on a person or object that's located somewhere other than the center of the shot (say, in one of the corners).

5. **Tap again to open the exposure tool, as shown in Figure 1-3, and then drag the slider up or down to make the photo brighter or darker.**

Figure 1-2: Your iPhone screen is your viewfinder.

See the section "Setting the exposure and focus" for more information.

6. **(Optional, iPhone 4s or later) Tap the Filters button, and then tap a special effect you'd like to apply to your photo.**

   You see the effect onscreen immediately, as shown in Figure 1-4, before you take the photo, but you can also add an effect when you edit the photo in Photos after it's taken.

7. **Tap the Camera button or press one of the Volume buttons.**

   A clicking noise lets you know the photo was taken. You can mute the shutter sound by moving the Ring/Silent switch to silent.

   If you have a hard time holding the phone still when tapping the onscreen button, you can place your finger on the shutter button, steady the camera, and then lift your finger.

   A thumbnail preview of the photo you took appears in the lower-left corner (in landscape mode, the lower-right or upper-left corner, depending on which direction you rotate your phone).

Figure 1-3: Tap the object you want to focus on and brighten, or darken, your subject.

Bursting on the scene

Hold the onscreen shutter button or one of the volume buttons to activate Burst mode, which takes a rapid succession of photos until you lift your finger, and works with regular or square photos. At ten frames per second, Burst is great for catching stills when there's a lot of action going on. iPhone 6 and 6 Plus offer Burst mode for the FaceTime camera as well. A counter tells you how many photos you took. We explain how to work with the photos later in this chapter when we discuss the Photos app.

Taking a panoramic view

A fun Camera feature is the possibility of taking 240-degree panoramic photos so you can capture the full width, or height, of your subject at hand. Here's how it works:

1. **Tap Camera on the Home screen.**

2. **Flick to the left across the screen until Pano is highlighted — it's the last choice on the right.**

   The arrow you see in the center, as shown in Figure 1-5, is a nifty tool that uses iPhone's built-in gyroscope to help you capture better images.

3. **Tap the Camera button and begin slowly but continuously moving your iPhone in one direction. Keep the arrow on the plumb line as you move in the direction of the arrow.**

   Left to right is the default, but just tap the arrow, before beginning to take the photo, to go the other way.

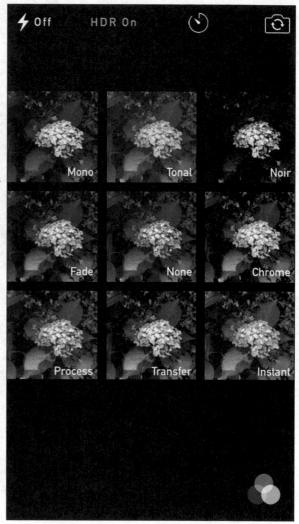

Figure 1-4: Tap to choose the filter you want to apply to your photo.

4. **Tap the Camera button when you finish capturing the panorama.**

   Your photo is saved in the Photos app as a Moment in Collections, which you open by tapping Photos in the Browse bar and in the Recently Added and Panoramas albums, found when you tap Albums in the Browse bar.

TIP

Turn your iPhone to landscape view and take a vertical panoramic shot. This is great for capturing tall buildings or boat masts in a single photo.

Setting the exposure and focus

The buttons at the top of the screen, as shown in Figure 1-2, appear when you open Camera. The first thing you want to do is choose where you want Camera to focus its attention. Your iPhone's default autofocus is the center of the image on the screen, where you see the yellow box.

iPhone 4s or later uses face detection and focuses on the most prominent face when you're taking a photo of people. Face detection balances exposure across up to ten faces. If you want the Camera to focus on a subject that isn't in the center, tap that area on the screen. You see the focus and exposure change to put your chosen subject in the best light. (Unless you want the subject in the center, in which case you should move your iPhone until you see the subject in the center of the screen.)

Figure 1-5: Keep the arrow on the line to capture captivating panoramic photos.

In addition to using the exposure tool, you can use the AE/AF Lock tool (Auto Exposure/Auto Focus), which changes the exposure (that is, the amount of light that is allowed through the lens) and then focuses on a different area. Tap and hold the area on the screen that has the amount of light you want the photo to have. A yellow box indicates the area used to gauge the exposure and the words "AE/AF Lock" (Auto Exposure/Auto Focus) appear at the top of the screen. Move iPhone to the subject you want to photograph, and then tap the Camera button. Tap elsewhere on the screen to unlock the AE/AF Lock.

For example, if you point your iPhone out a sunny window and activate the AE/AF lock, the natural light needs less exposure. Then point your iPhone at a subject indoors and take the photo. The exposure needed for the natural light is applied to the indoor setting and the photo comes out dark, even if the room seems well lit.

Lighten up

Depending on the model, your iPhone has one LED light (two on the 5s or later) next to the objective lens on the back camera that functions as a flash. You see the Flash button at the top left of the screen. Auto is the default position, meaning your iPhone turns the light on if it senses there's not enough light for the photo. Tap the Flash button to turn the flash on or off manually. When on, the Flash button is yellow; it's white in the auto or off position.

In addition to the flash, the Backside Illumination Sensor perceives low light conditions and makes adjustments to compensate. You can tap on areas that are too dark or too bright to adjust the lighting. The sensor corrects the contrast of the image as a whole.

To zoom or not to zoom

To zoom in on a portion of the subject you want to photograph, use the pinch-and-spread technique. iPhone's zoom is a digital zoom, which means it zooms by enlarging the image, not by getting closer to the subject. Digital zooming compromises the quality of the final image, so physically moving closer to your subject is by far the better choice. Try taking zoomed and normal photos to see if you can live with the compromise.

Macro mode kicks in automatically when you're about two inches away from the person or object you want to photograph. Tap the object you're focusing on to create a special effect where the main object is crisp and the background is blurry, as shown in Figure 1-6.

To help you visualize the distribution of objects in your photo and use the photographer's rule of thirds, turn on the Grid feature that puts a three-by-three grid overlay on your screen, dividing the screen into nine sections. To activate this option, open the Settings app, tap Photos & Camera, and tap the Grid switch to the on position.

Turning on iPhone's HDR

Digital photography is terrific in bright to shady situations, but in overly bright, very low-light conditions, or a shot that has both, the quality can be poor and result in overexposed or under-exposed photos. Using iPhone's High Dynamic Range (HDR) option can help you get better shots when the conditions aren't perfect. Like the flash, HDR has auto (iPhone 5s or later), on, and off settings. On the 5s or later, HDR is on auto by default; on earlier iPhone models, HDR is off by default. Tap it at the top of the screen to turn it on.

When HDR is in auto mode, your iPhone decides when the conditions merit using HDR. When HDR is used, Camera takes three photos with different expo-

Figure 1-6: Camera activates Macro mode when the subject is closer than two inches.

sures and superimposes them to create a better image. Taking images with HDR takes a few seconds longer than shooting normal photos, so try to hold iPhone steady and ask the subject to remain still. The iPhone 5s has a larger light sensor that provides greater light sensitivity, which means brighter, crisper photos.

The LED flash doesn't work when HDR is on. If both the flash and HDR are on auto, iPhone will use whichever option captures the best photo.

You can save both a normal version and an HDR version. In the Settings app, tap Photos & Camera, and then tap the Keep Normal Photo switch on. If you turn this off, only the HDR version is saved.

Book IV Chapter 1

Capturing, Editing, and Sharing Photos

Timing your shots

The Camera app in iOS 8 comes with a new feature: a timer that delays the photo for three or ten seconds, so you can prop your iPhone on a surface, position your group, then run over and put yourself in the photo, too. The timer works for taking regular or square photos and with both cameras. To take a delayed photo, do the following:

1. **Open the Camera app.**

2. **Tap the Timer button at the top of the screen, and then tap either 3s or 10s to select how many seconds you want the photo delayed.**

3. **Position your iPhone so your subject is framed as you want.**

4. **Tap the Camera button or one of the volume buttons.**

   The countdown is displayed on the screen and the flash blinks for each second. At zero, burst mode takes 11 photos, giving you a little extra time to join the group.

   Tap the Camera or volume button before the time's up to stop the timer.

Turning the lens on yourself

The Switch Camera button in the upper-right corner of the screen switches the active objective from the iSight camera on the back of your iPhone to the FaceTime camera on the front so you see yourself on the screen. This camera has lower resolution, no flash or zoom, but it can take advantage of the Back-side Illumination Sensor and takes both still photos and video. It's handy for self-portraits (or if you find yourself without a mirror and some lettuce in your teeth) and FaceTime.

To use the front camera — the one above the screen — follow these steps:

1. **Open the Camera app.**

2. **Tap the Switch button in the upper-right corner.**

   You see yourself on the screen. The objective is at the top of your iPhone (or the side if you rotate to the landscape position), so play around with tilting, raising, and lowering your iPhone for the most favorable photo.

3. **Switch to Square and add a filter if you'd like that style of selfie. Tap the onscreen shutter button or press one of the volume buttons.**

   If you flick beyond Square to Pano or beyond Video to Slo-Mo, Camera automatically switches to the iSight camera.

Other ways to obtain images

Taking photos with Camera isn't the only way to add images to your iPhone. We can think of at least five other ways:

✔ **Screenshot:** If you have an image on your screen — even during a FaceTime conversation — that you want to save or maybe send to a friend, tap the Home button while holding the Sleep/Wake button. You hear the shutter click and the image is saved as a Moment in Photos and to the Recently Added album.

✔ **Mail or Messages:** Tap the photo or video in the message that someone has sent to you. The photo opens in Quick Look. Tap the Share button and choose Save Image from the options.

✔ **Image Capture:** In Safari, tap and hold on an image on a web page. Tap Save Image from the options that appear. The image is automatically saved to Photos.

✔ **Photo Stream:** If you activate Photo Stream, photos taken with other iOS devices or added to iPhoto or Aperture on a Mac connected to iCloud's Photo Stream will be in the Photo Stream album on your iPhone.

✔ **From your computer:** Use iTunes to sync photos from your photo management software (see Book I, Chapter 5).

Browsing and Editing Photos

As soon as you take a photo with the Camera app, the photo is stored in the Photos app in at least three places: as a Moment in the Photos Collections, in the Recently Added album, and in the photo type album; for example, as soon as you take one panorama photo, a Panorama album is created, or capture one slow motion video and a Slo-Mo album is added. If you've activated the iCloud Photo Library or Photo Stream, you find your photos there, too — and we get to that a little later in this chapter.

Photos stores your photos in three ways, which you access by tapping the associated button in the Browse bar at the bottom of the Photos screen:

✔ **Photos:** These are photos you take with your iPhone or sync from Photos on your computer using iTunes. The photos are organized hierarchically by year; each year or group of years is a Collection, which is divided roughly by month. Each Collection is divided into Moments, as shown in Figure 1-7. Moments are grouped more or less by a time period or place. If Location Services for geotagging was on when the photo was taken, when you tap on the location, a map shows where the photos were taken.

TIP

When you tap a thumbnail to open the photo, the location, date, and time appear at the top of the screen above the photo.

▸ **Shared:** Stores the albums you create to share with others. See the "Sharing the (photo) wealth" section, later in this chapter.

▸ **Albums:** Here you find the Recently Added album that holds the most recent photos you took with your iPhone. You also find albums Photos creates automatically, including Favorites, which appears when you tag a photo as a favorite by tapping the heart button, and photo type albums, which are created when you take at least one type of photo such as square, panorama, or burst. You see albums synced from iTunes including Events and Faces, as well as albums you create on your iPhone. Events shows collections of photos divided by event, as set up on your computer, and Faces, which is supported only by photos imported from iPhoto or Aperture on a Mac via iTunes, sorts photos by identifying people in the photo.

Figure 1-7: The browse buttons at the bottom of the screen give you sorting and viewing options.

TIP

As soon as you delete a photo, Photos automatically creates a Recently Deleted album. When you delete a photo, it goes to this album for 30 days, after which it will be erased. You can recover photos from the Recently Deleted album within the 30 days or definitively delete it from this album before then. Tap Select in the upper right, then tap Delete All or Recover All to take the action on all photos or tap the photos you want to delete or recover, and then tap the appropriate button at the bottom: Delete or Recover.

When you take a burst photo, you don't see all the 47 or 86 or however many photos you took in Photos; you just see one thumbnail image in Moments or the Recently Added or Bursts album. Tap the preview thumbnail and then tap Select to see the series of photos. A gray dot under some of the photos indicates those images that Photos thinks are the best quality. Tap the photos you want to save and the circle on the lower-right corner of the photos becomes a check mark. Tap Done and then tap one of these two choices:

✔ **Keep Everything:** The selected photos become separate Moments but the other burst photos remain together as a Moment.

✔ **Keep Only (number of selected) Favorites:** The selected photos become separate Moments and the other burst photos are deleted.

Creating albums

You can create albums on your iPhone to make finding and viewing photos easier. Photos in an album can include those you take with your iPhone, as well as photos you sync from your computer through iTunes, Photo Stream, or iCloud Photos. You can sync albums from your computer to your iPhone, but albums you create on your iPhone don't sync to your computer.

Albums lets you put related photos together for easier viewing, although the original photos remain where you copy them from. To create a photo album, follow these steps:

1. **Open the Photos app.**

2. **Tap Albums at the bottom of the screen.**

3. **Tap the Add button that appears in the upper-left corner.**

   The New Album dialog appears.

4. **Type in a name for your new Album.**

5. **Tap Save.**

   The Add Photos screen appears.

6. **Tap Photos or Albums in the Browse bar to find the photos you want to place in the new album.**

   In Photos, tap a Collection to see thumbnail images of the Moments it contains. Tap Select next to a Moment to choose all the photos it contains or tap individual thumbnails to select them.

In Albums, tap Recently Added or another album to see thumbnails of the photos in that album, and then tap the thumbnails of the images you want to include in the album.

7. **Tap all the photos you want to include in the new album from various sources, and then tap Done.**

8. **Your new album appears in the Album list.**

9. **(Optional) To add more photos to the album, tap the album in the Album list to open the thumbnail view. Then tap the Select button in the upper-right corner. Tap the Add button at the bottom and repeat Steps 6 and 7.**

10. **(Optional) To Delete photos from an album, tap the album in the Album list, and then tap Select in the upper-right corner. Tap the photos you want to remove from the album and then tap the Delete button (the trash can).**

11. **(Optional) To delete an album, tap Albums at the bottom of the Photos screen. Tap the Edit button, and then tap the red and white minus sign to the left of the album name. Tap Delete, and then tap Delete Album in the pop-up menu to confirm your choice.**

12. **(Optional) To rename an album you created, tap Albums, tap the Edit button, and then tap the name. Tap the "x" to the right of the album name to erase it, and then type a new name. Tap Done.**

13. **(Optional) To change the order of albums on the Album list, tap the Edit button, and then touch and drag the Rearrange button to the right of the album name to move it to the position you want in the list, and then tap Done.**

Editing photos

The quality of the photos you take with your iPhone is pretty good, but you may want to edit your photos to make them even better. Here's how to use Photos' editing options:

1. **Open the Photos app.**

2. **Tap Photos or Albums — wherever the photo you want to edit resides.**

3. **Tap the photo you want to edit.**

   If you want to edit a photo in one of your Shared albums, you are prompted to duplicate the photo because you can't edit shared photos.

4. **Tap the Edit button, and then tap the magic wand that appears in the upper right of the screen.**

   Known as Auto-Enhance, this quickly adjusts the sharpness and contrast of the photo and automatically looks for redeye and adjusts it. Tap

Cancel if you want to revert to the original, tap Done if you like what you see, or go on to Step 5 to take advantage of the other editing tools.

5. **When you tap Edit, three buttons appear at the bottom of the screen (refer to Figure 1-8:)**

    • *Crop/Constrain:* Use your fingers to zoom and pan the image. Tap the Rotate button or use the dial beneath the image to change the orientation until the image is positioned as you want. Drag the corners of the crop grid to set the area you want to crop or tap the Aspect button to choose one of the preset ratios. Tap one of the other buttons to perform more edits or tap Done to save the changes you made.

    Tap Cancel if you don't want to Save your changes.

Rotate　Crop/Constrain　Meters　Aspect

Filters　Crop corner

Figure 1-8: Rotate or crop your image.

    • *Filters:* Tap to apply one of the color filters. A strip across the bottom shows you how each effect will affect your photo; tap the one you like and then tap Apply in the upper-right corner, or tap Cancel in the upper-left corner to leave the photo as is.

- *Meters:* Tap to access meters that allow you to adjust Light settings, such as exposure, shadows, and brightness; Color settings, including saturation and contrast; and Black and White settings, like intensity and grain. Tap the disclosure triangle next to the setting to see the list of options, as shown in Figure 1-9. Tap the option you want and drag the meter left or right to adjust the setting; you see the effect immediately. Tap the list button to return to the list of options and make further adjustments or tap Done to save your changes.

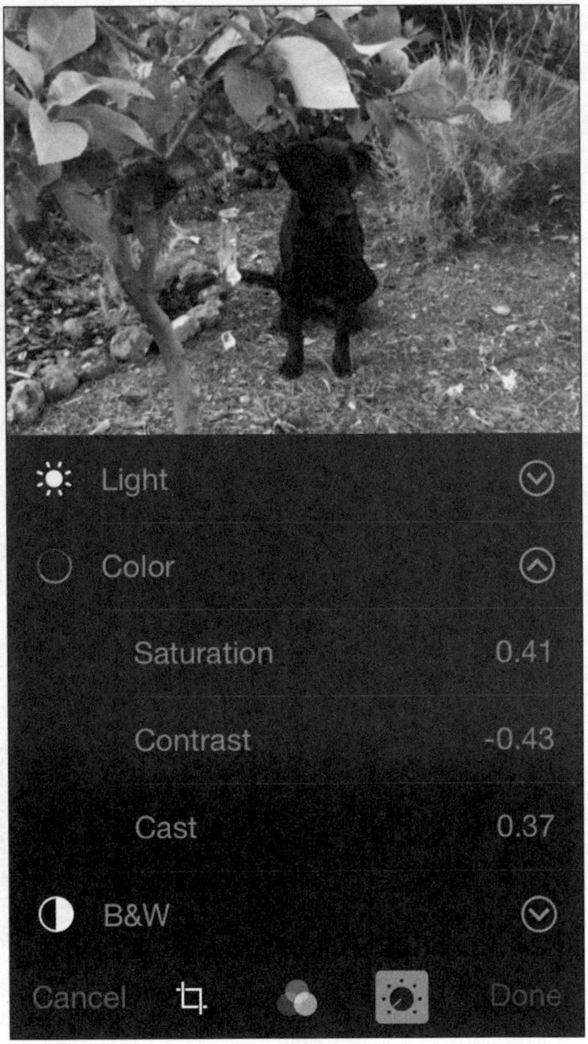

6. **Tap the previous button in the upper-left corner to return to the album where the photo resides; tap it again to return to the Albums screen.**

Figure 1-9: Adjust the color, brightness, and saturation of your image.

7. **Tap a button at the bottom of the screen to go to another album or press the Home button to leave Photos.**

Bonus Chapter 3 (online) suggests photo enhancement apps that you can download to your iPhone. For more on how to access the online bonus content, see this book's Introduction.

Sharing the (photo) wealth

After you're happy with your photos, you may want to share one or more electronically or as an old-fashioned print. Photos lets you copy, print, and send photos and videos to others by AirDrop or as email attachments or multimedia messages (MMS or iMessage), or upload them to Twitter, Facebook, or Flickr. Of course, you can also delete photos and videos from Photos. First, we look at how to do things with a single photo, and then we explain managing batches of photos.

To share one photo:

1. **Open the Photos app.**

2. **Tap the collection, moment, or album where the photo you want to share, copy, or print resides.**

   The thumbnail view opens.

3. **Tap the photo you want to use.**

   At the bottom of the screen, you see the Share, Favorite, and Delete buttons.

4. **Tap the Share button, and in the Share Sheet that then appears, tap the action you want to take, as shown in Figure 1-10:**

   • *AirDrop:* Send the photo to someone nearby who has AirDrop turned on and who is in your Contacts. Just tap the person's name or image and the photo is sent to them. From her iPhone, iPad, or recent Mac model running OS X Yosemite, she can accept or decline the photo.

Figure 1-10: The Share Sheet displays all available sharing options.

- *Message:* Pastes the photo in a New Message, which will be sent as an MMS or iMessage. Fill in the recipient and tap Send (refer to Book II, Chapter 2).

- *Mail:* The photo is pasted into a new message. Type in the address and a message if you want, and tap Send (see Book II, Chapter 4). You're asked to choose what size file you want to send: Small, Medium, Large, or Actual Size. The approximate file size is indicated; if your email service has size limits for attachments, choose an image that is about half the size of the limit (because the file sizes are approximate and if you stay at the limit, you're likely to have problems sending the file).

- *iCloud Photo Sharing:* Add the photo to a Shared Stream that you created, or you can create a new one. See the "Storing and Sharing Photos" section for more information.

- *Twitter:* Sends your photo to your Twitter account. You must be signed in to Twitter to use this feature.

- *Facebook:* Posts your photo to your Facebook profile. Add a comment and location if you like and tap Post. You must be signed in to Facebook to use this feature.

- *Flickr:* Posts your photo to your Flickr account. Add a comment and tap Post. You must be signed in to Flickr to use this feature.

- *Pinterest:* Sends your photo to your Pinterest account. Tap Board to choose the board you want to pin the image to, and then tap the PinIt button. You must be signed in to your Pinterest account from the Settings app to use this feature.

- *LinkedIn:* Posts your photo to your LinkedIn profile. Add a comment, choose who you want to share with, and tap Post. You must be signed in to LinkedIn to use this feature.

Tap the More button to add, or hide, social network buttons on the Share Sheet.

- *Copy:* Puts a copy of the photo in the Clipboard, which you can then paste in another app such as Notes or Pages.

- *Slideshow:* Opens a slide show of the images in the album or begins playing the video. See the section "Viewing slide shows" for the steps to take. If an Apple TV is detected on the network, you see an AirPlay option.

- *Assign to Contact:* Assigns the photo to a person or entity in Contacts. See Book III, Chapter 1 for complete details.

- *Use as Wallpaper:* Uses the photo as the background for your Lock or Home screen. We explain how to do this in the section "Using a photo as wallpaper," later in this chapter.

- *Print:* Prints the photo to a printer on your wireless network. See Book I, Chapter 2 for details about wireless printing.

If you want to share more than one photo, you can select others from the thumbnails at the top of the screen just by tapping them, and then tap the action you want to take.

Tap Cancel in the upper-left corner if you don't want to share the photo after all.

5. **After you tap your choice, the Share Sheet closes.**

If you want to delete a single photo, select it as above and then tap the Delete button (the trash can). If you want to add the photo to your Favorites album, tap the Favorites button (the heart).

Batches

Sometimes you have more than one photo that you'd like to print, email, or even delete. Photos lets you choose a group of photos and then take the same action for all of them at once. Do the following:

1. **Tap either Photos or Albums in the browse bar. Slightly different things happen depending on which you tap:**

   • *Photos:* Tap a Collection to see the Moments it contains and do one of the following:

   If the photos you want to share are in one Moment, tap the Share button next to the Moment that has the photo(s) you want to share, and then, as shown in Figure 1-11, choose Share This Moment, which

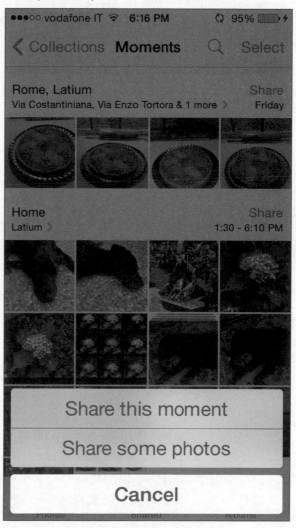

Figure 1-11: Send entire Moments or batch photos from an album to take an action on a group of photos.

shares all the photos in the Moment, or Share Some Photos, which opens another thumbnail view of the moment where you tap each photo you want to share.

If you want to share photos from several Moments, tap Select in the upper-right corner and then tap the photos you want to share.

- *Albums:* Tap the album that has the photo(s) you want to share. Tap Select in the upper-left corner and then tap the photos you want to share.

2. **Tap the Share button at the bottom of the screen.**

   Depending on the number and file size of the photos you choose, some sharing options may not be available. For example, Mail has a limit of five photos. The sharing options that can be used have active buttons. If you exceed the photo limits, the option doesn't appear in the Share Sheet.

3. **(Optional) Add the selected photos to a new or existing album by tapping Add To at the bottom of the screen.**

   The Albums list opens but only albums created on your iPhone are active and accessible.

   Tap the album you want to add the photos to or scroll to the bottom and tap New Album, in which case the New Album dialog opens; there you type a name and tap Save.

   The selected photos are added to the existing or new album.

4. **(Optional) Delete the selected photos by tapping the Delete button.**

When you Delete a photo from an album you created, the photo remains in the collection it came from, but it's removed from the album. Photos deleted from automatic albums, such as Favorites or Bursts, or from a collection are moved to the Recently Deleted album for 30 days, after which time they're permanently erased.

Using a photo as wallpaper

You can customize the wallpaper, or background image, that appears on your Lock screen and your Home screen. We explained how to do this from the Settings app in Book I, Chapter 4. Here we explain how to assign wallpaper directly from Photos:

1. **Select the photo you want to assign from any of the albums on Photos.**

2. **Tap the Share button in the bottom-left corner.**

3. **Tap Use as Wallpaper.**

   The Move and Scale screen appears.

4. **Pinch and spread the photo to zoom to the size you want and pan, or move, the photo around until the image is just how you want it on the screen.**

5. **(Optional.) If you have Reduce Motion turned off (in the Settings app, tap General and then tap Accessibility), you have a Perspective Zoom option. Tap it on, and your perspective of the image changes slightly when you move the screen, as if the image were behind the glass screen; when off, the image appears as if it were painted on the glass and doesn't move when you move the screen.**

6. **Tap the Set button.**

7. **Choose one of the options that appear:**

    *   *Set Lock Screen:* To use the image for the Lock screen.

    *   *Set Home Screen:* To use the image for the Home screen.

    *   *Set Both:* To use the image for both the Lock and Home screen.

    *   *Cancel:* If you decide to leave things the way they are.

If you're like us, sooner or later you'll find you have hundreds if not thousands of photos on your iPhone and finding the one you want to share can mean a lot of scrolling. Photos in iOS 8 has a Search option: Tap the Search button (the magnifying glass) at the top of the screen in either Photos or Albums view. You see two preset choices that include Nearby (photos that were taken near your current location) and Favorites (photos for which you tapped the Favorites [heart] button). You can search by any of the metadata attached to a photo, such as location or date or by an album name.

Viewing slide shows

With its larger Retina display, both iPhone 5 and later models show off your photos beautifully, but earlier iPhones are nothing to sneeze at. You can also connect to a television or monitor to play your slide show, which we explain in Book IV, Chapter 4. To view a slide show on your iPhone, follow these steps:

1. **Open the photo or album where you want the slide show to begin.**

2. **Tap the Share button and then tap Slideshow.**

    The Slideshow Options screen appears.

3. **Tap Transitions.**

    Choose the type of transition you want from the list. A transition is what happens on the screen between one photo and the next.

4. **Tap the Play Music switch on or off.**

    If you want music to accompany your slide show, tap on. The Music app opens so you can make a selection from any of the lists. After you tap your selection, you automatically return to where you were in Photos.

5. **Tap Start Slideshow.**

   The slide show plays from the photo where you begin through to the end of the album.

The Slideshow settings give you a few viewing options. Open the Settings app and tap Photos & Camera. In the Slideshow section, set the following:

✔ **Play Each Slide For:** Choose the duration of each image on the screen, from 2 to 20 seconds.

✔ **Repeat:** Plays the slide show in a continuous loop.

✔ **Shuffle:** Plays the images in a random order.

Moving photos from your iPhone to your computer is handled by your photo management software. On a Mac, this might be Image Capture, iPhoto, Aperture, or another application that you prefer. On Windows, you may use Photoshop Elements (8 or later), Live Photo Gallery, or Pictures Library. When you connect your iPhone to your computer with the USB connector cable, the photo management application you use recognizes your iPhone as it would any other digital camera. If import photo choices don't appear automatically, you may have to go to a command such as File➪Import and choose to import all the photos or select only some of the photos you want to import.

Storing and Sharing Photos

iOS 8 gives you two ways to store and share photos: iCloud Photo Library or Photo Stream. If you choose iCloud Photo Library, photos and videos from all your devices are stored in and accessed from iCloud, freeing up storage on your iPhone and other devices for other purposes.

Photo Stream is an alternative to connecting your iPhone to your computer with the USB connector cable. Up to 1,000 photos from all devices that are signed in to the same iCloud account with Photo Stream turned on are synced. Photos remain on your iPhone and other devices. You can have both iCloud Photo Library and Photo Stream turned on simultaneously, although we suggest you choose one after considering your storage needs. Here we look more closely at both functions.

iCloud Photo Library

iCloud Photo Library couldn't be simpler. Whenever you capture a photo or video with your iPhone, it automatically goes into your iCloud Photo Library and can be accessed and downloaded from any device, anytime, anywhere — as long as you have an Internet connection.

To activate iCloud Photo Library, open the Settings app, tap Photos & Camera, and tap the iCloud Photo Library switch on, as shown in Figure 1-12. iCloud Photo Library stores the original full-resolution photos. Below the iCloud Photo Library switch you can see when the library was last updated.

You can choose to have Photos manage downloaded images in one of two ways:

*✔ **Optimize iPhone Storage:** Tap this option to optimize any downloaded images for your iPhone screen, which occupy less room on your iPhone. The full-sized originals are stored in iCloud.

*✔ **Download and Keep Original:** Tap this option and any photos or videos you download maintain the full-resolution as they have on iCloud.

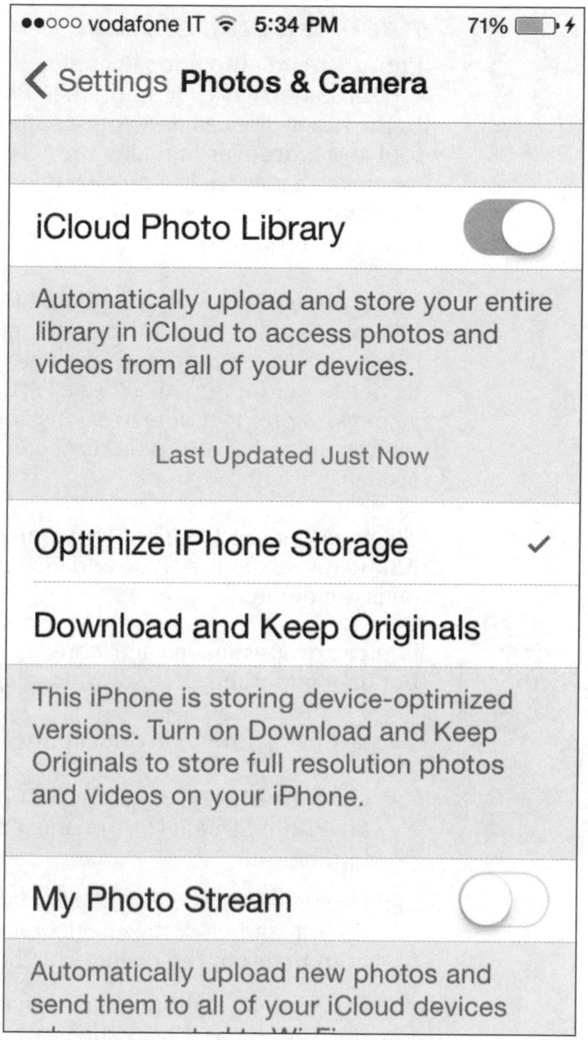

Photos are organized into Moments, Collections, and Years as on your iPhone, and you can edit photos and create albums and access them from all your other iOS devices and the web. The first 5GB are free, and if you need additional storage, plans begin at 20GB for $0.99 a month and 200GB for $3.99 a month.

●●○○○ vodafone IT 🛜 5:34 PM   71% 🔋⚡

❮ Settings Photos & Camera

iCloud Photo Library ⬤

Automatically upload and store your entire library in iCloud to access photos and videos from all of your devices.

Last Updated Just Now

Optimize iPhone Storage ✓

Download and Keep Originals

This iPhone is storing device-optimized versions. Turn on Download and Keep Originals to store full resolution photos and videos on your iPhone.

My Photo Stream ⬤

Automatically upload new photos and send them to all of your iCloud devices

Figure 1-12: Activate iCloud Photo Library on all your devices to share and store photos seamlessly.

Photo Stream storage

Photo Stream automatically uploads photos you take with your iPhone or other iOS devices to iCloud. Then Photo Stream pushes, or downloads, them to the other devices and your computer. We've found this to be a priceless tool and timesaver in taking the screenshots for this book — seconds after capturing a screenshot on our iPhone, upon opening iPhoto it shows up in the Photo Stream section under Recents as well as in Events on our Macs (no cable required).

Photo Stream also uploads photos from your computer. For example, if you take photos with a digital camera, and then move them to your computer, those photos are automatically uploaded to iCloud and pushed to your iOS devices, including your iPhone. You can view them on your iPhone for 30 days, giving you time to save a copy on your iPhone, too, if you like. Only photos uploaded after you turned on Photo Stream will be placed in Photo Stream.

The most recent 1,000 photos from all sources are stored in Photo Stream on iCloud for 30 days. As you add new photos beyond the 1,000 limit, the oldest ones are deleted.

Photos are downloaded and stored in full resolution on your Mac or Windows PC, but they're optimized for download speed and storage for your iOS devices.

To start using Photo Stream, do the following:

- **On your iPhone,** open the Settings app, tap Photos & Camera, and tap My Photo Stream On. You must be connected to Wi-Fi for Photo Stream to function.

- **On your Mac (OS X 10.7.5 or later),** open System Preferences, click iCloud, and click the check box next to Photos. Click Options and check both boxes in the dialog: My Photo Stream and Photo Sharing.

  In your Mac's photo management program, go to Preferences and click the iCloud tab. Check the box next to My Photo Stream to turn it on, and while you're there, click the box next to Photo Sharing, which we cover in a few paragraphs. Then choose how you want Photo Stream to handle your photos:

  - *Automatic Import:* Photos that are pushed to the Photo Stream library on your Mac are automatically imported to iPhoto or Aperture. With this box checked, your photos are permanently stored on your computer in Events, Faces, and Places when they enter Photo Stream from another device.

  - *Automatic Upload:* All new photos are sent from your computer to Photo Stream. Deselecting this box means you manually drag photos into the Photo Stream library or select the photos and then choose

Photo Stream from the pop-up Share menu at the bottom of the window. Although Photo Stream makes sure you don't exceed the storage space on your iPhone, manually managing photos that go from your computer to Photo Stream limits the number of photos pushed to the Photo Stream library on your other devices.

✔ **On a Windows PC (7 or 8),** download the iCloud Control Panel for Windows at `http://support.apple.com/kb/DL1455`. Open the iCloud Control Panel and click the check box next to Photo Stream.

On Windows, the process is manual: Drag photos you want in Photo Stream from your photo management application to the designated Photo Stream folder. The default folder is `C:\Users\<user name>\Pictures\Photo Stream\My Photo Stream`, which you can change by clicking the Options button next to Photo Stream in the iCloud Control Panel.

iCloud Photo Sharing

Passing your iPhone around the table from friend to friend isn't the only way to share photos. iCloud Photo Sharing lets you invite people to view albums you create and keep on iCloud. You create an album and invite specific people to see it. As you add more photos to the album, the invitees are notified that new photos have been added and can go view them. You can also make your album public, and even give others permission to add photos to your album. You and the people you share you album with can "like" a photo or write comments about it.

Here we explain how to create shared albums and how to share privately with a few people and with the public at large.

When you set up Family Sharing a Family album is automatically created in iCloud Photo Sharing. Photos and videos captured by family members on their devices show up in the Family album. Tap the Shared button in the Browse bar to access it.

Creating shared albums

You can create an album, choose whom to share it with, and then add or select photos, select the album to put them in, and then share the album. Make sure Photo Sharing is on in the Settings app under Photos & Camera, and follow these steps for the first option; we explain the second option next:

1. **Open the Photos app.**

2. **Tap the Shared button at the bottom of the screen to open iCloud Photo Sharing, which displays a list of shared albums.**

   The first item in the list, Activity, shows the history of photos and comments that were posted to the shared albums.

**Book IV
Chapter 1**

Capturing, Editing, and Sharing Photos

3. **Tap the plus sign in the upper left or New Shared Album at the bottom of the list.**

   A dialog opens and the keyboard appears on screen.

4. **Type a name for your new shared album, and then tap Next.**

5. **You can proceed in either of the following ways:**

   • Tap Create without selecting people you want to share the album with.

   Or

   • Tap the To field and type the email address of the person you want to invite to view your photos, or tap the Add button (it looks like a plus sign) to access your Contacts and choose recipients from there. Repeat Step 2 to add more recipients, and then tap Create.

   Your new album is added to the iCloud Photo Sharing list.

6. **Tap the album to add photos.**

7. **Tap the Add Photos button (the plus sign).**

   Thumbnail images of the Moments in Photos opens. Tap the Shared or Albums buttons in the Browse bar to choose photos from a different location.

8. **Tap the photos you want to add to that album.**

9. **Tap Done.**

   The iCloud dialog opens, as shown in Figure 1-13.

10. **Type a message if you want, and then tap Post.**

    The photos are added to the shared album on iCloud Photo Sharing and anyone allowed to see the photos is notified.

Sharing photos with a select few

You may find it easier to select your photos and then create an album. And, as you take new photos, you probably want to add them to a shared album. The steps to take are the same for both:

1. **Tap Photos on the Home screen.**

2. **Tap the Moment or Album that has the photos you want to share.**

   To share just one photo, open the photo and then tap the Share button and go to Step 6.

3. **Tap the Select button.**

4. **Tap the photos you want to share.**

5. **Tap the Share button.**

If you want to share all the photos in a Moment, tap the Share button above the Moment, and then tap Share This Moment.

6. **Tap iCloud Photo Sharing.**

   A dialog opens (refer to Figure 1-13). Type an optional comment and then do one of the following:

   • If the album name that appears next to Shared Album is the one you want to add photos to, simply tap Post.

   • If you want to add the photos to a different existing album, tap Shared Album and then tap the one you want to use.

   • If you want to create and share a new album, tap Shared Album and then tap New Shared Album. Create an album as explained in the section, "Creating shared albums."

Figure 1-13: Create shared photo albums on iCloud Photo Sharing.

7. **Tap Post.**

   Addressees receive an invitation to subscribe to your Shared Album.

8. **After someone joins your shared Shared Album, they'll be notified when new images are added.**

The people you invite to view your shared album have to have an Apple ID, which they use to sign in to it. Otherwise, follow the steps in the next section to turn Public Website On, and the email they receive will contain a link to the Shared Album.

Going public with your albums

To make a shared album available to the public through a URL, you have to first create the shared album in one of the two ways explained previously and then go into the album's settings. Follow these steps:

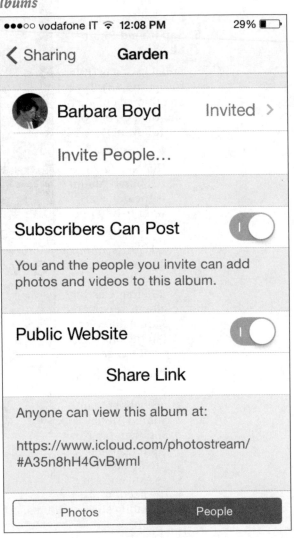

1. **Tap the Shared button at the bottom of the Photos screen.**

   The iCloud Photo Sharing list contains all the shared albums you created. The first album, called Activity, shows the history of everything you've done with shared albums.

2. **Tap the album you want to make public.**

   You see all the photos that are in the stream and two tabs at the bottom: Photos and People.

3. **Tap People.**

   You see the screen as in Figure 1-14 and can do the following:

   Figure 1-14: Go public with your albums.

   • Tap the disclosure triangle to the right of a name of a subscriber to resend the invitation or remove the subscriber.

   • Tap Invite People to invite others to see this shared album.

- Tap the Subscribers Can Post switch to the on (or off) position if you want invitees to be able to add photos or videos to this album.

- Tap the Public Website switch to the on (or off) position to change the status of this album. This creates a URL on iCloud so anyone who knows the link can view it.

- Tap Share Link, to share the link of a public album via Mail, Message, Twitter, or Facebook or to copy the link so you can paste it elsewhere, such as a newsletter or website.

- Tap Notifications if you want to receive alerts in the Notification center when subscribers interact with the album by liking, commenting, or adding photos.

- Tap Delete Shared Album to delete this shared album.

4. **(Optional) To stop sharing your album with someone, tap the person's name in the list at the top of the screen, scroll down the Info screen that appears, and then tap Remove Subscriber.**

Liking and commenting on photos

The basis of social networking is sharing and getting feedback on what you shared. If you're familiar with social networks such as Facebook or Pinterest, liking and commenting on photos will be second nature. Simply tap the Shared button in the Browse bar, and then tap the Activity album to see all the photos in all your albums or tap the specific album that has the photo you want. Tap the photo and then tap the Like button, if that's the action you want to take. Tap the Add A Comment field to write something about the photo, and then tap Send.

Chapter 2: Acquiring and Browsing Music, Videos, Movies, and More

In This Chapter

✓ **Matching your existing media**

✓ **Browsing and sampling**

✓ **Making your purchases**

✓ **Tracking down free iTunes promotional music and other goodies**

✓ **Reading up on iBooks**

✓ **Learning about iTunes U**

Apple sells more than hardware. Ancillary stores provide seemingly endless media to enjoy on your various devices. In this chapter, we introduce you to three of the four media outlets: the iTunes Store, your one-stop shop to download music, movies, TV shows, tones, and audiobooks; iTunes U, which offers a vast catalog of courses from universities around the world; and the iBooks Store, which offers paid and free electronic books from various publishers.

First, we take a close look at the iTunes Store, both on your iPhone and on your computer, and show you the ins and outs of browsing, sampling, and buying media. If you think iTunes is just for music, think again. We explore iTunes' other offerings, including movies, TV shows, audiobooks, and free promotional music. We visit the iBooks app and store to put some great works on your iPhone. And then we check out the courses at iTunes U.

After you have media to enjoy on your iPhone, go to Book IV, Chapter 3 to learn about using the Music and Podcasts apps and Book IV, Chapter 4 to start watching visual media in the Videos app.

Matching Your Media to iTunes

We explain how to sync your iPhone with media stored on your computer in Book I, Chapter 5, but not all your media is necessarily in iTunes. If you have a collection of CDs, you may not have copied them onto your computer because you didn't have any reason to. Or you may download music from other online sources. Wouldn't it be great to put some of that music onto your iPhone to listen to when you're away from your computer or stereo system? First, you have to move that music into iTunes on your computer, and here we explain the different ways to do that.

Media that's already on your computer

Moving media that you downloaded from another site like Amazon (www.amazon.com) or GoMusic (www.gomusic.com) is simple — just drag those files into your iTunes library. To make that task even easier, choose the Automatically Add to iTunes option when selecting the destination for saving a downloaded file, and the file shows up in your iTunes library.

An alternative to moving all your music into the iTunes app on your computer is to subscribe to iTunes Match. For a yearly fee of $24.95, iTunes Match "matches" up to 25,000 songs you have that are available from the iTunes Store and puts it in your iTunes in the Cloud library as an iTunes item. It also upgrades songs that are available in the iTunes Store to 256 Kbps (unavailable songs remain in the format you have them in). The upgrades alone could be good reason to purchase it, but because anything in your iTunes library is also in iTunes in the Cloud, with iTunes Match, even songs you didn't purchase through iTunes are available across all your devices. After the media is in iTunes, and you activate iCloud, you're just a syncing step away from having everything in your iTunes library accessible on your iPhone.

Media on a CD

To import media from a CD, follow these steps:

1. **Open iTunes.**

2. **Insert the CD you want to copy into the disc drive on your computer.**

   If the CD doesn't appear under the Library pop-up menu, choose Preferences (Mac) or Edit➪Preferences (Windows) and click the General tab of the Preferences dialog. Toward the bottom of the screen, you see the When You Insert a CD pull-down menu. Choose Show CD to see the CD under Devices. You can also change the default Settings here.

3. **Click the CD in the pop-up menu on the top left of the window.**

   The songs are listed and selected by default. If you only want to import some of the songs, deselect those you don't want.

4. **Click Import CD.**

   The Import Settings window opens. Click the pop-up menu next to Import Using to change the default settings. (See the sidebar for details about import settings.)

iTunes encoding music settings

When iTunes imports music, it automatically compresses the file with the iTunes Plus encoder, which plays at 256 Kbps in stereo (128 Kbps in mono). However, iTunes also gives you the option of using a different encoder to compress music you import. Click Import Settings at the bottom right of the iTunes screen to change your settings for the active import (set your own default import settings by choosing Preferences, clicking the General tab, and clicking the Import Settings button). You have five choices, each of which has an Auto setting and four of which have custom settings.

One minute of CD quality audio requires 10MB of storage. Compressing makes the file smaller so you can fit more songs on your personal listening device (that is, your iPhone). AAC and MP3 encoders compress the data by removing audio you wouldn't be able to hear unless you have bionic ears. AIFF, WAV, and Apple Lossless Encoders transform the data without removing any audio, so it can be played on your computer or iPhone.

Here's a brief explanation of the differences to help you choose if you decide to change the encoder you use to import music:

- **AAC (Advanced Audio Coding) Encoder:** Offers better sound quality and more flexibility at the same bit rate as MP3. Files are compressed and tags identify information about the song, such as artist, CD, and title.

- **AIFF (Audio Interchange File Format) Encoder:** AIFF and WAV offer the highest listening quality but don't copy tag information, such as the name of the artist, CD, or song (although iTunes does track that in its database, it won't show up if you

burn to another CD), and the files are large because they aren't compressed. AIFF files can be read and created on iTunes on both the Mac and Windows, but they're more commonly used in the Mac environment.

- **Apple Lossless Encoder:** Apple Lossless compresses files without removing (or losing) any audio so you have audio quality similar to AIFF/WAV but with slightly smaller files. It also sets tags like AAC and MP3 encoders. The downside is that most non-Apple devices don't support Apple Lossless.

- **MP3 Encoder:** Files are compressed and tagged. This is the choice to make for non-iOS MP3 players or if you want to burn an MP3 CD to play in a portable CD player or car stereo.

- **WAV Encoder:** iTunes on both Mac and Windows reads and creates WAV files. They're widely used with Windows and other operating systems.

To convert a song from one format to another, right-click the song and then click Advanced⇨Create ___ Version, where the ___ will be what you established in the Import Settings. Keep in mind there's no sense converting a lower-quality file to a higher-quality file (for example, converting an MP3 file to AIFF). The encoder can't add in audio that was removed. You can go from one encoder to another of similar quality, such as AIFF to WAV or Apple Lossless to MP3 with good results, albeit slight additional detail loss.

Your choice depends on how sensitive your ears are and what kind of output device you'll be using to listen to your music.

**Book IV
Chapter 2**

**Acquiring and
Browsing Music,
Videos, Movies, and
More**

5. **Click OK.**

   The status display at the top of the screen displays the songs that are being copied and the time remaining.

   When finished, the songs are stored in the Music library.

6. **Click the Eject button to remove the CD from your drive.**

If you have an active Internet connection when you copy a CD to iTunes, click the Options button and choose Get Track Names. iTunes will automatically scan the Gracenote Internet music database for any information related to the CD and copy it into the Info about that CD. After copying a CD to iTunes, download any album artwork that's available in iTunes by choosing File➪Library➪Get Album Artwork. You have to have an Internet connection and sign in to your Apple ID account to use this feature.

Browsing, Sampling, and Buying Music, Movies, and More at the iTunes Store

Have your Apple ID — or your finger if you have an iPhone with Touch ID — handy when you want to use iTunes because that's what you use to sign in and confirm your purchase. If you haven't yet created an Apple ID, see Book I, Chapter 5 for instructions.

When you first open the iTunes Store, it can seem overwhelming, and in a way it is: It offers more than 14 million songs. Besides all the music, iTunes also carries thousands of movies and TV shows, plus ringtones and audiobooks. Luckily, the iTunes Store, on your computer and iPhone, is organized to help you narrow your choices.

Shopping on your iPhone

iTunes on your iPhone is a streamlined version of the iTunes Store. Banners run across the top of the screen and then sections such as New and Noteworthy or This Week appear along with seasonal and media-specific sections. The recommendations are all there, but because of the smaller screen space, you see less of it at once — which may be a good thing. You need a Wi-Fi or cellular data connection to use iTunes on your iPhone. When you open the iTunes Store app, the screen shown in Figure 2-1 appears. The first time you open iTunes Store, the Music section appears, but if the last time you looked in iTunes Store you were browsing movies or audiobooks, when you re-open, that's what you'll see.

Tapping any of the buttons in the Browse bar at the bottom of the screen takes you to the corresponding section of the iTunes Store. Tap More to open a list of sections that aren't displayed in the Browse bar. To search for media, do the following:

1. **Tap any of the media browse buttons: Music, Movies, TV Shows, or Audiobooks or Tones from the More menu to look for that type of media.**

2. **Tap Genres to see a list of genres for that media (called Categories in the Audiobooks section).**

   Tap a genre and you see specific selections in either the Featured or Charts view.

3. **Tap the Featured tab at the top center to see the banner ads and icon; tap Charts to see the most popular items in each media category.**

   If you want to see the Featured or Charts for all genres in a media category, tap All Genres at the top of the list.

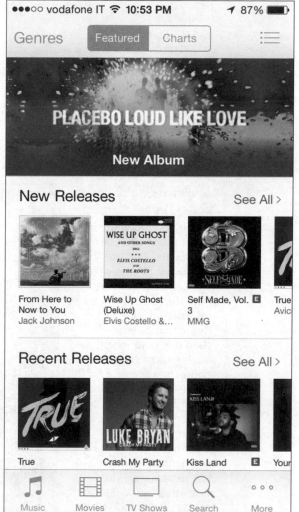

Figure 2-1: The iTunes Store on your iPhone.

Tap the History button in the upper-right corner to see your browsing history along with other lists of media that you expressed interest in in one way or another:

- ✔ **Wish List:** When viewing items, tap the Share button and then tap Add to Wish List.

- ✔ **Siri:** When listening to a song, hold the Home button to call on Siri to identify the song and tag it so you can order it later.

- ✔ **Radio:** Lists songs you heard while listening to iTunes Radio.

- ✔ **Previews:** See a chronological list of items you perused recently.

Book IV
Chapter 2

Acquiring and
Browsing Music,
Videos, Movies, and
More

Scroll down to the bottom of any Featured screen to access the following:

✔ **Redeem:** Opens a screen where you enter the code from any gift card or iTunes codes you have; the amount is added to your Apple ID account.

✔ **Apple ID:** Click to sign in if you don't see your Apple ID there. If you have a store credit, the credit balance appears under your account name.

Siri is always listening to ambient noise, at the ready for a command or to identify a song. Ask Siri, "What song is playing?" and it accesses Shazam, the song identification service. After Siri names the tune, tap the buy button to go directly to the iTunes Store to purchase and download the song.

Downloading to your iPhone

When you reach the center of the iTunes Store vortex and find the song, movie, or TV show you want to download, tapping the item opens an information screen. On items that have more than one component, such as an album that comprises songs, or a TV show that has multiple episodes, the information screen shows a list of each component, as shown in Figure 2-2. By the name and graphic of the item you see information such as the genre, release date, and star ratings. Below there are three tabs that give you the following information:

✔ **Songs** (in Music) or **Details** (Movies and TV Shows): Shows a description of the item and a list of songs or other details such as plot and actors for movies or a list of episodes for TV shows.

Figure 2-2: An iTunes Store information screen on your iPhone.

✔ **Reviews:** Shows star ratings, the total number of rankings, and written reviews. You can also write a review yourself by tapping Write a Review here.

✔ **Related:** Shows other items by the same artist or in the same genre and media, as well as other items people who bought this item bought.

To preview an item, simply tap it in the list. The Preview button transforms to a loading button and then a piece of the song or video plays.

You can preview video via AirPlay on Apple TV by tapping the AirPlay button.

To download an item:

1. **Tap the price or Free button to the right of the item.**

   The price button transforms to read Buy Song/Album/Movie/Episode/Season; Free becomes Download.

2. **Tap Buy Song/Album/Movie/Episode/Season or Download.**

   If you tap Buy by mistake, tap somewhere else on the screen, and it disappears.

   To purchase items, you must have credit or credit card information in your Apple ID account. Free items begin downloading immediately.

   In the Settings app, tap iTunes & App Stores and turn on the Use Cellular Data switch to process automatic downloads and iTunes Match through your cellular data service when Wi-Fi isn't available. Note that items larger than 50MB can't be downloaded over the cellular network. For files larger than 50MB you must connect to Wi-Fi or download them on your computer and then sync to your iPhone. TV shows and rented movies begin playing as soon as enough data has been downloaded to launch the video.

   Bonus songs, videos, and iTunes Extras (HD movies only) download to your iPhone; iTunes LP and digital booklets can only be downloaded to your computer. In iTunes on your computer, choose Store⇨Check for Available Downloads to retrieve these items.

3. **Downloaded items appear in the Purchased section found by tapping More.**

   Purchases are sorted by type: Music, Movies, and so on.

To share an item on one of the social networks or in a message, tap the Share button at the top of the screen to open the Share Sheet. Tap the sharing method you want to use and let your friends know about the great new artist you discovered on iTunes.

If Family Sharing is on, you can access the music and media that other family members have purchased. Tap More in the Browse bar, and then tap Purchased. Tap the name of the family member whose purchases you want

REMEMBER

REMEMBER

**Book IV
Chapter 2**

Acquiring and
Browsing Music,
Videos, Movies, and
More

to access. Tap the music you want to download or play in streaming, and it begins playing. See Book I, Chapter 5 to learn how to set up Family Sharing.

Browsing in iTunes

You'll see a few other options for iTunes on your iPhone. The default Browse bar contains:

- ✔ **Search:** Tapping the Search button opens a Search field. Tap in the field to open the keyboard. Type in the title or subject of the item you want to find, and then tap the Search button. iTunes lists potential matches to your search words sorted by media category, which you can scroll through or tap a tab at the top to see the result for only one type.

There are three more choices on the More screen that help you manage your iTunes Store experience. If you find you use one of them often, check out the Tip at the end of this section for rearranging the buttons you find on the Browse bar.

- ✔ **Purchased:** Choose the media type — Music, Movies, or TV Shows — and then choose to display by All (which is everything you've purchased on iTunes) or Not On This iPhone (where iTunes compares the media you've purchased and the media on your iPhone and shows you things that haven't been synced to your iPhone yet). Click the Download button to download those items to your iPhone.

- ✔ **Genius:** Genius makes recommendations based on your iTunes purchasing history. To use Genius, open the iTunes Store app, tap More, and then tap Genius. Tap the media you want recommendations for — Music, Movies, or TV Shows. Genius gives you a list of results it thinks you'll like. Tap any of the results to go to the information screen. Purchase and download as instructed earlier in this section.

- ✔ **Downloads:** Shows a status list of pending and in-progress downloads. Tapping the Pause button pauses the download until you start it again. If you lose your Internet connection, iPhone starts the download when the connection re-opens, or iTunes on your computer completes the download the next time you open iTunes. Pre-ordered items remain in the list until they're available and you download them. Tap the item for release date information. When it's available, tap the item and then tap the Download button.

From the More screen, tap the Edit button to rearrange the buttons you see at the bottom of the screen and those that appear in the secondary More screen. Just drag the icon of the button you want on the bar over the one you want to replace, and they exchange places.

On your computer

There's not much difference between the iTunes Store on your computer and on your iOS devices, including your iPhone. Click the iTunes Store button in the center of the toolbar and — perhaps returning to its roots — iTunes opens directly to the music promotions. Click the buttons on the upper left of the iTunes toolbar to shop for different types of media: Movies, TV Shows, Podcasts (Book IV, Chapter 3), iTunes U, Audiobooks, Apps (refer to Book IV, Chapter 5), and Tones. If you don't see all the categories, click the ellipsis and then click Edit in the pop-up menu; check the box next to the categories you want to see on the toolbar.

In each category, you see rotating banner ads across the top. Below the ads are sections along the lines of What's Hot or New & Noteworthy, as well as seasonal and themed sections. You can scroll horizontally and vertically, and clicking any of the ads or icons in this smorgasbord of offers takes you to an information screen about that item.

When you click on a song or album icon or name from anywhere in the iTunes Store, the album information window opens. Click a TV show and the season information screen opens. Click a movie and a movie information screen opens. These are the parts of an information screen:

- **Name (and artist if in the Music category):** Click the arrow next to the artist's name to see more songs and albums by the same artist.

- **Release date.**

- **Star ratings:** The number of ratings appear in the parentheses.

- **Buy button:** Click to download the media. Each option (for example rent or buy, standard or high-definition) has its own button. Songs can be purchased singly by clicking the button in the Price column or you can purchase the whole album by clicking the Buy button under the album; TV shows can be purchased singly or by season.

- **Share:** Click the triangle next to the Buy button to open a pop-up menu that has options to gift the item to a friend, add it to your own Wish List, tell a friend about it, copy the link, or share the item info via Facebook or Twitter.

    You can't use a store credit to pay for a gift. You must pay with a credit card or PayPal account.

- **Ratings:** For movies only. The ratings are the usual G, PG, PG-13, R, and so on for U.S. markets. Foreign films may have different ratings.

Three tabs give you different information:

- **Songs (Music), Details (all other categories):** The first few lines of the description of the item are visible. If the description is longer, click More on the right to expose the complete description. This is where you find

**Book IV
Chapter 2**

Acquiring and
Browsing Music,
Videos, Movies, and
More

the song list if you're viewing an album, the episode list for TV Shows and Podcasts, Chapters for Books, and lessons or lectures for iTunes U.

- ✔ **Ratings and Reviews:** Users can give a simple star rating, from zero to five, or write a review. Reviews help your downloading or purchasing decisions.

- ✔ **Related:** Lists items by the same performers and other items purchased by people who bought that particular item. A fourth tab appears when bonus items such as iTunes Extras or LP are available.

Tap the History button next to the Library button at the top of the window to see a list of items you previewed recently in any category. Here you'll also find your Wish List and your iTunes Radio history.

Finding music when you know what you're looking for

If you have a specific song or movie in mind, you can skip the rotating banner ads and lists of recommendations and search for the media you seek.

Pressing ⌘+F takes the cursor to the Search field. Type the name or a couple keywords in the Search field at the top right of the window, and then press return. A list of matching results appears. The results are culled from the entire iTunes Store but are divided by category. If you click Media Type in the list on the right, you'll see only that type of media.

Downloading media from iTunes

When you find something you like, click the Buy (or Rent) button and it's downloaded to iTunes. Either way, you have to sign in with your Apple ID account and pay the price. This happens two ways:

- ✔ **Credit card:** Enter your credit card information in your Apple ID account. You may have done this when you opened the account, or you can do it now by clicking your account name near the Search field in the upper right. If you haven't yet signed in to iTunes with your Apple ID you see Sign In; click to open the Sign In to the iTunes Store dialog, and then type in your Apple ID and password, and click Sign In. Click Account Info in the menu that opens when you click your account name. Type your password again and click the View Account button. Click Edit next to Payment Type to add credit card billing information. A window opens where you can choose the type of credit card you want to use (or PayPal) and type in the necessary information: account number, expiration date, billing address, and so on. Click the Done button when you complete the required fields.

- ✔ **Redeem:** You can redeem Apple or iTunes gift cards, gift certificates, or allowances. (You can set up a monthly allowance for yourself or someone else. A set amount is charged to your credit card or PayPal account and credited to the designated iTunes account.) Click your account name and then choose Redeem. Type in the code from the card or certificate or click Use Camera and hold the card up to your computer's camera.

The amount of the card or certificate is added to your account and appears to the right of the Apple ID account tab.

After you download the item, close the iTunes Store by clicking the My Music button in the toolbar — it may read My Movies or My iTunes U if that was the last type of media you were listening to or watching. You return to your iTunes library, which is non-store iTunes on your computer. Click the button in the toolbar for the type of media you downloaded (Music, Movies, and so on) to see your media. Use the menu under the Search field to sort the selection or edit your viewing options.

You can select Automatic Downloads so that whenever you download something on your computer or device, it's automatically downloaded to other computers or devices using the same Apple ID. On your computer, in iTunes, choose iTunes➪Preferences and click the Store tab. Check the boxes next to the media you want automatically downloaded to other devices: Apps or Music (Books as well on Windows). Books are managed by iBooks on a Mac running OS X 10.9 or later; choose iBooks➪Preferences and click the Store tab and then choose Download New Purchases Automatically. On your iPhone, open the Settings app, tap iTunes & App Store, and tap the switches next to Music, Apps, or Books On. While you're there, you can choose to use the cellular network to download purchases by tapping the switch by Use Cellular Data On, although there are size limits for downloading on the cellular network. Use a Wi-Fi connection to download larger files.

With iCloud, you can access rented or purchased media from all your devices. When you start watching on one device, you can pause there and begin playback on another device from where you paused on the first device. When you rent a movie, you have 30 days to begin watching the movie and 24 hours to finish watching once you begin, regardless of where you begin or finish watching.

Authorizing iTunes to play your purchased music, videos, books, and apps

When you open an iTunes account or Apple ID, you automatically authorize that computer to open videos, books, and apps purchased from the iTunes Store with your account. The media and the computer have to have the same authorization. You can authorize up to five computers, which means you can access your iTunes account from each of those five computers. Follow these steps to authorization:

1. **In iTunes, choose Store➪Authorize This Computer.**

   A pane opens asking you to type in your Apple Account name and password. That's what you established when you set up your account on iTunes.

2. **Click Authorize.**

   A message appears telling you how many computers are authorized with this account.

Book IV
Chapter 2

Acquiring and
Browsing Music,
Videos, Movies, and
More

Getting the goods for free

You probably noticed the word *free* floating around on iTunes. Some things, like lectures from iTunes U and podcasts, are always free. Temporarily free items are iTunes promotions. You can find them in different places:

- ✔ **iTunes Store Home page:** Take a look around. There's usually at least one link to something free in the banner ads. Scroll through the other sections. Free and discounted items are marked with a yellow triangle in the upper-right corner of the icon. At the very bottom of the page, there's a section called Free on iTunes. Tap See All to view the entire selection.

- ✔ **Music and TV Shows:** Click the Free link under Quick Links. Pilot episodes of new TV series are often free.

At some point, you may want to deauthorize an account — say, if you buy a new computer and donate your old one to the local homeless shelter. Instead of clicking Authorize This Computer, choose Store⇨Deauthorize This Computer. Type in your Apple ID name and password, and then click Deauthorize. Any videos, books, or apps associated with that computer are no longer available.

Reading Bestsellers in iBooks

You may think the screen is too small, but with its high definition and storage capacity, your iPhone is a good substitute for an iPad or Mac when it comes to reading e-books on iBooks. Think of those times when you're waiting for an appointment or your plane is delayed — having a good book at hand can help pass the time. And, if you don't have a book already downloaded, you can find one on the spot. In this section, we walk you through the stacks of the iBooks Store and show you how to adjust the iBook settings to best suit your eyes.

iBooks syncs across your iOS devices and Macs. You can also open the Settings app, tap iTunes & App Store, and tap the Books on in the Automatic Downloads section to simultaneously download books purchased on other devices to your iPhone.

Finding something to read

Like any major brick-and-mortar or online bookstore, the iBooks Store has a huge offering of fiction and nonfiction books on just about any subject you can think of and for different ages. To find a book that suits your fancy, just follow these steps:

1. **Open the iBooks app.**

   Your Library opens, as shown in Figure 2-3. (Tap My Books in the Browse bar if you see something different on the screen.) Your shelves will be empty if you haven't downloaded any books.

2. **Tap the buttons in the Browse bar to view the following:**

   • *Featured:* Opens the iBooks Store, which has the same layout as the iTunes Store with promotional banners and buttons filling the main part of the screen.

   • *Top Charts:* Helps you narrow your search. Tap the Categories button in the upper left to see top-selling books in a specific genre and tap the Paid or Free tab at the top of the screen to see books available for purchase or find some great freebies to download.

   • *Search:* Opens the Search field so you can look for a book with a specific title, by a specific author, or on a specific subject. You also see a list of Trending Searches to give you an idea what other readers are looking for.

Figure 2-3: iBooks displays your e-books on virtual shelves.

   • *Purchased:* Shows a list of all purchases you've made at the iBooks Store on any device, as well as a list of those not on your iPhone. You also find purchases made by other family members if you use Family Sharing.

3. **Tap a promotional button on the Featured screen or tap through the charts to find a book that interests you and then tap a book that you might like to read.**

Book IV
Chapter 2

Acquiring and
Browsing Music,
Videos, Movies, and
More

The Info screen opens and shows the usual information: Details, Reviews, and Related tabs, and Price (Free, if it is) and Sample buttons to either purchase the book or download a sample, respectively.

4. **After you find something you want to try or purchase, tap Sample, to download a sample to your iPhone, and then if you like it, you can purchase it later. Or tap the price (or Free) button, confirm that you want to purchase the book, and then either type in your Apple ID and password or touch your finger to the Home button to approve the purchase with your fingerprint (for iPhones with Touch ID only).**

The book is downloaded to your iPhone, and your Library opens. Your recently downloaded book is on the shelf with a "New" or "Sample" banner across it (refer to Figure 2-3). A small cloud on the corner of the book or document lets you know it hasn't been downloaded to your iPhone; this can happen if you download a book to another device but haven't selected automatic downloads for books in the iTunes & App Store settings.

Organizing your shelves

iBooks can store PDF documents as well as electronic books. By default you see everything on your shelves. To see only books or only PDF documents, tap the All Books button at the top of your Library shelves; the Collections screen opens. Tap PDF to see only PDF documents you downloaded or synced to your iPhone or tap Books if you only want to view books. When you tap a selection on the Collections screen, you then return to your library shelves and see only items in whatever collection you tapped (or you see everything if you tapped All).

When your shelves start to sag, you may want to create collections of related books or documents, for example, grouping books by the same author or all the PDF documents related to one project. To create a collection, tap New Collection on the Collections screen, and type a name, such as Nonfiction or Dickens. Tap Done and then tap All to see all your books. Tap Select in the upper right, and then tap the books or documents you want in the new collection. Tap Move at the top of the screen, and then tap the collection where you want the selected books to reside. You still see those books or documents when you tap All on the Collections screen but you can narrow your choices by viewing a single collection.

At the bottom of the Collections screen, you can tap the on/off switch next to Hide iCloud Books so you only see books that reside on your iPhone.

For your reading pleasure

Now that you have one or more books on your iBook shelves, you'll want to read them. Tap My Books in the Browse bar, tap a book on the shelf, and you can then do the following:

✔ The book opens to the table of contents. Tap the chapter where you want to begin reading.

✔ Tap the Font Size button in the upper-right corner, and a window opens as shown in Figure 2-4; tap the Font Size button again to close the window.

- Use the slider to adjust the screen brightness and tap the letters to shrink or enlarge the font on the page.

- Tap Fonts to change the typeface.

- Tap a theme to change the page and type colors.

- Tap the Auto-Night Theme switch to the on position to switch automatically to white text on black screen when it's nighttime.

Figure 2-4: Adjust the typeface style, size, and color to make for comfortable reading.

- Tap the Scrolling View switch to the on position to scroll vertically through the book instead of tapping to turn pages horizontally.

✔ Tap the Search button to look for a specific word or phrase or jump to a page number.

✔ Tap the bookmark in the upper-right corner to virtually dog-ear a page so you can find it later.

Book IV
Chapter 2

Acquiring and
Browsing Music,
Videos, Movies, and
More

✔ Tap and hold a word to select it. Drag the grabbers to select a phrase if you want, and then tap one of the tabs above the selection: Copy, Define, Highlight. Tap the arrow at the end of the menu to see the remaining options: Note, which lets you write a note in the virtual margin of the page, Search, or Share, which perform those tasks.

✔ Tap the Contents button (it looks like a list next to the Library button) to view the Table of Contents. Tap the Bookmarks or Notes tabs to see any of those you added to the book. Tap the Share button to recommend the book to someone via message or email. Tap Copy to copy a link to the book in the iBooks Store, which you can then paste to your website or a post on a social network. From the Contents screen, tap the Resume button to return to the book or the Library button to return to your bookshelves.

✔ Open the Settings app and tap iBooks to turn on options such as full justification and auto-hyphenation, and to set your syncing preferences.

To delete books or PDFs, tap the Select button at the top right of the Library screen, tap the items you want to delete to select them, and then tap the Delete button in the upper right. Tap Done when you're finished. If you delete books you purchased from the iBooks Store, you can download them again at a later date.

Enrolling in iTunes U

Although the iTunes U app doesn't come preinstalled on your iPhone, we highly recommend you download this free app and take advantage of all the interesting and informative media available in the iTunes U catalog.

Divided into 16 categories (think faculties), iTunes U features audio and video lectures from seminars and courses at universities around the world. iTunes U isn't limited to universities, however. You find lectures and presentations from professional meetings and conferences, such as TED and the Prostate Health Conference, as well as K through 12 and professional certification material. Aside from the vast selection of topics and the quality of the presentations, the best part is that the lectures are free!

Choosing courses

Here we briefly explain how the iTunes U course catalog is organized. As with the App, iTunes, and iBooks Stores, iTunes U lets you look at its offerings overall, by genre, by most popular, and, of course, by searching.

You see "courses" and "collections." *Courses* have a syllabus, study materials (which may be e-books or worksheets), and the lectures themselves as either audio or video files to be followed in chronological order as you build upon gained knowledge from one lesson to the next. *Collections* are stand-alone lectures related to a similar topic; you don't need to listen to or watch all of them to gain full knowledge. Here's how to find something that you want to learn more about:

1. **Open the iTunes U app.**

   The iTunes U catalog opens. The opening screen is probably familiar by now. Banner ads scroll across the top, Standout Courses and other categorical sections follow, and all are tappable buttons that lead to more information about that course. The other buttons are

   - **Categories (upper left):** Categories opens a list of the 16 "faculties" you can choose from. Tapping one of those faculties then opens a selection of courses on that topic displayed like the opening screen — banners, buttons, and the like. Choose All Categories from the Categories list to return to the full catalog selection.

   - **Library (upper right):** Library takes you to your collection of downloaded courses. We talk about that in the next section.

   The Browse buttons at the bottom are:

   - *Featured:* Banners across the top promote sponsored courses and then, scrolling down, you find sections such as Standout Courses and New and Notable. This same type of selection appears when you select a specific Genre.

   - *Charts:* Divided into Courses and Collections, this view lists the most popular — the most downloaded — courses and collections.

   - *Browse:* Choose the level you want — Higher Ed, K–12, or Other — and then scroll through the alphabetical list of institutions offering courses at that level.

   - *Search:* Tap to open the search field. Type your criteria and then tap the Search button. You can then view the results by collections, courses, or all, which includes collections and courses as well as a list of episodes (lectures) and materials that meet your search criteria.

2. **Tap a course or collection that interests you, and the Info screen opens, as shown in Figure 2-5.**

   - Tap Details to see descriptions, the course outline (if it's a course), and a list of lectures and materials. Tap More to see the complete information.

   - Tap Reviews to see what others have to say about the course or collection.

   - Tap Related to see other courses and collections on a similar topic that might interest you.

   - Tap the Share button to share a link to the course via AirDrop, Mail, Messages, Twitter, or Facebook, or copy the link to another app.

Book IV
Chapter 2

Acquiring and
Browsing Music,
Videos, Movies, and
More

3. **When you find a course or collection you want to watch or listen to, you have the following options:**

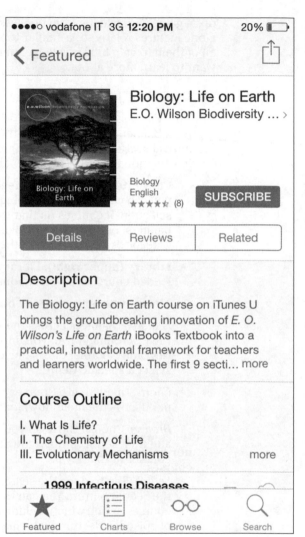

- **Tap Subscribe** to subscribe to the entire course. Links to the materials are added to your Library and updates are added as they become available (this is the default setting that we show you how to change later).

- **Tap the Download button** next to a single episode or material. The icon next to the download button indicates the type of file it is: A filmstrip icon means video; a speaker icon means audio; and a piece of paper icon means written materials, usually a PDF.

Figure 2-5: Subscribe to courses or single episodes from the Info screen.

4. **Tap the Back button in the upper left to return to the iTunes U screen where you were before.**

If you scroll to the bottom of the screen, you see your Apple ID, a Redeem button for adding iTunes Store card credit, your credit balance, and an Enroll button. Some courses have limited enrollment and you must request an enrollment code from the instructor to subscribe and attend. You can find more information about the instructor in the course description.

Attending class

After you subscribe to one or more iTunes U courses or collections, they're stored in your iTunes U library. Follow these steps to attend class:

1. **Tap the Library button in the upper right.**

   You see the courses and collections you subscribed to. The number tells you how many new episodes have been added since you first subscribed.

2. **Tap a course or collection to open it and begin learning.**

3. **Tap the episode to begin listening or watching, or tap a book if you want to begin reading course material.**

   Many of the interactive textbooks can be read-only on an iPad.

4. **Tap the Back button to return to the episode list for this course, and then tap Materials to see the materials list.**

5. **Tap Library to return to your iTunes U library shelf; tap Catalog in the upper-right corner to browse more courses.**

6. **(Optional) To rearrange the icons on the iTunes U shelf, touch and hold an icon until it gets a bit bigger, and then drag it to a new position.**

Collections display a simple list of the video or audio comprised, as in Figure 2-6. Tap the disclosure arrow next to the collection title to see more information, tap the Info (i) button to see more information about a

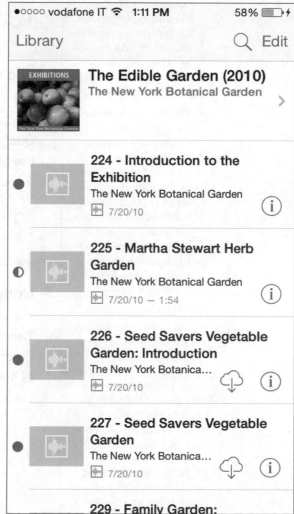

Figure 2-6: Collections display a list of episodes.

Book IV
Chapter 2

Acquiring and
Browsing Music,
Videos, Movies, and
More

specific episode, or tap the Download button to download an episode. Tap the Search button to search within the collection or a specific episode. Tap the Edit button to delete episodes you no longer want or remove the collection entirely.

Courses are interactive and you can access several different types of material and views. The buttons at the top do the following:

- Tap the Search button (the magnifying glass) to search throughout the course or within a specific episode.

- Tap the Share button to share a link to the course via Mail, Messages, Facebook, or Twitter; copy and paste the link in another app; or print what you see on the screen.

- Tap the Settings button (gear icon) to change the settings for that individual course: tap the Subscription switch on to receive updated information automatically; tap the Auto Download switch on to download new episodes and materials automatically.

- At any time, tap the button in the upper-left corner to return to the previous screen.

The Browse buttons along the bottom, as shown in Figure 2-7, contain the following:

- **Info:** Displays a list that includes buttons to open an Overview, which describes the

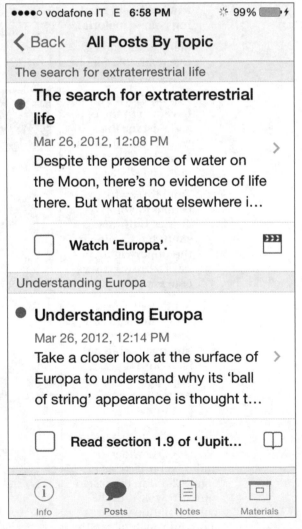

Figure 2-7: Courses offer diverse types of material and options.

course, the types of materials, what you can expect to learn, how long the course usually takes, and what education level it's appropriate for. The Instructor item describes the professor; you may find a link to send an email as well. Outline reveals the syllabus for the course. Tap the Info button in the upper left to return to the Info screen.

✔ **Posts:** These are the lessons and any supplementary material the instructor has provided (refer to Figure 2-7).

✔ **Notes:** Notes you take are neatly organized here. You can view all your notes together or your course notes, audio/video notes, or book notes. Tap the Plus sign at the top if you want to add a note from this screen.

You can also add notes while you are listening or watching an episode. Tap the Notes button in the upper-right corner and then tap the Add button (plus sign). The keyboard opens, as shown in Figure 2-8, so you can type a note related to the lecture, which continues to play while you take your note unless you tap Pause. The note shows the time during the lecture that the note was taken so you can easily return to the point related to your note. Tap Notes to see all your notes and then tap Done to return to the lecture. The red lines on the scrubber bar show where you took notes.

✔ **Materials:** Lists all the course materials (which sometimes must be purchased) and gives you the option to view by type: Audio, Video, and Books. Some books are readable only on an iPad.

Tap one of the choices to see the list of materials. See more information, download, and listen to or watch the episodes the same way as you would for an episode of a collection. Tap Edit in the upper-right corner to remove downloaded episodes.

The playback controls are similar to those you find for audio or video in other apps. You can go back 30 seconds, rewind, fast-forward, jump back or forward an episode, and control the playback speed.

Figure 2-8: Take Notes while listening to or watching a lecture.

**Book IV
Chapter 2**

Acquiring and Browsing Music, Videos, Movies, and More

In addition to the individual settings that you find when you tap the disclosure triangle next to the name of a course or collection in your Library, you can sync your notes with other iOS devices by opening the Settings app, tapping iTunes U, and tapping the Sync Notes switch on.

Chapter 3: Listening to Music and Audio

In This Chapter

- ✔ **Meeting and mastering the Music app**
- ✔ **Tuning in to iTunes Radio**
- ✔ **Searching Music for media**
- ✔ **Creating playlists**
- ✔ **Controlling music and audiobook playback**
- ✔ **Customizing Music's settings**
- ✔ **Listening to podcasts**

*W*hether you want some easy listening while you work or you need to block out the jackhammer on the sidewalk outside your window, the Music and Podcasts apps can help — especially if you pair them with the EarPods that came with your iPhone or one of the headsets or Bluetooth speakers we talk about in the online bonus Chapter 6.

In this chapter, we talk about Music, the app you use to listen to music and audiobooks and to tune in to iTunes Radio, Apple's new custom streaming service. We also talk about Podcasts, the app you use to listen to or watch — you guessed it — podcasts, which are free informational or entertaining episodes on just about every topic under the sun.

Meeting and Mastering the Music App

Music gives you the joy of listening to your favorite singers, bands, and audiobooks whenever you have your iPhone with you. First, we take you through the general layout of Music. Then we show you the basic commands for listening to music and creating playlists. Finally, we explain how to listen to your favorite type of music with iTunes Radio.

Open the Music app and you see a screen similar to that shown in Figure 3-1. You see five browse buttons across the bottom of the screen that help you find

4G 1:00 PM

Artists

🔍 Search

ADELE
1 album, 12 songs

David Bowie

and listen to recordings you have synced to your iPhone or stored in iTunes in the Cloud:

- **Radio:** Streams music from more than 250 genre-based stations or custom-built stations based on your music tastes.

- **Playlists:** Displays a list of playlists you've either created on your iPhone or synced from iTunes, including Genius playlists.

- **Artists:** Displays an alphabetical list of artists.

- **Songs:** Shows a list of songs, or spoken monologues or routines, in alphabetical order by title. Tapping the Shuffle button at the top of the screen begins playing all the songs on your iPhone in a random order.

- **More:** Brings up a list of additional viewing options:

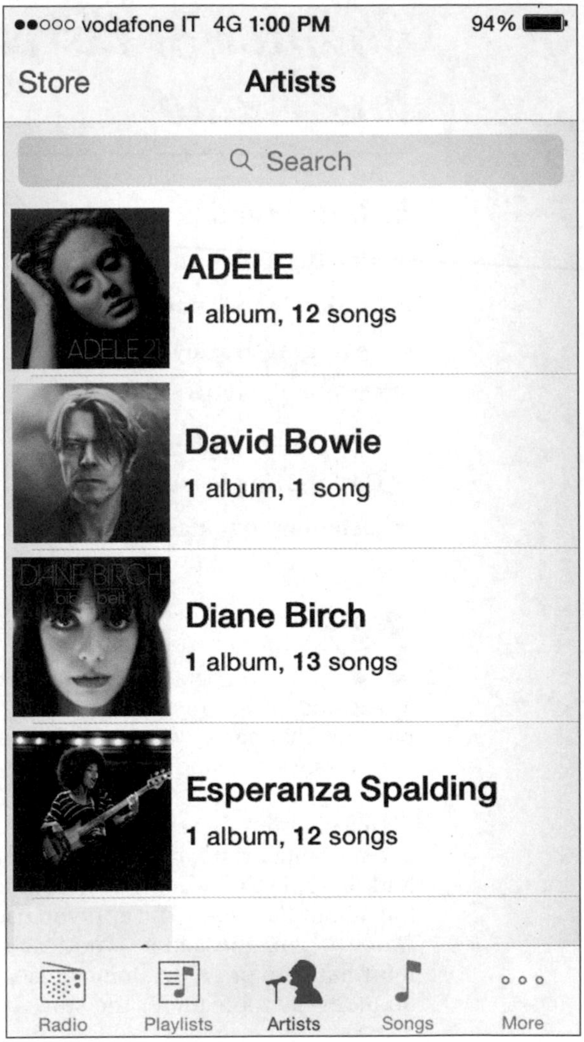

Figure 3-1: The Music screen.

- **Albums:** Shows a list of the albums the songs on Music come from. Even if you have only one song from an album, that album appears in the Albums list.

- **Genres:** Shows a list of genres. Tapping the genre opens a list of media you have in that genre.

- **Audiobooks:** Opens a list of audiobooks, if you have any on your iPhone.

- **Compilations:** Shows a list of compilations, which are often songs from different albums or artists put together as one.

- **Composers:** Displays an alphabetical list of composers. Tapping the name of the composer opens a list of songs written by that composer.

- **Shared:** Shows devices that are on the same Wi-Fi network and can share libraries or playlists that have been selected for streaming or can be seen by Home Sharing. Tap a different device to access music stored on that device. Home Sharing allows not only listening but also copying the content to the computer of the listener. See the section "Customizing Music's Settings" later in this chapter to learn about Home Sharing.

Tapping the Edit button in the top-left corner of the More screen opens a Configure screen. Tap and drag a button from the main part of the screen over one of the browse buttons. The two buttons exchange places. Tap Done when they're arranged as you like. This lets you put the buttons you use most in the Browse bar.

iTunes Radio

iTunes Radio is a great way to discover new artists in the genres you prefer and explore different types of music without making the immediate commitment to purchase. To use iTunes Radio, do the following:

1. **Tap Radio in the Browse bar at the bottom of the Music app.**

2. **Tap Start Listening the first time; subsequent times you see the screen as shown in Figure 3-2.**

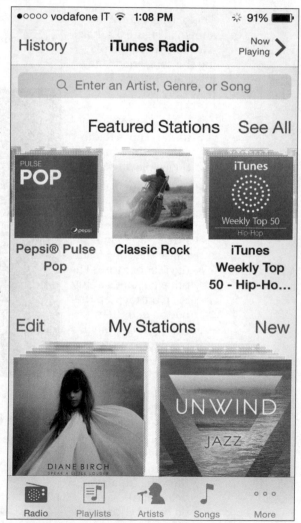

Figure 3-2: With more than 250 stations, you're sure to find something you want to hear.

You see two scrollable sections: Featured Stations, which scrolls horizontally and shows you iTunes created stations, and My Stations, which scrolls vertically.

3. **Tap a button that reflects the type of music you want to listen to.**

   The station either opens with a brief introduction audio that will be followed by a song or goes right into a song.

   You can ask Siri to play a station for you.

4. **Tap the Back button to return to the iTunes Radio screen.**

The playing screen, as shown in Figure 3-3, has a lot of options for playing the song and managing your stations. Here's how they work:

- **Back:** Tap to return to the iTunes Radio screen; the song continues playing.

- **Info:** Tap to get more information about or purchase the song.

- **Price:** Tap to purchase the song from the iTunes Store. The price becomes a Buy Song button; tap that button and then enter your Apple ID password or press the Home button to authorize your purchase.

- **Star:** Tap to add the song to your Wish List, play more songs like the one you're listening to, or block the song from ever being played again on that station.

- **Pause:** Tap to interrupt playback; tap again to play.

Figure 3-3: Pause or skip a song during playback.

✔ **Skip:** Tap to go to the next song on the station.

✔ **Volume:** Drag your finger along the slider to increase or decrease volume. The volume buttons on your phone or headphones control the volume, too.

If your phone locks during playback, the song artwork and playback controls appear on the Lock screen.

What's more, when you tap Info, you get several options for finding more stations, as shown in Figure 3-4. Tap Done when you finish with this screen to return to the playback screen.

✔ **Album Cover or List:** Tap to open the album the song is from in the iTunes Store.

✔ **Price:** Tap to purchase the song from the iTunes Store.

✔ **New Station from Artist:** Adds a new station to My Stations based on songs from different artists similar to this artist.

✔ **New Station from Song:** Adds a new station to My Stations based on songs similar to this song.

✔ **Add to My Stations (visible when you choose a station from the Featured Stations):** Tap to add the current station to My Stations.

✔ **Tune This Station (visible when listening to one of your stations):** Tap Hits, Variety, or Discovery to hear those kinds of songs in the genre of your station.

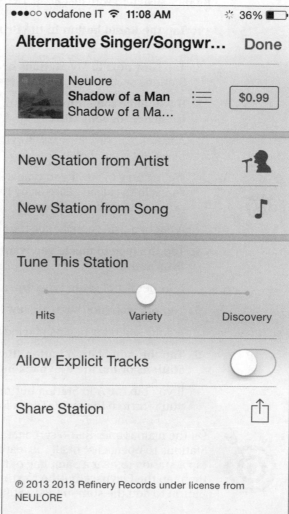

Figure 3-4: Use the playing song or artist as the basis for your favorite station.

✓ **Allow Explicit Tracks:** Tap on or off to include or exclude songs that use explicit language.

✓ **Share Station:** Tap to open the Share Sheet and let others know about the station either with AirDrop, a message, or a social network.

Adding new stations

Besides creating new stations based on a song or artist you like and are listening to, you can also create a station based on a genre you like. When you have different stations on iTunes Radio, you can hear the kind of music you're in the mood to listen to with just a tap. Here's how to add stations to My Stations:

1. **Tap the Radio button in the Browse bar of the Music app (refer to Figure 3-2).**

2. **Tap New next to My Stations or scroll down to the end of the My Stations section and tap the New Station button.**

3. **If you have something in mind, tap in the Search field and type an artist, genre, or song title.**

    A list of matches appears. Tap the one you want, and a station is created based on your choice.

    We're sorry to say if you type a specific song, that song doesn't play but songs in the same genre or by the same artist begin to play. And, like any radio, you can't replay a song.

    A list of music genres appears.

4. **Tap the type of music you want to hear — for example, Classic Alternative.**

    Another list of genre types opens.

5. **Tap one you like, such as New Wave, under Classic Alternative.**

    A song sampling begins playing in the genre you chose.

6. **Tap the Add Station button (the plus sign) to put that station in My Stations or tap the Playback button on the left to stop playback.**

    If you tap the Add Station button, the current sample begins playing and you return to the main iTunes Radio screen.

On the main iTunes Radio screen, tap the See All button next to Featured Stations to open a list of all the featured stations available. As with genres, tap a station to hear a sampling of the type of music that station plays, and then tap the Playback button to stop hearing samples or tap the Add Station button to add the station to My Stations and begin listening to that station.

Editing your stations

iTunes Radio lets you customize your stations in ways that make sense to you. Tap the Edit button on the Radio screen, and then do the following:

✔ To manage the station list, tap Edit (a second Edit button on the screen that opens) and then

- *Change the order of your station list:* Press and drag the reorder button to the right of the station name to move it up or down the list.

- *Delete a station:* Tap the red and white button to the left of the station name and then tap Delete, or without tapping Edit, drag across the station name and then tap Delete.

✔ To manage or delete a station, tap the station name. The screen shown in Figure 3-5 opens. Do the following:

- *Rename the station:* Tap in the Station Name field, tap the X at the right end of the field, and then type in a name that you like.

- *Tell your friends:* Tap the Share button to open the Share Sheet and spread the word about the station in the usual ways.

- *Customize your station:* In Play More Like This or Never Play This, tap Add Artist, Song, or Genre and then type in the artist, song, or genre you want to add to or avoid on this station. Your choices appear listed below each heading. Except for the first item in the Play More Like This section, you can swipe across your entries to delete them.

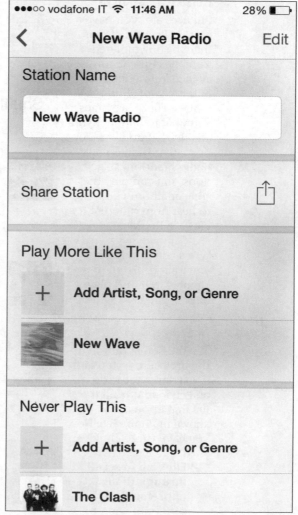

Figure 3-5: Customize your stations.

- *Delete the station:* Tap Delete Station at the bottom of the screen to eliminate it from your My Stations selections.

Tap the Back button to return to the My Stations list, and tap Done to return to the iTunes Radio screen in Music.

To see a list of what you've listened to or added to your wish list, tap the History button in the upper-left corner of the Radio screen. Your listening history is sorted by station, and tapping any song in the list plays a sample. You can purchase directly from the History list by tapping the price button.

Finding songs

Chances are, you have a great collection of music that you downloaded from the iTunes Store or synced from your computer to your iPhone via iTunes. There are times you want to listen to your absolutely familiar favorites rather than iTunes Radio's random selections. You can play the song or album you want to hear from different views in the Music app.

When you find the song you want to listen to, simply tap it and playback begins.

In Songs

Tap the Songs button in the Browse bar; tap More if you don't see it there, and choose it from the list that appears, as shown in Figure 3-6. Now you have three choices:

✔ **Flick up to scroll through the list until you find the song you want to hear.**

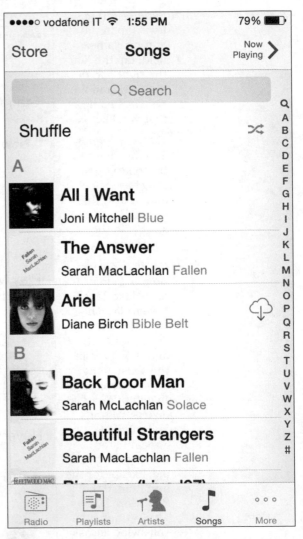

Figure 3-6: Songs shows an alphabetical list of all the songs on your iPhone.

✏ **Tap the letter of the first word of the song in the alphabet that runs down the right side of the screen.** *The, A,* and *An* don't count as first words.

✏ **Type the name of the song in the Search field at the top of the screen.** If you don't see the Search field, tap the Status bar at the very, very top of the screen or scroll the list down until you reach the top where the Search field resides.

In Artists

Tapping Artists in the Browse bar opens an alphabetical list of artists (refer to Figure 3-1), sorted by first name. Find the name of the artist you want by using the Search field or flicking through the list, or tapping the letter that corresponds to the artist's first name in the index that runs down the right side. The number of albums and songs by that artist in your Music collection appears beneath the artist's name. Tap the name of the artist to see a list of songs by that artist.

In Albums

Tapping Albums in the Browse bar opens a list of albums; tap More if you don't see it there, and choose it from the list that appears. Tap the album that has the song you want to hear, and you see a list of the songs on that album. The name of the artist and the album name appear to the right of the album cover image. The number of songs and album playing time are shown as well. The playing time for each song appears to the right of the song name.

With Search

From a screen in Music in any category (except Radio, which searches iTunes Radio rather than your music collection), you can open Search and look for a song, artist, or album. Scroll to the top of the screen or tap the Status bar and the Search field appears. Tapping in the Search field opens the keyboard. Begin typing the name of the artist, album, or song, and a list appears divided by category: artist, album, and song. The more letters you type, the narrower your search results. Search looks at all the words in a title, not just the first word, and gives you results for songs that are part of an album name that matches your search criteria. For example, search for "blue" and the results include all the songs on Joni Mitchell's album *Blue,* Diana Krall's version of the song "Almost Blue," as well as all the songs by the band Blue Sage, if you have those on your iPhone.

You can also search the iTunes Store: Scroll to the bottom of the result list to tap Continue Search in Store. The iTunes Store opens and displays songs, albums, and other media, such as audiobooks, ringtones, or movies that match your search words.

You can find media from outside Music, too. Open Spotlight Search by pulling down in the center of any Home screen, and type in a few letters or a word of the song or artist you seek. The results appear by app, so if a match is found in Music, it appears in the results list under the Music app.

Playing songs

When you find the song you want to hear, tap the song. The song begins playing and you see the Now Playing screen, as shown in Figure 3-7. If you have any other songs in your library that are from the same album, those subsequent songs play until they're finished or you tap the Pause button.

The main controls — Play/ Pause, Previous/Rewind, Next/Fast Forward, and Volume — are at the bottom of the screen.

- ✔ **Play/Pause:** Tap to begin playing the song or to pause. When the song is paused, it stays at that paused point even if you do other things on your iPhone. When you return to the song that was playing, it picks up where it left off.

- ✔ **Previous/Rewind:** Tap to jump to the beginning of the playing song, unless you're in the first three seconds of the song, in which case you jump to the previous song. The numbers above the album image tell you which song in the lineup you're listening to. Tap and hold to rewind.

- ✔ **Next/Fast Forward:** Tap to jump to the next song. Tap and hold to fast-forward the song you're listening to.

You can also fast-forward or rewind in a song by dragging the playhead (the red line on the bar) along the scrubber bar. Slide your finger down to use half-speed scrubbing or keep your finger on the scrubber bar for high-speed scrubbing.

Figure 3-7: The Now Playing screen shows the album cover of the song that's playing along with the Music controls.

When you tap a song from the Songs list, the Now Playing screen opens. The Previous and Next buttons take you to the song before or after the playing song in your songs list. Shuffle randomly plays all the songs in your songs list.

If you only want to hear songs from a specific album or a particular artist, tap the Album or Artist browse button and choose your first song from there. The Previous and Next buttons function within the limits of the album. Shuffle randomly plays the songs in that album. You see three buttons under the volume bar:

- ✔ **Repeat:** Tap to open a pop-up menu and choose Repeat Off, Repeat Song, which plays the same song continuously, or Repeat Artist, which plays consecutive songs by the same artist. Tap Cancel if you don't want to use the Repeat feature.

- ✔ **Create:** Tap to open a menu that lets you create a Genius Playlist, which is a playlist that goes well with the song you're listening to, or Create a New Station from Artist or Song in iTunes Radio. Tap Cancel if you touched the Create button when trying to pause the song. (If you don't see the Genius button, and you want to, open the Settings app, tap Music, and tap the Genius switch on.)

- ✔ **Shuffle:** Tap once and Music plays the songs of the album, playlist, or your entire song library in a random order (the button is highlighted and reads Shuffle All); tap again to turn off shuffle and hear the songs in the order they appear on the album or playlist (the button is white again). You can also shake your iPhone to Shuffle, unless you've deactivated that function in Music settings, which are explained a little later in this chapter.

Tap Repeat Artist and Shuffle together to hear the album, playlist, or your song library continuously in a random order.

The Back button at the top left of the screen returns you to the spot where you chose the song, which could be the album itself, the Songs list, the Artists list, and so on. You can also swipe to the right to go back.

The Track List button in the upper right switches between the Song Playing view, as shown in Figure 3-7, and the Album Playing view, as seen in Figure 3-8.

In the Album Playing view, you can assign a rating of one to five stars to each song. iTunes can then use your ratings to create a playlist based on your ratings (for example, a playlist of songs that have four or five stars). Red bars indicate the song that's playing. Tap Done to return to the Song Playing view.

Playing albums

You can go directly to an album by tapping Albums in the Browse bar (tap More in the Browse bar if you don't see it) and then choosing the album you want to hear from the list. Tap the first song and the album begins playing. You can also start the album from another song or tap the shuffle button to let Music choose a random playing order.

From the Now Playing screen, turning your iPhone to a horizontal position opens the Cover view. Flick from left to right to scroll through your album collection. Tap on an album cover to open the track list. Tap a song to begin playing. You can tap the Play/Pause button in the lower-left corner to use those two controls; however, you have to turn your iPhone to the vertical position to use the other playback controls.

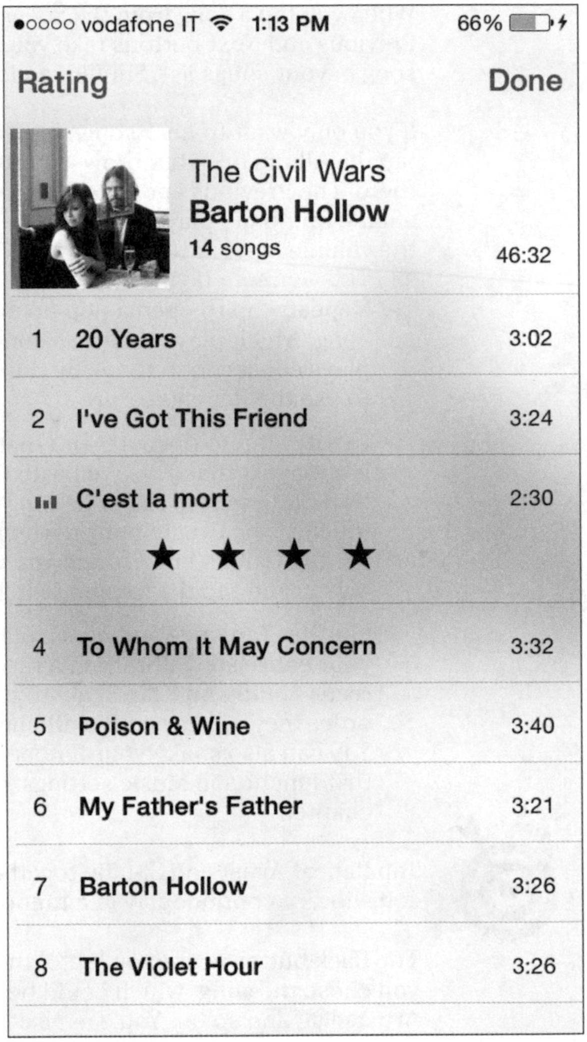

Playlists

Playlists are sort of like creating your own personal radio station that plays songs you like all the time. Oh, wait, isn't that iTunes Radio? Not quite, Playlists are limited to songs in your library;

Figure 3-8: The Album Playing view shows a list of the songs on the album and a rating for the song that's playing.

you mix and match the songs you want to listen to together, in the order you want to hear them, and save it to listen to again and again.

Tap the Playlists button in the Browse bar. The first two items in the list are Genius Playlist and Add Playlist. A playlist that iTunes creates for you using the music in your collection is a Genius playlist. A simple playlist is one you create yourself.

Creating Genius playlists

Make sure Genius is turned on in the Settings app under Music. To create a Genius playlist, you select a song and iTunes creates a playlist of 25 songs it thinks go well with the song you selected. To create a Genius playlist, follow these steps:

1. **Tap Playlists from the Browse bar.**

2. **Tap Genius Playlist.**

   If you don't see it, scroll to the top of the screen where Genius Playlist and New Playlist reside.

3. **Select the song you want iTunes to use as the basis for the playlist by tapping one of the browse buttons and scrolling through to find the song you want.**

4. **Tap the song you want to be the basis of the playlist.**

   You may see a message that says you don't have enough songs to make a playlist based on the song you chose.

   The Genius Playlist is created.

5. **Tap the playlist to see a list of songs it contains, as shown in Figure 3-9.**

6. **Tap the first song to begin playback.**

   The playlist plays until you pause the song.

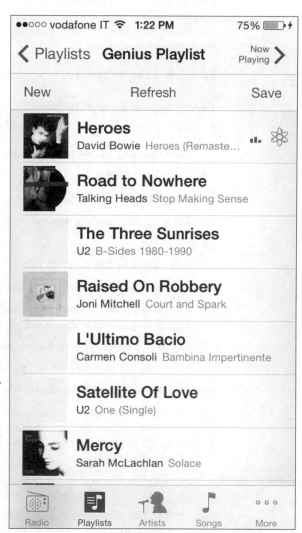

Figure 3-9: iTunes creates a Genius playlist based on a song you select; the Genius Playlist screen shows the songs in the playlist.

7. **Tap Save to save the playlist; it's given the name of the song you based it on.**

The name of the playlist is the name of the song you chose at the beginning. It appears at the top of the playlist list and the Genius icon is next to the name.

If you add more songs to your iTunes collection, you can update an existing Genius playlist. Tap the playlist to open it, and then tap the Refresh button. iTunes looks at your content and creates an updated playlist that may include songs you've added since the playlist was created, if any of those new songs meet the criteria of the old playlist.

To delete a Genius playlist, tap the playlist and then tap the Delete button.

Creating your own playlist

If you already have a playlist in mind, you can create it yourself:

1. **Tap Playlists in the Browse bar.**

2. **Tap Add Playlist.**

   A New Playlist box appears.

3. **Type a name for your playlist in the field.**

4. **Tap Save.**

5. **Tap Songs in the Browse Bar.**

6. **Tap the songs you want in your playlist.**

   After a song is selected, it's dimmed so you don't select it twice. You can also go to other views such as artist or album to choose songs.

7. **Tap Done when you're happy with your selections.**

   Your playlist appears on the screen.

8. **Tap the Edit button to do the following, as shown in Figure 3-10:**

   - Touch and drag the reorder buttons up and down to move the songs around in the order you want to play them. You can also let Music randomly reorder the sequence by playing the playlist with the Shuffle button.

   - Tap the red and white minus sign next to a song you want to delete and then tap the Delete button.

   - Tap the plus sign to add more songs. The songs list opens and you select songs to add as in the initial steps.

9. **Tap Done when you finish.**

10. **Tap the first song to begin playing your playlist or tap the Shuffle button to hear the playlist in a random order.**

If you want to change or delete your playlist at a later time, tap the playlist and follow Step 8 in the preceding list to add, delete, or reorder songs. Tap

Clear to clear the songs on the playlist and start over with the same title. Tap Delete to eliminate the playlist entirely. You can also swipe across a playlist in the Playlists list and tap the Delete button that appears.

Playlists created on your computer, including Smart Playlists, and those created on your iPhone are synced one to the other the next time you perform a sync if you sync your entire music library or choose to sync selected playlists.

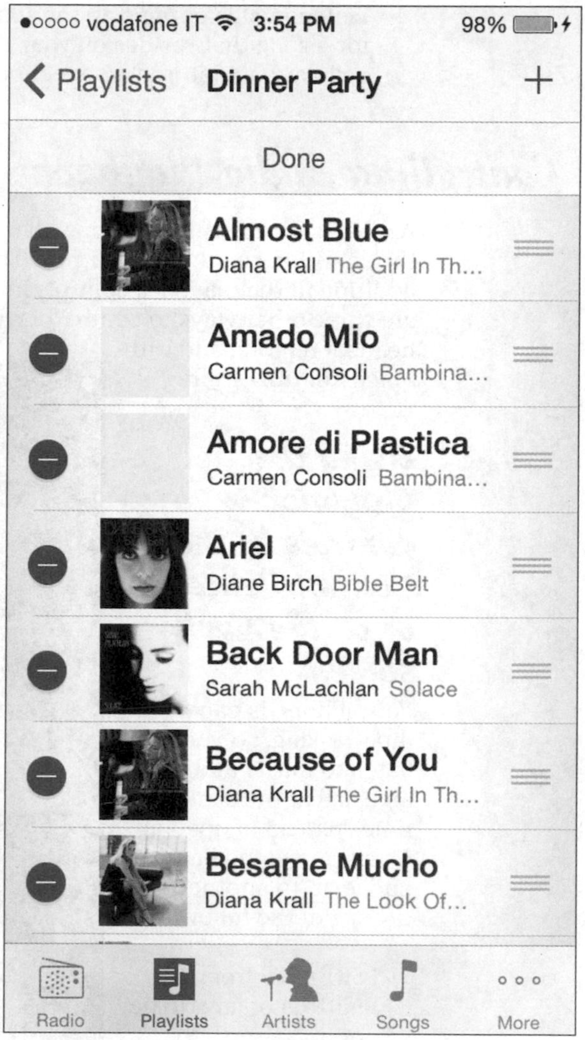

Keeping music in the cloud

One of the ways to free up storage space on your iPhone is to delete media such as songs from the Music app or video from the Videos app — but that doesn't mean you can't enjoy your music.

Media that you purchase from the iTunes Store, and/or songs you match with iTunes Match, remain with your iTunes

Figure 3-10: You can edit playlists you create.

account forever. Open the Settings app and tap iTunes & App Store. In the Show All section, tap the Music switch on. Even after you remove a song from your iPhone, the song titles appear in Music, but you see the Download button (the cloud with the downward-pointing arrow; refer to Figure 3-6) next to them. You have two options for listening to the song:

✔ **Put it back on your iPhone:** Tap the Download button and the song is stored on your iPhone anew.

✔ **Listen in streaming:** Tap the song to begin playback, just as you would for a song that resides on your iPhone. As long as you have a Wi-Fi or cellular data Internet connection, the song begins to play.

Controlling Audio Playback

As with so many things iPhone, there are multiple ways and places to access the same information or controls. The playback controls are no exception. In addition to the playback controls in Music on the Now Playing screen, there are three other ways to control playback: from the Control Center, using the headset remote, and with Voice Control or Siri.

Using the playback controls in the Control Center or on the Lock screen

Your iPhone is capable of multitasking, so you can listen to music and write an email at the same time. Instead of opening Music and going back and forth to another app, try one of the following:

✔ Swipe up from the bottom of any Home or app screen to open the Control Center. Adjust the volume and use the Rewind, Pause/Play, and Fast Forward buttons.

✔ Wake your iPhone by pressing the Home button or Sleep/ Wake button and adjust the playback controls, as shown in Figure 3-11.

Figure 3-11: The playback controls on the Lock screen.

Using the headset remote to control playback

You likely listen to music or other media with the headset or EarPods that came with your iPhone. Both have a microphone and a center button that you press to answer incoming calls and up and down buttons to control the volume of the incoming call. These three buttons control playback when you're listening to audio. Here's how to use them:

- **Volume:** Press the up or down buttons to increase or decrease the volume.

- **Pause:** Press the center button; press again to resume playing.

- **Next song:** Press the center button twice quickly.

- **Fast-forward:** Press the center button twice quickly and hold.

- **Previous song:** Press the center button three times quickly during the first few seconds of a song to go back one song or return to the beginning of the playing song if more than a few seconds have passed.

- **Rewind:** Press the center button three times quickly and hold.

If someone calls while you're listening to something, your iPhone rings both in the headset and from iPhone's speaker, unless you have the Silent/Ring button switched to Silent, in which case it just rings in the headset. You have these command options:

- **Answer the call:** Press the center button.

- **Decline the call:** Press and hold the center button for a couple seconds; two low beeps indicate you successfully declined the call.

- **Hang up:** Press the center button. After you hang up, the music or audio you were listening to resumes playing where you were before the call came in.

You can listen to music through a Bluetooth headset or speaker that you've paired with your iPhone. (Refer to Book I, Chapter 2 for Bluetooth pairing.) If the headset has volume buttons, you can adjust the volume with them. To listen to music with the iPhone speaker or another device, open the Control Center and tap the AirPlay button under Music, as shown in Figure 3-12; tap the device you want to use.

Listening to music with AirPlay

You can connect your iPhone to Wi-Fi and Bluetooth-enabled devices, such as speakers and headsets. With AirPlay-enabled devices (such as the Denon AVR-991 stereo), the connection is automatic. You can choose to broadcast music from your iPhone to speakers in different rooms of your house. You can also use AirPlay to stream audio to an AppleTV or to speakers that are connected to an AirPort Express Wi-Fi router. Follow these steps to set up AirPlay:

1. **Open the Music app.**

2. **Open the song, album, or podcast you want to hear to see the playback screen.**

3. **Tap the AirPlay button.**

4. **Choose the speakers you want from the list.**

   If the speakers don't appear on the list of AirPlay devices, check that both your iPhone and speakers are on the same wireless network.

5. **Tap the Play button.**

   The music plays on the speakers you've chosen.

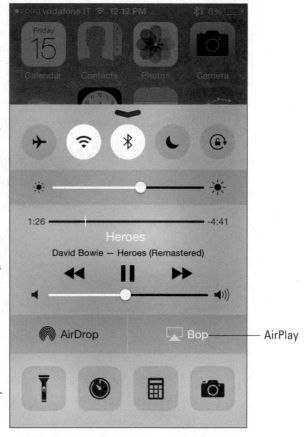

AirPlay

Figure 3-12: Use a Bluetooth device to listen to Music.

6. **To switch back to play on your iPhone, tap the AirPlay button again and then choose iPhone.**

If your speakers or stereo aren't specifically AirPlay-enabled but do support Wi-Fi or Bluetooth, you can connect them to your iPhone through the Control Center or Wi-Fi or Bluetooth in the Settings app.

Using Siri to control playback

We think Siri is great, especially when used along with the headset for an almost hands-free command center. Remember to speak slowly and clearly. If you find that Siri misunderstands you, try moving to an area with less ambient noise. If you still have problems, turn your iPhone off, wait a few seconds, and then turn it back on. To control playback with Siri, follow these steps:

1. **Press and hold the Home button until you hear a beep or Siri asks how she can help you.**

   If you're wearing the headset, press and hold the center button until you hear the beep, and then speak the commands.

2. **Say one of the following commands:**

   - "Play" or "Play Music" or "Play Station"

   - "Pause" or "Pause Music"

   - "Next Song" or "Previous Song"

   - "Play album/artist/playlist," and then say the name of the album, artist, or playlist you want to hear

   - "Shuffle" to shuffle the playlist or album that's playing

   - "Genius" or "Play more like this" or "Play more songs like this" to create a Genius playlist

   - Ask "What's playing?," "What song is this?," "Who sings this song?," or "Who is this song by?" to hear information about the song you're listening to

     Siri recognizes music playing in the background, too, and you can ask the same types of questions to identify the song that's playing.

   - "Cancel" or "Stop" to pause the song that's playing

Siri works when you have either a Wi-Fi or cellular data connection. When these are unavailable, you can turn Siri off in the Settings app and use Voice Control to command the Music app.

You can use the Clock app's Timer feature to set music to play for a certain amount of time and you can choose a song as your alarm in Clock's Alarm feature. See Book III, Chapter 2 to learn how to do both.

Customizing Music's Settings

You control a few of your listening options in Settings. These options affect everything in Music, not just one individual song. Tap Settings on the Home screen and then scroll down to tap Music. Consider these options:

✔ **Shake to Shuffle:** Just shake your iPhone to immediately change the current song.

✔ **Sound Check:** Often media from different sources plays back at different volume levels. Sound Check corrects so that everything plays at the same volume, saving you from turning the volume up and down with each media change.

✔ **EQ:** Tap to open a list of equalizer settings. Choose one that is best associated with the type of media you listen to most. You may have to try a few different ones to see which you like best.

Music, in general, drains the battery faster than some other common iPhone uses such as making phone calls and texting, or even reading an e-book, and EQ drains the battery a bit faster than the usual Music battery consumption.

The Late Night EQ setting lowers the loudest parts of what you're listening to and amplifies the quieter parts so you can listen on speakers and create less disturbance. When you use the headset, this setting improves the sound in areas with a lot of ambient noise, such as an airplane.

✔ **Volume Limit:** Tap to set a limit to how high your headphone volume can reach.

✔ **Lyrics & Podcast Info:** If this setting is on, any lyrics or podcast information available from iTunes is displayed when you tap the album cover or image on the Now Playing screen.

✔ **Group by Album Artist:** By default, this option is on and it groups artists by the information listed under Album Artist instead of information in the Artist field.

✔ **Show All Music:** Songs on your iPhone as well as those in iTunes in the Cloud appear in Music so you know what's available locally and remotely. When off, you only see songs that are stored on your iPhone.

✔ **Genius:** Tap on to enable Music to create Genius playlists.

✔ **iTunes Match:** This is a paid subscription ($24.95/year) where iCloud stores up to 25,000 music tracks along with playlists you have in iTunes on your computer.

✔ **Home Sharing:** Listen to music from your computer on your iPhone, if both are connected to the same network. In iTunes on your computer, choose File➪Home Sharing and sign in with your Apple ID. On your iPhone, type in your Apple ID and password in the Home Sharing section of the Music screen in the Settings app. In the Music app, tap More in the Browse bar and then tap Shared and tap the name of your computer. (You won't see the Shared option if iTunes isn't open on your computer or if your iPhone is connected to your computer.) Use the Music controls as you would for music on your iPhone. Tap More, tap Shared, and tap My iPhone to return to your music collection there.

Playing Audiobooks

The Music app isn't just for listening to music any more than the iTunes Store is just for buying tunes. You can download entire books on your iPhone and listen at your leisure. If you stop in the middle, when you open the book again, you pick up listening where you left off.

When a file is larger than 50MB, you have to connect to a Wi-Fi network or download the file to your computer and then sync.

To play an audiobook, the procedure is the same as for songs:

1. **Open the Music app.**

2. **Tap More, and then tap Audiobooks, which only appears if you have downloaded or synced audiobooks to your iPhone or are accessing them through Home Sharing.**

3. **Tap the item you want to listen to.**

   A list of the audiobook chapters appears.

4. **Tap the chapter you want to hear.**

   The audiobook begins playing and you see the Now Playing screen.

5. **The playback controls — Previous/Rewind, Play/Pause, Next/Fast-Forward, and the scrubber bar — are the same as for songs. The commands below the scrubber bar are slightly different:**

   • *Repeat:* Functions the same way as for music.

   • *15-second repeat/fast-forward:* Tap to replay the last 15 seconds or move ahead 15 seconds.

   • *Playback Speed:* Tap to change the speed — 1X is normal (the button is white), 1/2X plays at half speed, and 2X plays at twice the speed (both are orange).

Listening to Podcasts

If you like talk radio, documentaries, or the comedy hour or are just the curious type, you're going to love podcasts. The Podcasts app combines storefront, subscription and library management, and playback for audio and video podcasts. Dive into the next few pages to learn about finding, subscribing, and enjoying the world of podcasts.

Finding podcasts

If you have podcasts in iTunes and synced them with your iPhone, you find them in the Podcasts app Library and can skip ahead to the next section to learn about the playback controls. If you don't have any podcasts or want to add more to your library, follow these steps:

1. **Open the Podcasts app, and then tap Featured.**

   The Podcasts Catalog opens, as shown in Figure 3-13. If you've browsed or shopped at any of the Apple media stores, it will look familiar to you.

2. **Find a podcast that interests you by tapping one of the following:**

   - *Tabs:* Tap All to see selections for both audio and video podcasts; tap Audio or Video to narrow your choices by delivery type.

   - *Banners:* Tap an ad that interests you when it appears at the top of the screen.

   - *Buttons:* Scroll horizontally through a section, such as New & Noteworthy or tap See All to see a complete list for the section; scroll down to see more advertised podcasts and sections.

   - *Categories:* Tap to open a list of categories and then tap a category to see a list of podcasts in that category. Some categories have subcategories to help you find what you specifically seek.

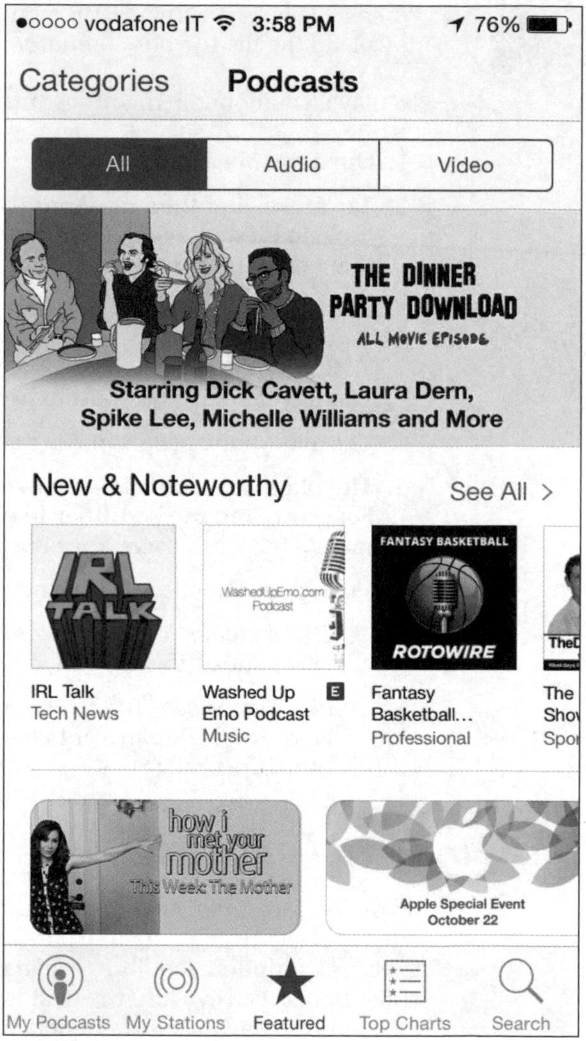

   Figure 3-13: Search for podcasts in the Podcasts app.

   - *Top Charts:* Tap the button in the Browse bar to see the top podcasts divided by audio and video, which you can narrow by tapping through the Categories list.

   - *Search:* Tap Search, and then type a search word or two to find something you like.

3. **Tap a podcast that interests you, and the Info screen opens, as shown in Figure 3-14.**

Here you can do the following:

- *Tap Subscribe* to subscribe to the entire podcast series. As new episodes are added, they appear in My Podcasts.

- *Tap the download button (the downward-pointing arrow)* next to a single episode. Some podcasts download immediately so you can listen to it later; others launch the podcast player. You can immediately listen to it as it streams.

If you want to hear other podcasts in the series and make sure you don't miss upcoming episodes, tap the Subscribe button. Most subscriptions and their relative podcasts are free, although some paid programming has

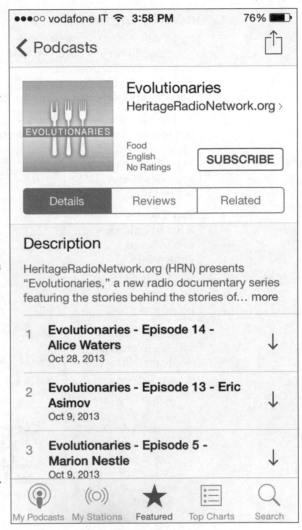

Figure 3-14: Subscribe to podcasts from the Info screen.

been added, and you can listen to downloaded podcasts offline.

- *Tap Reviews* to read reviews and add your own. You can also Like the podcast on Facebook from the Reviews screen.

- *Tap Related* to see other podcasts that are similar.

- *Tap the Share button (in the upper right)* to share a link to the podcast via AirDrop, Mail, Messages, Twitter, or Facebook, or copy the link to another app of your choice.

4. **Tap the back button in the upper left to return to the main Podcasts screen.**

Podcast playback

After you subscribe to one or more podcasts, the subscription is stored in your podcast library, where you manage and listen to them. Follow these steps to play back a podcast:

1. **Tap the My Podcasts button in the Browse bar.**

   Your podcast library appears as in Figure 3-15. Tap the Grid or List button to change the view (tap the Status bar if you don't see them). The number tells you how many unplayed episodes of that series you have.

2. **Tap a series to see a list of episodes, as shown in Figure 3-16.**

   You can do the following, from top to bottom of the screen:

   • *Tap the series title* to read a description.

   • *Tap the Share button* to share a link to the podcast via AirDrop, Mail, Messages, Facebook, or Twitter, or copy and paste the link in another app.

   • *Tap the Unplayed tab* to see a list of episodes you have yet to hear.

   • *Tap the Feed tab* to see a list of previous episodes.

   • *Tap the Info button* to read a description of the episode.

Figure 3-15: Manage podcast subscriptions in your Library.

- *Tap the Download button (the cloud with an arrow)* to download the episode to your library. You won't see the Download button if the episode is already downloaded.

- *Tap the episode (in the Unplayed or Feed list)* to begin listening.

The blue dot to the left of the episode indicates you heard the episode. A half blue dot indicates you began listening but didn't finish. A speaker means you're listening to the episode.

3. **The playback controls appear as shown in Figure 3-17, which shows audio playback controls (video playback controls have similar functions):**

   - *Play/pause button:* Does just that.

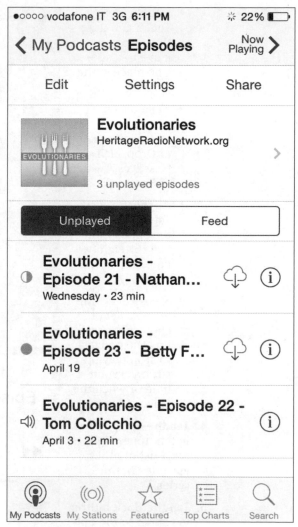

Figure 3-16: See episodes in different states of listening.

   - *Previous/Rewind:* Tap in the first few seconds of the podcast and you go to the previous episode. After that, tap once to return to the beginning; tap and hold to rewind.

   - *Rewind 15 seconds:* Goes back 15 seconds.

   - *Go forward 15 seconds:* Jumps ahead in the recording by 15 seconds.

   - *Next/Fast-Forward:* Tap to go to the next episode; tap and hold to fast forward.

   - *Volume slider:* Drag left and right to lower or increase the volume.

- *Scrubber bar:* Touch and drag the purple line to move to a specific place in the playback.

- *Share button:* Send a link to the episode via AirDrop, Mail, Messages, Twitter, or Facebook.

- *Playback Speed:* Tap to change the speed from half through two times the normal speed.

- *Sleep Timer:* Tap to see a list of choices for setting the podcast to stop playing after a certain time or when the episode ends.

4. **Tap the episode list in the upper right to see a list of other episodes in the series.**

5. **Tap the Back button to return to the episode list for this podcast on your iPhone.**

Figure 3-17: The playback controls appear while you're listening.

6. **Tap Featured, Top Charts, or Search to find more podcasts.**

 If your iPhone is filling up with podcasts and you want to delete some, tap Edit on the opening screen of My Podcasts and then tap the X in the upper-left corner to delete a podcast and the contained episodes. To delete episodes singly, open the podcast, tap the Unplayed tab, and then tap Edit. Tap the circle next to the episode(s) you want to eliminate, and then tap the Delete button.

Podcast settings

There are settings for individual podcast series and for the Podcasts app. To open settings for a series, tap the My Podcasts tab in the Browse bar. Tap the series icon, and then tap the Settings button (tap the Status bar or flick down if you don't see it). Here you can manage your subscription settings for specific podcast series, as shown in Figure 3-18. Make the following choices for the series:

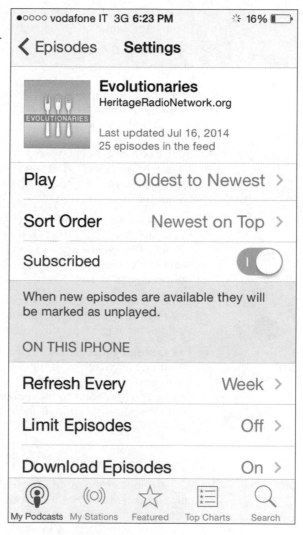

- ✔ **Play:** Choose to hear multiple podcasts from oldest to newest or vice versa.

- ✔ **Sort Order:** Choose how you want to see episodes: oldest or newest at the top of the list.

The following choices are found in in two places: within the series (where they apply only to the series) and within the Settings app under Podcasts; changes made in Settings apply to all podcasts you subscribe to.

Figure 3-18: Manage subscription settings on a podcast by podcast basis.

- ✔ **Refresh Every:** Set the default for how often you want to refresh the episodes of podcasts you subscribe to.

- ✔ **Limit Episodes:** When this option is set to All or Most Recent, either all episodes or the most recent episodes will be automatically downloaded when you subscribe to a new podcast.

✔ **Download Episodes:** When on, episodes will be downloaded so you can listen later; when off, you listen to episodes in streaming.

✔ **Delete Played Episodes:** Choose to keep or delete episodes after you hear them.

While you find the four previous settings in both the series and app settings, the following settings are found only in the Settings app under Podcasts and apply to all podcasts you subscribe to.

✔ **Sync Podcasts:** You may want to turn this on if you listen to podcasts on different devices. That way, you'll find the same subscriptions and episodes on your iPhone, iPad, or iPod touch or Mac or Windows computer.

✔ **Podcast Defaults:** If you want to treat all your podcast subscriptions in the same way, rather than change the settings one by one, you can set defaults that will be applied to all subscriptions. The options are the same as detailed previously for Refresh Every, Limit Episodes, Download Episodes, and Delete Played Episodes.

If you do want different settings for some subscriptions, set the defaults first (within the Settings app under Podcasts) then go in and change the settings for single, specific podcast subscriptions.

✔ **Use Cellular Data:** This setting uses your cellular data service for streaming playback or to download episodes to which you have activated automatic download. If you have a limit to your cellular data usage, you may want to leave this switch in the off position. In that case, your episodes are automatically downloaded only when you have a Wi-Fi connection.

Podcast stations

Podcast stations group up to four podcasts together. Podcasts builds two default stations: Most Recent and All Unplayed. When you subscribe to a podcast, episodes are added to these stations automatically. However, you can also create custom stations — for example, you could create an Arts station, and then subscribe to up to four art-oriented podcasts or even include single episodes you downloaded. First, find and subscribe to podcasts, or download episodes, you want on your station, and then do the following:

1. **Tap My Stations in the Browse bar.**

2. **Tap New Station, and type in a name when the New Station dialog opens, and then tap Save.**

   The list of your podcasts appears.

3. **Tap the podcasts you want to include, as shown in Figure 3-19, and then tap Done.**

4. **You see the new station on the My Stations list.**

Tap On-The-Go in the My Stations list and create a custom playlist by adding single episodes you want to download and listen to later.

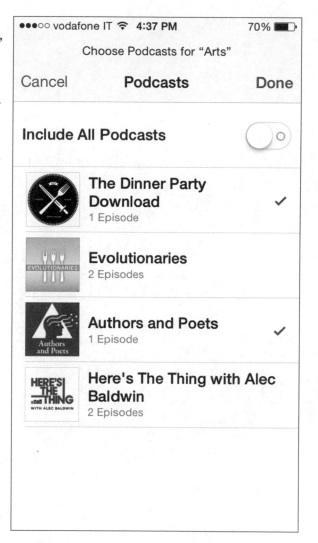

●●●○○ vodafone IT 🛜 4:37 PM   70% 🔋

Choose Podcasts for "Arts"

Cancel   **Podcasts**   Done

Include All Podcasts   ⚪

The Dinner Party Download   ✓
1 Episode

Evolutionaries
2 Episodes

Authors and Poets   ✓
1 Episode

Here's The Thing with Alec Baldwin
2 Episodes

Figure 3-19: Use My Stations to create custom listening "channels."

Chapter 4: Recording, Editing, and Watching Videos

In This Chapter

- ✔ Controlling playback
- ✔ Recording video with Camera
- ✔ Trimming video in Photos
- ✔ Slowing down the action
- ✔ Editing trailers and movies in iMovie
- ✔ Sharing your production

Your iPhone is great not only for watching movies, TV shows, and videos but also for creating your own movies. Whether it's to record an amateur sporting event or produce a full-length film, your iPhone has the capacity to capture, edit, and share videos that are limited only by your imagination.

In this chapter, we focus on onscreen action — specifically, watching videos you download and producing your own digital masterpieces. First, we review getting video onto your iPhone; then we give details of the video controls of the Videos app, and how to hook up your iPhone to a television so you can watch your videos on a bigger screen. We show you how to capture video with the Camera app — including slow-motion and time-lapsed video — and then trim it in Photos or create a full-blown movie, complete with trailer, in iMovie. Aaaannnd . . . action!

Getting and Watching Videos on Your iPhone

We use the term *video* as a generic term to mean a multimedia file, which combines audio with moving images. Video can be a music video, a movie, a television show, a podcast, a home movie, or pretty much anything that you watch, and you can watch most of them on your iPhone.

The first thing you have to do is get the video to your iPhone. You have several ways to do that:

- ✒ **Camera app:** Make a video directly on your iPhone, and then watch it in the Photos app on your iPhone. We explain how to do both in this chapter.

- ✒ **iTunes Store/Podcast Catalog/iTunes U:** Download a rented or purchased video from the iTunes Store, a video podcast, or an iTunes U lecture on your iPhone. See Chapter 2 of this minibook for the complete iTunes Store shopping guide. You watch video podcasts in the Podcasts app, which we talk about in Chapter 3 of this minibook.

    You need a Wi-Fi connection to download movies, television shows, and other videos if they're 50MB or larger — small videos can, and will, download over the 3G or 4G/LTE networks.

- ✒ **Streaming:** Watch a video directly from the Internet using Safari or another video app, such as Netflix or Hulu.

- ✒ **Your computer:** Watch video on your iPhone from your computer with Home Sharing or sync the videos on your computer to your iPhone via iTunes as explained in Book I, Chapter 5.

Your iPhone supports H.264 video up to 720 pixels (known as 720p video) and MPEG-4, part 10 video at 640 by 480 pixels, both at 30 frames per second with stereo audio in M4V, MP4, and MOV file formats. Motion JPEG (9M-JPEG) is supported at 1,280 x 720 pixels with stereo audio in AVI format.

If you copy a video to your iPhone and it doesn't open automatically, chances are, it isn't in one of the supported formats. To see the format of a video you synced from iTunes, open iTunes on your computer and click Movies, TV Shows, Podcasts, or iTunes U button in the toolbar, and then click the video you want information about. Choose File➪Get Info. Click the File tab; the video format is shown next to Kind.

To save the video in an iPhone-readable format, click once on the video in the list in iTunes. Choose File➪Create New Version➪Create iPod or iPhone Version. The file is saved in the MPEG-4 format with the same name as the original, so you'll want to rename it so that when you sync the file to your iPhone, you sync the one in the correct video format. (To rename the file, click the name. When it's highlighted, type in a new name or add something like "iP" to the filename, so you know it's iPhone's version.)

If you have a video that iTunes can't handle, you can try converting the file with a video transcoder utility on your computer such as HandBrake (www. handbrake.fr).

Controlling playback

After you have a video on your iPhone or as soon as you begin downloading from the iTunes Store, open the Videos app, and then tap the button in the Browse bar for the type of video you want to watch: Movie, Rentals, or TV Shows (you only see the categories in which you have media). If you have Home Sharing turned on, which we explain in the section "Streaming from your computer to your iPhone," later in this chapter, you also see a Shared button, as shown in Figure 4-1. Tap the video you want to watch.

Tap the video you want to watch and an information screen opens. Tap the Details tab to see a detailed description about the video, or tap the Related tab to see similar videos. Tapping a related video opens the iTunes Store to information about that item. Tap a TV show and you see a list of episodes you have. The number on the TV show button in the TV Shows screen indicates the number of episodes you have. There's also an option to show the complete season. When you tap that option, episodes you don't have appear on the list; you can purchase them directly by tapping the price button, as shown in Figure 4-2.

Tap the Play button to start the video. Even if it's still downloading you can begin watching. Most videos display in landscape view — the exception being if the video was recorded on an iPhone or iPad in portrait view.

Figure 4-1: See the assortment of videos on your iPhone from the Videos app.

Initially, you see the playback controls on the screen, which disappear after about six seconds. To open the playback controls, tap the screen; tap the screen again to hide them. Refer to Figure 4-3 for the controls explained here, from top to bottom:

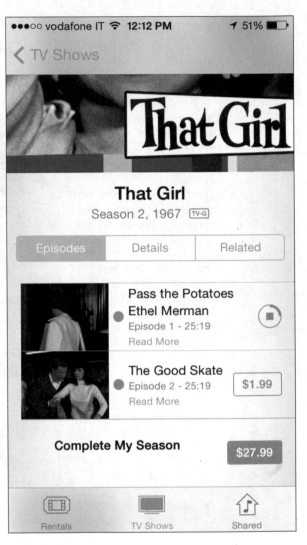

Figure 4-2: Get more details about the video from the information screen.

✔ **Done:** Tap when you want to stop watching and return to the Videos list. If you stop watching before a video is finished, when you start again, it picks up where you left off. You can also press the Home button to stop watching and return to the Home screen.

✔ **Playtime Scrubber Bar:** The time on the left is the time the video has played; the time on the right is the time remaining. Drag the white ball, known as the playhead, right and left on the scrubber bar to move forward and backward in the video. Slide your finger down as you drag the playhead to adjust the speed at which the video moves.

✔ **Volume Scrubber Bar:** Drag the white ball on the volume scrubber bar to raise or lower the volume. You can also use the volume buttons on the side of your iPhone.

✔ **Rewind:** Tap and hold to rewind; tap once to return to the beginning of the episode. If you're watching a movie that has chapters, tap twice to go back one chapter.

✔ **Play/Pause:** Tap to pause the video and tap again to resume playback.

✔ **Fast-forward:** Tap and hold to fast-forward; tap twice to go to the next chapter.

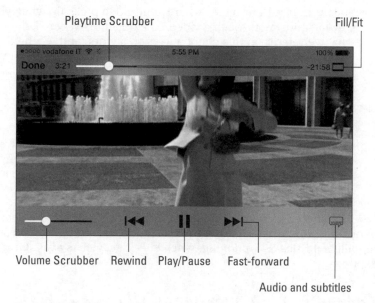

Figure 4-3: The video playback controls.

If you're wearing the EarPods that came with your iPhone, you can use the volume buttons on the microphone. You can also press twice on the center part to skip to the next chapter, or three times to go back a chapter.

You see a few control buttons only under certain circumstances:

✔ **Fill/Fit:** Tap the Fill/Fit button to toggle between two ways you can view video:

 • **Fit:** Choose Fit to see videos in their original aspect ratio, although you'll see black vertical or horizontal bands, called *pillarboxing* and *letterboxing,* respectively, depending on the ratio at which the original video was captured.

 • **Fill:** Choose Fill to fill the whole iPhone screen but lose some of the edges of the original version.

✔ **Audio and Subtitles:** Some movies have subtitle or language options. This button appears when they're available. Tap to see your options.

✔ **Audio Output:** Set the output device you want to use to view your video on another monitor.

Video settings

You have control over a few Video settings. Tap Settings on the Home screen and then tap Videos. These are your options:

- ✓ **Start Playing:** Determines where your video picks up when you stop viewing midway through a video. The default is Where Left Off, and it's what we refer to in this chapter — stop a video and when you restart, you pick up where you left off. The other choice is to start a video from the beginning when you restart. Tap Start Playing and check From Beginning if you prefer that choice.

- ✓ **Show All Videos:** Tap the switch on to see both videos that are downloaded to your iPhone and those that are stored in iCloud.

- ✓ **Home Sharing:** Sign in with your Apple ID and password to stream video from iTunes on your computer to your iPhone. See the section "Streaming from your computer to your iPhone," later in this chapter, for more information about Home Sharing.

You can turn on closed captioning and SDH (subtitles for the deaf and hard of hearing) in the Settings app by tapping General, tapping Accessibility, and tapping Subtitles & Captioning. When either service is available, you see captions.

Connecting to a monitor or TV via a cable

Your iPhone, especially if you have a version with 32GB or 64GB of memory, is a portable video warehouse, and the larger screen and Retina display on the iPhone 5 and later make watching a pleasure. Nonetheless, watching a documentary about the Himalayas on your iPhone really can't match the thrill of sweeping views that a large-screen monitor or television offers. You can watch the movies and TV shows — slide shows of photos, too — that are stored on your iPhone, on your iPhone, or you can connect your iPhone to a television or monitor and enjoy them on a bigger screen.

To attach your iPhone to a television, monitor, or projector, you need one of the following cables:

- ✓ **Lightning Digital AV Adapter (iPhone 5 or later) or Apple 30-pin Digital AV Adapter (iPhone 4s):** Use this adapter to connect your iPhone to an HDMI cable (sold separately) connected to your HDTV, video projection screen, or other HDMI-compatible device.

- ✓ **Lightning to VGA Adapter (iPhone 5 or later) or Apple 30-pin to VGA Adapter (iPhone 4s):** This adapter, along with a VGA cable (sold separately) connects your iPhone to your VGA TV, projector, or monitor.

- ✓ **Apple Composite AV Cable (iPhone 4s or earlier):** This connects your iPhone to your television's composite port. Older TVs usually have composite connections.

To play your movie or television show:

1. **Connect the cable to both your iPhone and your television or monitor.**

2. **On your TV, select the input device.**

   Refer to the instruction booklet for your TV if you don't know how to do this.

3. **Play the video from the Videos app as you normally would on your iPhone.**

   You see the images on your TV.

Playing video with AirPlay

You can stream video and images from the Internet across your iPhone and onto your TV if you have an AirPlay-enabled device or Apple TV. To play video wirelessly using AirPlay, follow these steps:

1. **Open the Videos app.**

2. **Open the video you want to watch.**

3. **Tap the AirPlay button.**

4. **Choose Apple TV from the list.**

   If Apple TV (or whatever you named your device) doesn't appear on the list of AirPlay devices, check that both your iPhone and Apple TV are on the same wireless network.

5. **Tap the Play button.**

   The video plays on your television.

6. **To switch back to play on your iPhone, tap the AirPlay button again and then choose iPhone.**

You can connect to a monitor or use AirPlay to play slide shows and videos from the Photos app by following the same steps.

Streaming from your computer to your iPhone

If you have a video stored on iTunes on your computer and you'd like to watch it on your iPhone, you can access the video with Home Sharing. You have to have iTunes 10.2 or later and both the computer and your iPhone have to be on the same Wi-Fi network. You also need an Apple ID and password. Follow these instructions:

1. **On your computer, in iTunes, choose File⇨Home Sharing⇨Turn On Home Sharing.**

2. **Enter your Apple ID and password, and then click Create Home Share.**

3. **On your iPhone, open the Settings app and tap Video.**

4. **In the Home Sharing section, type the same Apple ID and password.**

   You see Home Sharing only if you have an active Wi-Fi connection.

5. **Open the Videos app and tap Shared in the Browse bar.**

   The Shared screen opens with two choices: My iPhone and your Home Sharing username.

   You can use the same Home Sharing ID on several computers so the whole family — or you and your roommates — can share the movies in your libraries.

6. **Tap your username.**

   A list of the videos stored on your computer appears on your iPhone.

7. **Tap the video you want to watch and follow the previous instructions for playback control.**

8. **To return to the content on your iPhone, tap Shared and then tap My iPhone.**

Streaming media is when whatever you're watching or listening to is stored somewhere else, as opposed to being stored on your iPhone. The media plays as it comes across the local network or from the Internet and isn't saved or stored on your iPhone.

If Family Sharing is on, you can access the movies, TV shows, and video that other family members have purchased from iTunes. Go to the iTunes Store and tap More in the Browse bar. Tap Purchased and then tap the name of the family member whose purchases you want to access. Tap the video you want to download or play in streaming, and it begins playback as explained earlier. See Book I, Chapter 5 to learn how to set up Family Sharing.

Shooting Video with Camera

Watching movies and TV shows on your iPhone is fun, but there's nothing like the satisfaction of making your own video and then watching and sharing it with people you know.

iPhone 4s and later shoots video in high definition, up to 1920 x 1080 pixels (also known as 1080p) and 30 frames-per-second. This means you can make smooth, clear full-motion videos. Each video can be up to an hour long, although one minute of video takes about 80MB of memory or close to 5GB for an hour of video. As we mention in the intro, the Camera app captures slow-motion and time-lapse video, too, which we tell you about here.

To capture video, follow these steps:

1. **Open the Camera app.**

2. **Swipe the screen to the right to highlight one of the video options:**

   - *Video:* Captures real-time action.

   - *Slo-Mo:* Captures video at a higher frames-per-second speed, which then allows you to play the video at a slower speed. While you're recording, the screen looks the same, and then when you edit the video, you choose the part(s) to play back in slow motion. Choose Slo-Mo before recording; we explain the editing part in the next section.

   - *Time-Lapse:* Captures action over a period of time and then plays it back at a faster rate. For example, slow-moving clouds fly across the sky in a time-lapse video.

If you plan to record for a long period of time — say, a sunset or melting wax — putting your iPhone on a stand or propping it up helps capture steady images.

3. **Point your iPhone at the action you want to capture.**

4. **Tap the Flash button (Video or Slo-Mo only) to the on or auto position if you're in a low-light setting.**

   You have to turn the flash on before you begin recording your video.

   Flash isn't an option in Time-Lapse mode but you can increase or decrease the exposure and brightness by tapping the screen before beginning to record and dragging the slider up or down.

5. **Tap the Record button, which is the red dot in place of the shutter button, or press one of the Volume buttons.**

   The Record button becomes a red square in a white circle. While the video is recording, a timer appears at the top of the screen, as shown in Figure 4-4.

   You see "120 FPS" below or next to the Record button when recording in Slo-Mo (refer to Figure 4-4).

6. **(Optional in Video or Slo-Mo) Tap the shutter button above or next to the Record button to take a still photo while you're shooting video.**

7. **(Optional in Video or Slo-Mo) Tap the screen to bring up the exposure and brightness slider; drag to make your video darker or brighter.**

8. **(Optional in Video or Slo-Mo) Pinch and spread to zoom in and out on your subject while recording.**

9. **Tap the Record button or press one of the Volume buttons to stop recording.**

You can also press the center button on iPhone's EarPods to start or stop recording.

A thumbnail of your video's key frame appears next to the Record button.

Figure 4-4: Capture video in the Camera app.

Tap the Switch button if you want to capture video with the front-facing FaceTime camera, although there is no flash and the quality is lower.

Viewing and trimming videos

Watching a video that you've recorded is as simple as browsing your photos. Open the Photos app, and then tap Albums in the Browse bar. All your videos are kept together in one album. Tap the Videos album to see them.

You also find your videos mixed in with other photos in the Recently Added album and in Moments in Collections when you tap Photos in the Browse bar. The video icon and playing time stamped on the thumbnails distinguish videos from photos.

Tap the video you want to watch, and then tap the Play button (the triangle in the middle of the screen and at the bottom of the screen, where you see the Share, Favorites, and Delete buttons). The Play button becomes the Pause button when the video is playing, but the controls disappear almost immediately to give you a cleaner viewing screen. Tap the screen to see the controls again and tap the Pause button to interrupt playback.

Video recorded in Time-Lapse mode will replay faster than the action actually happened.

Photos gives you the possibility of trimming video captured in Video or Slo-Mo mode from the beginning or end of your video (but not in the middle):

1. **Tap the screen to make the controls visible.**

   A bar across the top of the screen displays the video frame by frame.

2. **Touch and drag the slider on the bar to move through the video in slow motion to identify where you want to trim.**

   It's often easier to work in landscape view, even if the video was shot in portrait.

3. **Tap and drag the left end of the bar to trim from the beginning of your video or tap and drag the right end of the bar to trim from the end.**

   The Trim button appears in the upper-right corner and the bar is highlighted in yellow, as shown in Figure 4-5.

4. **Tap the Trim button when you have the bracket positioned where you want.**

   It's a good idea to stop a bit before the actual point where you want to trim.

   Tap Save as New Clip, which keeps the original video and saves the trimmed video as an additional video in Photos and in the Recently Added and Videos albums.

   Video takes up storage space on your iPhone, and saving a new clip means you're storing not one but two videos. Consider moving your video to your computer and keeping only the necessary copies on your iPhone.

5. **Tap Cancel at any time if you want to start over.**

Figure 4-5: Trim removes frames from the beginning and end of your video.

Book IV
Chapter 4

Recording, Editing,
and Watching
Videos

Slowing down the action

The Slo-Mo option in the Camera app lets you designate a key sequence to play back in slow motion, something that shows a particularly rapid action such as a phenomenal triple flip from the high dive or the sleight of hand during a magic trick. When you record in Slo-Mo mode, the entire video is captured at a higher 120 frames per second (240 on iPhone 6 models), and you choose the segment you want to play back slowly by doing the following:

1. **Open the Photos app and tap open the video you recorded in Slo-Mo.**

   You find all videos in the Videos album; slow-motion videos are distinguished from other videos (and photos if you look in Moments or Camera Roll) by a circle in the lower-left corner of the thumbnail image.

2. **Drag the vertical black bars beneath the frame viewer to set the segment you want to view in slow motion, as shown in Figure 4-6.**

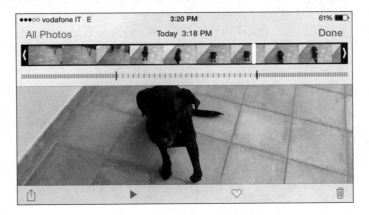

Figure 4-6: Slo-Mo lets you see fast action in slow motion.

If you want to share, mark as a favorite, or delete a video, use the buttons at the bottom of the screen in the same way you do for photos, as explained in Book IV, Chapter 1.

Directing iMovies

If you purchase a new iPhone, you're eligible to download the iMovie app for free. (Those who bought an iPhone prior to September 2013 can purchase iMovie from the App Store for $9.99.) This pared-down version of Apple's iMovie app for Mac lets you create trailers and movies from video captured on your iPhone. You can edit the video and add music, voiceovers, sound effects, still photos, and fades. Here we take you through the steps of creating a project and introduce you to the functions, but we encourage you to have fun trying the different effects and then sharing your production with your friends.

That said, to go a bit easier on your eyes, we recommend using the iOS version of iMovie on an iPad. For the full gamut of editing possibilities, the Mac version of iMovie is a better choice.

Creating a project

Viewing and trimming a video in Photos is fine, but if you want to assemble videos from various sources and add still photos, background music, titles, voiceovers, and special effects, iMovie is a good option.

Think of iMovie as a timeline illustrated with media. First, you insert the still and video images and define the transitions between the parts, and then you overlay titles, voiceover, effects, and background music. Here we take you step-by-step through the process of creating a new iMovie project, although you can pick and choose the type of media and overlays you want:

1. **Open the iMovie app.**

2. **Tap the Project button at the top of the screen, and then tap the plus sign (+) to create a new project or trailer.**

3. **Tap Movie.**

   A chooser opens, which displays themes for movies, as shown in Figure 4-7. Tap one, and then tap the Play

Figure 4-7: Choose a theme for your movie.

button to see a preview. Turn your iPhone to the horizontal landscape position to get a better view.

4. **After you decide on a theme (we use Simple for our example), tap Create Movie at the top right of the screen.**

5. **Do one or both of the following to insert video into your movie:**

   1. Tap the Media button (the filmstrip-musical notes combo) to insert existing media. A chooser opens that displays the media on your iPhone — video, photo, audio.

   2. Tap Video in the Browse bar to see the videos on your iPhone, and then tap the video you want to insert.

   3. Tap the Play button to watch the video.

   4. Tap the More (ellipsis) button to see other choices, such as inserting only the audio from the video.

   5. Tap the Insert arrow to place the video in your movie.

   AND/OR

   1. Tap the Camera button to record video for your movie.

   2. Camera opens and you record video as explained earlier in this chapter.

   3. After you tap the Record/Stop button to stop recording, three buttons appear at the bottom of the screen. Tap:

      • *Retake:* To substitute the recording you just made with a new one.

      • *Play:* To view what you recorded.

      • *Use Video:* To place the video you recorded in your movie and return to the iMovie app.

   If you don't want to use any recorded video, tap Retake, and then tap Cancel to return to the iMovie app.

   New and added video appears on the screen.

6. **To add still images, scroll through the video until the white line is in the position where you want to insert the photo.**

   If you want to insert the image in the middle of a video clip, double-tap the video clip, and then tap the ellipsis (in the lower-right corner), as shown in Figure 4-8. Tap Split. The video is divided and you can insert your still image right where you want it with these steps:

   1. Tap the Media button, and then tap Photos.

   2. Scroll through your albums to find the photo you want to insert.

Figure 4-8: Double-tap a video clip to see editing tools.

3. Tap the Photo. You return to the main project screen and your photo is inserted. You see a couple frames of your photo.

4. Tap the photo in the timeline once; refer to Figure 4-9 for the next steps.

   To see the tools at the bottom of the screen, double-tap a clip. Tap the video image to hide the tools. When you tap a clip, the appropriate tools appear.

Figure 4-9: Trim or lengthen the time the photo is onscreen.

5. On the image at the top of the screen, tap the Start arrow and then pinch or spread on the image to set the opening shot of your still image.

6. Tap the End arrow, and pinch or spread to set the closing shot of your still image.

7. Drag the yellow grabbers to lengthen or shorten the time the photo is on the screen. The time in seconds is shown at the top. During the length of time the image is on screen, it zooms from the opening shot to the closing shot as you set when you pinched it in Steps 4 and 5.

8. Drag the photo itself around in the upper part of the screen to position it; pinch to zoom.

7. Tap the Settings (gear) button to open the Settings screen within iMovie to do the following:

- Change the theme to stylize the transitions and titles.

- Turn on Theme Music to add background music associated with the theme; otherwise, you can add your personal music selection, as explained in Step 10, or make a silent film.

- Choose to fade in and/or out from black at the beginning and end of your movie.

- Choose whether the speed of the video affects the pitch of any audio.

8. Set the transitions.

Transitions are the seconds that occur between clips, and you can set the length of time at 0.5, 1, 1.5, or 2 seconds and choose the way one clip flows into the next.

1. Tap a transition between two clips (double-tap if the tools are hidden). Tap 1.0s (the default transition time) in the toolbar at the bottom of the screen, and then tap the length you want. Tap a transition style, and tap any choices available in the chosen style:

   - *None (known as a "jump cut" in video-editing jargon):* One clip goes directly into the next. This is the default that appears between two clips whenever you insert media.

   - *Theme:* One clip segues to the next following the colors and style of the selected theme.

   - *Cross Dissolve:* One clip melts into the next with an overlap between the end of one clip and the beginning of the next.

   - *Directional:* Tap either of the square transitions, as shown in Figure 4-10, to choose the direction that one clip flows into the next and whether the lead-in is a thick black line or just an unrolling of the next clip.

   - *Flash:* Choose between a black or white flash between clips.

2. Repeat for each transition.

9. Add titles to any of the still images or video clips by tapping the clip, and then doing the following:

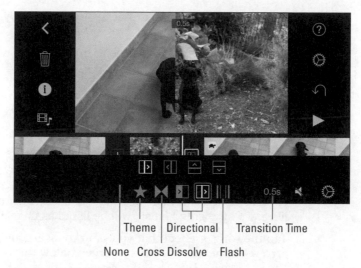

Figure 4-10: Transitions soften the shift from one clip to the next.

1. Tap Title at the bottom of the screen. (Double-tap the clip if you don't see the tools.)

2. Tap one of the title styles — None, Opening, Middle, or Closing — to define at what point in the clip the title will appear.

3. Tap the Type Style button (T) to choose how your text will appear.

4. Tap in the text box that appears on the clip in the upper part of the screen. Tap the X in the upper-left corner to delete the placeholder text, and then type the title.

5. Tap Done.

   Clips with titles have a T in the upper-left corner.

10. **Change the playback speed by following these steps:**

1. Double-tap the clip you want to slow down or speed up to reveal the tools at the bottom of the screen.

2. Tap Speed.

3. Drag the scrubber toward the turtle on the left to slow the video down or toward the rabbit on the right to speed it up. A turtle or rabbit icon appears on the upper-left corner of the clip that runs at a speed other than normal.

   Video you capture in Slo-Mo mode has a turtle icon, but you can change it to normal speed with this tool.

11. **Add a special sound effect or background music by following these steps:**

    1. Scroll to position the white line at the point you want to insert the audio effect.

    2. Tap the Media button.

    3. Tap Audio in the Browse bar.

    4. To choose music or sound effects from iMovie, tap Theme Music or Sound Effects. Submenus open that list music and effects. Tap the Play button next to each one to hear a sample.

       To choose music from your Music collection, tap one of the other choices such as Playlists or Songs, to see the list of music in that library. Copyrighted music will be listed as unavailable.

    5. Tap the song or effect that you want to insert, and then tap the insert arrow. It appears on the main screen below the video clips.

    6. Tap once to drag the grabbers and lengthen or shorten the audio.

    7. Double-tap to reveal the scrubber bar at the bottom of the screen. Drag the scrubber to adjust the volume, and then tap the ellipsis to add other effects such as changing the speed or adding a fade effect; tap the ellipsis again to see options for duplicating the audio or using it as the background audio.

    iMovie lowers the volume of background audio when other audio is playing, whether it's added audio or audio that was recorded with the video.

12. **To add a voiceover, follow these steps:**

    1. Scroll to position the white line at the point you want to insert the voiceover.

    2. Tap the Record Audio button.

    3. When you're ready to speak, tap the Record button. Three beeps provide a countdown to recording.

    4. Say, sing, clap, or do whatever you want to record and then tap Stop.

    5. Tap one of the buttons in the Recording Finished dialog as shown in Figure 4-11: Cancel, Retake (to try again), Review (to hear your recording), or Accept (to insert the recording in your movie).

    6. After you accept your recording, it appears on the main screen below your clips. If it overlaps with other added audio, it will appear below (refer to Figure 4-11); otherwise, it will be on the same line as other added audio.

    7. Edit the recording as instructed in Step 11.

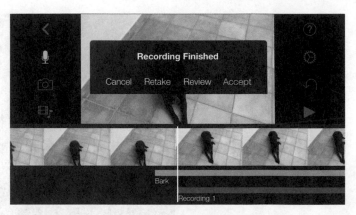

Figure 4-11: Add voiceovers while assembling your movie.

A few tips to remember:

- While you're creating your movie, tap the Play button to see how it is so far. Playback begins from the white line so scroll the clips left and right to begin from a specific point. Tap the Play button again to stop playback.

- Tap the Undo button (it looks like a U-turn symbol) to cancel the most recent action you took; tap again to redo what you undid.

- Hold and drag any of the parts of your movie to a new position.

13. **Tap the Back button to save and close your movie.**

Tap where you see My Project to open the keyboard. Tap the X to clear the field, type a name for your movie, and then tap Done.

Creating a movie trailer

After you've produced a movie, you may want to create a trailer to tease and entice viewers before they see the final cut. Here's a quick run-through of how to make a trailer:

1. **Tap the New Project (+) button, and then tap Trailer.**

2. **Scroll through the styles, and tap the Play button to preview the trailer style.**

Under the preview, you see the length of the trailer and the number of cast members, if there's more than one.

3. **When you've selected one, tap Create Trailer.**

The Outline and Storyboard screen opens, as shown in Figure 4-12.

4. **Tap in the Outline at the bottom half of the screen and type in the information, such as Movie Name, Studio Name, Director, and so on.**

   There's a pop-up menu for the Studio Logo Style.

5. **Tap the Storyboard tab.**

   Here you insert media that will be assembled into your trailer, as shown in Figure 4-13.

6. **Tap the placeholder in the storyboard.**

   Buttons for media choices appear at the top of the screen.

7. **Based on the description in the placeholder, tap the media type at the top of the screen.**

   For example, if the placeholder reads "4.3s Wide," you want to tap the Videos button at the top of the screen and select a video that's 4.3 seconds long with a wide-angle point of view. Or tap the Camera button and record 4.3 seconds of wide-angle video.

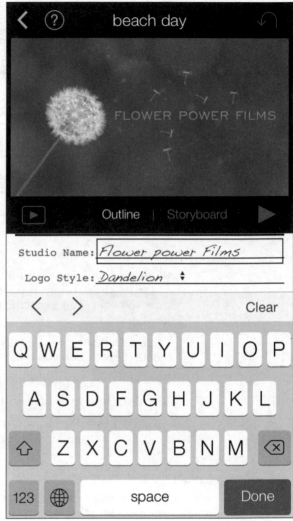

Figure 4-12: Add your movie credits to the Outline.

8. **Tap the media you want to use.**

   It's inserted and the next placeholder is at the ready for media to be inserted.

9. **Repeat Steps 7 and 8 until all the placeholders are filled.**

10. Tap any text fields on the storyboard. Tap Clear (just above the keyboard), and then type something applicable to your movie trailer.

11. Repeat Step 10 until you reach the end of the storyboard.

12. Tap the Play button on the right to preview your trailer in the editing screen or tap the Full Screen Play button (it looks like a playback arrow in a square) to play the entire trailer on your iPhone's screen.

    Tap the screen to see the playback controls, and tap Done to return to the project.

13. Tap the back buttons in the upper-left corner to return to the Projects chooser.

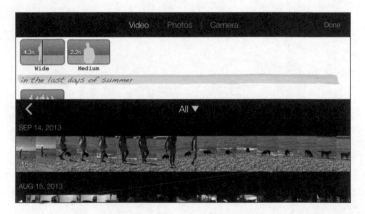

Figure 4-13: Fill the placeholders in the Storyboard to flesh out the trailer.

Chapter 5: Browsing, Installing, and Managing Apps

In This Chapter

↙ **Searching for and installing apps**

↙ **Deleting apps**

↙ **Updating apps**

↙ **Reviewing apps**

↙ **Stopping by the Newsstand**

↙ **Managing store cards with Passbook**

↙ **Playing around in the Game Center**

Apps exponentially increase the number of things you can do with your iPhone. To give you an idea, you can find apps for recipes, games, electronic readers, home banking, photo enhancement, conversion tools, and music identification, not to mention profession-specific apps such as radiation dosage calculators for oncologists or turbine calculators for mechanics. You find all those apps in the App Store.

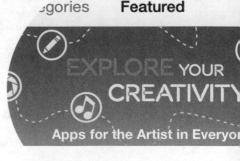

In this chapter, we tell you how the App Store works, give you tips for reading reviews to help you choose apps, show you how to install and delete apps, and explain how to reinstall them if you deleted them by mistake. We introduce you to three Apple apps that organize other apps: Newsstand, which organizes apps (those designed to work with Newsstand) for purchasing, subscribing, and reading periodicals on your iPhone; Passbook, which organizes cards and tickets for stores, airlines, coffee shops, and the like; and Game Center, which piques your competitive nature with multiplayer games and published leaderboards for games designed to work with Game Center.

This book's online bonus content gives a smorgasbord of apps that we recommend. Refer to the introduction to learn how to access the bonus content.

Discovering the Joy of Apps: "There's an App for That!"

A couple dozen apps — many included with your iPhone and the rest available to download, some for free — are developed by Apple, and the other 1,199,976 (give or take a few) are developed by third-party developers. You download apps from Apple's App Store, which you access either via your iPhone or other iOS device or via iTunes on your computer. The nice thing about the App Store is that it offers one-stop shopping. You don't have to shop from website to website for the best price or the latest version; everything is in one place. And Apple reviews the app before it goes up on the App Store, so you can be confident it'll work with your iPhone.

What's more, if you replace your iPhone with a newer model, acquire additional iOS devices, lose your iPhone, or if your iPhone or computer crashes before you've had a chance to back up the apps you've downloaded, the App Store has a record of everything you've downloaded and you can download your apps again (if they're still available) — without paying for them a second time. That's why you need an Apple ID to sign in to the App Store or iTunes Store, even to download free apps.

Free or for a price?

There are two kinds of apps: free and paid. Many, many apps are free although we have noticed a trend toward paid apps or in-app purchases. Rarely do you get somethin' for nothin'; apps that are free to download are often supported by ads, so after you take your turn in Words With Friends Free, a commercial for Foot Locker occupies your screen for 15 seconds before you can go on to your next turn, or an advertising banner may scroll across the bottom of your favorite recipe app. There's usually a paid, ad-free version available.

Nonetheless, we identify four types of free apps to help you choose:

- **Stand-alone apps:** Found in all categories, these apps work on their own and can be games, financial management, recipes, or just about whatever you can think of. They may or may not have ads.

- **Teaser or intro apps:** Pared-down versions of fee-based apps. Here, too, they may or may not have ads.

- **Support apps:** Vendors who provide an app that either is an iPhone version of their website or gives specific information. Home banking apps and real-time public transit information apps are two examples. Often, you find a link to the App Store on the website of the vendor or service provider. These usually only promote their own products.

✔ **Revenue-generating apps:** These apps provide frameworks for the real meat of the app. The app is free, but you pay for the content or to activate special features or purchase accessories.

We think of paid apps in two categories:

✔ **Low-priced:** Most are just 99 cents and the highest runs $5. Many ad-free apps are in this category and we find the price justified for apps we use a lot — those ads can get old fast. They run the gamut of categories.

✔ **Higher-priced:** More than $10. For the most part, these apps, such as scientific journals or productivity tools, give access to costly, copyrighted information or research and development investment on the part of the developer.

Double- (or triple-) duty apps

Look around and most people you see have one gadget or another in their hands. Having the same apps and the same information about those apps on each device makes work, and life in general, easier. *Universal apps* make working on multiple devices a breeze because they work on all iOS devices (iPhone, iPad, iPod touch). A plus sign in the upper-left corner of the price button indicates a universal app. When you look at an app's Info screen, which we explain in just a few paragraphs (refer to Figure 5-3), tap the Details tab and scroll down to the Information section. Next to Compatibility, you see which devices the app is compatible with.

Many iOS apps also have a Mac counterpart, often with more features, and are iCloud-enabled, which means you can create documents on one device, save them to iCloud, and open and edit them on another device. If you're a Windows user, you don't have to feel left out: You can access some of your documents through the www.icloud.com website.

Searching for and Installing Apps

Now that you know a bit about what you're looking for, we tell you how to get your hands on some apps. You can enter the App Store through iPhone or iTunes doors.

Searching the iPhone App Store

With more than 1.2 million apps, it's hard to know where to begin, let alone actually choose an app. Apple helps you by making some recommendations for apps, showing you bestsellers, best earners, and some Apple favorites. To begin navigating through the sea of apps on your iPhone, open the App Store app. A screen very similar to Apple's other media outlets — iTunes, iBooks, iTunes U, Podcasts — appears, as shown in Figure 5-1. Across the bottom, you see five buttons:

- **Featured:** Shows Apple-recommended apps divided into sections. Ads automatically scroll across the top. You can scroll horizontally through sections such as Best New Apps, and scroll down to see more sections.

- **Top Charts:** Tap one of the tabs — Paid, Free, Top Grossing — to see a list of apps sorted by those criteria.

You see apps under Top Grossing that are free, and you may wonder how a free app can be top-grossing. In a word: In-App Purchases. The app is free, but you then buy things within the app. For example, a poker game is free, but you buy 25 gold chips for

Figure 5-1: The App Store gives you many ways to find apps.

$1.99. You see the words *In-App Purchases* underneath the price or Free button of apps that offer them.

Both the Featured and Top Charts screens have a Categories button in the upper-left corner. Tap it to see a list of categories. Tap on one of the categories to see apps in that category. Some categories are divided into subcategories. Games and Newsstand are divided into subcategories. Some apps fall into more than one category, in which case it shows up on two different lists.

✔ **Explore:** Here, too, you find categories. At the top you find popular and featured apps from the selected category, subcategories, and even sub-subcategories (refer to Figure 5-2).

✔ **Search:** The screen opens with a list of Trending Searches. You can tap one of the trendy subjects in the list to see the apps that match it. To search for something else, tap the name of the app, if you know it, or a few keywords. The more words you type in the search field, the narrower your search results. Results appear in a scrollable list.

✔ **Updates:** Because the App Store knows which apps you've purchased and downloaded, it automatically sends you a notification when an update is available. The number you see in the badge

Figure 5-2: Explore shows popular and featured apps by category and topic.

on the Updates button is the number of apps that have updates. You can choose to have your apps updated automatically, in which case you never see the update notification. We talk about updates a little further along in this chapter.

You find your purchase history here, too, along with that of family members if you use Family Sharing. Tap Purchased at the top of the Updates screen to see a list that shows all the apps you ever purchased or only those that aren't on your iPhone. If you deleted an app and want to reinstall it, tap Not on This iPhone, scroll through the alphabetical list of apps, and then tap the Download button (it looks like a cloud with a downward-pointing arrow). After the download finishes, the Download button becomes the Open button. Tap it to open the app.

With iOS 8, developers can offer *app bundles,* several apps sold together for a discounted price.

To learn more about an app, tap either an icon or an item in a list in any of the screens. An Info screen opens, as shown in Figure 5-3. At the very top, you see the name of the app, the developer's name, the star ratings, and a button that displays either the price or "free." You may also see an Editors' Choice logo if the app has been deemed extra special by the App Store editorial team. Three tabs let you view

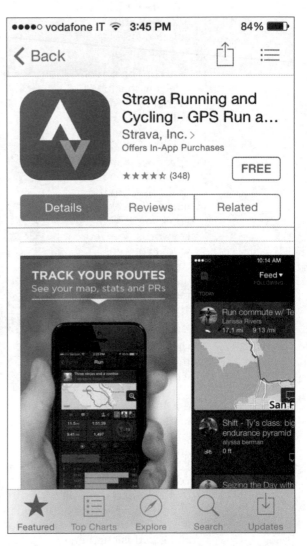

Figure 5-3: The app's Info screen gives detailed information about the app, including a description, screenshots, and reviews.

   ✓ **Details:** Scroll horizontally through screenshots of the app; some apps offer a preview video that shows you how the app works. Scroll vertically to read a description, information about the app such as the version and age rating, which indicates the minimum age considered appropriate for this app, as well as which devices it's compatible with, as mentioned earlier. You also find developer information, in-app purchases, the version history, and privacy policy. You may have to tap More or a disclosure triangle to read everything in the section.

Not all apps support Family Sharing, scroll down to the Information section, which tells you if Family Sharing is supported or if there are limitations.

✒ **Reviews:** You see the number of ratings and the average stars the app's been given as well as written reviews. If available, you can Like the app on Facebook. You can also write a review yourself or tap a link to go to the app support page.

✒ **Related:** Scroll horizontally through a selection of other apps by the same developer or other apps that were purchased or downloaded by customers who purchased or downloaded this app. Tap any of the icons to reach that app's information screen.

When you're choosing apps, read the description, which is written by the developer, to understand exactly what you should expect from the app. Then read the reviews with a discerning eye as to whether the app does what the description says it does, whether it's buggy, whether it's lame. Some reviewers write a bad review because they expected the app to do something that it never claimed to do. Look for a positive or negative consensus in reviews to help you make a downloading decision. And if it's free, just try it — you can always delete it if you don't like it.

Installing from the iPhone App Store

If you decide to download the app, tap the Free or price button on either the Info screen or the app in the list format. The button changes to Install or Buy. Tap the button. If you have an iPhone with Touch ID, confirm your purchase by resting your finger on the Home button. Otherwise, you may be asked to confirm the old-fashioned way by entering your Apple ID and password, as shown in Figure 5-4. (See Book I, Chapter 5 for more on setting up an Apple account if you haven't done so already.)

If you chose a paid app, you have to enter your credit card or PayPal account information, have your on-file charge card charged, redeem an iTunes or Apple Store card, or have a credit balance in your iTunes account. If this is the first time you've purchased something with this iPhone, you have to verify the account and payment information. A screen appears that asks for your payment information, where you must enter your credit card or PayPal information. Otherwise, you may tap None in the selection of credit card options, redeem an iTunes or Apple Store card, and then purchase items against the iTunes account balance. A second screen may ask your security questions to verify that you are who you say you are. After you enter this information the first time, you don't have to do it again until your credit card expires, your iTunes balance reaches zero, or you change devices.

If you frequently download items from the iTunes Store, you can associate a credit card with your iTunes account or purchase iTunes or Apple Store cards. Scroll to the bottom of the Featured screen and tap Redeem. If asked, sign in with your Apple ID and password. If the code on the back of the iTunes or Apple Store card has a box around it, you can scan it with your iPhone's camera by tapping Use Camera, pointing the iPhone lens at the code, and then tapping the camera button in the upper-right corner. Otherwise, tap You Can Also Enter Your Code Manually, and then type in the code. Apple charges your redeemed value first, and when that's consumed, will charge your credit or debit card. However, you have to redeem store cards before you make any purchases.

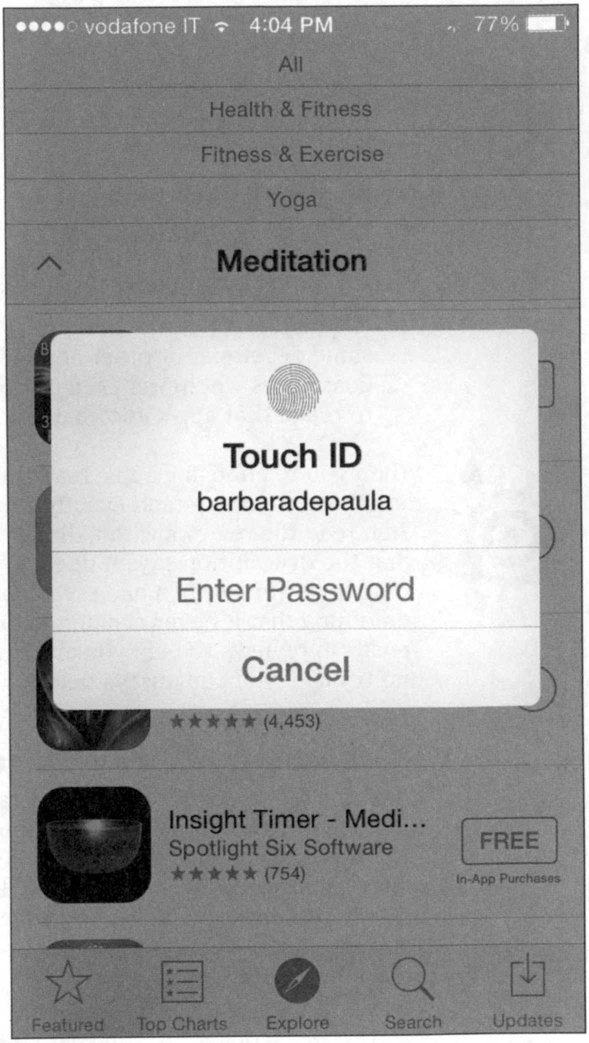

Whatever your payment method, you always have a chance to confirm or cancel your purchase after you hit the price button.

Figure 5-4: Confirm your purchase with Touch ID or type in your Apple ID and password when asked.

After the App Store has the information it needs from you, and you've confirmed that you want to buy the app, the price or Free button becomes a circle that rotates and when the app is downloaded, the button reads Open. You can continue shopping or tap the Home button, and the button of the new app appears. Across the bottom, the words *Waiting* or *Loading* appear beneath the app and a timer is displayed on the dimmed app button. If you're downloading with a Wi-Fi or 4G/LTE connection, your app may download so quickly it's finished by the time you get to the Home screen.

There are a few more things you should know about shopping at the App Store:

- ✔ You can't use store credits to give an app to someone as a gift. If you have both a store credit and a credit card on file and gift an app to someone, it will automatically be charged to your credit card.

- ✔ If you're the head of the household for a Family Sharing group, purchases made by members of the family are charged to the credit card you added when you created the family. You can activate the Ask to Buy feature for selected members (usually your children or someone with irresponsible spending habits), so the App Store prompts you to authorize purchases requested by those family members.

- ✔ Although you can window-shop the App Store from your iPhone to your heart's content, you can only download apps up to 50MB in size from your cellular network. To download apps larger than 50MB, you have to have a Wi-Fi connection on your iPhone.

- ✔ If you lose your Internet connection or for some reason the download is interrupted, the next time you have an Internet connection, the download starts again. If, instead, you open iTunes on your computer and sign in to your account with the same Apple ID you used to begin the download that was interrupted, iTunes completes the download.

Shopping for apps at the iTunes Store

If you do shop at the iTunes Store on your computer, you want to turn on Automatic Downloads so any purchases you make on one device, such as your computer or iPhone, are automatically downloaded to other devices linked to the same Apple ID.

To shop for iPhone apps from your computer, follow these directions:

1. **Open iTunes on your computer.**

2. **Click the iTunes Store button in the upper-right corner.**

3. **Click the App Store tab at the top of the window or click and hold the tab to open a pop-up menu from which you can click a specific app category.**

4. **Browse and shop as you would for other media.**

Here's how to set up Automatic Downloads:

1. **Open iTunes on your computer.**

2. **Choose iTunes⇨Preferences (Mac) or Edit⇨Preferences (Windows) and click the Store tab.**

3. **Under Automatic Downloads, check the type of media (Music, Apps, and/or Books) you want downloaded simultaneously to all devices.**

4. **Click OK.**

5. **On your iPhone, open the Settings app, tap iTunes & App Store, and then tap the switches on next to the items you want activated for Automatic Downloads (Music, Apps, and/or Books).**

Book IV
Chapter 5

Browsing,
Installing, and
Managing Apps

Sharing news about apps you like

Like many other iPhone apps, you can share what you find at the App Store. Tap the Share button at the top right of an app's Info screen to open the Share Sheet. From there, tap one of the sharing options — AirDrop, Message, Mail, Twitter, or Facebook — to send a link via one of those methods. You can also copy the link and paste it in another app. With paid apps, you have two more choices: Add to Wish List, to keep track of apps you want, or Gift, to send the app to another person.

To see your Wish List, tap the Wish List button in the top-right corner of the Featured or Top Charts screens. Apps listed are the same as in other lists: Tap the price to install the app as described previously. After an app is installed, it's removed from your Wish List. To delete an item from your Wish List without installing it, tap Edit, tap the circle next to the app to select it, and then tap the Delete button in the upper-left corner.

Apps that find you

Sometimes an app finds you. Many information providers (like newspapers or radio broadcasts), service providers (such as banks and FedEx), and social networks (like Facebook or Pinterest) caught on to the power of apps right from the beginning and developed slimmed-down versions of their Internet offerings.

If you visit the FedEx website via Safari on your iPhone, you'll be prompted to download the FedEx app so you can track deliveries or request pickups. Barbara's bank sent her an email invitation to download its online banking app. These apps give you direct access to the iPhone versions of their websites, which allow you to access the essentials without the extemporaneous fluff that takes a long time to load across a cellular data network.

Another way you can find apps for products and services you use frequently is to scan 2D barcodes, also known as QR (Quick Response) codes, which are those 1-x-1-inch square graphic images that look like a labyrinth. You have to download a 2D barcode scanning reader such as QR Reader for iPhone or i-nigma QR. After you have the reader app, you open the app and hold it over one of those barcodes. You're automatically sent to a mobile web page for the product or service associated with that barcode.

Deleting Apps

You may tire of an app or find you downloaded an app that's a dud and you want to delete it. We explain this in Book I, Chapter 3, but here's a quick review. To delete apps from your iPhone, do the following:

1. **Press and hold any app on the Home screen until all the app icons start wiggling.**

2. **Tap the X in the corner of the apps you want to delete.**

3. **Press the Home button when you're finished and the apps stand still.**

You can also go to the Settings app, tap General, tap Usage, and in the Storage section tap Manage Storage to open a list of all the apps on your iPhone. Tap the app you want to delete and then tap Delete App.

You can't delete the apps that came preinstalled on your iPhone.

After you download an app, it remains associated with your Apple ID on iTunes. If you accidentally delete an app from your iPhone, you can download again from the App Store, as explained later in this chapter.

Updating and Upgrading Apps

It seems almost every day an app or two on your phone has been updated. This is of no concern to you because in the App Store settings, you can choose to have apps automatically updated as updates become available. To make things even better, updates are free.

Upgrades, on the other hand, may have a fee attached. For example, if you download the free, barebones, or ad-laden version of an app but then want to upgrade to the full or ad-free version, you'll probably have to pay for it. Here we tell you how to put updates on automatic and how to find and install upgrades.

Setting up automatic updates

You aren't obligated to use automatic updates but we highly recommend you do; otherwise, you'll have to manually update your apps as explained in the next section. Follow these steps to turn on this feature:

1. **Open the Settings app.**

2. **Scroll down and tap iTunes & App Store.**

   The screen shown in Figure 5-5 appears.

3. **In the Automatic Downloads section, tap the Updates switch to the on position.**

   While you're there, tap the Apps switch on as well so whenever you download an app on one device, it's automatically downloaded on other devices on which you signed in to the same Apple ID.

4. **Tap the Use Cellular Data switch on (scroll down to see it) to download and update apps over the cellular data network.**

   Downloads and updates over the cellular data network are limited to 50MB; any apps larger than that have to be downloaded or updated using Wi-Fi or by syncing with iTunes.

Using iPhone's App Store to update

If you want to manually update your apps, ignore the preceding section and do the following:

1. **Open the App Store app.**

2. **Tap the Updates button in the bottom-right corner.**

   A list of apps that have updates appears. The version number is shown under the name of the app.

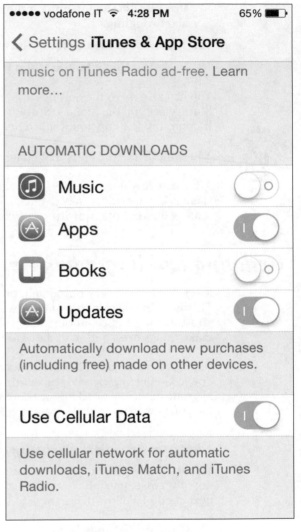

Figure 5-5: Automatic updates means you always have the most current version of an app.

3. **Tap What's New (it's written quite small under the version number) to see what changes or fixes the update made or tap the app icon to open the Info screen.**

   A list of changes pops open.

4. **Tap the Update button on the Updates list or the Info screen.**

   OR

   Tap Update All on the Updates screen.

Make sure to go to the Settings app, tap Notifications, tap App Store, and turn the Badge App Icon option on so you'll see a numbered badge on the App Store button when updates are available

Upgrading apps and buying content

Some apps let you know within the app that a new version is available. You may be playing a game and a notification appears telling you that a new version is available. Simply tap the link that appears to get the new version.

Within an app you may be invited to upgrade to the full or ad-free version. There may be a banner across the bottom that says something like "Tap here to play ad-free." The link usually takes you to the App Store, and there's usually a fee involved if it's an upgrade, from either a barebones or ad-laden version to a paid-for full or ad-free version.

Earlier in this chapter, we mention in-app purchases that could be chips you buy to play a poker game or extra tools to defend your avatar in a game or special effects in a video editing app. In-app purchases can also be content such as recipes or articles. To keep things simple, in-app purchases are managed by the App Store; however, you make the purchase directly from within the app. Some apps have a Store button in their in-app settings or info screens, which we tell you about in the next section.

App Info and Settings

After an app is installed, you may want to find out more about the app or adjust some of the settings. On your iPhone, information such as the version number and links to the support site are usually found within the app by tapping the Info (i) button, a help button, or one of the common icons such as a gear or list.

Some app settings are managed on your iPhone in the Settings app. Just open the Settings app and scroll down to the bottom. The last section you see is the list of apps that have settings you can change. Each app has different settings, so tap through and play around with the settings for the apps that you have.

Other app settings are managed from within the app. There's no cut-and-dried rule to follow. You can visit the support page for an app to learn where the settings are and what they do. Again, we recommend playing a bit with the apps you have and trying different settings to make the app useful and enjoyable for you.

In iTunes on your computer, select Apps from the Library pop-up menu to display all your apps. Click an app icon, and then choose File⇨Get Info. The app's Info window opens, which has several tabs across the top. You're probably most interested in the Summary screen, where you can see the version number of the app, its size and age rating, and when it was downloaded. You can also see what kind it is to determine if it works on both iPhone and iPad.

Reviewing Apps and Reporting Problems

Purchase decisions today are often based more on what someone else has to say about a product than on what the company says about its product. App reviews can help you decide whether to purchase an app. After you purchase and use an app, you can contribute to the improvement of the app world by writing honest, objective reviews and, when necessary, reporting problems. Your fellow app users will thank you and, at least in our experience, developers will be happy, too, not only for good reviews but also for a heads-up when there's a problem. When you have a good or bad experience, write a quick review or at least give the app the appropriate number of stars. If you encounter a recurring problem, let the developer know. Here's how to submit reviews and problem reports on your iPhone and through iTunes.

On your iPhone

Open the App Store app. Tap Updates and then tap Purchased at the top of the screen (tap the Status bar if you don't see Purchased). Scroll through the list of your purchased apps, which also includes free apps. You can only write reviews for apps that you've downloaded, whether free or purchased. Tap the app you want to review to open the Info screen and then do the following:

1. **Tap the Reviews tab.**
2. **Tap Write a Review.**

   You may be asked to sign in to your Apple account.

3. **Tap the number of stars you want to give the app, and then fill in the form and write your review.**
4. **Tap Send to submit your review.**

If you're having a problem with the app, tap the App Support button, which opens the developer's website. Follow the links there to contact the developer about any problems you're having.

On iTunes

To write a review from iTunes on your computer, locate the app in the App Store section of the iTunes Store and click the Write a Review button just under Customer Reviews. Fill in the form that appears and click Submit. To contact the developer about a problem, click Report a Problem on the Write a Review form or click the App Support button next to the Write a Review button.

If you're having a problem downloading or launching an app you recently downloaded, first try deleting it from your iPhone and installing it again. If that doesn't work and you want to report a problem to Apple, go into your purchase history by choosing Store➪View Account. Click See All in the Purchase History section and then click the arrow to the left of the app that's giving you trouble. Click Report a Problem and then follow the onscreen instructions.

Reinstalling Apps You Already Own

Mistakes happen. Computers crash. iPhones fall out of windows of moving cars. The result may be that an app is no longer on your iPhone, either because you deleted it or you have to unexpectedly replace your iPhone with a new one and you don't have a recent backup. (Or maybe you deleted all your game apps so you weren't distracted when you have work to do and now you want to reinstall them because you have some time off.) In any case, the App Store knows what apps you already installed and lets you download them again (if they're still available from the App Store), free of charge. Here's how to do it on your iPhone:

1. **Open the App Store app.**

2. **Tap the Updates button at the bottom right of the screen.**

3. **Tap Purchased at the top of the screen.**

   A list of apps you purchased appears.

4. **Tap All to see all apps you purchased or tap Not on This iPhone to see apps you purchased that aren't on this iPhone.**

   There are three buttons you may see when you tap All, as shown in Figure 5-6:

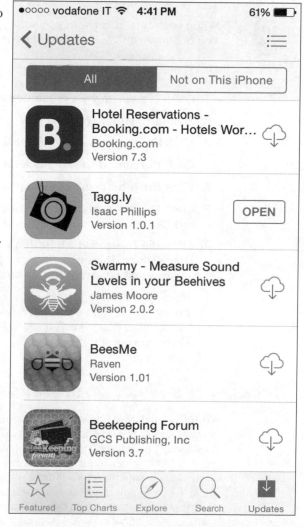

Figure 5-6: Access a list of purchased apps from the Updates screen.

- *Open,* which opens the app

- *Update,* which means an update is available for the app

- *iCloud icon,* which means that you previously purchased the app but it isn't on your iPhone — you see only this icon when you tap Not on This iPhone

5. **Tap the iCloud icon next to the app you want to reinstall.**

   The iCloud icon changes to a circle while the app is downloading and reads Open when the installation is complete. The app button appears on the Home screen.

When you reinstall an app, you automatically install the latest version even if you originally installed a prior version.

On iTunes, the procedure is similar:

1. **Open iTunes on your computer and click iTunes Store.**

2. **Sign in to your account if you aren't already signed in.**

3. **Click the Apps button in the toolbar.**

4. **Click Purchased in the Quick Links list.**

5. **Click the iPhone tab above the app icons.**

6. **Click the Not in My Library tab to the right to see which apps are missing.**

7. **Click the Download All button to download all the apps that aren't in your iTunes library to your computer or click the iCloud icon on a single app that you want to download.**

   The app is downloaded to iTunes and automatically downloaded to your iPhone too, if you've activated Automatic Downloads in iTunes preferences; otherwise, sync your iPhone with iTunes and the apps will be added to your iPhone.

Reading the News with Newsstand

With the quality of iPhone screens and the Display & Brightness settings that let you adjust the type size, reading on your iPhone has become a viable option to staying current with your reading material of choice. Newsstand isn't really an app but a folder in disguise that neatly organizes all your periodical subscriptions in one place. You find a publication's app (usually for free) by tapping the Newsstand button and then tapping Store. The Newsstand category of the App Store opens. (You can also reach it by opening the App Store, tapping Categories, and tapping Newsstand.) Scroll through as you would for any other kind of app as we explained previously. Tap the publication that interests you and tap Free to install the app.

The app icons appear like magazine covers or newspaper front pages on the Newsstand book-shelf, as shown in Figure 5-7. There are two ways to subscribe or pur-chase single issues :

✔ Tap Newsstand, and then tap the publica-tion. Not all periodi-cal apps are equal; to see a list of sub-scription options similar to those shown in Figure 5-8, tap the Library, Subscriptions, or Read button. Often you have the option of purchasing single issues or 3-, 6-, or 15-month subscrip-tions, as well as spe-cial issues.

✔ In the App Store, tap Search and type the name of the publica-tion you want or tap Categories, tap Newsstand, and then tap the category that interests you. After you locate the publi-cation app, open the Info screen and scroll to the bottom. Tap In-App Purchases to see what subscription options and issues are available. Tap the item you want to buy.

Figure 5-7: Newsstand stores your newspaper and magazine subscriptions in one place.

Press the Home button to exit the publication and return to the Newsstand shelf. Newsstand is really a folder on the Home screen so you have to press the Home button again to see the familiar Home screen buttons and bars.

The first time you tap the publication, a dialog lets you know the publication wants to send you notifications. Allowing this will send new issues to your

Book IV
Chapter 5

Browsing,
Installing, and
Managing Apps

iPhone immediately. Even if you don't allow new issues to be pushed, when new issues are released, a badge on the Newsstand icon indicates their availability. Tap the publication on the Newsstand shelf to download and read the latest issue.

Because each publication app is just that — an app created by a third-party developer — there's no set rule for the publication interface. Different publications use different buttons, and you'll have to poke around and see what you can do and how the app works. The first time you open a publication after you subscribe, you may have to enter login information, which may be your Apple ID or may be a different user ID and password the publication asked you to create. Some publications give you a free iOS subscription if you subscribe to the print edition, and you would enter your subscriber information, usually culled from the mailing label on the print edition, in the Settings screen, found when you tap the gear button in the upper-right corner. You may have other options within the publications on Newsstand, such as Search or Settings.

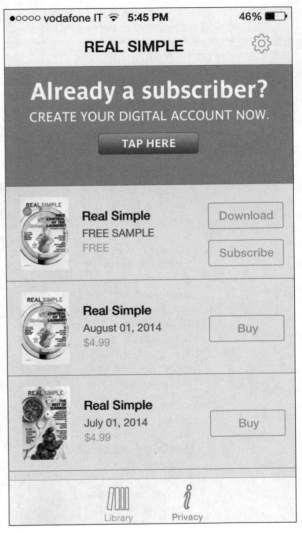

Figure 5-8: See subscription options from the publication's app.

Newspapers usually show articles in streaming, meaning they're frequently updated, and if you want to download an article to read later, you add it to a reading list in the app. Magazines, on the other hand, are usually downloaded to your iPhone, which means they occupy space. If you find you're running out of storage, see if the app offers an Auto Remove option, which deletes the issue after you read it and frees up storage space. As a subscriber, you can download it again at a later date.

Checking in with Passbook

In the ongoing effort to eliminate paper, Passbook steps in to provide electronic versions of boarding passes, movie tickets, coupons, and store cards. On iPhone 6 and 6 Plus, you can add credit cards to Passbook to use with Apple Pay. To give Passbook access to your credit card, tap the card and enter the security code from the credit card you have associated with your iTunes account. To add a different card, tap Add Card and then capture the card data with your iPhone's iSight camera or type it in manually.

Obtaining passes

Before you can use Passbook, you have to install Passbook-enabled apps on your iPhone. Follow these steps to do that:

1. **Open the Passbook app.**

2. **Tap Find Apps for Passbook at the bottom of the screen.**

   A list of apps that support Passbook appears.

   If you don't see the Find Apps for Passbook button, tap Passbook at the bottom of the screen.

3. **Tap the Free button next to the Passbook apps that interest you to install the app on your iPhone.**

4. **Tap Install.**

5. **Type in your Apple ID Password if requested.**

   The app is downloaded and the button now reads Open.

In addition to Passbook apps, there are two other ways to add passes:

- Tap Passbook and then tap the Scan Code button. The camera opens. Point it at the barcode on a product or a QR code in an ad to scan it; the pass or discount coupon is then added to passbook.

- You may receive email with a link or find URLs on websites that download coupons (www.coupons.com has many) or special offers to Passbook. Tap these links and the associated barcode or QR code is downloaded to Passbook, as shown in Figures 5-9 and 5-10.

Getting onboard

The fun and practical side of Passbook is using the passes. When you're ready to use one of the Passbook-enabled apps, open the app and do one of the following:

- Tap the Add to Passbook button and then tap the Add button on the coupon or follow the onscreen instructions to insert your username or number and password.

✓ For boarding passes, proceed with online check-in and then tap Download Boarding Pass to Passbook option.

After the passes are in Passbook, all you have to do is tap the appropriate one and scan it at the check-in counter or cash register. This means all you need is your pass-port and iPhone at the airport; when you reach the cash register at your favorite store, instead of shuffling a deck of store cards, just tap Passbook and then tap the appro-priate card. In no time, you're on your way down the tarmac, points are added to your account, or discounts are applied to your purchase.

Passbook is an iPhone-only app so it won't appear on your iPad and it doesn't have a com-panion app for your computer. What's more, iCloud doesn't sync your Passbook passes.

Figure 5-9: You find the Add to Passbook button in apps and on websites and online order forms.

Managing passes

Most of the passes in Passbook have options for automatic updates as well as some information about how the pass works. Tap the Information button in the lower-right corner of the pass to see the "back side" of the pass. Open the Settings app, tap Notification Center, and tap Passbook to choose to see Passbook on the Lock screen and the Notification Center. Then location- and time-based passes, such as boarding passes or theater tickets, appear on the Lock screen when you get to the airport or theater (as long as Location Services is on and you have a data connection). You can also eliminate a pass by tapping the Delete button in the upper-left corner of the pass.

Tap the Share button to send the pass to someone via AirDrop, Mail, or Messages, although they'll need to have an iPhone to do anything with it.

Figure 5-10: Theater tickets and discounts all in one app.

Making Apple Pay purchases

If you have an iPhone 6 with NFC technology, when you make a purchase at a store that supports NFC payments, you can simply point your iPhone at the NFC reader, select Apple Pay, and then rest your finger on the Touch ID sensor to approve your credit card purchase. The payment is charged to the first card you added to Passbook, but you can pay with a different card by tapping the card you want to use in Passbook at the time of your purchase. At any time, you can change the default card in the Settings app. You can also make online purchases with Apple Pay. Visit www.apple.com/iphone-6/apple-pay to learn which banks support Apple Pay and find stores and online retailers that accept Apple Pay.

Book IV
Chapter 5

Browsing,
Installing, and
Managing Apps

Playing Around in Game Center

Game Center pulls information from like-minded apps — games — in one place and enhances your experience by sharing your scores on leaderboards and allowing you to challenge friends who use Game Center to beat your score on a particular level or game. Game Center is part social network and part competitive playing field. When you sign in, any Game Center–enabled games you have on your iPhone are accessed by Game Center, and your playing history is recorded, but the app buttons remain on the Home screen. There are two types of games:

- **Single player:** You play by yourself, but Game Center tracks your scores for the entire game and individual levels and posts them on the leaderboard if you choose to go public with your playing habits. There are also achievements, which are specific actions within a game, such as unlocking a character, that garner points in Game Center.

- **Multiplayer:** You play with other people across either a Wi-Fi or Bluetooth network. Some games are immediately interactive, whereas others can be played leisurely, each player taking her turn when she wants, although this does hold up the progression of the game.

Signing in and making friends

Sign in to the Game Center with your Apple ID, and then choose a username or nickname for your Game Center profile that will appear as your moniker when you play multiplayer games or on leaderboards, sort of like choosing the top hat in Monopoly or calling yourself Curly at the bowling alley. You have to choose one that no one else is using and you can change it in the Game Center settings if you decide you want a new gaming identity.

The Game Center screen opens, and you find five buttons across the Browse bar at the bottom of the screen. Here's a quick rundown of what each one does:

- **Me:** From this screen you can type a status update and add or edit an image that represents you. Bubbles on the screen tell you how many games, turns, challenges, friends, and requests you have. Tapping the bubbles opens the same screens as tapping the buttons in the Browse bar.

- **Friends:** Here's where the social part of Game Center comes in. When you first sign in, Game Center lists friends who use Game Center and asks if you want to add them as Game Center friends. You can choose who you want to add. To add more friends, scroll through the list of recommendations and tap one you'd like to add as a friend. An info screen opens that tells you the person's username and shows his or her photo or image, which can help you make sure it's the person you thought. Tap the Send Friend Request button, and when your request is confirmed you can then see the games and scores of that friend, send challenges, and play multiplayer games together. You can also add friends by

- *Typing a name* in the Search field to find a specific friend and, if the person you want is found, sending a friend request.

- *Tapping the Add button* in the upper-right corner, which opens an email friend request. Type the email address or nickname of the person you want to send a friend request to.

- *Get more recommendations* by opening the Settings app, tapping Game Center, and tapping the Contacts and/or Facebook switches on in the Friend Recommendations section.

Tap the name of a friend to see that player's profile, as shown in Figure 5-11. Tap the bubbles to see more information. Friends

Figure 5-11: Learn about new games from a friend's profile.

shows that player's friends, and Games and Points show the games that player plays and the points he or she has racked up. If the player plays games you don't have, tapping the game in the Games or Points list opens a screen where you can download the game (after purchasing if it's not free). If you ever want to remove someone as a friend, tap the ellipsis in the upper-right corner of that friend's Info screen, and then tap Unfriend in the popup menu.

**Book IV
Chapter 5**

**Browsing,
Installing, and
Managing Apps**

✔ **Games:** Displays a list of the Game Center–enabled games on your iPhone. You also see how many achievement points you have for that app under the name. Tap a game to open the game information screen, as shown in Figure 5-12. Do the following from this screen:

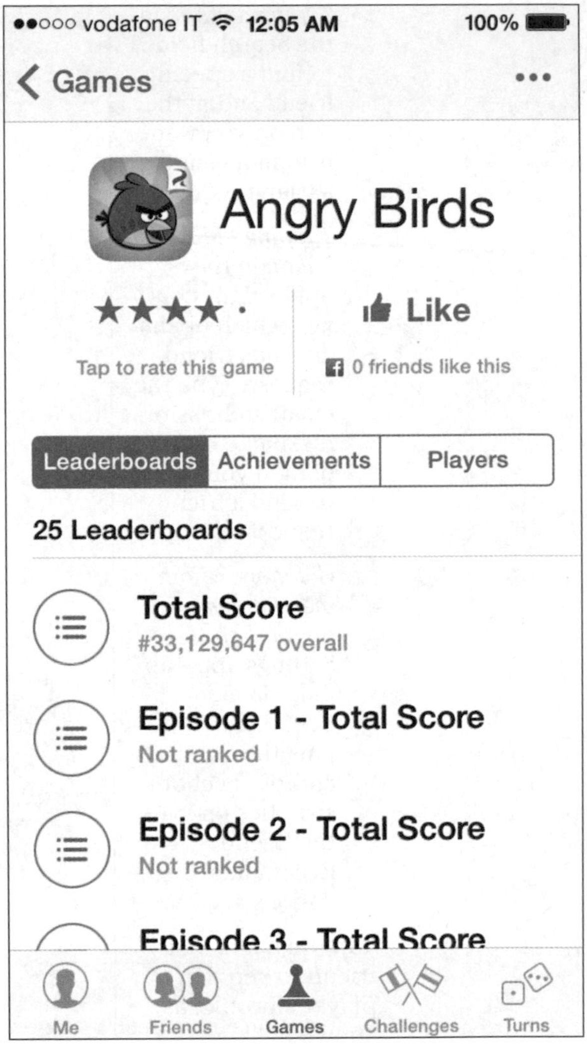

Figure 5-12: Access leaderboards and achievements from the game information screen.

- *Play or share* the game by tapping the ellipsis at the top-right corner.

- *Rate the game* by tapping the dots under the game icon.

- *Like the game* on Facebook by tapping the Like button.

- *Review the leaderboards* by tapping the Leaderboards tab, and then tapping the leaderboards for the total game score or top scores for a specific level. Tap a name in the leaderboard to view the player's profile and send a friend request.

- *See your achievements* by tapping the Achievements tab. Tap the achievement to share your accomplishment with your friends or challenge friends to master the same achievement.

- *See who's playing* when you tap the Players tab to see friends who are playing the game.

✔ **Challenges:** Lists challenges you send to and receive from other players. You have to be friends with a player in order to exchange challenges.

✔ **Turns:** Lists the games you're playing with others, along with the score and whose turn it is.

Challenging a friend

You can send challenges for a level you've already achieved, essentially challenging your friend to beat your score, or for an achievement. To send a challenge:

1. **Tap Games in the Browse bar.**

2. **Tap the game you want to send a challenge from.**

3. **Tap a level on a leaderboard or an achievement on the achievements list.**

4. **Tap the Challenge Friends bubble.**

   The Challenge screen opens and is addressed to friends who play this game but haven't completed the level or achievement to which you're challenging them.

5. **Type a message to accompany the challenge, if you want.**

6. **Tap Send.**

When you receive challenges, you see the number of challenges received in the Challenges bubble on the Me screen and a list of challenges on the Challenges screen. Tap the challenge to take. When you meet the challenge, your result is shared with your friend.

Taking your turn

If you want to play a multiplayer game, you have to invite friends to join in. Tap Friends in the Browse bar or on the Me screen, tap the person's Games bubble, and then tap a game you have in common. Tap the ellipsis in the upper-right corner to invite the friend to Play, and then tap Next to add more players. After all the invitations have been accepted, you can begin playing. Tap Turns in the Browse bar to see who's up next or when it's your turn to play.

Playing with the Game Center settings

Like most iPhone apps, Game Center has a few settings that customize how you use the app. Open the Settings app, tap Game Center, and turn the following on or off by tapping the switch next to the item:

✔ **Allow Invites:** When on, friends can invite you to play games. If you have a lot of fun, gaming friends, but want to limit your distractions, it may be a good idea to turn this off — but that kind of defeats the purpose of Game Center.

✔ **Nearby Players:** Lets Game Center users who are physically near you, invite you to play multiplayer games on Wi-Fi or Bluetooth.

✔ **Friend Recommendations:** Tap the Contacts and/or Facebook switches on to receive friend recommendations based on whom you know in those two apps.

You can adjust the types of notifications Game Center sends you in the Settings app by tapping Notifications and then tapping Game Center.

Index

About the Authors

Joe Hutsko: Joe is the author of *Green Gadgets For Dummies*, *Flip Video For Dummies* (with Drew Davidson), and *Macs All-in-One For Dummies* (with Barbara Boyd). For more than two decades, he has written about computers, gadgets, videogames, trends, and high-tech movers and shakers for numerous publications and websites, including *The New York Times, Macworld, PC World, Fortune, Newsweek, Popular Science, TV Guide, The Washington Post, Wired,* Gamespot, MSNBC, Engadget, TechCrunch, and Salon. Joe's website is www.joehutsko.com.

As a kid, Joe built a shortwave radio, played with electronic project kits, and learned the basics of the BASIC programming language on his first computer, the Commodore Vic 20. In his teens, he picked strawberries to buy his first Apple II computer. Four years after that purchase (in 1984), he wound up working for Apple, where he became the personal technology guru for the company's chairman and CEO. Joe left Apple in 1988 to become a writer and worked on and off for other high-tech companies, including Steve Jobs's one-time NeXT. He authored a number of videogame strategy guides, including the bestsellers *Donkey Kong Country Game Secrets: The Unauthorized Edition* and *Rebel Assault: The Official Insiders Guide.*

Joe's first novel, *The Deal,* was published in 1999, and he recently rereleased a trade paperback edition of it with a new foreword by the author (www.bit.ly/thedealjoehutsko).

Barbara Boyd: Barbara is the co-author with Joe of *Macs All-in-One For Dummies* and the previous editions of *iPhone All-in-One For Dummies.* She is the author of *AARP Tech To Connect: iPad* and *iCloud For Dummies In A Day,* and co-author of *Innovative Presentations For Dummies* (with Ray Anthony) and *The Complete Idiot's Guide to Pinterest Marketing* (with Christine Martinez). When not writing about technology, Barbara writes about food, gardens, and travel.

Barbara worked at Apple from 1985 to 1990, beginning as Joe's assistant and the first network administrator for the executive staff. She then took a position as an administrator in the Technical Product Support group. Barbara recalls working with people who went on to become top names in technology — it was an exciting time to be in Silicon Valley and at Apple in particular. That experience instilled a lifelong fascination with technology and Apple products. Her interest and experience led to subsequent jobs in marketing and publishing at International Data Group (IDG) and later for a small San Francisco design firm. In 1998, she left the corporate world to study Italian, write, and teach.

Presently, Barbara stays busy writing, keeping up with technology, grow-ing olives, and beekeeping. (She's a certified honey taster.) Barbara divides her time between city life in Rome, Italy, and country life on an olive farm in Calabria. You can find links to her books and read her blog at www.barbarajboyd.com.

Dedication

Joe Hutsko: I dedicate this book to my fabulously thoughtful, kind, caring, smart, creative, beautiful, and amazing co-author — and lifelong friend (and karmic life preserver) — Barbara Boyd.

Barbara Boyd: I dedicate this book to the memory of Dennis Cohen, witty and knowledgeable technical editor on most of the *For Dummies* books I've written.

Authors' Acknowledgments

You see the authors' names on the cover, but these books (like any book) are really a collaboration, an effort of a many-membered team. Thanks go to Aaron Black at Wiley for renewing this title and Kyle Looper for coming in during the final stages. We had the great pleasure to work with Elizabeth Kuball as our project editor and copy editor extraordinaire and Galen Gruman, whose vast technical experience and perfectionism offered a valuable contribution. Thanks, too, to the anonymous people at Wiley who contributed to this book — not just editorial, but tech support, legal, accounting, and even the person who delivers the mail. We don't know you, but we appreciate the job you do; it takes a lot of worker bees to keep the hive healthy, and each task is important to the whole.

We want to thank our agent, Carole Jelen, for her astute representation and moral support.

Thanks to the folks at Apple who developed such a cool product, and specifically to Keri Walker for her ongoing editorial product support.

Also, a special thanks to the app developers who shared their products and their time — their names are too many to list here, but please take our word for it when we say this book wouldn't have been complete without their support.

Thanks as well to you, dear reader, for buying our book — we had you in mind at every turn of a page.

Joe adds: Special thanks to the awesome team at Philadelphia's Walnut Street Apple Store for their assistance and support with earlier editions of this book.

Barbara adds: Thanks to my husband, Ugo de Paula. This book, like others before it, wouldn't have been possible without his loving support. And as always, extra special thanks to my co-author, Joe, for his kind, always-present friendship, which is more important than any writing project could ever be.

Publisher's Acknowledgments

Acquisitions Editors: Aaron Black and Kyle Looper

Project Editor: Elizabeth Kuball

Copy Editor: Elizabeth Kuball

Technical Editor: Galen Gruman

Editorial Assistant: Claire Johnson

Sr. Editorial Assistant: Cherie Case

Project Coordinator: Melissa Cossell

Cover Image: © iStock.com/Csondy

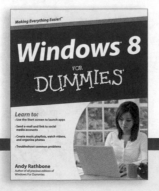

Math & Science

Algebra I For Dummies,
2nd Edition
978-0-470-55964-2

Anatomy and Physiology
For Dummies, 2nd Edition
978-0-470-92326-9

Astronomy For Dummies,
3rd Edition
978-1-118-37697-3

Biology For Dummies,
2nd Edition
978-0-470-59875-7

Chemistry For Dummies,
2nd Edition
978-1-118-00730-3

1001 Algebra II Practice
Problems For Dummies
978-1-118-44662-1

Microsoft Office

Excel 2013 For Dummies
978-1-118-51012-4

Office 2013 All-in-One
For Dummies
978-1-118-51636-2

PowerPoint 2013
For Dummies
978-1-118-50253-2

Word 2013 For Dummies
978-1-118-49123-2

Music

Blues Harmonica
For Dummies
978-1-118-25269-7

Guitar For Dummies,
3rd Edition
978-1-118-11554-1

iPod & iTunes
For Dummies, 10th Edition
978-1-118-50864-0

Programming

Beginning Programming
with C For Dummies
978-1-118-73763-7

Excel VBA Programming
For Dummies, 3rd Edition
978-1-118-49037-2

Java For Dummies,
6th Edition
978-1-118-40780-6

Religion & Inspiration

The Bible For Dummies
978-0-7645-5296-0

Buddhism For Dummies,
2nd Edition
978-1-118-02379-2

Catholicism For Dummies,
2nd Edition
978-1-118-07778-8

Self-Help & Relationships

Beating Sugar Addiction
For Dummies
978-1-118-54645-1

Meditation For Dummies,
3rd Edition
978-1-118-29144-3

Seniors

Laptops For Seniors
For Dummies, 3rd Edition
978-1-118-71105-7

Computers For Seniors
For Dummies, 3rd Edition
978-1-118-11553-4

iPad For Seniors
For Dummies, 6th Edition
978-1-118-72826-0

Social Security
For Dummies
978-1-118-20573-0

Smartphones & Tablets

Android Phones
For Dummies, 2nd Edition
978-1-118-72030-1

Nexus Tablets
For Dummies
978-1-118-77243-0

Samsung Galaxy S 4
For Dummies
978-1-118-64222-1

Samsung Galaxy Tabs
For Dummies
978-1-118-77294-2

Test Prep

ACT For Dummies,
5th Edition
978-1-118-01259-8

ASVAB For Dummies,
3rd Edition
978-0-470-63760-9

GRE For Dummies,
7th Edition
978-0-470-88921-3

Officer Candidate Tests
For Dummies
978-0-470-59876-4

Physician's Assistant Ex
For Dummies
978-1-118-11556-5

Series 7 Exam For Dum
978-0-470-09932-2

Windows 8

Windows 8.1 All-in-On
For Dummies
978-1-118-82087-2

Windows 8.1 For Dum
978-1-118-82121-3

Windows 8.1 For Dum
Book + DVD Bundle
978-1-118-82107-7

ℯ Available in print and e-book formats.

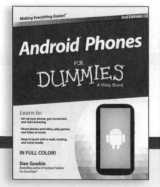

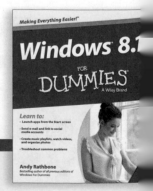

Available wherever books are sold. **For more information or to order direct visit www.dummies.com**

Take Dummies with you everywhere you go!

Whether you are excited about e-books, want more from the web, must have your mobile apps, or are swept up in social media, Dummies makes everything easier.

Leverage the Power

For Dummies is the global leader in the reference category and one of the most trusted and highly regarded brands in the world. No longer just focused on books, customers now have access to the For Dummies content they need in the format they want. Let us help you develop a solution that will fit your brand and help you connect with your customers.

Advertising & Sponsorships

Connect with an engaged audience on a powerful multimedia site, and position your message alongside expert how-to content.

Targeted ads • Video • Email marketing • Microsites • Sweepstakes sponsorship

Dummies products make life easier

- DIY
- Consumer Electronics
- Crafts
- Software
- Cookware
- Hobbies
- Videos
- Music
- Games
- and More!

For more information, go to **Dummies.com**· and search the store by category.

FOR
DUMMI

A Wiley